INSIGHT GUIDE

SOUTHERN SPAIN

INSIGHT GUIDE
SOUTHERN Spain

ABOUT THIS BOOK

Editorial

Managing Editor
Dorothy Stannard
Editorial Director
Brian Bell

Distribution

UK & Ireland
GeoCenter International Ltd
The Viables Centre
Harrow Way
Basingstoke
Hants RG22 4BJ
Fax: (44) 1256-817988

United States
Langenscheidt Publishers, Inc.
46–35 54th Road
Maspeth, NY 11378
Fax: (718) 784-0640

Worldwide
APA Publications GmbH & Co.
Verlag KG (Singapore branch)
38 Joo Koon Road
Singapore 628990
Tel: (65) 865-1600
Fax: (65) 861-6438

Printing

Insight Print Services (Pte) Ltd
38 Joo Koon Road
Singapore 628990
Tel: (65) 865-1600
Fax: (65) 861-6438

©1999 APA Publications GmbH & Co.
Verlag KG (Singapore branch)
All Rights Reserved
First Edition 1990
Third Edition 1999

CONTACTING THE EDITORS
Although every effort is made to
provide accurate information in
this publication, we live in a
fast-changing world and would
appreciate it if readers would
call our attention to any errors or
outdated information that may
occur by writing to us at:
Insight Guides, P.O. Box 7910,
London SE1 8ZB, England.
Fax: (44 171) 620-1074.
e-mail:
insight@apaguide.demon.co.uk

Southern Spain, or Andalucía, is one of Europe's most rewarding travel destinations. Spectacular scenery, fabulous Moorish monuments such as the Alhambra, the "white towns" of the sierras and the long blond beaches are just some of its attractions. It is also the home of two of Spain's most famous products, flamenco and sherry.

How to use this book

Insight Guide: Southern Spain is structured both to convey an [understanding of the region and]

◆ To understand modern-day Andalucía, you need to know about its past. The **Features** section, with a yellow bar, covers its history and culture in lively, authoritative essays.
◆ The main **Places** section, wit[h] a blue bar, provides a compre[-]hensive guide to the sights and areas worth visiting, beginning with the three great cities of Seville, Córdoba and Granada. Places of special interest are

coordinated by number with full-colour maps.

◆ The **Travel Tips** listings section, with a red bar, provides a convenient point of reference for information on travel, hotels, restaurants, shops and festivals. Information may be located quickly by using the index printed on the back cover flap – and the flaps are designed to serve as bookmarks.

◆ Photographs are chosen not only to illustrate the landscapes and buildings of the region but also to convey its diverse moods and the everyday activities of the Andalucíans.

The contributors

This new edition, edited by **Dorothy Stannard**, based in Insight Guides' London office, owes much to the work of **Mark Little**, a writer based in Mijas on the Costa del Sol. As well as contributing the new features Cathedrals of Wine and Wildlife, the information panels on Carmen (Seville) and Rock Talk (Gibraltar), and the picture stories on Festivals, Architecture, Andalucían Painters and Gardens, Little compiled a new Travel Tips section, with up-to-the-minute recommendations on where to stay and where to eat out, and a Decisive Dates table.

This edition of the guide builds on the original edition, edited by **Andrew Eames**. His team of contributors included **David Baird** (The Andalucían Character, War and Peace, Footprints of the Moors, Caves and Cave Living, **Jan Read** (history), **Thomas Hinde** (Málaga, the Costa del Sol, Gibraltar), **Alastair Boyd** (the White Towns, Ronda), **Jane Mendel** (A Cook's Tour), **Jan McGirk** (Morocco), **Mike Eddy** (Cádiz and Huelva), **Geraldine Mitchell** (Granada), **Nigel Bowden** (The Goodtime Costa), **Vicky Hayward** (Jaén and Almería) **Muriel Feiner** (Bullfighting Heroes), and **Philip Sweeney** (Flamenco).

The new edition includes many new images, in particular pictures by Apa photographers **Mark Read** and **Phil Wood**.

Travel Tips were edited by **Kate Mikhail**, and proof-reading and indexing completed by **Jane O'Callaghan** and **Lynn Bresler**.

Map Legend

▬ ▪ ▬ ▪	International Boundary
▬▬▬	Regional Boundary
– – –	Province Boundary
– ● –	National Park/Reserve
– – –	Ferry Route
✈ ✈	Airport: International/Regional
🚌	Bus Station
Ⓟ	Parking
❶	Tourist Information
✉	Post Office
⌂ † ††	Church/Ruins
†	Monastery
☾	Mosque
✡	Synagogue
▰ ▱	Castle/Ruins
∴	Archaeological Site
∩	Cave
𝟙	Statue/Monument
★	Place of Interest

The main places of interest in the Places section are coordinated by number with a full-colour map (e.g. ❶), and a symbol at the top of every right-hand page tells you where to find the map.

INSIGHT GUIDE
SOUTHERN Spain

CONTENTS

Maps

Southern Spain **138–9**

Seville **142**

Seville Province **159**

La Mezquita **168**

Córdoba **170**

Córdoba Province **175**

Granada **184**

Alhambra **186**

Around Granada **201**

Jaén Province **208**

Almeria Province **218**

Málaga Province **230**

Málaga **232**

Ronda **246**

White Towns **262**

Cádiz **273**

Cádiz Province **276**

Huelva Province **284**

Gibraltar **294**

Northern Morocco **306**

A map of Southern Spain is also on the front flap and a map of the region's main wildlife areas is on the back flap

Introduction

The Soul of Spain 15

History

Decisive Dates **16**

Mythical Beginnings **19**

The Moors March In **27**

The Christian Reconquest **35**

The Making of
Modern Andalucía................. **45**

Features

The Andalucían Character **59**

Footprints of the Moors **71**

Bullfighting Heroes **81**

Flamenco **89**

Cathedrals of Wine **97**

A Cook's Tour **105**

The Good-Time Costa **115**

Wild Andalucía **123**

The provinces depicted in *azulejo* in the Plaza de España, Seville

Information panels

Carmen 150
Olive Oil 213
Wrecks and Wreckers 272
Rock Talk 296

Insight on ...

Festivals 66
Architecture 76
Andalucían Artists 162
Gardens 178

Travel Tips

Getting Acquainted **314**

Planning the Trip **315**

Practical Tips **320**

Getting Around **323**

Where to Stay **324**

Where to Eat **334**

Culture **340**

Nightlife **341**

Sport **342**

Shopping **345**

Gibraltar **347**

Language **350**

Further Reading **354**

◆ **Full Travel Tips index**
  is on page 313

Places

Introduction 137
Seville and its Province 141
Córdoba and its Province 167
Granada............................. 183
Around Granada 199
Jaén and its Province 207
Almeria and its Province 217
Caves and Cave Living 225

Málaga and its Province........ 231
Ronda 245
Costa del Sol 253
Exploring the White Towns 261
Cádiz and its Province 271
Huelva & the Coto de Doñana 283
Gibraltar............................. 293
Going to Morocco 305

THE SOUL OF SPAIN

Andalucía is Spain par excellence, paradoxically and
simultaneously exuberant and desolate, crowded and quiet

Southern Spain is the source of Spanish cliché, of sherry, of flamenco, of *machismo*, of bullfighting and of coastal resorts crammed with ice cream-eating foreigners.

For package tourists, Andalucía means the cathedrals of the Costas – Torremolinos, Marbella and Fuengirola – and the miles of clubs, bars, cafés, golf clubs and white urbanisations that line what was once a rocky, unwanted coast. To cultural visitors, the highlights are the cities of Seville, Córdoba and Granada with their monuments – the Giralda, Mezquita and Alhambra. For lovers of wild, open spaces, there are some of the highest mountains in Europe (including one of Europe's southernmost skiing resorts) and marshlands crowded with camels and flamingos.

Moorish domination of the southern end of the peninsula for more than 700 years left a permanent imprint on the region and its people. The year of the Moors' final downfall, 1492, heralded a new era for Spain. Christopher Columbus sailed from Huelva on the historic voyage that brought the riches of the New World flowing back across the Atlantic. They turned Seville into a flourishing city but did little for the rest of Southern Spain.

Centuries of stagnation followed, and the poverty and lack of opportunity persuaded many Andalucíans (*andaluces* in Spanish) to emigrate. Many helped populate the Americas, while in the 1950s and 1960s thousands went to work in the factories of northern Spain and of other European countries. On the edge of Europe, between the Third World and the First, Andalucía continued to drift in a cultural and economic limbo. Change was slow in coming and at first was obvious only along the Costa del Sol, dedicated to the spending of money, legally or illegally, wisely or unwisely, in pursuit of a good time. But, following President Franco's death, the advent of democratic government and membership of the European Union, Andalucía is once more on the move – a trend stimulated by the colossal spending on infrastructure that preceded Expo '92.

Away from the raucous Costa and the cities, life is also changing in the *pueblos*, imperceptible though this might be to outsiders. Andalucía is a prosperous, booming region. These pages are a testament to its evolution, recalling the past, portraying the present and predicting the future. ❑

PRECEDING PAGES: rolling hills on the road to Granada; the lush gardens of the Alhambra; the white face of Alcalá de los Gazules; town houses beside the Giralda in Seville. **LEFT:** an expression of a rich and exuberant culture.

Decisive Dates

800,000 BC First indications of human habitation on the Iberian peninsula date from this time.
30,000 BC Last of the Neanderthals live in Gibraltar.
2500–2000 BC Megalithic civilisation flourishes in southern Iberia.
1100 BC Phoenician traders settle in Cádiz, the first of many Phoenician colonies along the southern Spanish coast.
800–550 BC The mineral-rich civilisation of Tartessos thrives near Huelva and Cádiz, then mysteriously vanishes.

237–228 BC Carthaginians, the heirs of the Phoenician trading empire, expand their territory in southern Iberia.
218–200 BC Romans occupy Iberia after defeating Carthaginians in Second Punic War; city of Itálica is founded near Seville.
61–60 BC Julius Caesar is governor of present-day Andalucía.
55 BC Seneca the Elder is born in Córdoba.
45 BC Julius Caesar defeats army led by Pompey's sons at the battle of Munda, near present-day Osuna, ending Roman civil war.
99 AD Itálica-born Trajan becomes Emperor of Rome.
409–415 Germanic tribes, including the Vandals, occupy Spain; Visigoths take over most of the penin-

sula at the behest of the crumbling Roman empire.
560 Birth of theologian, encyclopedist and archbishop St Isidore of Seville.
586 Visigoths convert from Arianism to Catholicism.
711 Tariq ibn Ziyad, a Berber commander, lands at Gibraltar and launches the Islamic conquest of the Iberian peninsula.
720 Christians defeat Muslims at Cavadonga in northernmost Spain, initiating the "Reconquest" of Iberia, which was to take 772 years.
756 Abd al-Rahman I establishes an independent Emirate in Córdoba, ruling most of the Iberian peninsula.
785 Construction begins on Cordoba Mosque.
929 Abd al-Rahman III proclaims the Caliphate of Córdoba. Al-Andalus reaches its zenith.
1010–1013 The city-palace of Medina Azahara is destroyed by rebellious Berbers; the Caliphate of Córdoba breaks up into a patchwork of petty kingdoms.
1086 Almoravids from northern Africa re-unite Islamic Spain.
1126 Birth of the Moorish philosopher Averroes in Córdoba.
1135 Maimonides, the Jewish philosopher, is born in Córdoba.
1147 Almohads from northern Africa invade Spain.
1212 Christian armies cross Despeñaperros Pass into Andalucía and defeat Moors at Navas de Tolosa, marking the beginning of the end of Moorish presence in Spain.
1236 Córdoba conquered by King Ferdinand III.
1238 Construction commences on the Alhambra in Granada.
1248 Ferdinand III conquers Seville.
1340 Islamic forces are defeated at the battle of Rio Salado near Seville, ending all efforts of invasion from northern Africa.
1348 Black Death sweeps many parts of Spain.
1364 King Pedro the Cruel orders construction of royal palace within Seville's Alcázar.
1391 Widespread pogroms against Spanish Jews.
1401 Construction begins on the cathedral in Seville.
1474 Isabella becomes Queen of Castile.
1481 Inquisition instituted in Spain.
1485 Columbus arrives in Spain.
1492 Ferdinand and Isabella conquer Granada, last Moorish kingdom in Spain; Columbus sails from Palos de la Frontera (Huelva) in search of the Indies; Jews who refuse to convert to Christianity are expelled.
1502 Last Muslims living in Spain ordered to convert to Christianity or leave; all save a few hundred choose to convert, and are known as Moriscos.
1519 Magellan sets sail from Sanlúcar de Barrameda to circumnavigate the world.

1559 First cultivation of tobacco starts in Spain.

1568 The Moriscos, converted Moors, revolt against Castilian overlords in the Alpujarra mountains south of Granada.

1587 Sir Francis Drake attacks Cádiz and sets fire to the Spanish fleet.

1596 Lord Essex emulates Drake's feat and ransacks the port of Cádiz.

1597 Cervantes is jailed in Seville accused of fiddling accounts while a tax collector; in prison he conceives his masterpiece, *Don Quixote.*

1599 The painter Diego de Velázquez is born in Seville.

1608 Publication of *Don Quixote.*

1617 The painter Bartolomé Murillo is born in Seville.

1700–14 Spanish King Carlos II dies childless, sparking War of Spanish Succession; Treaty of Utrecht grants throne to the Bourbon pretender; Gibraltar is ceded to Great Britain in perpetuity.

1768 Spain's first census shows the country has 10.2 million inhabitants.

1779–83 Great Siege of Gibraltar by Spanish and French.

1780 Last victim of the Inquisition is burned at the stake in Seville.

1785 Inauguration of the bullring in Ronda (Málaga), one of the oldest bullrings in Spain.

1805 Admiral Nelson defeats combined Spanish-French fleet off Cape Trafalgar in Cádiz.

1808 Napoleon replaces Spanish king with his brother, Joseph Bonaparte; Spaniards revolt against occupying French army.

181 Spain's first constitution is drafted in Cádiz.

1832 Publication of Washington Irving's *Tales of the Alhambra.*

1835 Church property in Spain, including numerous monasteries and convents, is confiscated and auctioned off.

1878 A plague of phylloxera (vine root louse) starts in Málaga and decimates vineyards in Andalucía.

1881 Pablo Picasso is born in Málaga.

1883 Members of the Black Hand, an anarchist organisation plotting against the wealthy class of Andalucía, are executed by garrotte in Cádiz.

1885 Devastating earthquake kills hundreds and destroys thousands of homes in the provinces of Granada and Málaga.

1898 Spain loses Cuba and Philippines in Spanish-American War.

1923 Primo de Rivera seizes control as dictator, with Alfonso XIII remaining as King.

1929 Ibero-American Exposition held in Seville.

1931 Spain becomes a Republic; King Alfonso XIII heads for exile.

1936 Spanish army revolts, led by General Franco, and three-year Spanish Civil War begins; the poet Federico García Lorca is shot in Granada.

1939 Spanish Civil War ends with Franco victory.

1947 The bullfighter Manolete is gored to death in Linares (Jaén).

1953 Spain agrees to US military bases on Spanish soil, ending 15 years of isolation.

1955 Spain joins the United Nations.

1966 US Air Force plane accidentally drops four non-activated atom bombs near the fishing village of Palomares, Almería.

1969 Spain closes border with Gibraltar.

1975 Franco dies, and Spain becomes constitutional monarchy under King Juan Carlos I.

1977 First free elections in Spain following restoration of monarchy.

1982 Andalucía becomes an autonomous region.

1985 Gibraltar border reopens.

1986 Spain joins European Community.

1992 Seville hosts Expo '92 to commemorate the 500th anniversary of the discovery of America. Money is ploughed into the infrastructure of the city and surroundings in preparation. ❑

LEFT: the Jews in Moorish Spain played an important role in society.

RIGHT: reading all about the death of Franco.

MYTHICAL BEGINNINGS

*Andalucía was united by force under the Carthaginians and
ruled by the Romans for seven centuries. Then came the Visigoths*

José Ortega y Gasset, the shrewd Spanish writer, once wrote an essay on *The Theory of Andalucía* in which he commented on the Andalucían stereotypes of bullfighting, flamenco and Carmen with a rose in her mouth. He maintained that such self-miming and narcissism is the product of long civilisation; and although Andalucía takes its name from al-Andalus, as it was called by the Moors who invaded it in AD 711, it is in fact one of Western Europe's oldest civilisations and trading communities.

Ortega y Gasset makes the further point that over the centuries Andalucía has been invaded by nearly all of the most warlike peoples of the Mediterranean, but that, like the Chinese, the Andalucíans have in the end "conquered" all their invaders by inculcating in them their own life-style and culture.

Mythical beginnings

The south of Spain was originally settled by the Iberians, a Mediterranean race of uncertain origin. However, the first inhabitants for whom there is firm historical evidence were the Tartessians of the Bronze Age in the 2nd millennium BC. Their land, known to the ancient Greeks as Tartessos and to the Hebrews as Tarshish, lay near Hades at the edge of the world where the sun sinks into the ocean and where Hercules was sent to fetch the fabled cattle of King Geryon. On his arrival, Hercules planted a couple of pillars on either side of the strait between Africa and Europe, before shooting the three-headed, three-bodied Geryon sideways through all three bodies with a single arrow and making off with his herd.

The German archaeologist Adolph Schulten spent much of his time between 1925 and 1945 in studying ancient sources and excavating the marshy Coto Doñana at the mouth of the River Guadalquivir in an attempt to discover the lost city of Tartessos, but without success; unlike Troy, this city has never been found. Nevertheless, quite by accident in 1957, Mata Carriazo, Professor of Archaeology at the University of Seville, picked up the bronze of a fertility goddess in a Seville junk shop, and was able to identify it as being of Tartessian origin.

This was followed by the discovery of a sculpture, The Mask of Tharsis, when a mining company opened up the galleries, unworked for centuries, of a mine near Huelva; and in 1961, during construction work at the Seville Pigeon Shooting Club in the hills across the river from the city, a workman's pick struck a metallic object. It proved to be only one of a hoard of Tartessian plates, bracelets and necklaces.

During recent years archaeologists have unearthed thousands of other artefacts, testifying to a knowledge of mining, industry and agriculture at a very early date and even bearing out the Greeks' description of Tartessos as a veritable El Dorado.

LEFT: the writings of Hernan Cortés, in safe hands in a Seville convent.
RIGHT: a Tartessian mask.

Aegean sailors were trading with Tartessos for copper, scarce in the Eastern Mediterranean, during the second millennium, long before the reign of King Solomon (circa 950 BC), of whom the Bible (Second Chronicles 9.21) reports that "the king's ships went to Tarshish with the servants of Hiram (King of Tyre); once every three years came the ships of Tarshish bringing gold, and silver, ivory, and apes, and peacocks."

Trading places

The Tartessians ventured far afield, fishing along the Atlantic coast and around the Canaries, and their sailors are reliably said to have sailed the "tin route" to Galicia and possibly as far as Cornwall. Strabo has a story of a Phoenician captain from Gadir (Cádiz) who kept the secret of the "tin islands" from a Roman ship that was shadowing him by purposely running his own ship aground, for which he was rewarded by his government. It was largely because of the abundance of tuna and the availability of tin, used in making bronze, and of other metals from the mines of Huelva that the Tartessians' trading partners and allies, the seafaring Phoenicians, established a factory at Gadir about 1100 BC.

There was peaceful competition from the Phocaean Greeks, who founded a trading post at Mainake near Málaga, and Tartessos was at its most prosperous in the 6th century BC during the long and peaceful reign of King Arganthonius, but suffered an abrupt change of fortune after the Battle of Alalia circa 535 BC.

Tartessos's allies, the Phocaeans, had established a colony at Alalia in Corsica and had inflicted enormous losses on the Carthaginians and Etruscans by pirating their ships. The battle was fought off Alalia with 60 Phocaean ships facing double the number of Carthaginian and Etruscan. The Phocaeans claimed victory, but lost 40 of their ships for 60 of the enemy's, while the remainder suffered major damage to their bows and rams. As a result the Carthaginians were able to close the whole Western Mediterranean to all but their own ships.

From then on Carthage, founded in the first place as a North African colony of Tyre, had a free hand in Spain and supplanted the Phoenicians. The kingdom of Tartessos disintegrated, and in the 3rd century BC, in a bloody campaign which cost the life of their commander, Hamilcar Barca, the father of Hannibal, Carthaginian forces

unified most of greater Andalucía by sheer force.

The Romans, now the emergent power in the Mediterranean, watched events in Spain with growing anxiety. They had made a pact with the Carthaginians that they should not advance north of the River Ebro.

Hannibal's attack on the city of Saguntum, which was south of the Ebro but under Roman protection, led to the outbreak of the Second Punic War (218–201 BC). Rome was now mistress of the seas and relied on a counter-attack in Spain, but was foiled by the speed of Hannibal's famous crossing of the Alps and invasion of Italy itself, in which he destroyed one Roman army

after another. Slowly the Romans fought back. In 211 BC they were defeated in Spain by Hannibal's brother Hasdrubal, but a new Roman commander, Publius Cornelius Scipio, was sent to Spain in 209 BC. He seized the Carthaginian base of Carthago Nova (Cartagena) by a surprise attack, and by 201 BC had driven the last of the Carthaginians out.

SHAPING HISTORY

The influence of the Romans cannot be underestimated, since it was to modify profoundly the Arabic civilisation of the Moors

Roman rule

It took long campaigning for the Roman legions to subdue the native tribes of Hispania, and

During the reign of Caesar's successor, Augustus (63 BC–AD 14), the country was divided into three provinces, of which the most southerly, Baetica, corresponded largely to present-day Andalucía. Hispania, and especially Baetica with its flourishing agriculture and mineral resources, was to become one of the Empire's richest provinces. The Romans greatly expanded the production of wheat, olives and wine. It was they who introduced the large earthenware jars or *orcae*, still used in Montilla for fermenting and storing wine,

there was also fierce fighting between the Romans themselves. The long-standing feud between Julius Caesar and Pompey came to its bitter end when Caesar annihilated the forces of Pompey's sons, Gnaeus and Sextus, at Munda, now Montilla, on 17 March 45 BC.

The Roman occupation of Spain was to last for some seven centuries, during which agriculture was reorganised; bridges, roads and aqueducts were built, and the Roman legal system was introduced.

LEFT: mosaic at the Roman site of Itálica.
ABOVE: Roman sarcophagus in the Alcázar museum in Córdoba.

and it has been estimated that by the 2nd century AD some 20 million *amphorae* of Spanish wine had been shipped to Rome, proof of which is the extraordinary artificial mountain of broken vessels from Monte Testaccio, still bearing their seals of origin.

Another export, from Cádiz (renamed Gades by the Romans), was the paste called garum, a product of the tuna fishing industry. This paste, made by marinating the belly meat of the tuna, as expensive as caviar is today, was believed by some, such as Pliny the Elder, to have curative powers. A similar garum in the form of a smooth paste of anchovies, black olives, capers and herbs, is still available in Catalonia.

Salt and sensuality

Martial, the Spanish-born poet, was, in fact, more interested in a different export of Cádiz, its sensual delights. The early 19th-century traveller Richard Ford describes Cádiz as "the centre of sensual civilisation, the purveyor of gastronomy etc." and adds that "It is quite clear that Cádiz was the eldest daughter of Tyre, and her daughters (i.e. descendants of settlers from Sidon) have inherited the Sidonian 'stretching forth of necks, wanton eyes, walking and minc-

> **FLAMENCO ROOTS**
>
> Flamenco as we know it today has also been influenced by the Moors and by the gypsies who arrived in Andalucía from India during the 15th century.

identifying the famous statue of Aphrodite Kallipygos (the Venus of the shapely buttocks) in the Naples Archaeological Museum as Telethusa in person, and there is another representation in the Villa Item in Pompeii of a naked *puella Gaditana*, with upraised arms and castanets in the act of dancing, startlingly like a flamenco dancer of today. And it seems beyond doubt that there is a strong historical connection between flamenco and these dances.

Roman cities the length and breadth of the

ing as they go' (*Book of Isaiah* iii.16)."

Dancers from Cádiz, the *puellae Gaditanae*, Byron's "black-eyed maids of Heaven formed for all the witching arts of love", were much in demand at entertainments in classical Rome, and Martial in particular returns to them time and again in his verses. So he writes about his mistress, the ravishing Telethusa: "She who was cunning to show wanton gestures to the sound of Baetic castanets and to frolic to the tunes of Gades, she who could have roused passion in palsied Pelias … Telethusa burns and racks with love her former master. He sold her as his maid, now he buys her back as mistress."

Richard Ford put forward good reasons for

Empire were built to a pattern, and many of those in Andalucía preserve the remains of their temples, forums, aqueducts, bridges and theatres.

So bridges survive at Córdoba (Roman name Corduba) and Espejo (Ucubi); aqueducts at Seville (Hispalis) and Almuñecar (Sexi); the-

> **FAMOUS SONS**
>
> Many illustrious Roman writers were born in Andalucía. Among them were Lucan, the Sénecas and Columella, who in his *De Re Rustica* wrote about the sherry-like wines from his native Cádiz. Even more famous were the Emperors Trajan and Hadrian, both born in Itálica.

atres at Málaga (Malaca) and Casas de la Reina (Regina); an amphitheatre at Écija (Astigi); a temple and baths at Santiponce (Itálica); while at Bolonia the ruins of Baelo overlooking the sea include a fortified precinct, streets lined with columns, a forum and fountain, temples complete with statues, an amphitheatre and the remains of houses.

These Roman cities were not large by modern standards, but their size belies their importance as the centres of power and culture. It has, for example, been estimated that the area of Roman Córdoba was around 70 hectares (170 acres) and that of Carmo (Carmona), then a place of importance, only 20 hectares (50 acres). Hispalis (Seville) probably ran to rather more than 100 hectares (250 acres), but its boundaries have not been accurately established.

The wealthy bourgeoisie often owned villas on the outskirts of the towns with extensive gardens and orchards, and beyond these lay the large estates or *latifundia*, worked by slave labour in Roman times. In modified form, these have survived over the centuries and have differentiated the rural economy and social patterns of life and work in Andalucía from those which developed in the rest of Spain.

Decline and fall

With the decay of the Roman Empire the first "barbarians" entered Spain via the Pyrenees during AD 407–409, but left little mark on the south. They were shortly followed by the Visigoths, a Germanic people, theoretically auxiliaries of the tottering Empire, who had lived in its shadow. This fiction persisted until 468, when the Visigothic king, Euric, broke with Rome. They had passed quickly down through the peninsula and met with little resistance in the south; the Andalucíans were, in Livy's phrase, *"Omnium Hispanorum maxime imbelles"* (Of all the Spaniards, the least warlike), and the Hispano-Roman nobility, dependent on a slave society, soon came to terms with the new rulers.

After the conversion of Visigothic King Reccared to Christianity in 568, the Church played a central role in unifying the country, but a crucial

weakness of the Visigothic kingdom, especially in Andalucía, was the division into haves and have nots, a situation which has largely persisted since then.

Further instability arose from the lack of a law of succession of the king by his son; of the 33 Visigothic kings who ruled Hispania from 414 to 711, three were deposed, 11 assassinated and only 19 died a natural death. So weak was the central authority that King Wamba resorted to calling up the clergy for service in his army.

Roderick, the last of the Visigothic kings, assumed power in 710. Legend has it that one of his enemies, Count Julián, sent his daughter Florinda to court at Toledo to receive the education befitting a princess, but that Roderick had seduced her, thus earning Count Julián's undying hatred and inducing him to conspire with the Berbers in North Africa.

Whatever the truth of this picturesque yarn, the Visigoths with their deeply divided leadership and lack of popular support had been lulled into a sense of false security by the apparent absence of any threat from the north or from Africa, and when an invasion came they were almost totally unprepared to meet it. ❏

LEFT: statue at Itálica, the centre of Roman rule.
RIGHT: the medieval caves of Antequera.

THE MOORS MARCH IN

Following the Moors' invasion, Córdoba became the capital of Islamic
Spain and the leading city of Europe – a place where poets and musicians thrived

In 711 Tariq ibn-Ziyad, Governor of Tangier, an outpost of the Damascus Caliphate, crossed the Straits of Gibraltar with some 7,000 men at his side and established himself on the flanks of Mount Calpe (subsequently to be known as Gibraltar, from the Arabic Jebel Tarik, "the mountain of Tariq"). His arrival caught King Roderick, the last Visigothic king, totally by surprise. Roderick nevertheless massed a large army and launched a frontal attack on the Moors, now reinforced and in a strong position near the present-day city of Algeciras.

The Visigothic king, at the centre, fought bravely, but the flanks of his army, commanded by renegades, treacherously turned tail. Roderick was either killed or took flight, never to reappear.

The advance into Spain marked the tip of an Arab thrust along the North African coast which had begun in the east in 642 with the annexation of Egypt by the second of the Umayyad caliphs of Damascus and was to be halted only in France by Charles Martel at the Battle of Tours in 732.

During the 30 years following the first incursion, Muslim governors of al-Andalus followed thick and fast and pressed northwards until al-Andalus, as the Moorish-occupied part of Spain became known, covered virtually the whole of modern Spain and Portugal apart from pockets of resistance in the far northwest and the Basque country.

The invaders were, however, split into different factions: the Qaysites and Kalbites of pure Arabian descent and also the North African Berbers, on whom Tariq and his successors largely relied in the conquest of the country. Al-Andalus was finally united by the establishment of the Umayyad dynasty of Córdoba which was to control its destiny for some 300 years.

PRECEDING PAGES: riches of the Moorish court.
LEFT: decorated dome of La Mezquita, Córdoba.
RIGHT: Mozarabic miniature of David and Goliath.

First of the line

Andalucía's founder, Abd-al-Rahman I (The Immigrant), was barely 20 when, in January 750, the Umayyads in Syria were irrevocably overthrown. The results were far-reaching. Abu al-Abbas, the founder of the Abbasids, was determined to root out and destroy every rep-

resentative of the fallen Umayyads everywhere in the world. Abd-al-Rahman was hunted from pillar to post, but with his brother succeeded in reaching the River Euphrates, with their pursuers still hard on their heels.

A contemporary chronicle, the Akhbar Majmua, describes what then ensued in the prince's own words: "We managed to reach the river ahead of them and threw ourselves into the water. When we got to the bank they began shouting: 'Come back; you have nothing to fear.' I swam and my brother swam; I was a little ahead of him. Half way across, I turned to encourage him; but on hearing their promises he had turned back, afraid of drowning. I shouted to

him, 'Come back, beloved'; but God did not will that he heard me. I swam on to the opposite bank. Then I saw that some of the soldiers were undressing to swim after me. They stopped, caught the boy and cut off his head in front of me. He was 13 years old."

Abd-al-Rahman's mother, Rah, was a Berber, and he succeeded in making his way along the North African coast to the family's ancestral home at Nakur in Morocco, from where he began negotiations with the Muslim leaders in Spain. In the event, the Muslim leaders

RELIGIOUS FREEDOM

Levying of tribute from converts to Islam was not permissible, so had there been conversions on a large scale the invaders would have suffered severe loss of income.

in al-Andalus had second thoughts about a Umayyad restoration in Spain, but Abd-al-Rahman was meanwhile gathering support on all sides and in 756 defeated his opponents near Córdoba.

The new regime

It has been argued that the Muslim invasion of Spain was a *jihad* (holy war). In truth, at no point did the victorious Muslims display any great enthusiasm to convert the indigenous Christians or Jews, far less to put them to the sword for a refusal to be converted.

BORN TO RULE

Abd-al-Rahman I was 26 when he became Emir. He is described by the 13th-century Moorish chronicler Ibn-Idhari as being "tall, fair, one-eyed, with shrunken cheeks and a mole on his forehead and wore his hair in two long ringlets." Something of the bitterness of his early struggles comes out in a poem which he wrote at the time:

I, and I alone, driven by a consuming anger, bared a two-edged sword,
Crossed the desert and furrowed the sea, mastering waves and wasteland.
I won a kingdom, gave it strength, and built a mosque for prayer.

In granting a large degree of religious freedom the invaders were not as disinterested as might appear at first sight. Some were desert nomads with little bent for cultivating the lands which they had seized, who preferred to move on to fresh conquests and quick booty. Others settled in the cities, leaving agriculture to the original owners. Always provided that they were People of the Book (i.e. Christians or Jews and not polytheists and worshippers of idols), the conquered people enjoyed local autonomy and freedom to pursue their own religion, subject to the payment of tax or tribute.

In all probability no more than 40,000 Arabs had crossed into Spain with the invading armies.

As time went on they married with the local women, and because of this intermingling of race the later Umayyads were more Spanish than Arab. However, the lustre of their royal origin survived and they remained fiercely proud of their Arab descent; this was to prove a two-edged weapon, since in the eyes of both Christians and Berbers they remained a foreign dynasty.

However, vivid testimony to their success in fostering a feeling if not an appearance of a national identity emerges from the *Indiculus*

> ## HEART OF ISLAM
> At its apogee Córdoba housed more than 100,000 inhabitants, many more than the London or Paris of the period.

by Abd-al-Rahman I from 785. Although the central portion has been vandalised by its conversion to a Christian cathedral, its vast spaces resemble nothing so much as a cool grove of palm trees. The double tiers of arches were probably suggested by Roman aqueducts, and the horseshoe arch, so typical of Moorish Spain, is in fact of Visigothic origin.

Around the mosque and schools the market sprang up, whose shops numbered around 8,000 at the height of the city's prosperity. A good idea of the layout of Córdoba at the time

luminosus of 854, quoted by T. W. Arnold in *The Preaching of Islam*: "Our Christian young men, with their elegant airs and fluent speech, are showy in their dress and carriage, and are famed for the learning of the gentiles; intoxicated with Arab eloquence they greedily handle, eagerly devour and zealously discuss the books of the Chaldeans (i.e. Muhammadans), and make them known with every flourish of rhetoric...".

The capital and heart of Islamic Spain was Córdoba, with its Great Mosque, reconstructed

LEFT AND ABOVE: life in Moorish Spain. The Moors were industrious agriculturalists, but also lovers of poetry and song.

can be gained from the old Jewish quarter of the city (the Judería) as it still exists today, with its narrow alleys criss-crossing and running at random, so providing shade from the beating sun; its white-washed houses with wrought-iron grilles over the windows; its secret flowered patios; and the sudden snatch of flamenco coming from one of its cool *tabernas*.

The workshops of the tailors, shoemakers, leather-workers, jewellers, weavers, dyers, smiths and armourers were situated in the market itself; other craftsmen, such as potters and tanners, who required more space for their kilns and pits, worked on the outskirts of the town.

The kings

Abd-al-Rahman and his successors, notably Abd-al-Rahman II (822–852), were lavish patrons of poets, musicians, scientists and philosophers, of whom one of the most colourful was Abu al-Hasan Ali ibn-Nafi, known for short as Ziryab because of his dark complexion; the Arabic word, appropriately enough, signifies a bird with black plumage. The most gifted singer and musician of his age, Ziryab is credited with the introduction to al-Andalus of the five-stringed lute, and influenced the whole

> ### MOORISH TASTES
>
> Today Andalucía owes many of its best and most typical dishes to the Moors, including the cold soups (*gazpachos*).

subsequent development of popular music and dance in Spain by introducing musical forms from Persia. More than a musician, he became the fashionable arbiter of taste in Córdoba. He instituted styles of dress for the different seasons of the year and also introduced toothpaste and set the trend for short haircuts.

Ziryab revolutionised the cuisine with recipes from Baghdad and, from his time, food was no longer served en masse, but as separate courses.

Abd-al-Rahman II was, in the elegant French of the great Arabist Lévi-Provençal, "*un grand amateur des femmes*", and according to the chronicler Ibn-Idhari his numerous wives and concubines presented him with 45 sons and 42 daughters. The management of this harem was entrusted to one Nasr, who became so powerful as to be described as "the proconsul of the keys, who administers the whole of Hispania".

Nasr finally overstepped himself and at the behest of one of the Emir's wives offered a poisoned draught to Abd-al-Rahman in the guise of a medicine. However, the doctor who had been blackmailed into preparing it warned another wife, the charming and devoted Fakr. The wretched Nasr was forthwith bidden to drink the poison himself and at once expired.

Glorious era

Al-Andalus reached its zenith under Abd-al-Rahman III (912–961). He found it on his accession in a disturbed and rebellious state, but soon settled accounts with dissidents within al-Andalus and then directed equally forceful operations against the Christians of the Marches to the north. Only on one occasion did he suffer a reverse, at the hands of the resolute Ramiro II of León – a defeat attributed by the Christians to the appearance of St James (Santiago) on the field of battle at Simancas.

Having successfully pacified his kingdom and secured its borders, Abd-al-Rahman III took the important step in 929 of declaring himself Caliph, so asserting his rights as an absolute sovereign.

As a symbol of his new status, in 936 he embarked upon the Medina Azahara, a palace of unparalleled magnificence on the outskirts of Córdoba.

> ### PALACE FIT FOR A CALIPH
>
> The construction of Abd-al-Rahman III's Madinat al-Zahra (which is now known as Medina Azahara) involved, according to Henri Terasse in *Islam d'Espagne*, "10,000 to 12,000 workmen; 15,000 mules and 4,000 camels transported the materials; and each day the works called for 6,000 items of dressed stone and 11,000 loads of lime and sand, without counting bricks and gravel."
>
> The centrepiece of the great pillared reception hall was a pool of quicksilver, reflecting a quivering light over the whole interior and giving an exhilarating overall impression of constant movement.

Extensive excavation has begun to reveal the full extent of the palace (8 km/5 miles west of Córdoba along the C431), which was destroyed stone by stone by the Berbers only 70 years after it was finished. It lay on three levels, a mosque on the lowest, above it gardens and above them the palace. Two of its pavilions, with their beautiful stonework, are in the course of reconstruction.

The mystic Ibn-al-Arabi witnessed the pomp and ritual of Medina Azahara at its peak. To impress an embassy of Christians from the north of Spain, the Caliph had mats unrolled for a distance of three miles from the gates of Córdoba to the entrance of the palace and a double rank of soldiers stationed along the route, their naked swords meeting at the tips like the rafters of a roof.

Ibn-al-Arabi also says that, inside the palace "the caliph had the ground covered with brocades. At regular intervals he placed dignitaries whom they took for kings, for they were seated on splendid chairs and arrayed in brocades and silk. Each time the ambassadors saw one of these dignitaries they prostrated themselves before him, imagining him to be the caliph, whereupon they were told, 'Raise your heads! This is but a slave of his slaves!' At last they entered a courtyard strewn with sand. At the centre was the caliph. His clothes were coarse and short: what he was wearing was not worth four dirhams. He was seated on the ground, his head bent; in front of him was a Koran, a sword and fire. 'Behold the ruler', the ambassadors were told."

The economy

The overflowing riches of al-Andalus and its ruler originated within the country and were dependent on agriculture and the exploitation of mineral resources rather than on foreign trade. The most important crops, as in Roman times, were cereals, beans and peas of various types, olives and vines.

The Arabs introduced a variety of new crops, herbs and fruits to Spain, notably bitter oranges and lemons and almonds, saffron, nutmeg and black pepper. They also planted a profusion of semi-tropical crops which depended on efficient irrigation, for which the Moors took over and greatly extended existing works instituted by the Romans.

Gold, silver, copper, mercury, lead and iron had been worked by the Romans, but the mines had fallen into disuse during the Visigothic period. They were reopened by the Moors, who also mined cinnabar (a source of mercury) at Almadén near Córdoba.

It was from here that al-Nasir ("defender of the faith", as Abd-al-Rahman was known after

assuming the title of Caliph) obtained the quicksilver for the pool at Medina Azahara.

For all its brilliance, the Caliphate suffered from an infrastructure which was to lead to disintegration and downfall. As time went on, the inhabitants of Al-Andalus, in their enjoyment of an increasing prosperity, preferred a life of peace and plenty, and paid mercenaries rather than defend themselves against the increasingly belligerent Christians of the north.

The sharp division of social classes into the monied and influential and an amorphous proletariat subject to the least whim of the caliph and his deputies resulted in a passivity and lack of initiative amongst the mass of the population –

LEFT: painting was encouraged as a courtly skill.
RIGHT: an ornate window displaying Islamic motifs in the Sevile Alcázar.

a state of affairs of which the Arabs had themselves taken advantage in over-running the earlier Visigothic kingdom. But before the final cataclysm there was one last outburst.

Intrigue

Abd-al-Rahman III's successor, the bookish al-Hakam II, was an efficient enough ruler, but he fathered a sickly and incompetent successor, Hisham, the son of a Basque concubine, Subh. His tutor, Ibn-Abi Amir, was a young man of boundless ambition and took the first step on the ladder to fame and power by making Subh his mistress. Soon he had made himself controller of the Mint and administrator of the prince's finances, and the one obstacle to his becoming virtual dictator was the army commander, General Ghalib.

Ibn-Abi Amir thereupon abandoned Subh and married Ghalib's daughter, the talented and intelligent Asma. This did not placate the loyal old soldier, who took up arms on behalf of his Umayyad master and joined battle with Ibn-Abi Amir at San Vicente near Atienza in July 981. The gallant Ghalib spurred into the melée to encourage his soldiers, his red scarf streaming from his golden helmet, but, as Ibn Hazam relates, was thrown from his horse. His hand was cut off and, with the ring still on his finger, delivered with his head to "the accursed hunchback".

Ghalib's death removed the last check to Ibn-Abi Amir's ambitions. Without actually deposing the caliph, he had him confined to the palace of Madinat al-Zahra while he assumed the title of *al-Mansur bi'llah* ("victor with the help of Allah") or Almanzor in Spanish.

Whatever his faults, al-Mansur was a superb soldier and led many an expedition against nearby Christians. Among the most important were those of 985 against Barcelona; of 998 against Vermudo II of León, during which Coimbra, Zamora and León itself were occupied; and of 994 against Sancho García of Castile.

However, of all al-Mansur's successes, the most spectacular was the great expedition of 997, undertaken by way of Oporto, which struck at the very heart of Christian Spain and destroyed the church of Santiago de Compostela. It was a disaster for the Christians which resounded far beyond the peninsula, for Santiago (St James) was the patron saint of Spain and his shrine in the far northwest of Spain was one of the most celebrated of medieval Christendom, and the popular goal of a multitude of pilgrims from all over Europe.

> **MILITARY PROWESS**
>
> As a soldier al-Mansur is credited with no less than 57 successful expeditions against the Christians of the north and west.

The city and its cathedral were razed to the ground, only the actual tomb of St James being left intact at the express command of al-Mansur. The army marched back to Córdoba through Lamego, carrying with it an enormous booty, which included the bells and doors of the cathedral. These were carried by Christian captives and used to embellish the Great Mosque.

Later, when Córdoba fell to the Christians, the bells were carried back to Santiago, this time by Moorish prisoners.

Poisoned fruit

When al-Mansur died in 1002, with Hisham II still titularly caliph, he was for all practical purposes succeeded by a younger son Abd-al-Malik, who had already proved his worth as a soldier in North Africa. Things went well enough for six years until, on the way back to Córdoba after a successful campaign against Sancho García of Castile, Abd-al-Malik complained of pains in the chest and died. It was suspected that he had been poisoned by his own younger brother Sanchuelo, who, according to one story, offered to share an apple with him and cut it with a knife which had been smeared with poison on one side.

The vain and pleasure-loving Sanchuelo was no soldier or administrator like his dead brother. His debauched parties with his boon companion Hisham II became the byword of Córdoba, and it was not long before he was deposed and executed in a palace revolution.

The sorry events of the next two decades have been eloquently summarised by Lévi-Provençal in his masterly *Histoire de l'Espagne musulmane*: "In the whole history of Muslim Spain, no period was more troubled or tragic. Córdoba raised the flag of revolt; the civil war soon spread to the provinces and the more distant parts of the Marches. At the beck and call of rival factions, sovereigns came and went, in almost every case ending in bloodshed and lasting more often for months rather than years… In brief, this was chaos which engulfed and irretrievably wrecked the patient work of the great princes of the dynasty and ended the political unity they had made so many efforts to achieve."

The disintegration of the caliphate, abolished by a council of ministers in 1031, marks a turning point in the history of Moorish Spain, though it was another four centuries before Granada, the last of the independent kingdoms into which it broke up, fell to the Christians.

Towards the end it was undoubtedly the presence of large numbers of restless and warlike Berbers which led to the ruin of the caliphate. And ironically, it was the all-conquering warrior al-Mansur, with his massive infusion of Berbers into the army, who paved the way for the final and irrevocable disaster that was to befall the Moorish empire. ❑

LEFT: part of the ruins of Medina Azahara.
RIGHT: the Moors' invasion of Spain is remembered today in re-enactments, as it is here in Baeza near Granada.

THE FINAL FALL

Weep for the splendour of Córdoba, for disaster has overtaken her.
Fortune made her a creditor and demanded payment of the debt.
She was at the height of her beauty; life was gracious and sweet
Until all was overthrown and today no two people are happy in her streets.
Then bid her goodbye, and let go in peace since depart she must.

– from the Bayan al-Mughrib of Ibn-Idhari.

THE CHRISTIAN RECONQUEST

The Christians of the north began to claw back power in the south in the 11th century, but it was another 400 years before their reconquest was complete

By the end of the caliphate al-Andalus had disintegrated into some 30 small principalities governed by so-called *reyes de taifas* or "party kings". In the east the Slavs (mercenaries from northern Europe) and the eunuchs of the palace guard carved out their kingdoms for themselves in Valencia and the Balearics; Granada and Málaga were taken over by Berbers; while in the western heartland of Seville and Córdoba, Muslims of both Arab and Spanish descent held sway.

Meanwhile the Christians of the north, inspired by a new religious zeal, began making inroads into al-Andalus under leaders such as Ferdinand I of León-Castile, his son Alfonso VI of León-Castile and that scourge of the Moors, the freebooting El Cid. The most brilliant soldier of his generation, El Cid, having quarrelled with his liege lord Alfonso VI, began his private campaign against the Moors, culminating in the capture of Valencia in 1094.

Christian comeback

In a sudden reversal of roles as the reconquest got underway, it was increasingly the Muslims who became tributaries of the Christian kings. Impoverished as they were, these kings were, to begin with, only too pleased to accept this arrangement. The adjustment seems to have been made without much difficulty, since Muslims and Christians had been used to living side by side and pursuing their different religions. And in any case the caliphate had evolved a civilisation and customs of its own, and the large majority of its people thought of themselves as belonging to al-Andalus, rather than Africa.

Of all the *taifas*, the Abbasid kingdom of Seville most nearly approached the fallen caliphate in the extent of its territories and the splendours of its court. Its founder, al-Mu'tadid (1042–69), extended his realm as far as southern Portugal. Ruthless, cruel and sensual,

he planted flowers in the skulls of his decapitated enemies, using them to decorate the palace gardens, and had his first son put to death on suspicion of plotting against him.

He was succeeded by the gifted and intellectual al-Mu'tamid, under whom 11th-century Seville saw a remarkable flowering of culture.

His vizier, Ibn-Ammar, was one of the most accomplished poets of his time, and it was through him that al-Mu'tamid met the captivating and wilful Rumaykiyya.

It happened that the king was one evening walking by the banks of the Guadalquivir, when, struck by the appearance of the water in the light breeze, he improvised the following couplet:

The wind scuffs the river
And makes it chain mail...

He turned to Ibn-Ammar to complete the verse, but for once the poet was unable to oblige. A passing slave-girl then broke in:

Chain mail for fighting
Could water avail

LEFT: view of Granada from the west.
RIGHT: hooded penitent, symbol of the Reconquest, during Holy Week, Seville.

So impressed was al-Mu'tamid with the girl that he sent a eunuch to bring her to the palace and asked her who she was.

"My name is I'timad," she said, "but I'm usually called Rumaykiyya, because I am the slave of Rumayk and drive mules for him."

"Are you married?" he asked.

"No, your Majesty."

"Good," said he, "I shall buy you and marry you."

Al-Mu'tamid remained in love with her until their last tragic banishment to Africa.

> **AL-MU'TAMID'S CHOICE**
>
> In Al-Mu'tamid's own words from the chronicle *Al-holal al-mawshiya*: "I would rather drive the camels of the Almoravids than be a swineherd among the Christians."

The initial idyll was not to last. Al-Mu'tamid might be as a lion to the rulers of the other *taífas*, but was no match for Alfonso VI of León-Castile. There is a picturesque story that when Alfonso first advanced on Seville in 1078, he was tricked by Ibn-Ammar, who had a magnificent chess set inlaid with gold. The king was so enamoured of it that Ibn-Ammar challenged him to a game, promising him the set if he won. If, on the other hand, Alfonso lost, he must grant a wish. Ibn-Ammar won with ease and promptly demanded the raising of the siege; Alfonso kept to his word, but doubled the tribute.

However, Alfonso captured Toledo in 1085, declared himself Emperor of Spain and issued a peremptory demand for the surrender of Córdoba. The writing was on the wall, and with much heart-searching Al-Mu'tamid took the momentous step of summoning aid from the fanatical Yusuf ibn-Tashufin, the leader of the Almoravids in North Africa.

Men of war

The Almoravids, a warlike and puritanical sect devoted to a return to the original purity of the Koran, had swept across half of North Africa. Their leader, Ibn-Tashufin, already 70 years old, dressed in wool; partook only of barley bread, milk and the flesh of the camel; and viewed with repugnance the wine-imbibing, the music and culture of al-Andalus.

Caught unawares by the landing of the Almoravids in June 1086, Alfonso marched to meet the invading army, swelled by the forces of al-Mu'tamid and other party kings, at Sagrajas near Badajóz. Here, for the first time, the Christians faced the tactic of compact and well-ordered bodies of infantry, supported by lines of Turkish archers and manoeuvring as a unit to the command of thunderous rolls from the massed tambours of the Moors.

Used, as they were, to single combat, where personal valour counted above all, the Christians broke and fell into confusion. Only 500 horsemen, most of them wounded, survived, among them Alfonso.

Defeat for all

The battle of Sagrajas set back the cause of reconquest in al-Andalus for some 60 years, but the rulers of the *taífas*, soon to be expelled from their kingdoms, were equal losers. All al-Mu'tamid's misgivings about Ibn-Tashufin were justified. In September 1091, after heroic resistance and a desperate plea for help from the erstwhile enemy Alfonso VI, Seville was overrun by the Almoravids. Al-Mu'tamid and Rumaykiyya were exiled to Aghmat in the Atlas Mountains and lived in penury until the end of their lives.

However, in spite of a publicly proclaimed austerity, even the Almoravids, and particularly the officials charged with the everyday conduct of affairs, fell victims to the easy lifestyle of al-Andalus. A new Christian champion had meanwhile arisen in the shape of Alfonso El

Batallador ("The Fighter") of Aragón, who in 1125 struck deep into the south, reaching the Mediterranean near Málaga.

By now the power of the Almoravids was effectively spent; once more al-Andalus seemed ripe for reoccupation by the Christians, but yet again they were still to be cheated for another century. The Almoravid empire in North Africa was finally overwhelmed in 1145 by that of the Almohads, also religious in inspiration but with a broader interpretation of Islam and bitterly opposed to the narrow doctrines of the Almoravids.

It was not until 1171 that Abu-Ya'qub Yusuf

Holy war

Al-Andalus, extended by the conquest of most of present-day Portugal, remained firmly in Almohad hands for the rest of the century. In 1195 at Alarcos the Christians suffered one of their worst defeats in the history of the reconquest.

Nothing daunted, Alfonso VIII, the lion-hearted king of Castile, worked tirelessly with the Archbishop of Toledo to cement a grand alliance, and his efforts were recognised by Pope Innocent III, who in 1211 declared a crusade against the Moors. By May of that year Alfonso VIII had assembled a huge army, swelled by some 60,000 crusaders from beyond the Pyre-

embarked on the systematic subjugation of al-Andalus. The rulers of a second generation of *reyes de taifas*, who had filled the vacuum left by the downfall of the Almoravids, trimmed their sails to the wind and swore allegiance to the new Almohad caliph, one of whose lasting achievements was the building of the Great Mosque of Seville, of which the minaret, the Giralda, 93 metres (305 ft) high and containing a ramp wide enough to make the ascent on horseback, still survives.

LEFT: Christian and Muslim playing chess.
ABOVE: the Moors admit defeat before the Catholic monarchs. Granada was the last kingdom to fall.

RULE OF IRON

Under the zealous and puritanical Almoravids, Seville was shorn of its former glories. The common people at first welcomed their new rulers, but soon found that they had exchanged the flamboyant liberalism of the Arabo-Andalucían aristocrats of the *taifas* for the uncompromising rules of Muslim theologians, the *faqihs*. It was now the Christian kingdoms of the north which tolerated a symbiosis of religions and cultures; and although the Christians and Jews suffered most under the Almoravids, poets, philosophers and scientists also soon experienced the full force of a religious inquisition.

nees, and in July he faced the Moors under Muhammad al-Nasir strongly positioned at Las Navas de Tolosa in the Sierra Morena.

It was a fiercely fought battle. According to one account, the caliph had a premonition of disaster and his negro guard were hemmed around him with iron chains. At the end of the day the Moors were routed, the plucky Archbishop Arnold of Narbonne who took part putting their dead at 60,000, for the loss of 40,000 Christians.

During the 13th century Moorish resistance

AN EMPIRE LOST

Las Navas de Tolosa was more than an episode in a war: it presaged the overthrow of the Almohad empire and the disintegration of al-Andalus.

Ferdinand III of Castile and of his son Alfonso X (The Wise). Baeza and Ubeda in the east were taken in 1233, Córdoba in 1236, Jaén in 1245 and Seville in 1248.

New rulers

The lands retaken from the Moors were made over to the knights and barons who had fought beside the kings. Many land grants were small or medium-sized, but vast tracts of land were also ceded to families such as the Guzmáns, forebears of the Dukes of Medina Sidonia; and

in al-Andalus crumbled under the hammer blows of James the Conqueror of Aragón, of

these huge *latifundios*, akin to the *latifundia* of Roman and Visigothic times, were to be the cause of the agrarian problems which have beset Andalucía until the present day.

The Guzmáns, probably of German origin, had distinguished themselves at the battle of Las Navas de Tolosa and in the capture of Seville. Don Alfonso Pérez de Guzmán (El Bueno, the Good) is famous for his heroic defence of Tarifa in 1294. His son was captured by the Moors during the siege; faced by the Moors with a demand for surrender, failing which the boy would be killed, he defiantly tossed down a dagger from the walls – which they promptly used to kill his son.

A NATION OF SCHOLARS

The greatest triumph of the Almohads was posthumous and lay in the achievements of the 12th and 13th-century Toledo school of translators in transmitting to Western Europe the work, not only of Andalucían scholars and scientists, like Averroës (1126–98), but also, via Arabic translations, that of Euclid and Aristotle. Another event of major importance was the introduction of Arabic numerals (which we still use today) in place of the clumsy Roman system.

It is to the credit of the new Christian rulers that, initially, they reverted to the tolerant policies of the earlier Moorish regimes, Muslims and Jews remaining free to practise their religions, subject to a capitation tax. *Mudéjars* (Muslims living in the reconquered Christian areas, as distinct from *Moriscos,* who were Christian converts) formed most of the agricultural workers, and estates were taken over by their new Christian owners without changing the pattern of country life.

By the time the Catholic Monarchs, Isabella

> **CREATIVE TALENT**
>
> As artisans and craftsmen the Mudéjars were unrivalled, especially in such techniques as decorative plaster work, marquetry and wood carving.

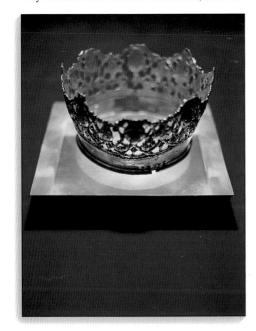

and Ferdinand, became joint rulers of Spain in 1479, the sole remaining Moorish enclave was the Kingdom of Granada, which also comprised Málaga and Ronda. At its peak it extended only 180 km (112 miles) from east to west and 80 km (50 miles) from the sea to its inland border. Towards the end of the Moorish rule as many as 100,000 people crowded into this small area.

Last bastion

That Granada lasted so long was because Ibn-al-Ahmar, the founder of its Nasrid dynasty, had

LEFT: Ferdinand and Isabella, royal crusaders.
ABOVE: Isabella's crown.

become a vassal of Ferdinand III of Castile and had actually assisted in the capture of Seville in 1248. Also, Ibn-al-Ahmar further helped Ferdinand's successor, Alfonso X, to overthrow the remaining emirates in the south.

Thereafter the Nasrids cleverly played off their North African Marinid allies against the Castilians and, by keeping a low profile and by the unwilling payment of tribute, staved off a frontal attack. Ibn-al-Ahmar nevertheless took the precaution of constructing a chain of watchtowers along the mountainous borders of his kingdom. Though little remains of these defences, the picturesque village of Alhama de Granada on a by-road from Granada to Málaga (C340) is still worth a visit.

The fall of Granada in 1492 cannot be explained simply by internal weaknesses or by the feud between its leaders which left it a prey to the advancing Christians. By the beginning of the 14th century, signs of religious and racial conflict began to appear, which grew increasingly bitter during the reign of the Catholic Monarchs.

Racial conflict

The Christians in the reoccupied territories were uneasily aware of the abilities of the Mudéjars as workmen and artisans, and of the Jews as administrators, doctors and merchants. From this it was a short step to postulate that such employment was unworthy of a Christian, and any attempt by the Jew or Mudéjar to better his status was fiercely resented.

Once the doctrine of *limpieza de sangre* (purity of blood) had been declared, it became a disgrace for any convert to Christianity to be even remotely tainted by Jewish blood. Only those who could claim complete purity of blood were admitted to positions of public authority.

Starting with the setting up of the Inquisition and the first *auto de fé* – the pronouncement of sentence on heretics and their burning at the stake – in Seville in 1481, the Catholic monarchs issued a decree in March 1492, giving Jews a choice between baptism or expulsion and allowing unbaptised Jews four months to liquidate their property and possessions.

When it became apparent that the Jews were emigrating *en masse*, even the harsh conditions of the decree were dishonoured and many of the

émigrés were stripped of their possessions and had to leave the country destitute. The Moriscos were soon to suffer the same fate as the Jews. Apart from the human suffering inflicted by the expulsions, Spain was also deprived of the services of its best doctors, administrators and financiers, who were Jewish, large numbers of skilled Morisco artisans and a sizeable part of its agrarian labour force.

It is difficult to tell whether the rulers of Granada in their isolated mountain fastness understood the full significance of these events

or realised that, once Christian Spain had absorbed the idea of nationhood bound by a single religion, the traditional multi-religious co-existence was no longer possible. By 1482 the Catholic monarchs began to make concerted plans for the overthrow of Granada and another crusade was declared by the co-operative Pope.

Meanwhile a family feud had broken out in Granada. The emir, Abu'l-Hasan, returned from a military expedition to find that the garrison of the Alhambra had revolted and declared in favour of his son, Muhammad Abu-Abd-Allah, known as Boabdil. Abu'l-Hasan was forced to take refuge with his brother, the only member of his family still loyal.

FINAL SETBACK

The Christians suffered a major reverse when Queen Isabella's tent caught fire and the conflagration swept through their camp.

The campaign against Granada began disastrously for the Christians. So confident were they of success that their army was accompanied by a train of merchants anxious to profit in the anticipated spoils. In the event the invading force was routed in March 1483, and the merchants spent their gold in buying their own freedom.

Unlucky king

Boabdil's reign began as disastrously as it was to end – not for nothing was he named The Unlucky by his subjects. Over-reaching himself in an attack on the Christians, he was taken captive and released by King Ferdinand on condition that he acknowledged vasselage to Castile and took the part of the Christians against his father and his uncle, al-Zaghal.

During the next 10 years, Ferdinand's forces moved in relentlessly on Granada. Málaga was taken after an epic resistance in 1487, and Ferdinand decided to make an example of it. The town's citizens were deported en masse to other parts of Spain and those unable to pay crippling ransoms were sold into slavery. Boabdil had been living under the delusion that he would be left in possession of Granada, but after the final defeat of al-Zaghal was bidden to deliver up the city. This caused an immediate public outcry and Boabdil belatedly decided to fight.

In 1491 a Christian army of 40,000 foot-soldiers and 10,000 cavalry invaded the lush *vega* below the city. They were beaten off by the gallant Moorish general Musa ibn-Abu l-Ghazan and Ferdinand then decided to sit it out and set up the huge tented encampment outside the city.

It was only a matter of time before the besieged town was starved into submission. After prolonged negotiations the capitulation was signed on 25 November 1491.

So, in a minor key, almost 800 years of Moorish rule in the peninsula came to an end. Boabdil had surrendered the last outpost without a fight to the end, and the bitter reproach of his mother, A'isha, rings down the centuries: "Weep like a woman for what you could not defend like a man." ❑

LEFT: the Moors are driven back to Africa.
RIGHT: the treaty agreeing the surrender of Granada, with the signatures of Ferdinand and Isabella.

Ey ... esbrad los offos mayores y garamos
z garamal. El este que omn noles und qn vil del
tpo dmomte ... que ... ynedi mas ... y ...
Nome le des garamos le ... onla nada ... orgfen
... llema algund ... ...

Nos El Rey Alla ... de Castilla de leon Aaragn de ... z ...
porla presente Seguramos ... leamos de med e ... da y aylt
adolo en aquella capitulaço ... e ante ... ynambe ...
mes ... con otro alos plazos ... a ... e ... mania
enda ... Se ... z ... ago ... que ello ... y fraude
algune ... z por Seguridas dello ma damos dar la presente
firmada de nuros nombres e ... da ... mro ... fecha el
... plaze ... a veynt e ... dias del mes de
Nombre ano de myle z ... e novera y anos

yo ... ...
... ... por ... mdad 388

& 575

THE MAKING OF MODERN ANDALUCÍA

It was from here that Christopher Columbus set sail to the New World.
His discovery transformed Andalucía into a world trade centre

In January 1492, with the surrender of Granada signed and the Christian army about to enter the city, Christopher Columbus, a lonely and Quixotic-looking figure on a mule, rode into the encampment of Santa Fé. It had been six years since he had first petitioned Queen Isabella for support in his project for reaching the Indies by sailing to the west. The project had been ridiculed and rejected by a commission of enquiry; Columbus was in despair and staying at the monastery of La Rábida near Huelva before taking ship for France.

While there, he discussed his hopes with one of the friars, Juan Pérez, who had been the Queen's confessor. Pérez wrote to Isabella; what he said has not been preserved, but it was of such consequence that Columbus was immediately sent money to return to court and seven months later his three ships set forth from the small port of Palos on their epic voyage of discovery.

Andalucía was thus associated from the outset with the discovery of the New World. The three little ships were crewed mainly with sailors from Palos, Moguer and Huelva; many of the Conquistadores and most of the first colonists were from Andalucía or neighbouring Extremadura; and in 1503, within 11 years of Columbus's first voyage, Seville was playing such a central role in trade with America that Queen Isabella established a Casa de Contratación there to regulate all trade with the New World. Its functions included the furnishing of embarkation permits; the inspection of ships; the supplying of mercury needed for refining silver; the registration of merchandise and the handling of the gold, silver and pearls destined for the royal exchequer. It further administered justice, saw to the despatch of missionaries, and served as a centre for navigational studies.

PRECEDING PAGES: defeat of the Spanish Armada.
LEFT: Seville prospered thanks to Columbus.
RIGHT: *In the Blink of an Eye*, painted by the Seville artist Valdés Leal.

Gateway to a new world

Seville (and later Cádiz in 1717, when the Guadalquivir river silted up and was no longer navigable for large ships) thus acquired a virtual monopoly of the trade with America. This

was not, as is often thought, simply a matter of the Catholic monarchs and their successors exploiting its position. The ships of the time were limited in range, and depended on the trade winds and a staging post in the Canaries to make the voyage at all; the Andalucían ports were therefore much better placed than those of the north or the Mediterranean,

J. Vicen Vives, for example, in his *Moments Crucials de la Historia de Catalunya*, has cogently put the technical reasons for the absence of Catalan shipping on the Atlantic route: "It was not feasible for a caravel to make the passage of the Strait of Gibraltar from west to east, against current and winds, without los-

ing much time and risking men and ships. It required the nautical revolution of the early 18th century, especially the introduction of sails known as focs, and an enlarged cruising range before the Mediterranean peoples could hope to participate in the American trade. Málaga, an important part of the Kingdom of Granada, with a hinterland rich in wheat, wines and silk, did not take part in commerce with America until 1778, although expressly awarded the privilege of free trade by Charles V in 1529."

IN FEAR OF DRAKE

Such is the terror Sir Francis Drake inspired that mothers in that part of Spain still frighten rebellious children by threatening them with the ghost of 'El Draque.

Spain's decision to embark on the ill-fated invasion of England with his massive Armada. Andalucía was the first to feel the effects when Drake made his pre-emptive strike on Cádiz.

Raid on Cádiz

In April 1587 the harbour of Cádiz was jammed with some 60 vessels, from hulks and coasters to the tuna fishing fleet and large merchantmen, many of them laden with supplies for the Armada, which was assembling in Lisbon. Drake's fleet, flying no colours

Another compelling reason for routing shipping through Seville or Cádiz was to organise convoys. To begin with, ships sailed singly or in groups unguarded; but as buccaneers and pirates began preying on the treasure ships of the Spanish Main, fleets were assembled at Seville, Cádiz or Sanlúcar de Barrameda and sailed under the protection of heavily armed galleons. The practice survived until the mid-18th century, when even eight or ten galleons could no longer protect the fleets against the depredations of the British Navy.

The attacks on Spanish shipping by Sir John Hawkins and Sir Francis Drake during the 1570s and 1580s contributed to Philip II of

so as to avoid identification, burst into the outer haven and within 24 hours had destroyed or captured some 24 ships. But for the prompt arrival of the Duke of Medina Sidonia with reinforcements, it would probably have captured the city.

The immediate result of the raid and the subsequent destruction of shipping and supplies along the Portuguese coast was to delay the sailing of the Armada for a year.

When the Armada finally did sail in May 1588, it was under the command of Don Alfonso Pérez de Guzmán, Duke of Medina Sidonia, Andalucía's premier noble. The fleet included a strong squadron of 11 ships from

Andalucía with a complement of 780 seamen and 2,325 soldiers under the command of Don Pedro de Valdés. His flagship, *Nuestra Señora del Rosario*, was one of the most heavily-gunned in the Armada and was therefore assigned the role of "troubleshooter" and charged with the defence of all the slower moving and more vulnerable craft.

By ill luck the vessel was an early casualty of the first clash in the English Channel, when, having gone to the aid of

SHERRY GALORE

By seizing some 2,900 pipes of sherry, or "sack" as it was then known, in the raid on Cádiz, and releasing it on the English market just when it was scarce, Drake contributed to a lasting demand for the drink.

Rivers of gold

During the early years of trade with the Americas, "rivers of gold" poured into Seville; it has been said that the emeralds from Colombia and pearls from Darien were traded around the cathedral in the same sacks used for chick-peas.

There was ostentatious spending on public works, palatial houses and churches. Perhaps the most grandiose project was the construction during the late 16th and early 17th centuries of the Lonja de Mercaderes, or exchange, now the Archive of the Indies, which was financed with just one quarter of 1 percent of the silver arriving from the Americas.

Another source of wealth was the export to the colonies of olive oil and wine; in return, Andalucía received new plants and foodstuffs, such as maize, tobacco, peppers and chocolate.

Andalucían writers, such as one Antonio Domínguez Ortíz in his *Andalucía Ayer y Hoy*, comment on a failure to grasp the enormous opportunities afforded by Seville's near trading monopoly during the early period. This has been put down to a number of causes, in particular to the lack of industry, except on a small artisan scale – for example, the manufacture of textiles and tiles. The textile industry could not, however, compete with northern Europe, and though much has been made of Seville's monopoly, most of the textiles exported to the Americas through Seville were not made in Spain but came from England and the Low Countries.

By the time of Philip IV (1621–65), because of the decision of Count Duke of Olivares to

another ship, she was disabled in a collision with the *Santa Catalina*, also of the Andalucían squadron, and captured by Drake.

The Armada's losses were appalling. After a battering in the Channel by the English fleet, the survivors were driven by gales up the North Sea and round the north of Scotland; of the 130 ships which had sailed for England, only 60 made the return journey to Spain. Medina Sidonia survived the disaster, sick in body and spirit, with a flagship that limped into Santander near to foundering.

ABOVE: *The Victory being towed into Gibraltar with the body of Nelson* by Clarkson Stanfield.

OPPORTUNITIES LOST

Much has been made of Seville's failure to take advantage of its virtual trading monopoly in the early years. Shipbuilding would have seemed an obvious opportunity; but, because of their poor quality, ships built in Andalucían yards were prohibited by royal decree from being used on Atlantic routes. There was a wide-open opportunity for Seville to establish itself as the banking centre of the Western world; but, perhaps because of the ill-judged expulsion of the Jews, all attempts to establish a viable banking system collapsed, with disastrous repercussions on the mercantile community.

squander American silver and human resources on a fruitless war in Flanders, inflation was rampant. The Atlantic trade had declined considerably and the most valuable export that Andalucía could offer was that of its own people.

Emigration from Andalucía and neighbouring Extremadura from 1493 to 1600 is reliably put at 40 percent. The result is a prevalence of Andalucían customs in South America and the close resemblance of Spanish as spoken in Latin America to Andalucían.

UNDER ATTACK

A desperate shortage of supplies during the Spanish siege of Gibraltar was made good when Admiral Rodney broke the blockade.

hopelessly outnumbered and outgunned by an Anglo-Dutch fleet, and after a siege of only three days the governor surrendered to Prince George of Hesse as the representative of the Archduke Charles.

Gibraltar was ceded to Britain in 1713 as part of the Treaty of Utrecht, by which the war was brought to an end. The Spanish were soon to question Britain's right to its possession. During 1779–83, at the time of the American War of Independence, it underwent one of the famous sieges of history, when it was beset both by sea and land by the armies and fleets of Spain and France. It was, however, well prepared, with storage galleries cut into the rock and the latest types of artillery capable of raking the attackers at low angle.

The siege culminated with the French throwing in 10 floating batteries "fortified 6 or 7 ft thick ... with green timber bolted with iron, cork and raw hides; which were to carry guns of heavy metal and be bomb-proof on the top with a descent for the shells to slide off." The British found an answer to them in firing off red-hot cannon balls; and after subjecting the defenders to a tremendous hammering, all 10 of the platforms caught fire and sank or blew up.

The argument over Gibraltar rumbles on, with Spaniards naturally resenting the presence of a foreign enclave on Spanish soil and some regarding the polyglot and fiercely anglophile population as little better than a gang of smugglers, while the British government finds itself in a cleft stick when every referendum results in a near 100 percent preference for the status quo.

Debating point

The issue of Gibraltar at the southernmost tip of Andalucía has now for almost three centuries soured relationships between Spain and Britain. The dispute dates from the War of the Spanish Succession (1701–13), when Charles II of Spain died without heir and the choice of a successor lay between the Archduke Charles of Austria and Philip of Anjou. After Philip was crowned with the support of Louis XIV, war broke out between Spain and France on the one side and Austria on the other, supported by Britain, Holland and Portugal.

In 1704 the allies decided to open a new front by seizing Gibraltar. The Spanish garrison was

Bonaparte's attack

During the next major conflict on Spanish soil, the British were for once allies instead of enemies. In writing about the Peninsular War of 1807–14, during which Napoleon's armies overran the whole of Spain and Portugal, Richard Ford remarks: "The Spanish have two objects: one to detail the ill-usage which they have sustained from the invaders; the second to blink as much as possible the assistance afforded by England." A fair statement of what happened is that the British troops would have had no chance of beating Bonaparte and the French in open battle but for the relentless resistance of the Spanish, especially the guerrillas,

any more than the Spanish could have continued the fight without the inspiration of Wellington's victories.

The French assault on Andalucía began in January 1810 after a series of disastrous Spanish defeats. Marshal Soult and Joseph Bonaparte, with 40,000 men, were faced by 23,000 Spanish extended over a front of 240 km (150 miles).

Córdoba fell without a fight on 24 January. The Junta which had been ruling the country from Seville decamped for Cádiz on the 23rd, followed by the military commander, the Duke of Albuquerque, with his troops. The city fell into the hands of an excited mob; nothing was done to destroy the arsenals, the largest in Spain; and vast quantities of munitions, as well as tobacco to the value of £1 million were lost to the invaders when they took over on 29 January.

Soult lost no time in despatching General Victor to take Cádiz, but he arrived too late to intercept Albuquerque's 12,000 troops, who had entered the city two days before, blowing up the only bridge over the wide salt-water channel between the mainland and the Isla de León on which Cádiz is built.

Despite a French blockade lasting for years, Cádiz was under no serious threat thanks to the presence of gunboats in its harbour and larger units of the Spanish and British navies further out. In the hour of their peril the Spanish forgot earlier fears about the landing of British troops, and in February 1810, 3,500 men under General William Stewart landed to reinforce the garrison.

Meanwhile, all the rest of Andalucía lay open to the ravages of Marshal Soult, a connoisseur of other people's paintings, who accumulated his extensive collection simply by theft, and of General Sebastiani, the plunderer of churches.

French occupation

Sweeping as the French victory had been, their hold on Andalucía was tenuous and confined to the larger towns and cities. The French were never safe from the activities of the guerrillas, which tied down huge numbers of troops.

Ferdinand VII's repudiation of the liberal constitution of Cádiz was far from being the end of the matter. A first fruit of his autocratic policies was the revolt and loss of the American colonies between 1810 and 1824; and the strug-

gles between liberals and absolutists rumbled on through the 19th century with the outbreak of the two Carlist wars.

The road to Europe

Spain entered the 20th century minus most of its remaining overseas possessions, lost in the Spanish-American War of 1898. Alfonso XIII, at the head of a shaky constitutional monarchy, was king of a country plagued by increasing civil unrest. In 1923, the Jerez-born General Miguel Primo de Rivera seized power although the King retained the throne. Primo de Rivera's was a more or less benign dictatorship which

counted on considerable popular support and saw enormous activity in public works, but he was an incurable optimist and totally hopeless at economics, driving Spain to the brink of bankruptcy, and was ultimately deposed by more constitutionally correct Spanish military. The Spanish king was forced into calling municipal elections, which were won overwhelmingly by proponents of a Spanish republic. Taking the hint, the chagrined king headed for exile, and Spain's Second Republic was born.

It was a short-lived exercise, as confrontation between left- and right-wing supporters gathered steam. In 1936, the Spanish army posted in Morocco rose up against the government,

LEFT: early industry – rollers used for pressing olives.
RIGHT: Alfonso XIII ponders affairs of State.

under their commander General Francisco Franco. The word was sent out to military commanders all over Spain, many of whom joined the revolt. Andalucía was split in two. The sanguinary Quiepo de Llano seized control of Seville and Granada fell shortly afterwards, leading to bloody reprisals in which thousands of Republican supporters were executed, including the Granada-born poet García Lorca. Málaga was captured in 1937 after bombardment from navy ships and the arrival of tough Italian troops seasoned by

HUNGRY FOR WORK

During the terrible depression of the post-war years hundreds of thousands of Andalucíans emigrated to factory jobs in France and Germany.

the wars in Abyssinia. The support of Italy and Nazi Germany, aside from Franco's superior fire power, were decisive in the insurgents' final victory in 1939.

Franco's iron fist

Franco, who was ruthless and incorruptible in equal measure, was to decide the destiny of Spain for the next three and a half decades. Although officially neutral, Spain was sympathetic to the Axis during Word War II and afterwards Spain was an outcast from the community of nations. Franco's government preached an extreme form of isolationism, hoping against hope to rely on the country's own

resources. The devastation of war was followed by a prolonged drought which led to the "Years of Hunger". Andalucía was especially hard hit.

Things were to change in 1953 when Spain agreed to cooperate with US efforts in the Cold War, and allowed four American bases to be built, including an enormous naval base at Rota, near Cádiz.

Fuelled by a fresh inflow of cash, Spain edged its way into the 20th century. While Franco still held the country in his iron grip, a number of the more repressive rules were relaxed, and Spaniards began to enjoy a measure of middle-class comforts, including the ubiquitous Seat 600 car.

But the true revolution was triggered by the arrival of curious foreign visitors. The first were artistic types, artists and writers seeking the cheap life in the sun. Next came the trendies and the hippies. Finally, the first planeload of package tourists landed at Malagá airport in the late 1960s, and there was no stopping the flood.

Hotels sprouted along the Andalucían coast, farmers abandoned their land to become waiters and cooks. More importantly, Spaniards came into contact with foreign ways and ideas, and they were perfectly prepared when Franco finally died in 1975 and the newly proclaimed King Juan Carlos I, to the surprise of many observers, led Spain painlessly into democracy. The first democratic elections were held only two years after Franco's death, and Spain was welcomed back into Europe, joining the European Community in 1986.

For much of Spain's post-Franco history, the country was governed by the nominally socialist PSOE party, headed by the charismatic Felipe González. Before world recession enforced a spell of belt-tightening, the government were profligate with public spending and Spain lived through a boom period. Andalucía was a main beneficiary of new roads and injections of cash, much of it European funds.

The whole world was invited to a party to witness the Andalucían miracle: Expo '92 in Seville, when Spain celebrated the 500th anniversary of Columbus's historic voyage to the New World. ❑

LEFT: troops in the Sierra Nevada in the Civil War.
RIGHT: Italian planes bomb the Republicans.

THE ANDALUCÍAN CHARACTER

Andalucía has at last taken itself into the modern age,
but old traditions and local rivalries die hard

For a long time Andalucía was the poor relation among Spain's regions, crushed by the burden of poverty and feudal legacies, drained of its manhood and its brightest minds. Some Spaniards even viewed it as part of the Third World and as being inhabited by a mix of decadent aristocrats and illiterate rustics with laughable accents.

There was some truth in the stereotype. Until the 1960s Andalucía still seemed "a land bottled for antiquarians", as the English traveller Richard Ford described it early in the 19th century. Many of its ways and values had changed little since medieval times. It was a pleasantly picturesque world, provided you were comfortably off or only passing through: a land of whitewashed villages, vast estates and daunting sierras with bull-breeders and sherry barons, flamenco dancers and gypsies lurking around every corner. The injustices and the misery were masked by the beauty of the region and the graciousness of its people.

Andalucía remains unique. The ritualised lifestyle of one of the oldest of Western civilisations continues. The flamboyance, the anguish and the passion are still there. But now the region is rushing into the 21st century. Mass tourism turned rigid mores upside down along the Mediterranean coast. Poverty still exists, particularly among the farm labourers, but these days the car parks are packed outside those temples of consumerism known as *hipermercados*.

Age of change

Nobody laughs at the Andalucían accent these days. After all, the country's longest-serving post-Franco prime minister, Felipe González Cames, comes from Seville. High society, which once spurned Andalucía's lack of culture, flocked to classes to learn the *sevillana*, a spirited flamenco dance. European Union funds reinvigorated agriculture and the colossal investment and interna-

tional contacts created through Expo'92, marking the 500th anniversary of Columbus's voyage to the New World, stimulated the economy.

Teenagers whose parents can barely read tinker with computers and dance to the same loud music as counterparts in other European countries. "Andalucía is Europe's California," claims

the propaganda. Well, not quite. It is a society moulded by layers of ethnic, social and cultural influences. Andalucía's history has roots in Africa and Asia as well as Europe.

Mattress tactic

Time and again it has demonstrated its ability to absorb and adapt new invaders, whether they be Phoenicians, Moors or Castilians. In his perceptive essay *Theory of Andalucía*, José Ortega y Gasset, one of the most eminent 20th-century Spanish intellectuals, drew comparisons with China in the region's capacity to accommodate conquerors through the "mattress tactic". Andalucía's tactic before violent attack was "to give

PRECEDING PAGES: pre-Lent Carnival band; the annual Jerez horse fair; girl in the Plaza de España, Seville. **LEFT AND RIGHT:** timeless Andalucían good looks.

way and be soft. In this way it always ended up intoxicating the harsh impetus of the invader with its delightfulness."

The microchips may be down now that Andalucía is part of Europe, but it is difficult to imagine the *sevillano* or the *malagueño* giving up his three-hour lunch or his addiction to the bulls. Andalucíans inhabit an area which is naturally bountiful and their culture has always been fundamentally an agrarian one.

The grand stage

What particularly sets the Andalucían apart is his taste for making a show of himself for keeps his personal relationships well-tuned. This is carried to extremes at the Seville Fair, where Andalucíans uninhibitedly put themselves on show to all, but an outsider soon finds that he is attending a week of personal reunions.

Julian Pitt-Rivers, whose study of the mountain village of Grazalema (Cádiz) is regarded as a landmark in anthropological research, pointed out that: "In a pueblo community, personal relationships have a higher priority than legal considerations."

When the English researcher Ronald Fraser arrived in Mijas (Málaga province) in 1957, he immediately noticed that "the pueblo was the

strangers. Anybody visiting Seville can be forgiven for thinking he has strayed on to a grand opera stage. Ortega y Gasset suggested that this collective narcissism, this propensity to contemplate himself and delight in himself, while it could produce affectations, resulted in the Andalucían reaching a better and clearer self-knowledge than that attained in other societies. Thus it was easier for Andalucíans to remain consistent in their customs and faithful to their own culture.

Socialising is a vital ritual to the Andalucían. The old custom of the *tertulia*, whereby friends meet regularly to discuss everything under the sun, still endures. In local bars and clubs a man

PERSONAL MATTERS

Everything is personal to an *andaluz*, including religious matters. The men rarely attend church – that is usually considered the domain of the womenfolk – but he will fiercely proclaim the virtues of this Virgin as opposed to that of any other community. Isidoro Moreno, a leading Spanish anthropologist, felt that the intensity of personal relations explains a good deal about Andalucían society and its segmentation. "It appears very open," he commented. "But people fool themselves. Their personalised relations encourage many groups of a few persons and it is difficult to penetrate them."

focus of life; it had the 'urban' quality that is so dear to the Andalucían of human concourse and discourse. The strength of family life... was its cement. Exaggeratedly, it appeared that everyone was related, that the village was one extended family."

Usual suspects

Forty years after the tourist boom foreigners are still looked on with suspicion and influential contacts are considered the best means of getting on in life. This reflects a cynicism ingrained by centuries

REBELLIOUS SPIRITS

Democracy, a novelty, has still to prove itself in a land where taking to the mountains as an outlaw was a frequent recourse under oppressive regimes.

Sundays, but not many would let it be known that they occasionally did the washing-up. That would be inviting gibes about their masculinity.

Spanish television daringly ran advertisements trying to persuade men to help wives with kitchen chores. That campaign underlines the extent to which the machismo cult still rules. Women are only beginning to challenge their accepted role. Exaggerated pride is one of the negative aspects of this manliness; bigheartedness and grand gestures are two of the appealing characteristics.

of oppression. Andalucíans are not surprised when politicians indulge in cronyism; experience has taught them to distrust authority and that using *enchufes* (connections) is the best way of obtaining satisfaction from government.

Despite the drift to the cities, the family still rules supreme, revolving around the mother, a venerated figure and willing slave. She reigns over the home and raising the children is generally left to her. More independent-minded young fathers may be seen pushing the baby pram on

Local rivalry

Poor communications and illiteracy contributed to the Andalucían's suspicion of everything beyond his own community. Isolation has led to intense rivalry between towns and villages. Denigrating other towns is popular. Rhyming slander is popular, on the lines of *"Loja, la que no es puta es coja,"* (In Loja, the women are either whores or lame) and *"Buena es Granada, pero junto a Sevilla no vale nada,"* (Granada is all right, but it is worth nothing compared to Seville).

Courtship and canes

But attitudes are changing. The *moto* (motorcycle) has helped. Until the 1970s, rural com-

LEFT: card sharps enjoy a game in a bar in Priego de Córdoba. **ABOVE:** women flutter fans, essential summer accessories, in a shop in Ecija.

War and Peace

Buried in the files of Spain's town halls are tales of many a forgotten conflict and Quixotic confrontation. Nevertheless, the revelation in the early 1980s that two humble Andalucían municipalities were at war with powerful European nations did provoke a certain amount of local astonishment.

Inspired by local pride, fearless in defence of Spanish honour, Líjar and Huescar had been engaged in hostilities with Denmark and France since the 19th century, a challenge of which unaccountably neither Copenhagen nor Paris seemed aware. A flurry of diplomatic activity

was necessary before peace was finally declared in two of the region's remotest and most tranquil areas.

Small and poor, the village of Líjar lies in the heart of the harsh Sierra de Filabres in Almeria province. The 650 inhabitants scrape a living from the arid soil and from their work in nearby marble quarries. But their spirit is indomitable. How else could they have carried on a 100-year war against the might of France?

Don Miguel García Saéz, fervent monarchist, lawyer, journalist and crusader, was the instigator. As Líjar's mayor, he was indignant when he heard that King Alfonso XII had been insulted and stoned by the mob while passing through Paris. At a meeting of the seven village councillors on 14 October 1883, he formally declared war on France, contemptuously reck-

oning that each Líjar inhabitant was equivalent to 10,000 Frenchmen. Don Miguel noted that Spain had more than enough valour to "wipe the cowardly French nation off the map".

Although the war lasted a century, there was no bloodshed. Few tourists, let alone soldiers, managed to negotiate the winding roads that lead up to the hamlet.

Yet, when news of the war leaked out, many of Líjar's inhabitants were reluctant to drop the matter. They felt France's recent stance towards Spain, not least the attacks by French farmers on Spanish agricultural products, hardly justified a change. Finally, however, after intense diplomatic negotiations, France despatched its consul from Málaga and a peace treaty was eventually signed with the required pomp on 30 October 1983.

Huescar, a town of 10,000 people in the northeast of Granada province, had forgotten all about its war with Denmark until a diligent local historian unearthed town hall records dating back to 1809, when a good part of Spain was occupied by Napoleon's forces. The Spanish government, which was lodged at that time in Seville, issued a royal order declaring war on Denmark as an ally of Napoleon.

When news of this reached Huescar, the local council issued its own declaration expressing its "eternal contempt for the enemies of Spain". Somehow Huescar forgot to revoke that declaration.

For 172 years hostilities dragged on without casualties. Indeed, Denmark appeared unaware even of Huescar's existence until news of the find in the archives was broadcast by a Danish radio correspondent.

This prompted swift action by the Danish ambassador in Madrid who wrote to say: "It is surprising that this bellicose matter has not been resolved. But I believe it is never too late and I hope to have the opportunity to put matters right."

For reasons of political expediency, a number of Huescar's councillors favoured maintaining a symbolic state of war. But even they had to agree that Huescar's armed forces, consisting of eight municipal policemen, might not be sufficient to combat Danish tanks. Peace talks finally went ahead on the condition that "they preserve the honour of our city and promote understanding with the Danish people".

Before a treaty could be signed, Huescar did take two prisoners of war. They were journalists from Denmark who were lightheartedly handcuffed when they arrived at the town hall to report on the event. When it was decided to remove the handcuffs, however, the key had been mislaid and they had to be escorted to a blacksmith to be freed. ❑

munities were often inbred because youngsters had no way of visiting neighbouring towns and villages and only chance encounters could lead to marriage outside. Even courting a girl from the same village was a laborious process, since the *novio* was required to spend countless evenings visiting his girlfriend's family but never, in theory at least, being permitted to spend time alone with her.

CHANGING TIMES

Today girls have unheard-of liberty, until early marriage chains them effectively to the home.

One of the great opportunities to break out occurred on the Mediterranean coast with the cane-cutting season every spring. Hundreds of

Easier communications and a more relaxed moral code are contributing to marriages between communities which in the past turned their backs on one another. In the Alpujarras, a teenager said: "It wasn't so long ago that they tossed in the fountain a lad from the next village who dared to come here at fiesta time to court one of our girls."

Links with the past are most strongly in evidence in the fiestas. Some old customs are believed to date from neolithic times, such as the cult of the dead (on the night before All Souls' Day relatives hold a vigil in

young men spent several weeks engaged in this gruelling task, chopping the sugar-cane with machetes. The workers lived in conditions that were often abysmal and their pay was low, but it was a rare moment of freedom, a chance to earn extra cash and meet girls away from family pressures.

The sugar-cane business has slumped but today most youngsters can afford a motorcycle or car. No longer confined to their own villages, their choice of *novias* is no longer restricted to second cousins and the girl next door.

LEFT: villagers in Líjar's Plaza de la Paz.
ABOVE: the young favour an increasingly open society.

DIVIDED THEY STAND

In the mountain village of Frigiliana the people look down physically and figuratively on the neighbouring town of Nerja, which was dirt-poor until recently but is now a flourishing tourist resort. "Not too long ago they were penniless fishermen. They came here to beg. Now they act as though they're superior. The truth is that they are not *gente seria* [literally, serious people]. You can't rely on them," complain the locals, mixing past history and recent envy. The new rich of the tourist resort polish their new cars, pack their modernised houses with veneered furniture and scoff: "Those sierra bumpkins! They don't even speak Spanish up there."

cemeteries and light candles before the tombs of the departed).

Virgin worship

As in all agrarian societies, the earth has an almost mystical importance and explains the astonishing emotions aroused by the Virgin, who – as American Hispanist Allen Josephs convincingly argues in his book *White Wall of Spain* – is a Christian incarnation of the earlier pagan earth-mother and goddess of fertility.

One of the Virgins which excites most fervour is *La Blanca Paloma* (The White Dove), Queen of the Marshes, and it is easy to see pagan connections with the pilgrimage which attracts a million or so people to her sanctuary at El Rocío, in the marshes near the mouth of the Guadalquivir. Fanaticism, piety and non-stop singing, dancing and drinking coalesce in a spectacular release of emotion. As Josephs points out, "the ecstatic wine-dance of antiquity is still practised as religious ritual, incor-

porated now into the worship of the Virgin, but unchanged as dramatic ritual and devotion-diversion". Andalucíans' capacity to launch themselves into another dimension on such occasions sets them apart from more "developed" urban man who has become so removed from his primordial roots that he has to rationalise existence on a psychiatric couch.

The *andaluz* remains a creature of nature, childlike in his enthusiasms, with an urge to live each moment vividly. He may never read a newspaper but poetry excites his deepest sentiments; he may not be baptised García Lorca, Antonio Machado, Vicente Aleixandre or Rafael Alberti, but he is a poet at heart.

Gypsy flavour

Perhaps it is this poetic licence in Andalucíans which leads them to create their own myths. Once a personality has been elevated to this mythological status, he or she is untouchable. This is particularly so in the bullfight and flamenco worlds where gypsies are among the leading performers. Matador Curro Romero is capable of magic when the conditions and mood are right. More often, however, shaking with fear at the sight of the bull, he simply refuses to fight and

VIOLENT PREJUDICE

In January 1984, a thousand inhabitants of Torredonjimeno (Jaén) tried to lynch a gypsy family and five people were badly burned when their house was torched.

Flamenco would not exist in its present form had not the gypsies wandered in from Egypt during the 15th century. True to form, the Catholic monarchs issued an edict in 1499 ordering the "Egyptian" to settle down and get regular jobs within 60 days instead of wandering about the kingdom. If they refused they would receive 100 lashes and exile the first time; the second time, their ears would be cut off and they would be permanently expelled.

Harsh treatment has always been the gypsies'

disappointed fans hurl seat-cushions after him.

"The amazing thing is that inside the *plaza de toros* people may scream abuse," mused the matador Antonio Ordoñez. "But with every step Curro takes away from the plaza the public's memory becomes shorter. By the time he has covered 100 metres people are telling him what a great job he has done."

Another adored gypsy matador, Rafael de Paula, was arrested for conspiring to kill his wife's lover. Far from ruining his career, this made him more popular.

LEFT: bullfighting plays a key part in local culture.
ABOVE: the Verdiales fiesta in Málaga in full swing.

lot. Although today there is no longer legal discrimination they often face hostility. *Payos* (non-gypsies) are ambivalent in their feelings towards these nomadic nonconformists. García Lorca, however, was lyrical: "The *gitano* is the highest, the deepest, the most aristocratic, the blood and the alphabet of Andalucían and universal truth."

Gitano fire has played its part in creating the Andalucían character. It is a complex, contradictory character, one which fits as easily into the computer age as does La Virgen del Rocío and the fiesta associated with her. Building "Europe's California" in the land where the Kings of Tartessus and the Caliphs of Córdoba once held sway is going to be a fascinating exercise. ❏

FIESTAS FOR ALL SEASONS

The Andalucían character shines at fiesta time. Singing, dancing, prancing horses, food and wine...these are the basic ingredients of a fiesta

Andalucían fiestas come in seasonal cycles, and many trace their roots to pagan times. Even the deeply solemn Semana Santa procession has pagan roots, as a celebration of spring. Not for nothing is Easter held on the first Sunday after the first full moon after the vernal equinox. Other celebrations are unabashedly pagan, such as the eve of San Juan (23 June), when bonfires are lit, effigies burned, and the tradition is to leap through the flames and then bathe in the sea to cleanse the spirit.

Most fiestas are light-hearted affairs. Two weeks after Semana Santa, Seville holds its April Feria. Every city and village holds an annual *feria*, usually in summer. The end of summer marks harvest season, when every wine-growing area has its Fiesta de la Vendimia, the biggest being in Jerez. Other crops are similarly honoured, everything from raisins to olives.

SOLSTICE CELEBRATION

The winter solstice has been celebrated since the dawn of mankind, although now we know it as Christmas. In Spain, Christmas goes on for two weeks, starting with *Nochebuena* ("the good night"), on Christmas Eve. People greet *Nochevieja* ("the old night"), New Year's Eve, in front of the clock in the main square, where they eat the 12 grapes of good luck, one for each chime. Finally comes the Epiphany, or Feast of Three Kings, when Spanish children receive their presents.

The cycle ends with Carnival, the final fling before the abstemious Lent period leading up to Holy Week and a new round of fiestas.

▷ **PASSION PLAY**
Christ's passion and death are re-enacted in outdoor plays in many towns, such as Riogordo (Málaga), whose *Paso* (passion play) spans two days.

△ **FIESTA RHYTHM**
Girls clap their hands to the rhythm of a *Sevillana* song during the April Feria, a week-long party featuring singing and dancing, horse parades and bullfights.

△ **HARVEST FEST**
Recalling wine-making methods of days gone by, grapes are trod in front of the main church during the September harvest festival in Jerez de la Frontera.

◁ **VIRGIN OF THE SEA**
In fishing communities the image of the Virgen del Carmen, patroness of fishermen, is taken out in sea-borne processions in July.

VIRGIN WORSHIP

The story is repeated in countless villages: a hunter, a shepherd or a farmer stumbles across an image of the Virgin Mary, concealed in a grotto or in the hollow trunk of a venerable old tree, presumably to hide it from the heathen Moors. He tries to take it back to the village, but falls asleep and, on waking, finds the Virgin has miraculously returned to her original hiding place. Word of the miracle spreads, a shrine is erected, and it becomes a place of pilgrimage. Some of these pilgrimages called *romerías*, after the custom of gathering wild rosemary (*romero*) along the route, have become mass events, such as the pilgrimage of the Virgen de la Cabeza in Andújar (Jáen), the pilgrimage of the gypsies in Cabra (Córdoba), the sea-borne processions to honour the Virgen del Carmen (*photo above*) or, the biggest of all, the Romería del Rocío, on the edge of Doñana, which attracts around one million people every Whitsuntide.

◁ **EASTER PENITENT**
An image harking back to the Middle Ages – a hooded penitent in one of Málaga's Holy Week processions. He is a member of a *cofradía*, the brotherhoods which organise the processions. These can last eight, 10 or even 12 hours.

△ **HORSE PLAY**
Carriage at the Jerez de la Frontera's annual Horse Fair in May. No town takes its horses as seriously as the sherry town, birthplace of the Carthusian breed.

▽ **PRE-LENT REVELRY**
Troubadours sing satirical verses during Carnival. Such songs were banned under Primo de Rivera and also under Franco – apart from in Cadíz.

△ **FESTIVE COLOURS**
Flamenco costumes are worn for a fiesta in Lebrija (Seville). Most Andalucían towns hold their *feria* during summer, when returning migrants can join in.

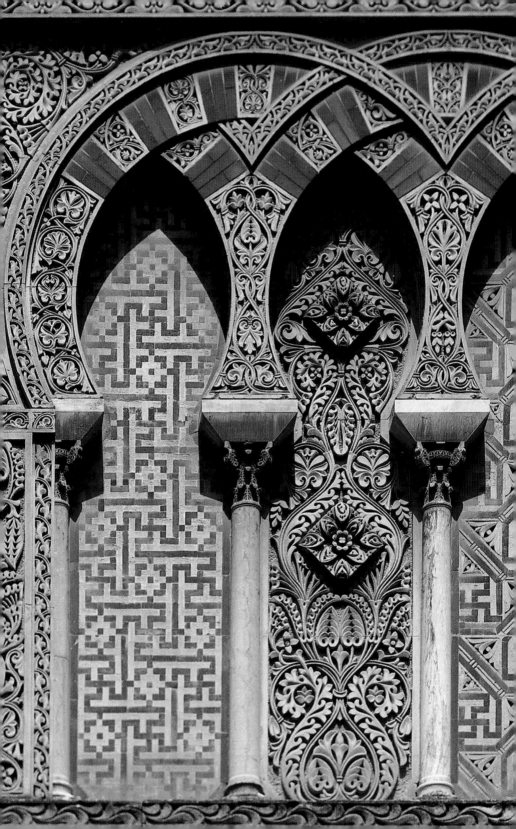

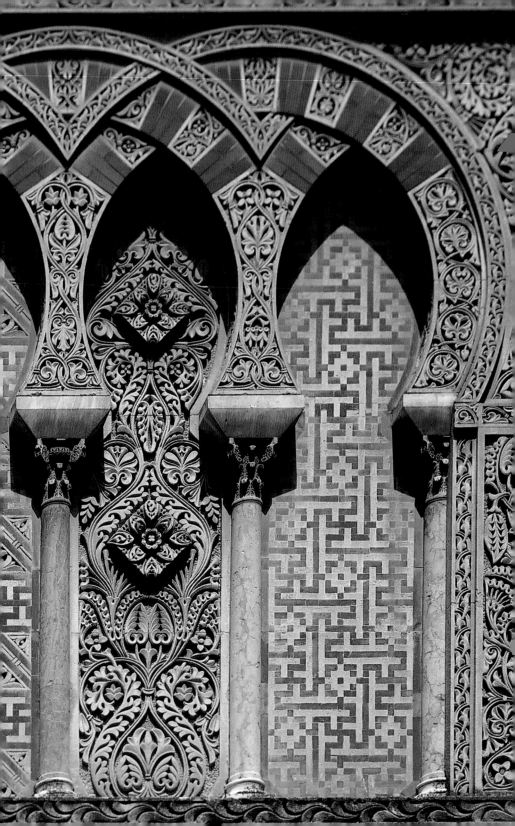

FOOTPRINTS OF THE MOORS

Traces of Andalucía's Moorish history can be found everywhere: in its architecture, irrigation techniques and even in the people's physical characteristics

When King Hassan of Morocco made his first official visit to Spain in 1989, he was presented with the freedom of Madrid. Holding the symbolic key to the gates of the city, he declared that he intended to lose it so that the doors of friendship between the two countries could never be locked.

The remark struck a chord among both Moroccans and the people of Andalucía. Residents of Morocco's ancient city of Fez are said to dream even now of returning to al-Andalus, the land of milk and honey that they were forced to flee 500 years ago. They listen to groups playing "Andalucían music", a style reflecting the origins of flamenco, and some of them are said to still hold on to the keys of their old homes in Granada.

Andalucía has absorbed, changed and been changed by successive waves of settlers. The Moors (derived from the Roman mauri or maurusci, a name applied to the Berbers of the Atlas Mountains) left perhaps the deepest imprint during their stay of 700 years on Spanish soil. In the end they suffered pain and persecution, but retained their attachment to the region.

The same may be said of the Jews, who contributed profoundly to Andalucían commercial and intellectual life before being brutally and foolishly expelled.

Artistic influence

One meets with the Moorish inheritance at every turn in Andalucía, although at times the influence is so subliminated into local culture that its origin is almost invisible. The most striking aspects to a visitor are obviously the architectural gems, such as the Alhambra palace of Granada with its delicate stucco designs and light-as-air pillars and patios, the Great Mosque of Córdoba with its red-and-white arches marching into the shadows, the Giralda tower soaring over Old Seville. Almost every community – many bearing clearly Arab names

such as Almachar, Benamahoma, and Zahara – is dominated by the crumbling (or recently restored) walls of an *alcázar* (fort).

Many of the region's churches are built on the site of mosques and traces of Moorish-style structures are common in the brickwork, archways and roof tiles.

Indeed, distinguishing features of Mudéjar art – strictly, work executed by Muslims living under the Christians – continued to be used in buildings throughout Spain and beyond long after the Moors had been ousted. Even today, potters from Granada to Seville carry on the tradition, turning out products little different from those used in medieval times, employing similar techniques and designs to those used by the Moors.

In the Alpujarras region of Granada province, which was the last stronghold of the Moriscos (Muslims that converted to Christianity), the flat-roofed houses strongly resemble the Berber dwellings of the Atlas Mountains in Morocco.

PRECEDING PAGES: facade of La Mezquita, Córdoba.
LEFT AND RIGHT: Moorish-style craftwork.

Work and speech

Irrigation techniques owe much to the Moors, who worked hard and ingeniously to transform Andalucía into a garden. Many of today's channels carrying water from mountains to fields follow ancient routes that they first traced. The Moors are credited, too, with introducing sugar-cane, peaches and apricots to the peninsula.

The Spanish vocabulary is crammed with words adapted from the Arab tongue. A *fonda* (inn) was a *funduq* to the Moors. *Jaque mate* (checkmate) comes from *al-sah mat* (the king has died). *Alfaque* (bank or shoal), *alcornoque* (cork tree), *aljibe* (cistern) and *aljama* (Moorish or Jewish quarter) are just a part of the linguistic legacy.

And as for the cries of "Olé!" that greet a matador's fine pass in the bull-ring or the emergence of the Virgin from her temple, linguistic researchers claim these are the echo of the Muslim exclamation "Allah! Allah!"

And in recent years, after centuries in which the term *moro* has been used as pejorative, the

> **CREATIVE FORCE**
>
> Poetry and silk-weaving, leatherwork and literature flowered under the Moors, and Caliph al-Hakam II collected 400,000 books in his personal library.

> **ANCESTRAL REMNANTS**
>
> It is possible to see signs of the Moorish inheritance in the way Andalucíans look and act: those smouldering dark eyes, hawk-like noses, and jet-black hair; the flaring of temperament and flare for show; the Oriental flavour of the anguish distilled in cante jondo, a variation of flamenco; a taste for haggling; the love of fine language and indifference to niceties of time.
>
> Too much, however, can be made of characteristics which are shared by many Mediterranean peoples, and it is easy to draw many more comparisons, as academics often point out.

Andalucíans themselves have joined the search for Arab roots.

The expulsion of thousands of Moors and Moriscos from the region to be replaced by settlers from the north diluted the Arabness of Andalucía. The fanaticism that inspired those purges also plunged Spain into dark centuries of religious persecution and intellectual stagnation.

Initially, the *Reyes Católicos* (Queen Isabella and King Ferdinand), flush with their 1492 victory over the Moorish Kingdom of Granada, were generous towards the Muslim population, guaranteeing them the right to practise and conserve their customs, but this attitude soon changed.

End of an elite

The Spanish Inquisition had been set up in 1478 (the Inquisition already existed, most strongly in France and Italy). Eventually it was to investigate the Moors who feigned conversion but were found to be still following Islam. Primarily, however, it was intended to deal with the "evil influence" of the Jews.

> **FLAMES OF INTOLERANCE**
>
> Two thousand heretics were burned in Seville in the year 1481. The Jews were suspect both because of their religion and their wealth, which provoked jealousy.

Persecution had not been unknown to the Jews living in al-Andalus, but during the Golden Age of the Caliphs around the 10th century, they, the Christians and the Moors, had managed to live peacefully alongside one another, and intermarry.

This was an era when art, trade and agriculture flourished in a climate of tolerance. Recognised as valuable members of the community, the Jews were skilled artisans, weavers, financiers and merchants with connections in Baghdad and Damascus.

Some were influential in government. Hadai Ben Shaprut, diplomat and doctor, was a powerful adviser to the Caliph of Córdoba, Abd-al-Raman III, and a promoter of Talmudic studies. An 11th-century philosopher, Bahya Ben Paquda, exercised profound influence on Jewish mysticism with his writings, first composed in Arabic. Among those who attended Córdoba's Talmudic school was Moses Maimonides, later to distinguish himself as physician to the Sultan Saladin and as a great thinker.

Lucena, a Jewish stronghold in the Córdoba caliphate, was virtually independent. According to one contemporary writer, "The Jews who dwelt within its massive walls were richer than in any other region subject to Islam and were much on guard against their rivals."

When the crusading armies of Castile conquered Andalucía, Arab and Hebrew books were consigned to the flames. Soon heretics were joining them on the bonfires.

Although historians disagree over the number of victims of the Spanish holocaust, it is believed some 2,000 were killed during the tenure of the first Inquisitor General, Tomás de Torquemada, himself a *converso* (converted

Jew). The Jews were suspect both because of their religion and their wealth, which provoked envy. In 1492, Torquemada persuaded Isabella and Ferdinand to issue an edict giving the Jews three months to be baptised or leave the country. It was forgotten that the conquest of Granada would not have been possible without Jewish finance.

More than 170,000 Jews refused to renounce their faith and were driven out of Sepharad (the Hebrew name for Spain) where their ancestors had lived for 2,000 years.

Scattered about the world, half a million Sephardic Jews today still use the Judaeo-Spanish tongue known as *Ladino*. Some families, like the ousted Moors, claim still to possess the keys of their Spanish homes.

Loss of an elite

At a stroke Spain lost an educated elite. To complete the impoverishment of Andalucía, the monarchy soon made life impossible for the Moors, closing their mosques, torturing them and denying them basic rights.

In 1567, King Philip II decreed: "You must abandon your language, your religion, your traditions, your customs, clothing and finery and,

LEFT: stucco detail from the Córdoba synagogue.
RIGHT: a mosque in Marbella, built by the Saudi Arabian royal family.

above all, that mania of yours, so little Christian, of bathing yourselves daily. You must forget your ancestors, and baptise yourselves and give yourselves names like ours." The bloody War of Granada resulted, and in 1609 all Moriscos were ordered out of Spain.

Although the Inquisition claimed thousands of victims, the numbers have often been exaggerated. It should also be remembered that this was a brutal era; according to some estimates, at around the same time more than

300,000 "witches" were burned in Europe, two-thirds of them in Germany and an estimated 70,000 in England.

After the purge

The Arabs had been too long in Spain for their influence to be completely wiped out. Moriscos remained in Spain, either adopting Christian names while concealing their true beliefs or embracing Catholicism. Their blood, and that of the Jews, had mingled with that of the conquerors and not all the statutes of *Limpieza de*

> **SPANISH INQUISITION**
>
> This was a time when merely refusing to eat pork was enough for somebody to be suspected as a heretic and dragged to the torture chambers.

MOROCCAN MIGRATION

Another stifling summer day dawns in Algeciras, a grimy seaport on the southern tip of Spain. As the sun's first rays etch in the harbour, a convoy of loaded vehicles chugs aboard a Morocco-bound ferry.

Most of the boat's passengers are Moroccan migrant workers who have spent up to two days waiting on the quay. Their waterside vigil is usually preceded by a sleepless, 1,600 km (1,000-mile) dash through France and Spain. The discomforts and dangers of this epic trek (migrants often carry large sums of money and expensive presents for their families back home and are targets for modern highwaymen) do not deter these industrial nomads. For these

Moroccans, a fortnight or possibly a month's rest in the desert and the chance to see their families justifies the annual purgatory that begins when the farms and factories of France, Germany and the Low Countries close for summer holidays.

Over four weeks from the end of July, over 750,000 Moroccans cross Spain towards Algeciras. From here it is a 2½ hour journey across the Straits of Gibraltar to Tangier or a one-hour crossing to Ceuta, a sliver of Spain in North Africa. When migrants reach this Spanish enclave near Tetouan, they are just 3km (2 miles) from home: after customary delays at the frontier, the cavalcades lurch forward and disappear into the tawny haze of Morocco.

sangre (literally cleanliness of blood) could change that fact. Semitic features are not hard to find in modern Spain.

Descendants of the *conversos have* played prominent roles in Spain's public life. They included Santa Teresa of Avila and great writers of the Golden Century of Spanish culture. Renewed religious freedoms, beginning in the 19th century, allowed Jews to return to Sepharad and they are once more in evidence in the arts, business and government.

THE POWER OF ISLAM

Spanish converts to Islam have created their own communities in the main Andalucían cities, sometimes demonstrating the special zeal to be found among all converts.

other than Catholicism to establish themselves in the country and this was the signal for a revival of the Islamic faith and for mosques to spring up in many locations.

Spanish Islam

Possibly 200,000 persons now follow the Muslim creed in Spain. The majority of these are of Moroccan origin, while some are from the Middle East oil states.

Members of the Saudi Arabian royal family are among the many Arabs from the Gulf States

Seville's labyrinthine Jewish quarter, known as Santa Cruz, and Córdoba's Judería, complete with synagogue, attract many visitors. Names such as Platero (silversmith) indicate a connection with the Jewish artisans of the past and it cannot just be coincidence that Córdoba has an unusually large number of silver-workers and jewellers.

With the approval of a democratic Constitution in 1978, Spain once more allowed religions

who have bought property on the Costa del Sol. They have even established their own mosque at Marbella. Along this increasingly cosmopolitan coast, signs in Arabic compete for attention with those in English. At Pedro Abad, near Córdoba, the Ahmadiya sect from Pakistan has established a mosque in an effort to widen its influence.

Some Spanish remain wary of such developments. For instance, proposals to erect a mosque in the Albaicín, Granada's old Arab quarter where a number of converts live by making handicrafts such as hand-painted ceramics and embossed leatherware, have met with opposition from many *granadinos*. ❑

FAR LEFT: documenting an annual ride home to Morocco from Paris. **LEFT:** breaking the journey. **ABOVE:** Moorish inspiration in the modern hotels along the Costa del Sol.

BUILDING ON THE PAST

All the great civilisations to settle in Andalucía left outstanding monuments, a legacy that presents a living history of architecture

Three millennia in the mainstream of Mediterranean civilisation have given Andalucía its fair share of great monuments. The most feverish construction took place under the Romans, who were great builders of roads, theatres, bridges, aqueducts and new towns, such as Itálica near Seville.

The Moors improved on what had preceded them, including the horseshoe-arch developed by the Visigoths and put to such splendid use in the grand mosque in Córdoba. With the arrival of the austere Almohads, Moorish architecture was less ornate (the Giralda in Seville is an example), but the twilight years of Islam in Spain brought a flourishing of a delicately exuberant style, embodied in the Alhambra.

CHRISTIAN FORMS

Even after the Moors' dominion, the Moorish influence was strong. The Mudéjars, Moorish craftsmen living under Christian rule, combined Moorish and western forms. Conquest by the Christians coincided with the late Gothic and renaissance periods, which left outstanding collections of palaces in Baeza and Ubeda, and the renaissance Palace of Carlos V in the Alhambra. These styles and the baroque which followed are best appreciated in the great religious constructions: because they took so long to build most Andalucían cathedrals provide a visual catalogue of Western architecture.

◁ **CARVED COLUMN**
Column from the Roman theatre in Itálica, near Seville. Founded in 206 BC, the city is the largest Roman site in Andalucía.

△ **BURIAL CHAMBER**
The Cueva de la Menga, one of several megalithic dolmens near Antequera was built 4,500 years ago out of 31 stone slabs.

◁ **ADOPT AND ADAPT**
The *mihrab* in Córdoba's mosque. The horseshoe arch, developed by the Visigoths, was perfected by the conquering Muslims.

▽ **MORE THAN MOORISH**
Neo-Mudéjar influences can be seen in modern buildings such as the bullring in Puerto de Santa María (Cádiz), opened in 1880.

THE COLOURS OF ANDALUCÍA

△ **EXPRESSION OF WEALTH**
The facade of the Palacio de Jabalquinto in Baeza, Andalucía's best example of Isabeline architecture, a variant of renaissance.

▽ **SEVILLE SHOWCASE**
Expo '92 was a showcase for new architecture, such as the Puente del Alamillo, a tensile structure supported on a single column.

▽ **ELABORATE FLOURISHES**
The baroque Iglesia de la Aurora in Priego de Córdoba, near Córdoba.

Although mosaics of coloured stones were a common decorative element in Roman Andalucía, it was under the Moors that the decorative tile was born. Moorish ceramic tiles, used on floors, walls and roofs, showed a definite Oriental influence.

Their Spanish name, *azulejo*, comes from the Arabic *az-zulayj*, or "little stone". Originally, small single-coloured tiles of various shapes were arranged in geometric patterns, as in the Alhambra.

Crucial to the development of the *azulejo* was glazing, which fixed the colours on the tile and made it more durable. Gilded tiles were used to cover roofs and copulas, such as that which originally crowned the Giralda in Seville. The art further evolved under the Christians in the 15th and 16th centuries, especially in Seville, where the individually-coloured tiles were replaced by square tiles containing several different colours. These could be arranged to form shapes and pictures, and Seville's *azulejos* were a prime export to Europe.

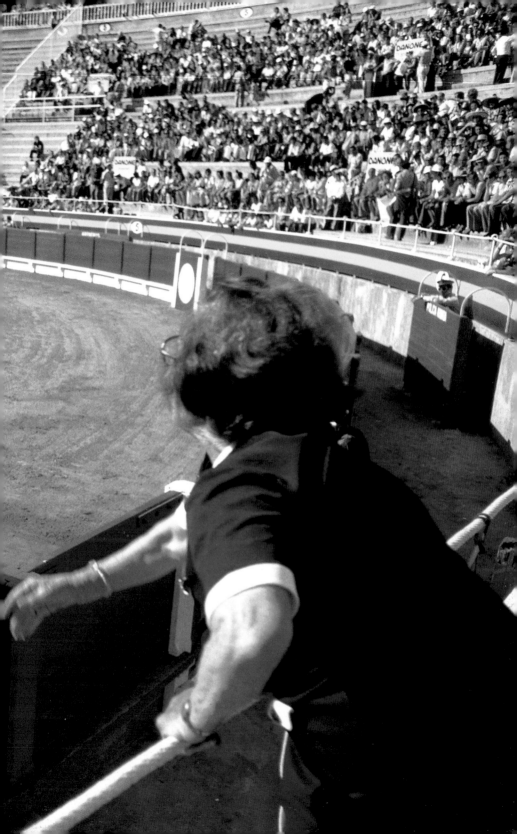

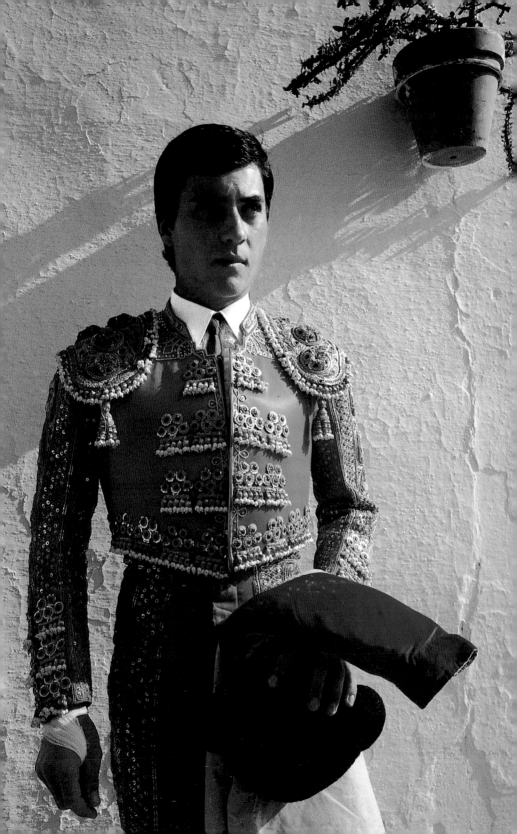

BULLFIGHTING HEROES

Bullfighting is a passion passed from one generation to the next.
Dynasties are made in the bullring but often at great expense in terms of human loss

Alfonso the Wise, King of Castile and León, could hardly have imagined, when he declared the profession of bullfighter to be disreputable in his Code of Laws, that one day whole families would take up and sustain this dangerous profession. Today's bullfighters are often members of dynasties similar to the lineage of royal sovereigns.

The dynasties of *toreros* – and bullfighting itself, for that matter – all began around 300 years ago in the Andalucían city of Ronda (see page 245), set in the mountains behind Marbella, where one of the country's oldest bullring still stands. The oldest known bullfighting dynasty, the Romeros *(see below)*, originate from Ronda, and one of today's top young bullfighters, Francisco Rivera Ordóñez, is not only the heir to three truly great families in the history of bullfighting – Dominguín, Ordóñez and Rivera – but also claims indirect ties with that Andalucían town.

First fighters

Francisco Romero was born in Ronda at the beginning of the 18th century. He started the tradition of bullfighting simply, on foot, equipped with a sword and *muleta* (small cloth). But his greatest merit really lies in having fathered a whole dynasty.

Juan Romero, son of Francisco, had no less than four bullfighter sons – José, Pedro, Gaspar and Antonio – a circumstance not at all unusual at that time, considering that it was common for children to adopt their father's trade. Antonio had the misfortune of being killed by a bull in 1802, but Juan's second son, Pedro, was eventually proclaimed the "Father of Modern Tauromachy" (bullfighting).

Born in Ronda in 1754, Pedro Romero is credited with having killed over 5,600 bulls in his career without ever suffering a major injury.

PRECEDING PAGES: an appreciative bouquet is thrown for a knight of the bullring.
LEFT: a young matador waiting for his moment.
RIGHT: *Cuadrilla*, by Daniel Vazquez Diaz.

From a family noted for its longevity – his father lived to 102 – Pedro Romero killed his last bull in the Madrid bull-ring at the incredible age of 79. He also founded the very first bullfighting school in Seville, under the auspices of Ferdinand VII, a forerunner of the dozen schools which exist in Spain today.

Heroic era

Another important dynasty was that of the Cándidos, who stood out during what is referred to as the heroic age of bullfighting – called thus because of the ferocity of the animals and the great risks taken by the *toreros*, who had not yet developed the fully refined techniques of today.

José Cándido was noted for killing a bull armed with a dagger in one hand, and his hat, used as a lure, in the other. Cándido was killed by a bull in Puerto de Santa Maria, but not while he was performing the aforementioned death-defying feat but while rushing to the aid of a *banderillero* in danger, he slipped in a

pool of blood on the sand and was fatally gored.

Jerónimo José Cándido was only nine years of age when his father died, but in the end he, too, chose to follow in his father's footsteps by first joining the *cuadrilla* (squad) of Pedro Romero.

The next major family of bullfighters, the Costillares, began with brothers Juan and Joaquín Rodriguez, the latter of whom was the first to adopt the rather unusual nickname of "Rib Cage".

Joaquín Jr, born in Seville in 1748, was the

HIGH ART

Belmonte was responsible for redefining the very ground rules of bullfighting, converting the popular spectacle into the refined art of today and not a mere display of athletic skill and ability.

recognised creator of the *volapié* sword manoeuvre, the manner in which most bulls are killed today. The *volapié* involves positioning the bull, encouraging it to charge, and moving in simultaneously to a potentially deadly encounter between man and beast.

Until this innovation all bulls had been killed by the difficult *recibiendo* method, in which the matador adopted a firm, immobile stance, incited the bull to charge, and then plunged in the sword as best he could.

Francisco Arjona Cuchares was the most famous of the Arjona dynasty, a capable and versatile *torero*, who set off for Cuba at the age of 50 to perform in a bullfight there, only to fall sick and die of yellow fever soon after his arrival in the West Indies.

Intense rivalry

During the height of bullfighting's popularity the most passionate rivalry ever encountered in the ring existed between two *sevillanos*, Joselito el Gallo and the so-called "revolutionary" Juan Belmonte.

The Gallos were of pure, gypsy lineage. An inspired, unpredictable, intensely superstitious bullfighter, when in the ring Rafael el Gallo could simultaneously perform some of the most memorable and artistic work imaginable, then flee scandalously from the bull, by jumping headfirst, most undecorously into the *callejón* (the protected area of the ring). It was Rafael el Gallo, the gypsy *torero* personified, who defined bullfighting as "having a mystery to tell… and then trying to tell it".

His father José was the classic, cerebral, masterful *torero*, the prototype of what every bullfighter should be: dominating, superior, arrogant, brave and elegant. He made his debut at 13 and dominated the ring until Juan Belmonte came along.

Short and without the physical prowess of his rival Gallos, Belmonte was forced to create a new fighting technique, in which the bull was the one to move about and not the bullfighter. In order to dominate the animal, he obliged it to charge.

Never were passions so high as during this Golden Age, when everyone from the butcher to figures from the literary and art world ardently

THEN AND NOW

It was the custom during the heroic age of bullfighting that an aspiring bullfighter began learning his trade as one of the three *banderilleros* (assistants) in the *cuadrilla* (squad) of an experienced matador and only when he was sufficiently practised did he break out on his own. Nowadays, things work backwards. *Banderilleros* are customarily *novilleros* (novice bullfighters) that have failed to make the grade or matadors that are past their prime and have decided to join the *cuadrillas* of younger, up-and-coming bullfighters. *Banderilleros* assist in handling the bull by using a cape and in placing *banderillas* (sticks) in the bull's shoulders.

defended their favourites. Belmonte lived on to become one of the most important bullfighters of all times, but one thing was lacking to convert him into a legend to match his rival, according to writer Ramón de Valle Inclán, who recorded the following exchange with the matador: "All you are missing, Juan, is to die in the ring," said the writer, to which Belmonte replied: "I will do my best." Sadly, an ailing Belmonte eventually committed suicide on his Seville ranch in 1962, just six days short of his 70th birthday.

MODERN DYNASTIES

The Bienvenida dynasty is represented today by the retired and respected Angel, Luis and Juan, who had less glittering, and safer, professional lives.

of "Papa Negro", the Black Pope of Bullfighting.

Papa Negro had six bullfighting sons, each of whom stood out for his art, courage, elegance and refinement, both in and out of the ring, although unfortunately luck did not smile on them. Among them, the oldest of the boys, the "almost perfect" *torero* Manolo, died at the age of 25 from what was most probably cancer. The solid, classic, scientific Pepe, who had never suffered a serious injury in his entire career, finally succumbed, at the age of 54, to a heart attack while bull-

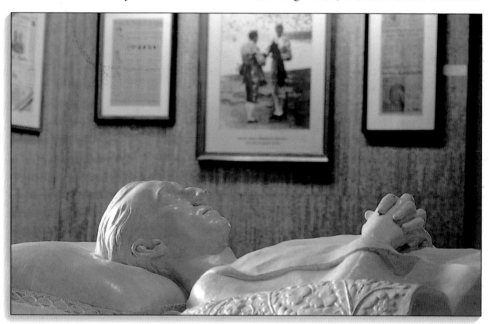

Tragic family

One of the longest dynasties in bullfighting history was nicknamed "Bienvenida", because its founder was born in the small town of Bienvenida in the province of Badajoz way back in the middle of the 19th century. Manuel Mejias Rapela adopted his father's bullring pseudonym and became a truly popular matador until a bull from the Trespalacios ranch abruptly terminated his career with a near-fatal goring during a fight. Mejias earned a sobriquet in his own right, that

LEFT: Rafi Camino, the latest in a long dynasty.
ABOVE: effigy of a bullfighting hero in the Bullfighting Museum, Córdoba.

fighting in Lima, Peru. Rafael, meanwhile, had passed away under mysterious circumstances at the age of just 16.

Antonio was the best loved of them all and a favourite son of the demanding Madrid public; he was the epitome of elegance, both as a bullfighter and as a gentleman and will always be remembered for his artistic and intelligent handling of the bulls. He died of spinal injuries resulting from a tossing while fighting a calf "for fun" on a country outing.

Role model

The great Antonio Ordoñez, his father Cayetano (nicknamed "Niño de la Palma") and his four

brothers, Cayetano, Juan, Pepe and Alfonso, were natives of Ronda. Cayetano Sr was Ernest Hemingway's bullfighter model in *The Sun Also Rises*, although Hemingway later became Antonio's most ardent fan.

Antonio Ordoñez, considered one of the greatest *toreros* of all time, interpreted the art of bullfighting with the maximum purity, classicism and bravery. He appeared on the scene at the beginning of the 1950s to challenge his future brother-in-law Luis Miguel Gonzalez Dominguín, the capa-

SUMMER OF LOVE

Ernest Hemingway was inspired to write a series of essays on bullfighting for *Life* magazine, which were later published in a book, *The Dangerous Summer*.

Manuel was killed by a bull in Málaga in 1926. Manuel's half-brother, Miguel III, became the leading matador of the 1950s, noted for his unmatched bravery, forming a striking duo with Madrid-born Julio Aparicio.

Among today's bullfighters, at least 40 matadors and just as many *novilleros* have some direct or indirect relationship with previous *toreros:* Jose Mari Manzanares, Emilio Oliva, Luis Francisco and Juan Antonio Esplá, El Boni, Rafi de la Viña and Juan Mora are all sons of bullfighters

ble, technical and powerful rival of Manolete in the 1940s.

Today's heroes

One of the most successful young fighters today, Miguel Baez Litri is the son of an immensely popular *torero* in his own right. Miki (Miguel's pet name) took the *alternativa* in the Nîmes bullring. The *alternativa* ceremony, granted by a senior bullfighter, converts a novice into a fully-fledged professional.

The saga of the Litris began in their native Huelva, where the first Miguel Baez Litri was born at the beginning of the 19th century. He was followed by Miguel Litri II whose son

of varying fortune who have entered the ring.

Another, more recent source of bullfighting talent have been the official bullfighting schools established in various parts of Spain during the 1980s. Their graduates have included successful fighters such as Cristina Sánchez – not the first female bullfighter in history, but the first one to be taken seriously – yet even she comes from a bullfighting background. Her father, Antonio Sánchez, was a *subalterno*, an assistant bullfighter.

It is understandable that the children of not overly successful *toreros* are encouraged or freely choose to follow in their footsteps in an attempt to achieve the glory denied their fathers,

but it is more difficult to understand why the son of a *torero* who has attained the coveted top status of *figura de toreo* would risk life and limb in the rings. There are only eight or 10 top fighters and the price they must pay for the honour is steep.

High pressure

Top *toreros* perform in up to 70, 80 or even 90 *corridas* a year, for wages varying according to the size and category of the ring, from 1½ million pesetas in a small town to more than 5 million pesetas for the major San Isidro Fair in

> ### ADVICE FROM THE TOP
> Often their seniors did everything they could to discourage young *novilleros* from pursuing this immensely difficult and self-sacrificing profession.

Madrid. These apparently impressive fees are reduced considerably after the salaries of a minimum of eight employees are deducted, along with all their hotel, food and travel expenses, the manager's commissions, taxes and the cost of publicity, sequinned suits, capes, swords and other paraphernalia.

Sacrifices must be made

In summer, the schedule is extremely pressing and bullfighters criss-cross the country with

LEFT: putting on a show, Roberto Dominguez and some supporters.
ABOVE: a moment of prayer before the fight.

barely enough time to rest before the *corrida*.

Amongst the true bullfighting fraternity drinking, smoking and partying are frowned on, but many young, ambitious *novilleros* make these sacrifices willingly, seduced by the overwhelming desire to reach the zenith of their profession, only later to experience remorse about adolescent years spent with no friends, no teenage diversions, and under the burden of an eternal sense of fear and responsibility.

From father to son

Litri Sr kept the most spirited calves on his ranch for his son to fight in the hope that the spectacular bumps and bruises Miguel received from them would discourage him from continuing in the trade; but they didn't. Litri said he knew he would be a bullfighter from the first moment he stood before a brave, fighting calf, when "the strangest sensation came over me". He was a mere eight years old at the time.

There is something in the blood of the best-known dynasties that keeps them returning to the ring. In Francisco Rivera Ordoñez Jr are the seeds of three important bullfighting dynasties, the Ordoñez family through his mother, the Dominguíns, through his maternal grandmother, the late Carmen Gonzalez, and the Riveras, inherited from his father. Francisco Rivera Paquirri was killed by a bull in 1984 when at the height of his career – an event that shocked the bullfighting world but failed to discourage his son, who has been fighting calves on his father's and grandfather's ranches ever since he can remember, from following in his father's footsteps.

Although Francisco Jr's financial prospects were secure no matter which road he chose to follow in life, he was very clear about his future. He told his mother the day of his father's funeral: "Now, I am more convinced than ever, mama, that I want to become a bullfighter." He was then nine years old.

Most towns in southern Spain have bullfighting during the appropriate season. Unfortunately the displays on the Costa del Sol are often not of good quality, and do not make a fitting introduction to the art. Try to see your first fight at one of the best-known rings, with a well-known matador. ❑

FLAMENCO: FROM KITSCH TO PUNK

With its gypsy past behind it, flamenco survived the Franco years,
emerging with new vitality and ready to absorb the sounds of contemporary music

The earliest origins of flamenco, a synthesis of music and dance which has come to be identified with the essence of Spain, are unclear. Flamenco crystallised in the gypsy communities of southern Andalucía in the mid-18th century, and much speculation as to its ancestry has focused on the Middle Ages, when gypsy tribes from Rajasthan in India migrated through Egypt and North Africa into Spain.

Today's flamenco certainly shares common features with Indian and Arab song, and other linguistic evidence supports the Arab connection – the word flamenco may have come from the Arabic *felag mengu*, meaning "fugitive peasant". Gypsies have always adopted and adapted the musical styles of their host communities, however, and flamenco also contains strong traces of Jewish and Byzantine Christian religious music, as well as regional Spanish folk styles.

Gypsy cult

The historic heartland of flamenco is the triangle of flat delta between Seville, Jerez and Cádiz, but the music spread with the movements of the gypsies. Catalonia, home of the great dancer Carmen Amaya, and Asturias spawned powerful local styles. The songs known as *farrucas*, for example, originated in the non-flamenco north and arrived in Cádiz with Galacian and Asturian sailors. *Payo*, or non-gypsy artists, acquired the flamenco arts, at first by marriage into gypsy families, and later, as the genre became a professionally dispensed commodity rather than a closed private entertainment, by choice and study.

The rise of flamenco to an art appreciated by the educated and moneyed fits the familiar pattern of similar musical forms such as the Blues, which started as rough but vital lower-class entertainment. The word "flamenco", both an adjective and a noun, denotes a way of life, and

---

PRECEDING PAGES: the real thing in Granada's Sacromonte. **LEFT:** classic pose.
RIGHT: international star Joaquín Cortés mixes flamenco, jazz and modern dance.

a person who is unsettled, uncommitted, emotional, unpredictable, quite possibly criminal, in every sense anti-bourgeois. In this sense, the new young flamenco-rockers, of whom more later, are truer to the origins of the music than some of the established concert performers who have built professional careers.

Types and styles

The flamenco repertoire is based on songs with specific uses or contexts – songs about work or religion, dance tunes, or semi-spontaneous musical expressions of the joys and sorrows of everyday life. The oldest and most typically gypsy songs, such as the *tonás*, are sung unaccompanied, except for some basic percussion. The *martinetes*, originally created in the blacksmiths' forges of the old gypsy district of Triana, in Seville, are still sometimes recorded with the clang of a simulated hammer and anvil.

The numerous styles of flamenco are sometimes divided into the categories of *cante grande* (great song), *cante intermedio* (intermediate) and

cante chico (little). The *cantes chicos* are brighter, lighter, and often accompanied by dance. Examples are the very common *bulerías*, *alegrías* and *tangos*. A small number are re-adaptations of hybrid rhythms created in the Hispanic-American colonies. These styles, which include the *guajira*, the *rumba*, the *colombiana* and the *milonga*, are much in evidence in new flamenco.

The pinnacle of the true flamenco singer's art is the body of great songs, often referred to as *cante jondo* (deep song), the *soleares* and *seguiriyas*, which are expressive of the deepest, most heartfelt emotion and,therefore, most difficult to perform and most prized.

Deep song

It is in the *cante jondo* that the quality known as *duende*, literally spirit or demon, is most crucial. *Duende* is considered to be a form of involuntary inspiration which takes over a performer and exalts his singing to a high art, provoking a murmur – or roar – of "*olés!*" from the audience as a particularly gut-wrenching *copla*, or verse, spirals to its fierce climax.

Just as *duende* is not programmable, so the art of flamenco is at odds with the concept of rehearsal. Flamenco was, and at its best still should be, an impromptu communal activity that grows with the feeling of the moment (plentiful

supplies of alcohol helping matters considerably).

The major development of flamenco into a public entertainment started in the 1850s, with the growth of café *cantates* featuring established gypsy artistes, among them the first flamenco stars such as El Planeta and El Fillo. From this period dates the *cuadro flamenco* – the group of four to a dozen singers, guitarists and dancers, taking turns at solos.

Gaudy kitsch

By the 1920s, the so-called Golden Age of flamenco had become a tinsel age, with the popularity of the art leading to increasingly cheap, gaudy and inauthentic spectacle. This period con-

tinued through the Franco years, though by the late 1950s a process of regeneration had started.

The Franco dictatorship saw a broadening of Andalucían-based music into a flamenco-tinged range of song styles, a process which the government encouraged as the music was politically uncontentious, easy to identify for tourists, and colourful. The light but dramatic song form known as the *tonadilla* became popular, interpreted by Spanish Piaf-equivalents such as Conchita Piquer, Juanita Reina and, later, Rocio Jurado. The *fol-*

FLAMENCO KINGS

The southern French group, the Gypsy Kings, were to score world success with a sound very similar to flamenco rock.

Rock stars

On the pop/rock front, the Cano Roto sound, named after a rough gypsy suburb of Madrid, was born around 1973. Young gypsy-dominated groups, such as Los Chorbos, Los Grecas, Los Chunguitos and Los Chichos, mixed electric and acoustic guitars with bass and drums to create a fast pop sound based on the rumba rhythm.

In pure flamenco, two young performers who were to assume huge stature consolidated their careers. The brilliant *payo* guitarist, Paco de

clóricas – Lola Flores, Isabel Pantoja and others – purveyed a similar, glossy flamenco cabaret music.

Flamenco's associations with Franco, of course, alienated large numbers of youthful, progressive Spaniards and the general image of the music of the south, including pure flamenco, in the 1960s and 1970s was old-fashioned. But by the time Franco died in 1975, a number of developments in flamenco and flamenco-linked music were under way, which were to herald the return to form of Andalucían music.

Lucía, began his work of combining an impeccable technique with an explorative approach which included the incorporation of a range of Latin-American melodies and rhythms, as well as a number of jazz and rock collaborations.

Most importantly, a young gypsy *cante jondo* singer from near Cádiz built a major reputation, as much for his rock-and-roll lifestyle as for his searing, *duende*-inhabited voice and charisma. El Camarón de la Isla combined the qualities of rock and flamenco.

Camarón died in 1992, a victim of his frantic lifestyle, but he had by then secured a position among the flamenco greats. There is a before and after Camarón, for he influenced a genera-

LEFT: Manuel de Paula performs.
ABOVE: lights, camera, action.

tion of flamenco performers which emerged in his wake, including his protegée, Niña Pastori.

Flamenco's rhythms continue to spread into other genres. A key influence in the incorporation of flamenco traits into the world of rock and fashion was Kiko Veneno, a Seville-based guitarist whose 1977 punk-influenced album, *Veneno*, featured the guitar playing of the brothers Rafael and Raimundo Amador, descendants of an old Triana flamenco dynasty.

Controversial Cortés

Each new instance of "flamenco fusion" brings out groans of protest among the purists. This is especially true of flamenco dance. While the dancer Joaquín Cortés drew mass crowds in Spain and abroad with his fusion of flamenco, jazz and modern dance, flamenco diehards dismissed his performances as a bastardisation, pointing to El Guito or Farruco as the true custodians of the art. Yet it has been precisely in dance where the greatest evolution has taken place throughout the history of flamenco. In its earlier form, the dance was a sort of tribal performance involving a circle of people; the movements were much slower, and in the case of women involved only the waist up. It was Carmen Amaya who revolutionised the *baile flamenco* in the 1930s with her tempestuous, foot stomping renditions

Fashion boom

While flamenco-rock experiments have continued traditional flamenco has flourished too. Local government-funded festivals provide abundant audiences for the old custodians of the authentic *cante*, singers such as Pepe de la Matrona, as well as younger stars like the Habichuela family, Tomatito, Enrique Morente, el Lebrijano, Vicente Soto and el Cabrero.

The inventiveness of Andalucían music seems undiminished. El Camarón's 1989 album *Soy Gitano*, recorded with London's Royal Philharmonic Orchestra, reaffirmed him as a major innovator as well as an established traditional star, and made his early death all the more tragic. Experiments combining flamenco singers with Moroccan groups – El Lebrijano with the Orchestra of Tangier, José Heredia Maya with the Orchestra of Tetouan – look set to be repeated with increasing popularity. ❑

LEFT: flamenco school, Granada.

CATHEDRALS OF WINE

Sherry, the world's most famous aperitif, comes in many guises.

Here's how to tell your palo cortado from your oloroso...

There was a wine maker in Jerez de la Frontera in the mid-19th century named Manuel González who did a healthy trade exporting the dark, sweet, nutty wine of the region to England. He had an uncle, José Angel de la Peña – Pepe for short – who was fond of a type of wine which, unlike the popular sweet sherry, was crystal clear in appearance and bone-dry to the palate. There was a section in the wine cellar where uncle Pepe kept a few barrels of the stuff, for his personal enjoyment and for sharing with friends.

One day, one of Pepe's barrels was included in a shipment to England. Word soon got back from the importers. Could they have some more of that rare, clear stuff, please? So the winery started making more of this style of wine, naming it after the vintner's uncle: Tío Pepe. Thus was a Jerez legend born, and today Tío Pepe is one of the top-selling wines in the world.

The land of sherry abounds in such anecdotes, accumulated over the centuries. Few tipples have the mystique surrounding those from this corner of the province of Cádiz, where a unique combination of soil, grape, climate and ageing methods give rise to the world's most popular aperitif wine. The names of some of its makers – Domecq, Osborne, Terry – have an almost legendary ring to them, conjuring images of a charmed life surrounded by thoroughbred horses, solicitous lackeys and fine women with olive complexions.

Fine cellars

Reposing in the cellars of Jerez there are some one million wood barrels – the large sherry *botas*, or butts, each containing 500 litres of liquid gold. These veritable cathedrals of wine are the best place to learn about the different types of sherry and how they are made. The wineries, some of which resemble cities in miniature, welcome curious travellers and have become the town's major attraction, with tens of thousands of visitors a year.

A typical tour will last between 40 minutes and an hour, After an audio-visual show about sherry and the winery's history, a guide will lead you through the cellars, with their endless

PRECEDING PAGES: sampling local sherry, Córdoba.
LEFT: the late José Ignacio Domecq was popularly known as "the Nose".
RIGHT: barrels marked with famous names

rows of casks (many of them signed by celebrities who have visited in the past), explaining the *criadera* and *solera* system used for blending the different vintages, and the difference between *finos, amontillados* and *olorosos*. The tour ends in the *sacristía,* or sacristy, with a tasting of the wines, drawn from the cask by the *venenciador,* who uses a small cup attached to the end of a slender rod.

The Golden Triangle

Sherry is born in what has been called the "Golden Triangle", a wedge of gently rolling country in western Cádiz. At one corner is Jerez itself. At the two other corners are El Puerto de Santa María, the port from which sherry was traditionally shipped, and Sanlúcar de Barrameda, at the mouth of the Guadalquivir. Each has a distinct character: where Jerez is aristocratic and proud, El Puerto is a workaday port, and Sanlúcar a relaxed fishing town. Between them lie the expanses of brilliant white, chalky soil, carpeted with the vines.

Most sherry is made with the Palomino grape. It is a high-yielding white grape, but aside from that there is nothing much to be said for it: white wines made from Palomino are thin, flabby, and prone to oxidation (darkening). Yet,

TYPES OF SHERRY

Fino: Clear and bone dry, with a delicate, almondy aroma; the favourite drink at Andalucían *ferias*.

Manzanilla: *Fino* aged in Sanlúcar, even paler in colour than Jerez *fino*.

Amontillado: Darker than *fino*, and equally dry; obtained by adding alcohol during ageing which kills off the flor yeast and induces a partial oxidation. Alternatively, the *fino* is left to age longer and the flor dies off naturally.

Oloroso: Dark amber-coloured, dry sherry, in which the coating of flor has not participated, as the wine is fortified to 18° alcohol from the start, preventing the yeast from growing; dry, full bodied, with a nutty flavour.

Palo Cortado: In Jerez, they say that "you can't make *palo cortado*, it just happens". Usually described as half-way between an *amontillado* and an *oloroso*.

Cream: The term "cream" refers to sweetened sherry. All Palomino sherry is originally dry, but can be sweetened with the addition of sugar or sweet wine.

Pedro Ximénez: A dark, sweet fortified wine, made with Pedro Ximénez grapes. After harvest the grapes are left to toast in the sun, inducing partial raisining.

Moscatel: Sweet wine made with the white Muscat grape.

Brandy de Jerez: Jerez brandy, made with wine spirits produced with grapes from La Mancha or Extremadura.

in Jerez, it goes to new heights thanks to an almost magical combination of circumstances.

First, there is the soil, the chalky *albariza*, which has the characteristic of soaking up the water from the torrential winter rains and storing it so that the deep-rooted vines can survive the long, hot summer months.

Then there is the prevailing humidity, due to the area's proximity to the Atlantic and the wetlands of the Doñana park. When the wine is put into barrel, a coating of yeast – called the flor – forms on the surface,

FOR THE ANGELS

All the precautions cannot prevent part of the wine evaporating: around five percent is lost, known as "the angels' share".

are compacted sand which is watered down regularly. Even the gardens surrounding the wineries are for a purpose: they help maintain a cool, humid microclimate around the cellars.

The ageing process

After the grapes are pressed and fermented, the wine is aged for a year or two, then it enters the *criaderas*, rows of barrels that hold blends of different vintages. A portion of wine is drawn off from the casks, called the *solera*, which contain the oldest blend for bottling. These

thanks to this humidity, and this seals the wine, protecting it from the air, feeding on the sugars and giving the wines their exceptional dryness. In Sanlúcar, the most humid part of the region, the layer of flor is thicker and the resulting wine, called *manzanilla,* even drier.

Every detail of the wine cellar is designed to keep the vital flor happy. High vaulted ceilings keep summer temperatures down; windows, covered with esparto mats which can be raised or lowered to control ventilation, are oriented to trap the damp westerly winds. The cellar floors

LEFT: the grape harvest gets under way.
ABOVE: traditional barrel-maker at work.

casks are topped off with wine from casks containing the second-oldest blend, which in turn is replenished from yet another row of casks, right on up to those containing the youngest blend, which are topped off with the most recent vintage. The system evolved from the need to keep stocks relatively fresh and consistent in flavour. Therefore, with one or two exceptions, there is no vintage sherry; practically all are blends.

Sherries are fortified wines, which means extra alcohol is added just before bottling for *fino* sherries or before they age for *olorosos*. They should be drunk within a year or two of bottling.

Just as important to the local economy is Jerez Brandy, also produced by the sherry wineries,

which make 90 percent of Spain's brandy. Somewhat sweeter than French brandy, it acquires its distinctive character when the basic wine spirits (for which grapes from other Spanish regions are used) are left to age in casks which have previously held sherry wine. Its discovery came about quite by accident. In 1860, the Domecq winery received an order for 500 barrels of *"holandas"* (as clear wine spirits were called, Holland being the main customer), but payment was not forthcoming and the shipment never left the

MOORISH INVENTION

The invention of the stemmed sherry glass with rounded bottom and narrow mouth is attributed to Ziryab, court musician and arbiter of style under Abd-al Rahman II.

and a grape vine in the other. The local wines were shipped to Rome, and the export business has continued unabated ever since. Even the Visigoths recognised the importance of the vineyards and ensured their continuity. As for the theoretically abstemious Moors, it seems they found a loophole in the Koran's prohibition of imbibing. Not only did wine-making continue uninterruptedly, medicinal purposes being proffered as an excuse when one was needed, the Moors in fact improved the methods used to make it.

cellar. Instead, it sat forgotten in old sherry casks for five years, until it occurred to the foreman to sample it. He found it had turned a golden colour and acquired a good flavour and aroma. Thus was another Jerez legend born: Fundador brandy.

Venerable tradition

Although legend has it that wine making was introduced to Jerez by the mythical King Geryon of Tartessos, it is believed the Phoenicians or perhaps Greeks from Phocaea planted the first vines. The area around Jerez rose to prominence under the Romans who, it's said, conquered the world with a sword in one hand

They introduced distilling to Jerez – the word alcohol and the Spanish word for still, *alambique*, are both Arabic in origin – and expanded the acreage of vineyards.

In more recent centuries, the wine trade of Jerez became inextricably linked to England. It is not certain whether the British taste for sherry dates from before Sir Francis Drake's day, or whether he was in fact responsible for introducing it to England when he attacked Cádiz in 1587 and made off with nearly 3,000 barrels of the stuff.

England's thirst for sack, as it was known, (Spaniards called wine destined for export *saca*, literally "removed") knew no bounds. In the

18th and 19th centuries, many of the English wine merchants, along with others from Ireland, France and Holland, settled in Jerez to take an active part in the production side of the business, and from this time date some of the classic Jerez wineries that operate today.

Social connections

The wealthy merchants married into Spanish society and formed the new aristocratic class of Jerez. They lived in style in palatial abodes. The May horse fair and the September harvest festival were practically private parties, when the various members of the Sherristocracy

a highly competitive world market the trade needed modernising. The wineries underwent sometimes painful restructuring, with the number of workers plummeting from 10,000 to 2,000 in 15 years.

Yet when you attend the *feria,* with proud men and women parading on their horses, you know that Jerez will always have some of that old spirit. And in a reversal of history, in 1998 members of the González-Byass family bought back the 30 percent share of the *bodega* which they had sold to a British multinational in 1992, the winery thus becoming family-owned once again. Tío Pepe would have approved. ❑

could flaunt their riches and impeccable taste. When the multinational drinks companies such as Allied Lyons and Seagrams started buying into the sherry trade in the late 20th century, many thought it was the beginning of the end of the grandiose Jerez lifestyle.

Big business

Today nearly 100 million litres (26½ million gallons) of sherry is produced a year. With around 80 percent of that sold abroad, it continues to be Spain's most exported wine, but in

LEFT: the family-owned Gonzalez Byass.
ABOVE: sherry pouring at the *feria,* Ronda.

THE OSBORNE BULL

One of the most familiar landmarks in Spain are the billboards in the shape of a black bull which loom on hillsides beside many roads. The first ones were erected in the 1950s to advertise the Osborne winery's brandy, Veterano, and they grew in number to more than 100, each one 12 metres (40 ft) tall . Yet not long ago they were threatened with extinction. A 1988 law ordained that advertising be removed from the sides of national roads. Such was the outcry that the authorities decided to make an exception. Today, the 21 "bullboards" still standing in Andalucía are protected as part of the region's heritage.

A COOK'S TOUR

From tasty tapas to sensational seafood, the cuisine of Andalucía
combines simplicity with delicious subtlety of flavour

Andalucía covers a lot of Spain, from the peninsula's highest mountains to the golden beaches of the Mediterranean, from dry, scrubby hillsides to lush river valleys. The cooking reflects this diversity. It can be as subtle and refined as a cool sherry sipped in the dappled shade of a grape arbour, as brash as a noisy *tapas* bar, as simple as the aroma of bread baking in wood-fired ovens.

Delicious morsels

The best introduction to authentic Andalucían food in all its diversity is the *tapas* bar, a very special way of life in southern Spain. In a *tapas* bar, wine, sometimes served from the barrel, is dispensed along with a huge variety of foods, both hot and cold, which are usually consumed while standing at the bar.

Tapas themselves may be as simple as plates of fat, herb-scented olives; toasted almonds; hard-boiled quails' eggs; paper-thin slices of salt-cured, raw serrano ham; sliced sausages such as paprika-red *chorizo*, peppery *salchichon*, smoky *longaniza*; aged cheese; and prawns in their shells.

Then come *tapas de cocina*, those that are cooked. These include croquettes; batter-dipped prawns; ham rolls stuffed with cheese (*flamenquines*); bite-sized pieces of crisp-fried fish; vegetable fritters. And salads, such as *pipirrana*, a tomato-onion-pepper relish; campera, made with sliced potatoes, onions and olives in a lemon-flavoured dressing; *remojón*, an exotic combination of oranges, onions and cod; *pulpo*, with diced octopus with tomatoes, garlic and parsley; roasted peppers.

Seafood selections might include *gambas al pil pil*, prawns sizzled with garlic; clams or *mussels a la marinera*; *cazon en adobo*, tangy marinated, fried fish; *boquerones al natural*, fresh anchovies dressed with garlic and vine-

gar. Other dishes encompass meatballs, rabbit in almond sauce, chicken with garlic, tiny pork cutlets, stewed tripe with *garbanzos*, kidneys in sherry sauce, spicy Moroccan-style kebabs, lamb stew, sautéed mushrooms, and, of course, *tortilla*, a thick potato omelette. Some *tapas* bars specialise in just a few selections, others

may have as many as 40 different dishes, sometimes listed on a blackboard. A *tapa* really is just a nibble – in some bars, served free with a *copa* of wine. Those wanting a larger serving should ask for a *ración*.

The drink of choice is dry *fino*, either sherry or Montilla, both made in Andalucía. These are fortified wines, so the small portions of food serve to temper the effects of the alcohol.

Meal times are late in Andalucía: 2–3pm for the *comida*, or midday meal, which for Spaniards is the main meal of the day, and 9–10pm for the *cena*, evening meal. So *tapas* bars are places to pass a pleasant few hours snacking before dinner.

PRECEDING PAGES: superb seafood abounds.
LEFT: paella to go. Paella is originally from Valencia but now every region of Spain has its own variation.
RIGHT: *tapas*, tasty appetisers or a meal.

Other popular eating places are *ventas*, country restaurants serving rustic country food, and *chiringuitos*, shanty restaurants set up on the beach. Here you should try *espetones*, a simple speciality of fresh sardines speared on sticks and grilled on a fire.

Simple yet subtle

Perhaps it's because Andalucíans like to do their eating standing up that other Spaniards claim Andalucía has no cuisine of merit. In fact, this region arguably has the finest fruits and vegetables, seafood, hams,

> **RICH PICKINGS**
>
> Country people foraged for wild asparagus, mushrooms and wild herbs and greens, all of which still play a part in the cuisine.

cheeses, nuts, oil and wine in the country. It is, certainly, simple fare without pretensions, but the subtlety of flavourings, the combinations and the freshness of the raw materials make it special.

Once Andalucían cuisine was considered the most refined in of Europe. The use of spices, herbs, almonds, rose water, orange blossoms and other exotic flavourings is its Oriental heritage, brought to the region by the Moors.

Of course, not everybody lived like a king or a caliph. Andalucía has also been a land of

> **FRUITS OF THE EAST**
>
> The Arabs brought the first orange trees to Spain. These were bitter oranges, sour as lemons, but wonderful in marmalade. These are still used ornamentally in southern Spain, where their blossoms perfume courtyards and their juice is used in cooking, but the fruit is left to rot.
>
> These invaders from the East also contributed rice, spices such as saffron, cinnamon and nutmeg, as well as aubergines and many other fruits and vegetables, which thrive in this temperate zone. While northerners were existing on coarse grains and simple gruels, the people of Andalucía were developing a cuisine and elevating cooking into a high art.

intense poverty. People learned to exist on the barest essentials and yet still make them palatable. Thus, something as simple as *gazpacho*, the region's well-known cold soup which is still popular today, is both nutritious and delicious, yet is little more than bread, oil, garlic and a few vegetables. People lived off the land wherever possible, consequently wild rabbit and partridge, free for the taking, were once more common than chicken.

The basics of Andalucían cooking are olive oil, tomatoes and peppers (both from the New World), garlic and onions together with fish on the coast and pork products inland. Potatoes are a staple, either fried as a side dish, or cooked in

a casserole with other ingredients to make a sturdy main dish. Though Valencia, land of *paella*, is famous for rice, Andalucía actually grows more rice than the Levante. *Garbanzos*, dried beans and lentils, usually cooked with locally made sausages and vegetables, are daily fare.

Bread of heaven

Andalucía is also known for the quality of its bread, baked fresh daily. In the old days a country family living far from town would bake bread in outdoor clay ovens, little changed

SECRET OF SUCCESS

Each area has its speciality sweets, some of which are made by nuns who have kept the recipes secret for centuries.

is served with rice or noodles as a first course, followed by the meat and vegetables. These are home-cooked meals, however, not often found in restaurants.

Andalucían hams are also famous. These are called *serrano* or mountain hams, because they're usually made in cool, dry mountain regions. Salt-cured and aged from seven months to several years, they are served raw as an aperitif.

The most appreciated hams are those with surnames, such as de Jabugo (Huelva), de Pedroches (Córdoba) and de Trevelez (Granada),

since Roman days. Enough bread would be made to last a week. Nothing was ever wasted, explaining why many soups and sauces in Andalucían cookery are thickened not with flour but with stale bread.

Home cooking

The *cocido*, also called *puchero or olla*, is another basic all over Andalucía. Chicken, ham bone, meat, sausages, *garbanzos*, vegetables and potatoes are all cooked together. The broth

and, in particular, those made of *pata negra*, a breed of black-footed, brown Iberian pigs, which roam semi-wild and feed on acorns. Their flesh is incredibly sweet. *Patanegra* hams are very expensive.

Moorish sweets

The sweets of Andalucía, richly flavoured with aniseed, cinnamon, sesame and bathed in honey, especially show the Moorish influence on the area's cuisine. One sugary speciality is *yemas*, a sweet rich in egg yolk. In the wine-making regions of Jerez and Montilla, vast quantities of egg whites were once used for the clarification of the new wine. The remaining

LEFT: avocados in Europe's winter vegetable garden.
ABOVE: Andalucía's mountain hams are salt cured and aged from seven months to several years.

yolks were then donated to the convents, where the nuns devised myriad ways of turning them into delicious sweets.

There's still a large variety of biscuits to be found today. *Tortas* are round, flat cakes, studded with aniseed, often eaten for breakfast; *soplillos* are almond macaroons; *huesos de santo* or saint's bones, typical of All Souls' Day, are shaped to look like bones; *borrachuelos*, *pestiños* and *empanadillas* are fried pastries, dipped in honey or sugar syrup; polóvorones,

ox-tail; *ternera mechada*, beef pot-roast; *huevos a la flamenca*, a flouncy version of eggs baked with ham, peas, asparagus, tomato sauce and *chorizo* sausage; *soldaditos de Pavia*, frittered bits of salt-cod.

This is the city where *tapas* originated, and you'll probably eat better in *tapas* bars than in most restaurants. Authentic *yemas de San Leandro*, egg yolk sweets, are available only at the monastery of the same name (Plaza San Ildefonso 1). Other convents also make sweets and pastries.

SEAFOOD GALORE

Cádiz is a wonderful place to eat fish and seafood, both in the city and coastal environs. Here are prawns, lobsters, crabs, oysters, clams, mussels at their freshest.

mantecados and perrunas are crumbly biscuits, especially loved at Christmas time, as are roscos, ring-shaped biscuits, which are either fried or baked.

Some specialities, such as *gazpacho*, belong to all of Andalucía. But each province has its own culinary character and part of the fun of travelling is to enjoy the local food.

Seville, cosmopolitan heart of Andalucía, is famous for its olives, generally served with sherry, but also cooked with meat, chicken and duck. Try, also, the home-cured olives, which have been cracked open and cured in brine with garlic, thyme and fennel. Good Seville dishes are *menudo*, veal tripe; *rabo de toro*, braised

GASTRONOMIC JOURNEY

One doesn't have to be a train enthusiast to enjoy a journey on the Al-Andalus Express, a vintage train ride through some of the loveliest landscapes in Andalucía. The train is also known for its excellent food and wine, including plenty of Andalucían specialities.
The train operates from April–October, with two 7-day itineraries available (departing from and returning to Madrid or Seville). One tour travels from Seville to Córdoba, then on to Granada to visit the Alhambra and Generalife gardens, continuing with a stop at the sumptuous Bobadilla hotel near Loja for lunch, through Ronda and Carmona to Jerez and back to Seville.

Seafood specialities

Following the great River Guadalquivir to the two Atlantic ocean provinces, Cádiz and Huelva, visitors will find an area prodigiously endowed with seafood. In Huelva try *chocos*, tiny squid stewed with beans; swordfish in saffron sauce; fresh tuna in tomato sauce; skate in paprika sauce. *Mojama*, called the "ham of the sea", is salt-cured dried tuna, served in slivers as an aperitif.

> **KITCHEN TIPS**
>
> The genius of Málaga cooking is in having the oil at the right temperature, so the fish emerges crisp and golden and still moist.

But not everything in Huelva comes from the sea. The province boasts strawberry fields for-

the bay from Cádiz to Puerto Santa Maria. Here on the promenade facing the port are various *cocederos* and *freiduras,* where you can buy 20 or more different kinds of freshly cooked shellfish and fish, wrapped in paper cones.

Prawns from nearby Sanlúcar de Barrameda are incomparably sweet and worth seeking out, and the fresh, fried sole tastes as if it had jumped straight from the sea into the frying pan. Restaurants and *tapas* bars here and in Cádiz proffer a vast number of interesting fish dishes, including the following which are

ever, the popular, sweet fruit being exported to Europe. Especially delicious is *lomo de cerdo,* fresh pork loin from Huelva's Iberian pigs. The province also has excellent game and lamb, and much sought-after wild mushrooms and white truffles. The famous *pata negra* hams can be purchased straight from the manufacturers in Jabugo, Cortegana and Cumbres Mayores. Huelva has its own wine region, Condado, which produces light white table wines.

For a real seafood treat, take a ferry across

all recommended: *urta a la roteña*, a bream casserole; *abajá de pescado*, fish stew; *lisa en amarillo*, saffron-tinted mullet. Cádiz also has both a "dog" soup, *caldillo de perro*, a fish soup flavoured with sour oranges, and a "cat" soup, laced with garlic.

Not far from Cádiz is Jerez. Sherry, which varies from pale, dry aperitif wines to velvety-smooth dessert wines, is much used in cooking throughout Andalucía. Try *riñones al jerez*, kidneys braised in sherry; mushrooms stewed in sherry, sweetbreads with *oloroso*, chicken sautéd with sherry. Sherry vinegar, available in Jerez and in select supermarkets, has been around for a long time, but is now very trendy.

LEFT: the dining-car on the Al-Andalus express, a luxury hotel on wheels. **ABOVE:** a bar in Seville fills up for early evening drinks.

The dessert to try in Cádiz is *tocino del cielo*, tiny squares of dense, rich custard.

Along the Costa

With more than 137 km (85 miles) of coast, the province of Málaga, too, is famous for its superb seafood. Try *fritura malagueña*, a mixed fish fry of fresh anchovies, so crisp you can eat them bones and all; try also fried rings of tender squid, prawns, and a piece of a larger fish such as hake. Other local fish dishes are *pescado al horno*, sea bream

> ### MOUNTAIN TROUT
> Trout comes from Riofrio, making it an ideal place to stop off for a memorable lunch when breaking the journey between Málaga and Granada.

and peppers cooked with saffron and spaghetti. On the cosmopolitan Costa del Sol, however, you can eat French, Italian, Danish, Thai, Moroccan, Chinese, Indian and many other cuisines. In fact, you might have to do some hard looking to find any authentic Spanish food.

East of Málaga the coast extends through a stretch of Granada and on to Almería. This is Europe's winter garden, with miles of plastic-covered fields ripening all sorts of veg. Besides seafood and rice dishes, there are veg-

baked with layers of potatoes, tomatoes, onions and peppers; *rape a la marinera* or anglerfish (not in fact rape), sailor's style; and *lubina a la sal,* a whole sea bass baked in a case of coarse salt, which seals in all the juices. Here you can also find superb fish soups, such as *sopa viña* , a creamy, sherry-spiked brew, and *cachoreñas,* flavoured with orange.

Besides the standard version of the cold tomato-based soup, *gazpacho,* Málaga has another delightful summer soup of its own, *ajo blanco con uvas,* a tangy white soup made of crushed almonds, garlic and grapes. *Paella* can be ordered at many restaurants and beach bars. A variation is *cazuela de fideos,* seafood, peas

etable stews with wheat berries and a paprika-flavoured soup, *pimentón.*

Inland bounty

Granada province varies from the snow-covered peaks of the Sierra Nevada to the fertile plain to the subtropics of the coast where bananas, custard apples, avocados, mangos and sugar-cane are all grown.

Almond groves cover the inland hillsides; ground almonds are used as seasoning with rabbit, chicken and fish dishes and in a Granada speciality, *sopa de almendras*, almond soup.

From the Alpujarras mountain region come *serrano* hams. Try broad beans fried with

chunks of ham or fresh trout sautéed with ham. Other favourites are: the *tortilla sacromonte*, an omelette made with ham, sweetbreads, kidneys and peas and *choto al ajillo* which is either baby kid or lamb laced with garlic.

North of Granada are the inland provinces of Jaén and Córdoba. Wheat fields and olive groves dominate the landscape, except where it rises steeply in the north in the Sierra Morena. Here, venison, wild boar, partridge, hare and other kinds of game are found. Lamb, excellent in

DISH OF THE DAY

If passing through Córdoba try a *revuelto* which is a dish made up of creamy scrambled eggs with wild mushrooms and other vegetables.

white *gazpacho*, which is made with almonds and spiked with apples or melon.

The Restaurant Caballo Rojo in Córdoba features Moorish and Sephardic cuisine, with dishes such as anglerfish *mozárabe*, with raisins; lamb braised with honey and a touch of vinegar;and Sephardic-style broad beans with herbs. *Pastel cordobés* is a dessert of flaky pastry filled with sweet "angel's hair", candied threads of a melon-like fruit.

The town of Puente Genil in the province of

both these provinces, is usually served braised.

In Jaén, *ajoharina* is a delicious way of cooking potatoes; *andrajos*, which literally means "rags", is a game dish with squares of pasta; *perdiz en escabeche* is marinated partridge.

Córdoba is known for its vegetable dishes, especially artichokes, which might be braised with clams, in a Montilla wine sauce; cardoons, another thistle similar to the artichoke; wild asparagus; and aubergine. Summer specialities include *salmorejo*, which is similar to a very thick *gazpacho*, served with pieces of ham, and

Córdoba is the main centre for the production of *dulce de membrillo*, a local quince jelly.

The Córdoba province also makes world-class wines, in particular those of Montilla and Moriles. After visiting a *bodega*, have lunch at Las Camachas in Montilla, a rustic restaurant on the main highway, where the local landed gentry used to dine. You can get a good *revuelto de trigueros*, eggs scrambled with wild asparagus and mushrooms, or a plate of good ham to accompany your *fino*.

A final word of warning: menu in Spanish always refers to the fixed-price meal of the day; if you want the *à la carte* menu, you should ask to see *la carta*. ❑

FAR LEFT: torta Española. **LEFT:** Jabugo hams.
ABOVE: *Jabugitos* are hung up to dry.

THE GOOD-TIME COSTA

Once the preserve of the wealthy yacht set,
Costa del Sol now embraces a complete social spectrum

At the base of the jagged piece of Spain that reaches out towards Africa is the Costa del Sol. Thanks to over-development it is devoid of most of the attributes that normally constitute paradise, but this stretch of coast has, nevertheless, managed to persuade the world that this once neglected slice of the Mediterranean is a land of heavenly delights.

The metamorphosis of the section of Andalucían seashore once described by English author Laurie Lee as "beautiful but exhausted... seemingly forgotten by the world" has been such that writer and critic Kenneth Tynan more recently described it as an "inbred and amoral" land of Sodom and Gomorrah.

Name changes

Back in the 1950s, before the tourist boom exploded along the Spanish Mediterranean, the Costa del Sol was a diffuse title applied to the coastline between Almería province and Gibraltar. Local jealousies and a surge of self-confidence have since persuaded large chunks of this coastline to throw off the blanket term.

To the east of what is now recognised as the Costa del Sol lies the Costa de Almería and the Costa Tropical of Granada. To the west is the most recent satellite: Costa Gaditana, the sweep of coast that takes in the desirable development of Sotogrande. Today, the description Costa del Sol really applies to just a 110 km (68 mile) rump of coast pertaining to the province of Málaga.

The precise date of birth of this rough diamond of Spain's monolithic tourist industry is not known. The first signs of life flickered back in the 1920s when Marbella, a dirt-poor fishing village, was popular with British army officers and their families on leave from Gibraltar. During this period, the iron ore mine in the hills behind Marbella was run with British expertise; this handful

of mining engineers represented the Costa del Sol's first resident expatriate community.

Prehistory

The year 1932 is regarded as the turning point in the making of the Costa del Sol. So legend has it, a lady called Carlota Alessandri pur-

chased a piece of barren hillside at Montemar, west of Torremolinos. Asked what she intended to plant there, she replied haughtily: "Plant? I shall plant tourists! This could be the beginning of the Spanish Riviera."

This budding Spanish Riviera died suddenly in the summer of 1936 when the Spanish Civil War erupted. Foreign residents unable to flee the conflict were scooped up by a Royal Navy destroyer and deposited in the British colony of Gibraltar.

After World War II, the Marquis of Najera, a Spanish nobleman, took up residence in Torremolinos. In his wake came well-to-do Spanish families, and an unusual collection of European

---

PRECEDING PAGES: conspicuous wealth, Puerto Bánus.
LEFT: enjoying the good life.
RIGHT: Prince Hohenlohe, founder of the Marbella Club.

diplomats and colonial officials unable or unwilling to adjust to a retirement devoid of constant sunshine.

The dash of blue blood and large measure of eccentricity brought to the newborn Costa del Sol by these disaffected noblemen and exotic bureaucrats provided an excellent cocktail in which artists, writers, film stars, and their acolytes could flourish. These halcyon days probably saw the coining of what has become the Costa del Sol's unofficial motto: "It's not who you are, it's who you say you are that counts."

> **A LA MODE**
>
> Torremolinos and its environs gained a much-needed niche on the "place-to-be" circuit.

Centre of the fringe

In the 1960s Torremolinos became the pivot for bohemians who were drawn like moths to the bright lights of the Costa del Sol. The basic requisites of hedonists – wine, drugs and a dive with a sea view – were cheap in T-town, the patronising name this strange fauna gave to a hamlet which had once been proud of its water mills. Among this colourful and cosmopolitan flotsam-and-jetsam swam literary giants like Ernest Hemingway and James Michener, the American novelist who based his book

> **THERE TO STAY**
>
> Not all the beautiful people were just passing through. A curious selection took up long-term residence, living off the Coast's flamboyant image. The Costa del Sol's jet-and yacht set contingent included maverick Spanish nobleman and ageing rake Don Jaime de Mora y Aragón, and Gunilla von Bismarck, a descendant of the Iron Chancellor. The monocled, immaculately dressed Don Jaime, who once eked out a living playing the piano at the Marbella Club, and the imposing, flaxen-haired Gunilla, who has made self-promotion an art form, became essential guests at all the best Costa del Sol "happenings".

The Drifters on characters plucked from amongst the Costa del Sol's lotus-eaters.

While Torremolinos throbbed with life on the lunatic fringe, further down "The Coast" (as the Costa became known in fashionable circles), Marbella began to lose its importance as a mining centre. Spanish nobleman Ricardo Soriano, the Marquis of Ivanrey, introduced his wealthy friends to the village, which he promoted to them as an up-market destination.

The Marquis's nephew, Prince Alfonso von Hohenlohe of Liechtenstein, was so impressed that, on his father's instructions, he bought a decaying farm house and a 24-acre (9.6-hectare) fig tree plantation on the outskirts of the primi-

tive fishing village for £2,000 (US$3,000).

In 1953 the pudgy prince turned the farmhouse into a hotel, and put up some small bungalows on the land. His rich and titled friends came to stay in droves at the seafront accommodation that Prince Alfonso named the Marbella Club.

It was the opening of the Marbella Club that attracted the "café society" to the now snobbish Costa del Sol. This exclusive tag was secured by a stream of famous visitors that included King Leopold of the Bel-

TOURIST EXPLOSION

To cater for the demand in sunshine homes for sun-starved northern Europeans, concrete wedding cakes sprang up on the seashore, and instant Andalucían villages spread like measles.

taste for themselves the good life they had read about in the papers.

Increasing numbers of these holidaymakers decided that the Costa del Sol was to be their playground too, with many staying on to set up bars and restaurants. The fortunate few who had sat around their pools and talked wistfully of lost thrones, fading empires or forfeited estates, discovered they had neighbours who sat around their pools and talked wistfully of the East End, Eindhoven or Essen.

gians, the Duke and Duchess of Windsor, Gina Lollobrigida, Sophia Loren and Frank Sinatra.

Bucket stops

Inevitably, the rest of the world refused to be left out of the fun and frivolity that engulfed the "Sun Coast", and so between Torremolinos and Marbella a string of bucket-and-spade resorts sprang up to cater for the deluge of package tourists who had to come to the Costa del Sol to

In the 1970s two events occurred which completed the Costa del Sol's evolution from up-market tourist destination to international playground that is dubbed the California of Europe: the 1973 oil crisis and Middle East turmoil persuaded many rich Arabs to seek safer havens for their sudden riches; and in 1979, Margaret Thatcher swept to power in Britain.

Arabs and Brits

The Arab invasion of the Costa del Sol was led by King (then Prince) Fahd of Saudi Arabia. Together with 60 relatives and minions, he set up one of his many homes just down the road from the Marbella Club in a multi-million dol-

LEFT: Costa regular Antonio Banderas.
ABOVE: Sean Connery, a long-time devotee of the Costa del Sol until 1998, when persistent intrusion by the media forced him to put his house on the market.

lar palace which was built to resemble the White House in Washington. The complex comes complete with mosque and heliport.

Among the Arab multimillionaires to encamp on the Costa del Sol was Adnan Khashoggi, a Saudi Arabian arms merchant whose obscene banquets and outrageous fiestas actually managed to offend the jaundiced tastes of the Costa del Sol's home-grown debauchees. His sumptuous yacht moored in Puerto Banus did, however, draw droves of tourists to the kitsch marina.

Caddishly, Khashoggi's fair-weather friends and apologists on the Coast remained silent

when Khashoggi was indicted in the United States on charges of embezzlement.

The Costa del Sol had always been popular with the British even before Margaret Thatcher was first elected prime minister in 1979. But it was her removal of exchange controls that allowed thousands of Britons to invest their golden handshake, black money or red-hot cash in a little villa in the sun, thereby laying claim to large swathes of the Costa del Sol. They helped shove the Spaniards into the minority in picturesque townships like Mijas, where Spanish is spoken only by the maid or the gardener on sprawling vila developments such as Miraflores and Calahonda.

Crooks on the Costa

If it was Arab and British money that cemented the Costa del Sol into its present position as an international investment centre, it was the Costa del Sol's proximity to the cannabis plantations in Morocco's Rif Mountains just across the Straits of Gibraltar, and the absence of an extradition treaty between Spain and Britain that helped the coast gain the dubious title of the Costa del Crime.

The fortunes generated by drug trafficking have seen the growth of a sophisticated extension of the European underworld. A booming local economy and the ease with which a foreign face goes undetected aid the crooks that haunt the Costa; in addition, the hostility of nearby Gibraltar to the local Spanish authorities proves a stumbling block to solving many crimes and gathering evidence, a complaint persistently made by Spain.

The snatch in the late 1980s by French gangsters of Melodie Nackachian, a fragile creature of Lebanese-Korean parentage, as she was being chauffeured to her posh English school in Marbella, demonstrated how deeply foreign mafias had infiltrated the community. For a week, hundreds of Spanish police combed the "Costa del Kidnap". The huge police drag net that eventually rescued the child flushed out other international delinquents including a gunman wanted for various murders in four European countries. The Spanish government's response was to reinforce the Coast's overstretched police with detectives trained to hunt down foreign criminals.

Despite constant tales of bank robbers and drug barons living it up in their sunny hideaways, of property sharks defrauding pensioners, of drug-crazed muggers preying on paraplegic tourists, and of the recession of the 1990s that blew a chill wind along the coast and led to reports of its demise, the Costa del Sol's reputation as a good-time girl who is kind to everyone remains intact. It is perhaps the fusion of fact and fantasy that makes the Costa del Sol so alluring. The Costa del Sol is, after all, whatever you want her to be. ❏

LEFT: Gunilla von Bismarck, veteran socialite and party hostess.
RIGHT: a waterchute at Torremolinos, one of the many amusements providing fun for a different kind of good-time seeker.

WILD ANDALUCÍA

Andalucía's soaring sierras and extensive wilderness areas

harbour exciting fauna and rare flora

In a special enclosure high in the Sierra de Cazorla in southern Jaén, five lammergeiers have been slowly adapted to conditions in this mountainous area of Andalucía. With a wingspan that can reach 3 metres (10 ft), the lammergeier, or bearded vulture, is the biggest bird in Europe, and one of the rarest. In Spain, its last major refuge, these impressive birds are known as *quebrantahuesos*, or "bone busters", for their habit of dropping bones from a great high to crack them open and get at the nutritious marrow. Cazorla's five specimens were found wounded in other parts of Spain and carefully nursed back to life. Though these birds will never fly again, they form the basis of an ambitious breeding plan to reintroduce the species to the park, where the last bearded vulture was spotted in the 1980s.

Waking up to nature

Similar programmes are taking place all over Andalucía, as a wide variety of plant and animal species are closely monitored to ensure their survival, and unspoilt nature areas are earmarked for official protection.

It is a reflection of a new awareness among Andalucíans that wildlife is something to be treasured. Spaniards have never had a great reputation as nature-lovers, but in recent years education in the classroom and television documentaries on wildlife have given rise to a new generation of green Andalucíans who are very serious about protecting their natural heritage.

And a rich heritage it is indeed, with 17 percent of Andalucía's territory afforded official protection as wilderness area, more than double the national average of five percent. In all, there are more than 80 different locations classified as nature parks (*parque natural*), nature reserves (*reserva natural*) or nature enclaves (*paraje natural*). Some may be small, inaccessible

lagoons which happen to be crucial to migrating birds, others are large extensions covering many square kilometres, such as the 2,140 sq. km (825 square mile) Cazorla nature park.

The Andalucían wilderness is amazing both in its quantity and its variety. Surprising as it may seem, within an hour of the tourist beaches

of the Costa del Sol one can find a landscape of limestone rock formations sculpted by the wind and rain at El Torcal; the largest breeding colony of flamingos in Europe at Fuentepiedra lagoon; a herd of wild ibex grazing on rocky crags in the Sierra Blanca, a mere 16 km (10 miles) from Marbella; snow capped peaks in the Sierra de las Nieves, home to a rare type of fir tree found nowhere else in Europe. All this without even leaving the province of Málaga.

The Doñana National Park

The crown-jewel of wild Andalucía is the Doñana National Park, 500 sq. km (193 square miles) spreading at the mouth of the Guadalquivir

PRECEDING PAGES: impressive limestone formations at El Torcal, near Antequera.
LEFT: views across the Sierra Nevada near Lanjarón.
RIGHT: a goshawk on the watch for food.

river. About two-thirds of the park consists of marsh and wetlands, the most valuable in Europe, for they provide a breeding ground for more than 100 species of birds, and are a wintering ground or stop-over on the migration route for many others.

The extremely rare imperial eagle soars in its skies here, while scattered trees provide convenient perches for spoonbills, storks, egrets and herons.

The park was once a hunting estate used by the Dukes of Medina Sidonia, whose palace was located across the river in Sanlúcar de Barrameda. In 1563 the Duke married Doña Ana. The place became known as the Coto de Doña Ana – the Hunting Ground of Doña Ana. Hunting continued to be the main activity here for centuries, but in the 1960s intensive farming threatened: water drawn off for irrigation reduced the wetlands from more than 1,800 sq km (700 sq miles) to 310 sq km(120 sq miles), and only the area's designation as a nature park in 1969 saved it from disappearing altogether.

WEIRD AND WONDERFUL

The Doñana continues to change even today as sand dunes advance to engulf pine forests then shift on to reveal the weird shapes of the dead trees.

RURAL TOURISM

Andalucía's wealth of wildlife and unspoilt scenery has brought about a dramatic rise in environment-oriented holidays and outdoor activities. Especially during spring and autumn, bands of birdwatchers and botanists from all over the world, some travelling with specialised tour companies, can be seen scrambling over countryside in the hopes of sighting some rare specimen. In summer, nature areas are alive with trekkers, campers, horse-back riders and off-trail bikers.

During the 1990s, Andalucía acquired numerous establishments to provide the legions of outdoors lovers with bed and board. The region now has dozens of small country hotels where once the choice was limited to a handful of lowly *fondas.* In addition, many farm houses and country cottages have been adapted for "rural tourism", offering inexpensive self-catering or bed-and-breakfast lodgings. The biggest network is the *Red Andaluza de Alojamientos Rurales,* which has hundreds of properties on its books (Apartado 2035, 04080 Almería).

Some rural hostelries organise courses in painting, photography or cookery. And nearly every large nature park has at least one company or co-operative of local guides to show you the sights; they can usually be contacted through the park reception centre.

Gazing over the expanse of Doñana, you might be tempted to think you're contemplating a view that hasn't changed in a million years but in fact it is a landscape of relatively recent vintage. Two thousand years ago, this was a vast brackish estuary, peppered with islands, but gradual silting up of the Guadalquivir river created the marshes.

Europe's desert

At the opposite end of the region, Almería's landscape provides a sharp contrast to the wetlands of Huelva. Tabernas is the only true desert in Europe, with less than 20cm (8 inches) of rainfall

also protected as a nature park, a landscape of volcanic cliffs, isolated coves of black sand, and hillsides covered in prickly pear cactus (which, although now a familiar feature of the Andalucían landscape, is a species introduced from the Americas). Even this moonscape supports wildlife, with animals sharing space with numerous bird species, and plants including types of snapdragon and lilies unique to this area.

Not long ago, the coast of Cabo de Gata was accessible only to millionaires on private yachts or those with a taste for long treks over goat trails, but new roads have opened up the area to travellers, and campsites, hotels and restaurants

a year, and its landscape of parched, eroded hills has served as a backdrop for countless western movies. A bit north of here, at Sorbas, is one of the world's largest gypsum deposits, occupying what was at one time an inland sea. When it drained, it carved hundreds of cavities out of the crystallised gypsum, forming karstic caves whose walls glitter with crystals.

Nearby, the equally arid landscape stretching from the Cabo de Gata, the southeastern tip of Andalucía, up the coast to Carboneras is now

LEFT: shepherd with his flock in the foothils of the Sierra de Grazalema.
ABOVE: Cazorla National Park.

have sprung up to serve them. The same is happening all over Andalucía, where "rural tourism" is the latest trend. More and more visitors are taking to the great Andalucían outdoors, which leads to debates over whether tourism and nature are compatible. The Cazorla park, for instance, receives around half a million visitors a year.

Primeval forests

That places like Cazorla, Doñana or Cabo de Gata have survived at all is a minor miracle, for Andalucía's wilderness has been at odds with humanity for the last 2,000 years. The Romans were notorious choppers-down of trees – for building, mining, fuel, warfare – and the trend

continued more or less unabated until our time.

To get an idea of what the primeval forests that covered much of Andalucía looked like before the arrival of man, head for the mountains that straddle the provinces of Cádiz and Málaga. Near the coast is the Parque de los Alcornocales 1,700 sq. km (650 square miles) of cork oak, holm oak and Lusitanian oak which provide shade for an undergrowth of oleaster, laurels and rhododendrons.

Sierra de Grazalema

As you ascend towards Ronda, following the old tobacco smugglers' route from Gibraltar, this gives way to the heights of the Sierra de Grazalema, home to numerous raptors including one of . Europe's largest colonies of griffon vultures, in addition to the curious-looking Egyptian vulture, peregrine falcons and eagle owls. Among the trees found here is the rare *Abies pinsapo*, a fir which grows nowhere else in Europe. It requires shaded valleys at high altitude and constant humidity, which it finds here and in the neighbouring Sierra de las Nieves near Ronda.

The wet weather used to be considered a curse by locals, and few visited the mountains, aside from a handful of eccentric foreign birdwatchers and plant lovers. Today, the Sierra de Grazalema

BIRDS ON THE WING

The Strait of Gibraltar, where Africa seems so close you could almost touch it, is the point where birds which spend the winter in Africa and the summer in Europe make the crossing during their northern migration in spring and return journey in autumn. This is when Andalucía acts like a giant funnel as tens of thousands of birds converge on the southernmost tip of Iberia to await favourable conditions for the crossing.

The migration is one of the most spectacular nature experiences in Europe, and even the lay birder, armed with a simple pair of binoculars and a decent field book for identification, is bound to spot a few rarities. The birds'

arrival in spring is staggered (from February to June), so the best time to observe the migration is on the birds' return flight to Africa. Return traffic is busiest at the end of September and throughout October.

Among the best spots to watch the passage are the lookout points over the Strait of Gibraltar, just east of Tarifa and from the Rock itself.

In addition to large numbers of storks, some 250,000 raptors make the crossing, including honey buzzards, vultures (Egyptian, griffon), Montagu's harriers, ospreys, kestrels, short toed eagles, booted eagles, goshawks and many more.

is a favourite holiday venue, and authorities have had to restrict visitors to the valley with the highest concentration of pinsapo firs to 60 a day.

Friends and foes

Tourists aside, the 20th century brought new perils to Andalucía's wildlife. Although trigger-happy hunters – in Andalucía, there are approximately 300,000 of them – are often thought to be nature's worst enemy, they are in reality more interested than anybody else in preserving Spain's wilderness areas.

> **WET WET WET**
>
> Surprisingly for a region known for its sunny weather, Grazalema is the rainiest spot in Spain: the average annual precipitation is 225 cm (88½ inches).

things going for it: the sheer size of the region, the fact that much of it consists of inaccessible mountains and, sad though it is to say, social injustices of the past. When Andalucía was conquered by the Christians and the Morisco farmers ultimately expelled, most of the territory fell into the hands of absentee landowners, lords of vast estates known as *latifundia*, who were more interested in counting gold from the New World or hunting for wild boar than in turning their properties into working agricultural concerns.

A far more serious threat has come from agriculture (for example, water for irrigation depletes underground sources and pesticides and artificial fertilisers poison the land); toxic waste from industry and mining; ill advised reforestation in the past with fast growing non-native pine trees and eucalyptus; introduction of alien animal species either for hunting or breeding purposes, everything from mouflons to rainbow trout and Louisiana crayfish which crowd native species.

Fortunately, wild Andalucía has had several

LEFT: wolves were once common in the sierras.
ABOVE: the lynx, one of the rarest mammals in Europe. There are no more than 1,000 left in Spain.

Emigration, uninterrupted for centuries, left much of rural Andalucía under-populated, so nature was allowed to go its own way more or less unhindered.

Man's contribution

In a few of Andalucía's wilderness areas, man became an essential ingredient in the ecosystem. This can be seen for example in the *dehesa* of Huelva, a landscape of scattered holm oaks and cork oaks covering the hills in the north of the province, the Sierra de Aracena. Human activity here has always been linked to the land: hunting, forestry, cork harvesting, and especially the breeding of the free-ranging Iberian pig, whose

salted and air-cured hams are a delicacy. This primitive breed of pig, smaller than its more domesticated cousin, is released during the autumn to forage on acorns. Come January, they are rounded up again for the slaughter. Without the landscape of the *dehesa*, the Iberian pig could not exist as such. Without the Iberian hams, priced three times as much as standard *serrano* ham, locals would not be inspired to preserve the wild oaks which provide the pigs' diet.

The Sierra de Aracena occupies the western extreme of the Sierra Morena, the mountain range that separates Andalucía from Castile. A string of protected nature areas – the Sierra del

Norte in Seville, Sierra de Hornachuelos and Sierra de Cardeñ–Montoro in Córdoba, Sierra de Andújar and Despeñaperros in Jaén – form a wild corridor nearly 320 km (200 miles) long. The further east you go, the more rugged and mysterious is the mountain scenery.

The last wolves

The woods in these parts were the home of the last of Andalucía's wolves. Much maligned in folklore and literature, the wolf was ruthlessly persecuted by farmers and hunters, and some villages even retained an official wolf hunter. No wolves have been spotted here in years, and it is assumed they are extinct. But another, even more

cunning hunter continues to survive in the mountains of the Sierra Morena, the Iberian lynx.

The missing lynx

One of the rarest mammals in Europe, the lynx is the animal which best embodies Andalucía's struggle to protect its wildlife. Only one thousand of them are left in the whole of Spain, in the most optimistic of estimates, scattered in different communities, with Andalucía accounting for around half the population.

Some lynx have been run over by cars, or died after eating poisoned baits, or killed by misguided hunters, but the biggest cause for their dwindling numbers was a myxomatosis plague which all but wiped out their main diet, rabbits. In Doñana, one of the lynx's last refuges, they are afforded special attention, with intensive radio tracking and observation. The largest population lives in Jaén's Sierra de Cardeña–Montoro.

The lynx's fate hangs in the balance, but some species are making a comeback. White storks, considered a sign of good luck, returned to nest in Ronda after an absence of 20 years. The white-headed duck, not long ago on the verge of extinction, is finding new breeding grounds in the lagoons of southern Spain. The chameleon, which for decades had been fighting a losing battle with real estate developers, are on the increase again, with colonies detected in Almería and Granada.

Rare flowers

Like the prehistoric-looking chameleon, some of the most striking examples of Andalucían wildlife are among the smallest. Southern Spain is a botanists' paradise, with over 4,000 different plant species, more than 150 of which are endemic, not being found anywhere else in the world. They have evolved in unique microclimates such as those of Cazorla, where the Cazorla violet grows, or Sierra Nevada, also protected as a nature park. Contemplating the windswept heights around the popular ski resort, where no trees will grow, the landscape looks barren and forlorn following the spring thaw. But look closely, and you might spot the rare Nevada daffodil (*Narcissus nevadensis*) or Nevada saxifrage (*Saxifraga nevadensis*), just two of 70 catalogued. ❏

ABOVE: a golden eagle.
RIGHT: one of some 300,000 hunters in Andalucía.

PLACES

*A detailed guide to the entire region, with principal sites
clearly cross-referenced by number to the maps*

The autonomous region of Andalucía is Spain's most populous, with 7 million inhabitants in its eight southernmost provinces. The area it covers is huge, totalling 89,800 sq. km (34,700 sq. miles), an expanse the size of Portugal and twice the size of the Netherlands.

Within these confines the variety of landscape is tremendous. To the north is the long ridge of the Sierra Morena, a mountain range that effectively seals the region off from the rest of Spain, where the rich *sevillanos* go hunting; to the south is the Costa del Sol, playground of foreigners, where Europe's working classes rub shoulders with aristocrats and the famous. In the centre lies the flat agricultural plain of the Guadalquivir. To the east are the arid desert lands of Almería and the mountains of Granada, and to the west the marshlands of the Coto Doñana nature reserve. On the horizon from almost anywhere is North Africa, whose influence is felt in the history and the towns of this southernmost region of Spain and of Europe.

Each of Andalucía's old cities, Seville, Córdoba and Granada, has a major Moorish monument of world significance: in Seville it is the Giralda, in Córdoba the Mezquita and in Granada the Alhambra. But others have their claims to fame: Cádiz, the home of the Armada and the signing of the first Spanish constitution: Ronda, the birthplace of bullfighting; Huelva, Columbus's stepping-off point for the New World. In the province of Almería the landscape is so jagged and surreal that it's a popular location for shooting westerns; nearby Jaén is the undulating, soft heartland of the olive growing industry, and has been for centuries.

Here, too, is mile upon mile of urbanisation, ranging from the most select villas of Marbella to the worst excesses of Torremolinos tower blocks, where Spanish is a minority language. And tacked to the bottom of Andalucía, like a plug on the bottom of Europe, is Gibraltar, for long a source of dispute between Spain and Great Britain and no doubt long to remain so.

Distances between provinces and cities are not enormous, but travel times may well be longer than expected, either because of the winding mountain roads, or because of the weight of traffic, particularly in the coastal areas. Places of interest are numbered in the text and can be cross-referenced with the maps. Map locations are shown by the map icon in the top right corner of every right-hand page. ❏

PRECEDING PAGES tile panel from Seville encouraging early tourism; the Seville Fair; Patio de los Mirtos, Alhambra. **LEFT:** view over Jaén.

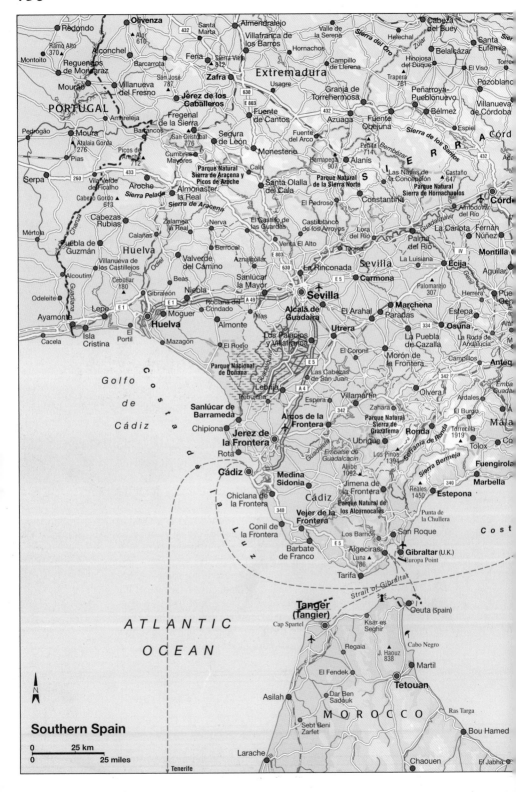

Redondo • Olivenza • Santa Marta • Almendralejo • Villafranca de los Barros • Valle de la Serena • Helechal • Cabeza del Buey

Ramo Alto 370▲ • Alor 610▲ • 432 • Hornachos • Sierra del Oro • Zújar • Santa Eufemia

Montoito • Alconchel • Barcarrota • Feria • Sierra Vieja 812 • Campillo de Llerena • Hinojosa del Duque • Belalcázar • El Viso

Reguengos de Monsaraz • San José 787▲ • Zafra • **Extremadura** • Trapera 781 • Pozoblanco

Mourão • Villanueva del Fresno • **Jerez de los Caballeros** • Usagre • Granja de Torrehermosa • Peñarroya-Pueblonuevo • Villanueva de Córdoba

PORTUGAL • Amareleja • Fregenal de la Sierra • 630 • E 803 • Fuente de Cantos • 432 • Azuaga • Fuente Obejuna • Bélmez • Espiel • Córd

Pedrogão • Moura • Barrancos • San Cristóbal 776 • Segura de León • Fuente del Arco • Peñita 714▲ • Sierra de los Santos • 432 • Ada

Atalaia Gorda 276 • Picos de Aroche 712▲ • Cumbres Mayores • Monesterio • Llemapega 907 • Alanís • Bembézar • R R A

Pias • 433 • Cala • Parque Natural Sierra de Aracena y Picos de Aroche • Santa Olalla del Cala • Parque Natural de la Sierra Norte • S • Las Navas de la Concepción • Castaño 647 • Parque Natural Sierra de Hornachuelos • Córd

Serpa • 260 • Vila Verde de Ficalho • Aroche • Sierra Pelada • Almonaster la Real • Sierra de Aracena • El Pedroso • Constantina • Almodóvar del Río

Cabezo Gordo ▲ 613 • Cabezas Rubias • Zalamea la Real • Nerva • El Castillo de las Guardas • Castilblanco de los Arroyos • Lora del Río • La Carlota • Fernán Núñez

Mértola • Puebla de Guzmán • **Huelva** • Calañas • Berrocal • Aznalcóllar • Venta El Alto • E 803 • Tocina • Palma del Río • Montilla

Alcoutim • Villanueva de los Castillejos • Odiel • Ceballar 180 • Valverde del Camino • 630 • La Rinconada • **Sevilla** • La Luisiana • **Écija** • Aguilar

Odeleite • Gibraleón • Beas • Niebla • Rociana del Condado • Sanlúcar la Mayor • E 5 • **Carmona** • Palomarejo 307 • Herrera • Pue Ger

Ayamonte • Lepe • E 1 • E 1 • Moguer • Pilas • Alcalá de Guadaira • El Arahal • **Marchena** • Estepa

Cacela • Isla Cristina • El Portil • **Huelva** • Almonte • Mazagón • Los Palacios y Villafranca • **Utrera** • Paradas • 334 • **Osuna** • Atar M

El Rocío • Morón de la Frontera • La Puebla de Cazalla • La Roda de Andalucía • **Anteq**

Parque Nacional de Doñana • E 5 • Las Cabezas de San Juan • El Coronil • Campillos • 342 • Emba Guada

Golfo • C o • Lebrija • **A 4** • Villamartín • Olvera • Ardales • Mála

de • s • Trebujena • Espera • 342 • Zahara • El Burgo • Torrecilla 1919 • Co

Cádiz • t • Sanlúcar de Barrameda • Arcos de la Frontera • Parque Natural Sierra de Grazalema • **Ronda** • Tolox

Chipiona • **Jerez de la Frontera** • Embalse de Guadalcacín • Ubrique • Los Pinos 1394 • Sierra Bermeja • **Fuengirola**

Rota • Aljibe 1092▲ • Reales 1450 • **Estepona** • **Marbella**

Cádiz • Medina Sidonia • Jimena de la Frontera • 340

Chiclana de la Frontera • **Cádiz** • Parque Natural de los Alcornocales • Punta de la Chullera • C o s t

Conil de la Frontera • 340 • Vejer de la Frontera • Los Barrios • San Roque

Barbate de Franco • E 5 • Algeciras • **Gibraltar** (U.K.) • Europa Point

Luna 786▲ • Tarifa

Strait of Gibraltar

Tánger (Tangier) • Ceuta (Spain)

Cap Spartel • Ksar es Seghir • Cabo Negro

A T L A N T I C • Regaia • J. Haouz 838 • Martil

O C E A N • El Fendek

Dar Ben Sadouk • **Tetouan**

Asilah • Ras Targa

M O R O C C O

Southern Spain • Sebt Beni Zarfet • Bou Hamed

0 — 25 km
0 — 25 miles

Tenerife • Larache • Chaouen • El Jabha

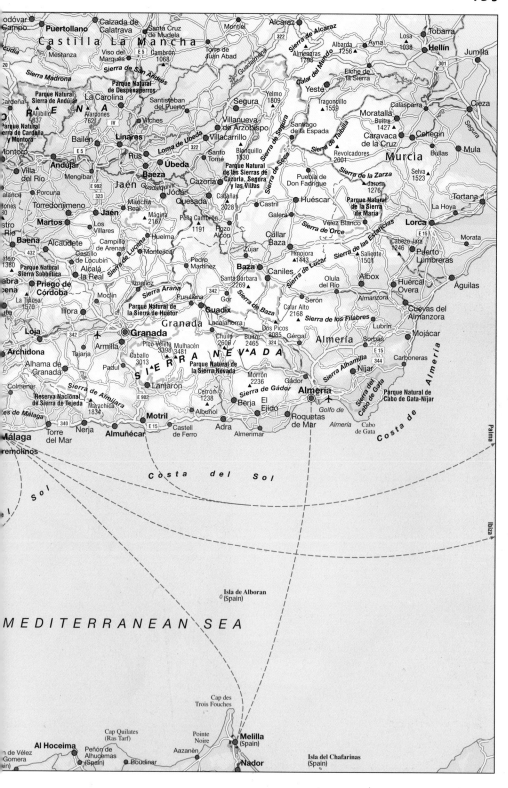

Castilla La Mancha

odóvar
Campo
Puertollano
Calzada de
Calatrava
Santa Cruz
de Mudela
Montiel
Alcaraz
322
Sierra de Alcaraz
Albarda 1256▲
Ayna
Losa 1038
Tobarra
Hellín
Jumilla
Mestanza
Viso del
Marqués
E 5
Cambrón
1068
Torre de
Juan Abad
Guadalmena
Almenaras
1798
301
Sierra Madrona
Sierra de San Andrés
Elche de
la Sierra
Parque Natural
de Despeñaperros
La Carolina
Santisteban
del Puerto
Segura
Yelmo
1809
Yeste
Calar del Mundo
Tragoncillo
▲1559
Calasparra
Cieza
Cardeña
Parque Natural
Sierra de Andújar
R E N A
Aljibillo▲
837
Alfardones
762▲
IV
Vilches
Villanueva
de Arzobispo
Santiago
de la Espada
Moratalla
Buitre
1427 ▲
Sierra
Parque Natural
erra de Cardeña
y Montoro
Bailén
Linares
Loma de Ubeda
Villacarrillo
Sierra de Segura
Caravaca
de la Cruz
Cehegín
Montoro
E 5
Rus
322
Santo
Tomé
Blanquillo
1830
Revolcadores
2001
Bullas
Mula
Villa
del Río
Andújar
Úbeda
Parque Natural
de las Sierras de
Cazorla, Segura
y las Villas
Murcia
Mengibar
Baeza
Cazorla
Puebla de
Don Fadrique
Sierra de la Zarza
Selva▲
1523
alance
Porcuna
Jaén
Guadalquivir
Jódar
Jarosa
1276
Tortana
ones
Torredonjimeno
323
Mancha
Real
Quesada
Cabañas
2028
Castril
Huéscar
Parque Natural
de la Sierra
de María
La Hoya
Martos
Jaén
Mágina
2167
Peña Cambrón
1191
Galera
Vélez Blanco
Lorca
E 15
Morata
Baena
Alcaudete
432
Los
Villares
Huelma
Fozo
Alcón
Cúllar
Baza
Sierra de Orce
Cabezo Jara
1246 ▲
Puerto
Lumbreras
atejo
1360
Castillo
de Locubín
Campillo
de Arenas
Montejicar
Zújar
Hinojora
▲1443
Sierra de las Estancias
Saliente
1501
Águilas
abra
cena
Alcalá
la Real
Pedro
Martínez
Baza
Caniles
Sierra de Lúcar
Albox
Huércal
Overa
Priego de
Córdoba
Iznalloz
Santa Bárbara
2269▲
Olula
del Río
Almanzora
La Tiñosa
1570
Moclín
Purullena
342
Gor
Serón
Calar Alto
2168
Cuevas del
Almanzora
Illora
Parque Natural de
la Sierra de Huétor
Guadix
Sierra de Baza
Sierra de los Filabres
Lubrín
Loja
342
Granada
Lacalahorra
Dos Picos
2085
Gérgal
Almería
Mojácar
Archidona
Granada
Pico Veleta
3398
Mulhacén
3481
Chullo
2608
Buñor
2465
324
Sorbas
Armilla
Tajarja
Caballo
3013
S I E R R A N E V A D A
E 15
Carboneras
Alhama de
Granada
Padul
Parque Natural de
la Sierra Nevada
Morrón
2236
Sierra Alhamilla
Níjar
Costa de Almería
Colmenar
Sierra de Almijara
Lanjarón
Cerrón
1238
Sierra de Gádor
Gádor
Almería
Sierra del Cabo de Gata
Parque Natural de
Cabo de Gata-Níjar
Reserva Nacional
de Sierra de Tejeda
Navachica
1834
E 902
Albuñol
Berja
El
Ejido
es de Málaga
Motril
Adra
Almerimar
Roquetas
de Mar
Golfo de
Almería
Cabo
de Gata
Torre
del Mar
Nerja
Almuñécar
E 15
Castell
de Ferro
Málaga
remolinos

C o s t a   d e l   S o l

S o l

Palma

Ibiza

Isla de Alboran
(Spain)

M E D I T E R R A N E A N   S E A

Cap des
Trois Fouches

Cap Quilates
(Ras Tarf)
Pointe
Noire
Melilla
(Spain)

Al Hoceima
Peñón de
Alhucemas
(Spain)
Aazanèn
Isla del Chafarinas
(Spain)

n de Vélez
Gomera
Boudinar
Nador

SEVILLE AND ITS PROVINCE

*Seville is undeniably romantic with its gracious architecture,
clip-clopping caleches and shady orange trees.
But it is also an exhilarating modern city*

Maps:
Area 159
City 142

If Andalucía is the embodiment of the Spanish clichés of flamenco, gypsies, fiestas and bullfights, then **Seville ❶**, its capital city, is its heart. This is the home of the temptress Carmen, of the lover Don Juan, and of Figaro, the Barber of Seville.

At one time this was Spain's largest city, through which all the riches of the New World poured. Today, with a population of 700,000, it is a prosperous hub of commercial and industrial activity, but you wouldn't guess it. Such is the *Sevillanos'* laid-back attitude to life and devotion to fun and fiestas that visitors will wonder how they ever accomplish any work.

For *Sevillanos,* it's almost as if no other place existed. Other Andalucíans tend to regard *Sevillanos* as conceited and unreliable, but for the traveller, few places are as enchanting as this city with its attractive old quarter of narrow streets permeated with the scent of orange blossoms and its surprisingly easy-going ambience.

Glory and decay

Although it had long existed as a settlement on the river Guadalquivir, the Romans first put the city they called *Hispalis* on the map. In their wake came the Moors, whose various rival factions tried to outdo each other by embellishing their city with rich palaces and mosques.

Seville reached its richest and busiest in the 15th and 16th centuries when it functioned as the major gateway to the New World discovered by Columbus. The treasure ships landed their cargoes on wharves on the banks of the Guadalquivir river, and the plunder passed through the royal counting house and into the treasury coffers.

At the time Seville, with a population of 85,000, of whom 7,000 were slaves, was probably the fourth largest city in the world, after Naples, Paris and Venice. The ships departed and returned in convoys (in 1608 alone there were 283 sailings from Seville to the New World), thus creating periods of great activity and great inactivity. During the times of inactivity chaos ruled.

Seville had a vicious underworld whose gangs were always at each other's throats. Such was the vast wealth passing through – and being filtered off by – the city that corruption was common, and the justice system was the cause of endless complaints to the king in Madrid. In the busy jails the condemned included clerics penalised for forgery and sodomy; city records detail the executions and tell many a grisly story. A man convicted of bestiality was burned and his donkey (his partner in the act) hanged; a con-

LEFT: the Giralda.
BELOW: a good-looking city.

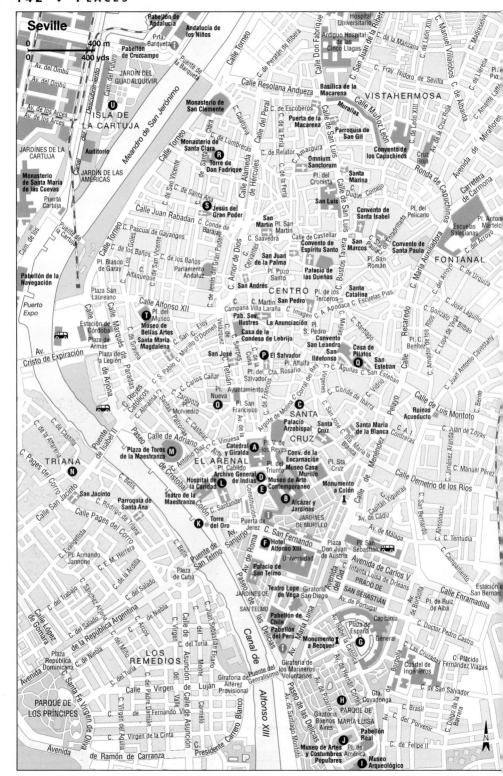

demned Moor on the gallows complained bitterly that a tavern still owed him half a flagon of wine, and he didn't want to leave this world before he'd collected the debt.

The streets were full of people with no particular employment but plenty of work – if they were prepared to do it. *Regatones* (street-hawkers) and *progerones* (vendors) were stationed at every corner. The *progerones* were licensed to sell on behalf of individual members of the public and thus functioned as the city's pawnbrokers; the *regatones* sold parts of cargoes that hadn't necessarily followed their legitimate path. It is these street scenes in particular that are recorded by one of Seville's best-known artists, Bartolomé Murillo (*see page 1162–3*), whose work is on show at many locations in the modern city, including the Fine Arts Museum (Museo de Bellas Artes) (*see page 156*).

The river brought good and bad. With the gold on the ships came disease, and in bad epidemics up to 600 people died every day. But the trade couldn't go on for ever and eventually a combination of increasing ship size, increased river silt, improvement of facilities at Cádiz and a decreasing flow of desirable goods from America dragged the business down. Seville lapsed into a quiet, almost provincial, country town.

Orientation

A visitor to Seville intent on seeing most of its attractions needs a keen sense of direction. This narrow-streeted city is confusingly built, and it is easy to stumble upon a landmark without any prior warning.

The biggest and best of the monuments are located in a small band of the city stretching from the Cathedral southwards down to the Parque de María

He who has not at Seville been Has not, I trow, a wonder seen

– RICHARD FORD A Handbook for Travellers in Spain (1855)

BELOW: the Guadalquivir in Seville.

LEGENDS OF THE GUADALQUIVIR

Ancient myth and history interweave in Andalucía and particularly along the 600 km (400 miles) of the Guadalquivir. One of the first bridges on the river is said to have been built in one night, while Queen Isabella slept, so that she would not wet her feet on the long march to conquer Granada.

In Seville, legend says that the Torre del Oro (Tower of Gold; *see page 153*), which commands the river in the centre of the city, acquired its name through King Pedro the Cruel's obsession for a beautiful woman with long golden hair. The king seized her from the convent where her husband had left her while he was away at war, and locked her in the tower. To deter the king, she tried to destroy her beauty by cutting off her hair and ruining her face with acid. The enraged monarch forced his attentions on her, then sent her back to the convent to die. Her husband, seeking revenge, joined Pedro's brother in bloody rebellion against the king.

In Córdoba province, the Guadalquivir curves around the well-preserved Almódovar castle. The bats that flutter at twilight from the battlements and fly over the river are said to be the spirits of those who suffered there, crying unheard pleas for mercy.

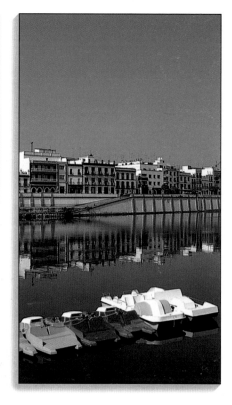

The Maria Luisa park marks the southern boundary of central Seville

Luisa and the Plaza de America. This band of history is one of the richest, most densely packed and varied centres in the world.

Landmarks

The **Cathedral** (Catedral y Giralda) (open daily; admission charge) is listed in the *Guinness Book of Records* simply for being big, but the close-packed streets that cluster around this vast edifice make it hard for one to appreciate it as a whole from the outside. Perhaps it is appropriate thus, for the building is composed of different structures from different periods, and its immensity is best appreciated from within.

A faded photocopy of the *Guinness Book of Records* certificate sits in the glass information case alongside the Cathedral's floor plan: 126 metres (413 ft) long by 83 metres (272 ft) wide by 30 metres (100 ft) high, the cathedral has the largest interior in the world, and is the third largest cathedral overall in Christendom, after St Peter's in Rome and St Paul's in London. The immensity of this inner area may not instantly be apparent, however, both because of the gloom and because the centre of the building is occupied by the choir (*coro*) and **Capilla Mayor**, which reduce the open space and prevent any real impression of the building's shape.

It is worth visiting the Cathedral at least twice: once in the morning at around 9am when the Capilla Mayor is illuminated and in use, the cathedral roof echoing with the dim voices of the red-robed clerics. At this time most of the gleaming nuggets around the walls will be in darkness, but the huge golden altarpiece or *retablo* (begun in 1482 by Flemish sculptor Pieter Dancart) at the back of the Capilla Mayor is at its best. The altarpiece, which is of gilded hardwood, con-

BELOW: the Barrio de Santa Cruz.

tains 36 tableaux of the life of Christ and measures 20 metres (66 ft) in height, almost to the roof.

You will have to revisit, however, to see the Cathedral's other qualities, and the whole is not as beautiful as the sum of its parts. On the northern side of the building, the **Patio de Los Naranjos** (viewed from an entrance from the street) is still, as its name suggests, filled with orange trees. This, with the Giralda tower, is the most accessible evidence of the original Moorish mosque (built in 1172) that preceded the Cathedral on this site.

The bulk of the present Cathedral was built between 1401 and 1507; thus the principal structure is Gothic, with additions in the shape of the *coro*, altar and Sacristía de los Calices, which are late Gothic (1496–1537); the Capilla Real (1530–69) at the eastern end is plateresque and further additions to the southern end are baroque.

Various exhibits are open to the public; these include a wealth of silverware within the treasury (**Sacristía Mayor**), a rather grand and gloomy chapel with display areas on either side. The **Sacristía de los Cálices** (with a very pretty arched roof) contains an exhibition of paintings including works by Goya, Valdés Leal and Zurbarán, although these are not labelled.

Beyond exhibitions of illustrated manuscripts and clerical vestments from the 18th century is the **Sala Capitular**, restored but still sadly neglected. This is the most glorious and unusual of rooms, built in elliptical shape with leather seats and marble floor specifically for the purpose of hosting the meetings of the Cathedral Council.

At the eastern end is the **Capilla Real** (Royal Chapel), the most used and most ornate of the side chapels, with the tombs of Alfonso X and Ferdinand III.

Map, page 142

BELOW: cathedral portal.

Next to the southern entrance is the grand but rather comic monument to Christopher Columbus, the great man's tomb carried by four figures who represent the four kingdoms that made up the Spanish crown at the time of his voyage – Castile, Navarre, Aragón and León. Columbus is probably not buried here; despite considerable confusion, his bones are believed to lie in Santo Domingo.

The Giralda

Literally and figuratively, the highspot of the Cathedral has to be the tower, that much-photographed, much-imitated 94-metre (308-ft) minaret which has been admired ever since its inception at the orders of Moorish ruler Abu Ya'qub Yusuf in 1184. The **Giralda** is said to be the best relic of the Maghreb dynasty anywhere in the world and was held in such esteem by the Moors that they wanted to destroy it rather than let it fall into the hands of the Christians. Every museum or gallery in Andalucía seems to have a painting of the Giralda, every souvenir shop has a model and every town an imitation: it is Seville's Eiffel Tower, and it probably deserves the affection it gets if just for its history and its excellent view.

Two different hands are clearly at work in its construction: the lower part is the original Moorish tower, most of which was destroyed in an earthquake in 1356. The Giralda was then rebuilt by Hernan Ruiz in 1558, and topped by a figure of Faith with her shield standing on a globe which rotates with the wind (the figure had to be removed in 1997 due to four centuries of wear and tear). Whatever you make of the Giralda from below, you should walk up the ramps within it (designed so that horsemen could ascend) to look out over the city, particu-

ABOVE: bell in the Giralda. **BELOW:** the monument to Christopher Columbus.

larly as this affords a rare opportunity of relating one Seville landmark to another. This was once the site of the first public clock in Spain (circa 1400), and today's bells make a dreadful row. From up here you can see the full immensity of the Cathedral, which is more visually interesting from above than it is from the side.

Map, page 142

The Alcázar

The second architectural jewel in Seville is within striking distance of the Giralda, hidden behind imposing battlemented ochre walls. Much of the older part of the **Alcázar** ⓑ (Alcázar y Jardines) (open Tues–Sun, closed Sun pm and Mon; admission charge) was built by Pedro the Cruel in 1366 (who, among other things, murdered some of his guests), in Mudéjar style. Its architecture echoes the Alhambra in Granada, although additions have been made since (including kitchens built specially for General Franco's visits). The *azulejos* or wall tiles are at their best here: their impact is undoubted and many a visitor is silenced by the delicacy of the work.

The palace fronts the inner courtyard (Patio de la Montería). On the right-hand side is an **audience hall** and chapel founded by Queen Isabella in 1503; the audience hall has various 18th-century paintings depicting the overthrow of the Moors. In the **chapel** (fine artesonado ceiling) the altar painting has a nautical theme appropriate to the rooms, which were specifically built for the planning of naval expeditions. A figure hidden in the Virgin's skirts is supposed to be Christopher Columbus.

The main entrance to the Moorish palace is surmounted by an inscription to Pedro the Cruel. Inside (turn left) it is the *azulejos* that dominate the eye, and

ABOVE: handle on the door of the main entrance to the Alcázar.
BELOW: view of the Giralda.

make every room, although bare, look different and richly furnished. The entranceway leads into the **Patio de las Doncellas** (maids of honour), the central courtyard which gives access to the other rooms. Tiled and pillared in similar fashion to the main patio at Granada, this courtyard has a more compact grace and quieter beauty.

Notable in the apartments are the **Ambassador's Hall**, the biggest of the side rooms, which has a domed roof (unfortunately dimly lit) and superb geometric and floral carvings on the walls. The hall has often been featured by the Moroccan film industry. Beyond is the small **Patio de las Muñecas** (dolls), which was the private gathering place of the family and is named after two tiny faces at the foot of one of the arches; the faces have been eroded by time and are now more sinister than pretty.

The Catholic Monarchs also made their mark on the Alcázar in a style which is more familiar, notably in the Charles V apartments, built at Charles's behest. These are located down the covered walkway that leads off to the left of the Patio de la Montería and across the inner garden. Underneath the walkway are the baths of Maria Padilla, mistress of Pedro the Cruel, who herself is said to have had several lovers. Men of the court lined up for the strangely erotic act of drinking her bathwater – all except one who excused himself on the grounds that "having tasted the sauce, he might covet the partridge".

The decor of the **Charles V apartments** seems clumsy in comparison with the Moorish craftsmanship elsewhere. The tapestries (which depict Charles's expedition to Tunisia) are much faded; they were completed in 1554 by the Dutch artist Vermayen, who included a self-portrait in his upside-down map of the Mediterranean.

Opinions vary on the source of the name azulejo, which some say derives from the overriding use of blue ("azul") in the tiles, but more likely derives from the arabic "al-zulayj", meaning little stone (see side panel, page 77).

BELOW: the Alcázar Gardens.

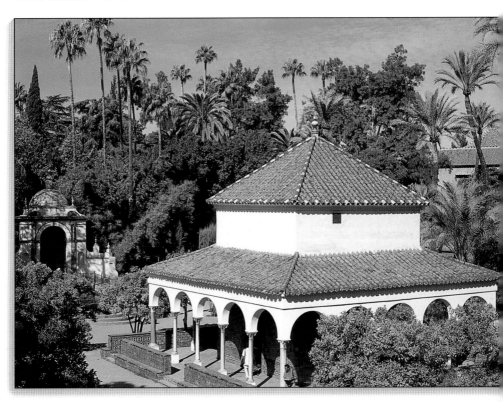

Return to the walkway for access to the Alcázar's **gardens**, which display characteristic features of Moorish design, including fountains, fish ponds, box hedges and small orange groves. These gardens are a welcome oasis in a city which is sadly under-supplied with places to sit and watch the world go by.

Santa Cruz

The northeastern wall of the Alcázar borders on the **Barrio de Santa Cruz** Ⓒ or former *Judería* (Jewish quarter), entered by a forbidding little archway in one corner of the Patio Banderas. This corner of Seville maintains some of the expected clichés: the Seville patio is here in super-abundance, with courtyards decorated with *azulejos* visible through wrought-iron gates; here young men play and sing flamenco in the small squares. In the summer the narrow, white-washed streets are cool and as quiet as on a Sunday morning until the bars fill up in late afternoon. The Plaza de Santa Cruz is the site of the best known of the three traditional flamenco venues in town, Los Gallos.

Complainants will say that Santa Cruz, with its carefully tended squares and hanging baskets, is overly prettified, but it remains the best place to be on a sum-mer evening, with its many bars, restaurants and shops. Out of the host of shops for tourists in this quarter, perhaps the most atmospheric is Antonio Linares's souvenir shop on Plaza Alianza, which contains a bizarre and extensive collec-tion of junk and quality antiques.

Monuments

Between the Alcázar and the Cathedral is a square, rather unappealing, sober building, once the **Lonja** (stock exchange), which now houses the **Archivo**

The Archivo General de Indias documents Spain's discovery of the New World.

BELOW: in the Barrio de Santa Cruz.

Looking for Carmen

When it was built between 1728 and 1766, the *Real Fábrica de Tabacos* (Royal Tobacco Factory) was the second largest building in Spain after the Escorial in Madrid. Here, thousands of women, known as *cigarreras*, worked to produce cigars and powdered snuff. The place was surrounded by tight security, for the Spanish State enjoyed a lucrative monopoly on the tobacco trade.

The tobacco factory, which functioned as such until the 1960s, is known as the home of Carmen, one of the most memorable literary stereotypes Spain has inspired. In the story by Prosper Merimée (1845), the brigadier José Navarro becomes smitten with passion for the gypsy *cigarrera* he must accompany to prison. He allows her to escape, then deserts and becomes a smuggler and bandit for her sake. But Carmen isn't faithful, and José stabs her to death outside the Maestranza bullring after he finds her flirting with a toreador.

Most remember Carmen from Bizet's opera, premiered 30 years after Merimée's story appeared. It marked a turning point in the genre, and continues to be the most popular opera in the world.

Carmen came to represent the classic Andalucían temptress, demure and defiant, feminine and independent at the same time, capable of turning men mad with desire. Did Merimée base his heroine on a real person? To find out, one has to cross the river to the modern new building in the Los Remedios district which houses Seville's new tobacco factory. On the third floor are the archives from the old tobacco factory – thousands of ledgers, each containing lists of the women who worked at the factory, with specific descriptions of each one.

The books list quite a few women named Carmen or María del Carmen, any one of whom could have served as a model for Merimée, such as one "María del Carmen García, from Seville, unmarried, aged 15, small, light coloured, black eyes, who was dismissed for having spoken insulting and scandalous words to her companions, and for throwing a pair of scissors at Concepción Vegue". The custodian of this peculiar archive believes Merimée's Carmen was a composite of the women who worked there when the author visited in 1840.

The Seville factory, in which up to 3,500 *cigarreras* would be working at one time, was Spain's biggest employer, and provided the first opportunity for women to be financially independent. They were the breadwinners in many a household, while their idle husbands loitered on street corners, smoking the cheroots their womenfolk had smuggled out of the factory. They worked in teams, one member of which was appointed to look after her colleagues' children. Their spirit of camaraderie and their self-confidence must have made an impression on Merimée. ❏

LEFT: Gonzalo Bilbao's *Las Cigarreras* (1915) in the Museo de Bellas Artes.

General de Indias ❿ (open weekday mornings). This collection comprises some 80 million pages relating to the discovery of the New World and the establishment and rule of Spanish colonies. Although it is not instantly obvious from the outside (go up the marbled staircase and fill in the visitors' book), a small exhibition is maintained in one of the long galleries, while elsewhere academics study the bulk of the documents. The exhibition usually includes a page or two from Columbus's diary or letters.

Map, page 142

Alongside the Lonja in Calle Santo Tomás (barely noticeable entranceway) is the **Museo de Arte Contemporáneo ❺** (Museum of Contemporary Art) (open Tues–Sun; mornings only in summer; closed Sat–Sun pm and Mon; admission charge), which features work principally by artists from Andalucía. The last room at the top contains the best of a patchy collection, particularly some fine Sevillian ceramics by Francisco Cortijo.

On the other side of the Puerta Jerez roundabout at the southern end of the Avenida de la Constitución is the **Hotel Alfonso XIII ❻**, a pompous, luxurious, old-fashioned hotel with uniformed, autocratic staff. The hotel was built in imitation of the Seville patio style specifically for the 1929 Ibero-American exhibition, and it is worth having tea there.

Alongside the hotel is one of the biggest buildings in the western world, erected in 1750 to house the **tobacco factory** in which the mythical Carmen supposedly worked with 3,000 other *cigarerras* (*see opposite page*). Now this rather grim building echoes with the cries of students, for this is the **University's** (open weekdays) faculty of science and law. To glimpse life in the factory in its heyday, visit the Museo de Bellas Artes (Fine Art Museum) (*see page 156*), where there are a number of paintings showing the factory women at work.

BELOW: neighbourhood bar.

Park properties

Beyond the University are the beginnings of María Luisa park and the site of Seville's Ibero-American exhibition of 1929, of which some buildings remain. These include the biological research station for the Coto Doñana nature reserve (Avenida de Chile), which is not open to the public but has a striking courtyard in pink marble littered with animal carvings.

Most notable of the remains of the exhibition is the **Plaza de España**  surrounded by a semi-circular building which took 15 years to build and functioned as the Spanish pavilion at the time. It now houses government offices and, apart from the tile pictures featuring Spain's every province on the outside, is rather a disappointment. Still, the Plaza itself, with its shaded waterway and bridges, is pleasant.

Better still is the jungle that is the **Parque de María Luisa** ⬢ itself. A judicious mixture of careful manicuring and rank outgrowth, of delicate landscaping and unharnessed riot, of familiar European plants and flowers and more exotic species from Africa and the Americas, the park is an essential picnic space in a city that at times becomes stiflingly hot. It is full of small sources of amusement: the *azulejo* benches buried deep under foliage; sweating joggers; ceramic frogs spouting water; duck sanctuaries full of doves.

The **Plaza de América** marks the end of the park. Surrounded on three sides by museums or government offices, the Plaza is packed with greedy doves which can readily produce an experience worthy of Alfred Hitchcock.

The **Museo Arqueológico** ⬤ (Archaeological Museum) (open Tues–Sat; admission charge) on one side of the square has an extensive collection from local excavation sites, with representative material from the earliest recorded his-

ABOVE: tile picture in the Plaza de España showing the province of Alava. **BELOW:** boating below the Plaza de España's Spanish pavilion, built in 1929.

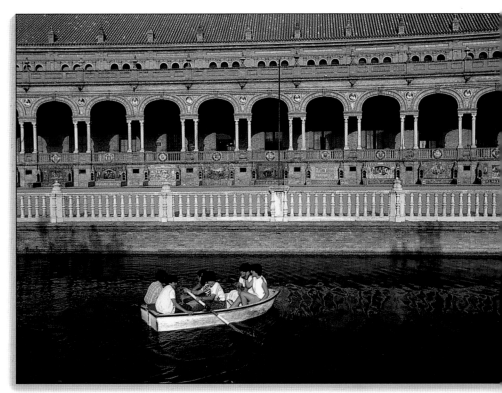

tory (neolithic and Tartessian) through to Roman and Moorish times. Pottery and silver and goldwork reflect the trading connections of Andalucía, with fine Phoenician painted ceramics. The Roman collection, in particular, is impressive, symptomatic of the significant Roman cities that once surrounded Seville, of which there is a map (with both Latin and Spanish names) on one wall.

Opposite, the rather sleepy **Museo de Artes y Costumbres Populares** ❶ (Arts and Folklore Museum) (open Tues–Sun mornings only; admission charge) promotes the expected aspects of Andalucía – bullfighters, the Seville Fair, gypsies and costume (with excellent background classical music). More surprising is a massive ploughing exhibition and a display of Christian paraphernalia; some of the mocked-up house interiors are worth lingering over.

Map, page 142

Waterside attractions

Back towards the centre of town, the 13th-century **Torre del Oro** ❿ (once covered with glittering tiles, thus the name) stands like a chess piece on the bank of the river. The tower once served a defensive purpose by anchoring a chain that stretched across to the other bank. It houses a **Maritime Museum** (open Tues–Sun mornings only; admission charge) which, although it contains nothing of any significance, is stuffed with fascinating odds and ends, from shark's jaws to paintings of the famous navigators. Murals here show how Seville in the 1700s was surrounded by a girdle of boats.

A street back from the river is the **Hospital de la Caridad** ❶ (open Mon–Sat; closed 1.30–3.30pm and Sun pm; admission charge). Founded in 1674 as a charity hospital for the homeless and the sick by Don Miguel de Mañara, this building still serves that purpose. It is best known to visitors, however, not for

BELOW: the Torre del Oro, once clad in glittering tiles.

For atmospheric bars, visit Calle García de Vinuesa in the Arenal near the bullring. It is lined with old-fashioned *bodegas*, stacked high with sherry barrels and with walls plastered with old bullfight posters.

BELOW: Plaza de Toros de la Maestranza.

the rather picturesque old gentlemen who hobble about the courtyard, but for the quality of the chapel. The latter, one of the most complete in Seville, has paintings by Murillo and Valdés Leal; Leal's two works above and opposite the entrance are particularly poignant, showing the transitory nature of life which passes *in ictu oculi*, in the blink of an eye.

Leaving the hospital you will see a statue of its founder, Don Miguel de Mañara, considered by some to be the role model for Don Juan, the cynical lover who had 1,003 Spanish mistresses. Decide for yourself if this man looks like a reformed seducer or a repentent Don Giovanni. The hospital became a point of call for romantic visitors who believed Seville to be the hot-bed of the lascivious South. Byron explained why in his own *Don Juan*:

What men call gallantry, and gods adultery,
Is much more common where the climate is sultry.

A little upstream to the north is the modern **Teatro de la Maestranza** opera house, built in 1992, and beyond it the **Plaza de Toros de la Maestranza** Ⓜ (Maestranza bullring) (open daily; closed Sat–Sun pm; admission charge) which seats 14,000 spectators and is the second oldest in the country after that at Ronda. If you don't want to see a fight, go on a guided tour. The ring was started in 1758, but in all its history only one matador has been killed within its premises. In the bullfighting museum the head of the mother of the bull that did the deed is mounted on the wall; what happened to the bull itself no one knows; it was rather hard luck on the mother to have had a courageous son. To make the spectacle complete, the bullring has its own mini-hospital for the quick treatment of injured fighters.

A bridge to the north crosses the river to the **Triana** Ⓝ district, once known

as the gypsy quarter but now principally visited during the day for the ceramic factories which still work here and at night for its restaurants and bars (expensive along the riverside **Calle Betis**; cheaper along **Calle Castilla** and nearby side streets). A favourite for local specialities is **Casa Cuesta**, officially called the Cerveceria Ruiz, on the corner of Castilla and San Jorge. Opposite, a dark, dank and dangerous seeming alleyway, appropriately named the **Callejón de la Inquisición** (Seville witnessed some of the Spanish Inquisition's greatest purges), leads down to the river.

Map, page 142

Shops and markets

From the top of García de Vinuesa the Avenida de la Constitución leads up to the **Plaza Nueva O**, which has the **Ayuntamiento** or town hall (built 1572) on one side. Behind it is the Plaza San Francisco, once used for tournaments. To the north is the **Calle Sierpes**, which runs through the heart of the shopping area.

Narrow streets from the top right of the Plaza San Francisco lead to the church of **El Salvador P** (open daily) surrounded by shops selling wedding dresses. This church, which is rather ramshackle from the outside and filled with gold *retablos* on the inside, was built on the site of a mosque and has Arabic inscriptions above the side door. From its northeastern corner narrow streets lead up to the **Plaza Alfalfa**, a busy little square with an excellent patisserie, which hosts the pet market (particularly birds) on Sunday mornings, well worth visiting.

A little further east is the **Casa de Pilatos Q** (built 1480) (open daily; admission charge), property of the Duke of Medinaceli, and so-called supposedly because it imitated Pilate's house in Jerusalem. It is in Mudéjar style, but does not match up to the Alcázar. You enter first through a Roman-style triumphal arch,

ABOVE: songbirds for sale on Sunday morning at Plaza Alfalfa.
BELOW: courtyard of the Casa de Pilatos.

Seville's Fine Arts Museum contains a superb collection, with works by El Greco, Goya and Velázquez. For information on painters associated with Andalucía, see pages 162–3)

crossing the *apeadero* (carriage yard) to its central patio where arcades of Moorish arches are echoed by Gothic ones on the floor above.

This courtyard contains some of the finest tiles in Spain: dazzling puzzle-book patterns in brilliant colours that include some extraordinary quasi-Impressionist designs, and impressive Roman statuary. To the right is the chapel and Pilate's study, which leads into an enchanting small garden with fountains and bougainvillea. A monumental staircase leads up to a late Mudéjar cupola (1537).

Opposite the Casa de Pilatos is the **Convento San Leandro**, a closed-order convent, whose contact with the outside world is via the sale of its famous *yemas* (candied egg yolks).

The other Sunday market is further north still on the **Alameda de Hércules**, a broad avenue marked at one end by two pillars topped by statues of Julius Caesar and Hercules. The market is largely junk, but the people are interesting. This is the red-light area of Seville; the houses are often deserted and decaying, and much of the city hereabouts is empty. One or two churches are worth visiting in this quarter, however: notably the **Monasterio de Santa Clara R** (Convent of Santa Clara), with the ancient **Torre de Don Fadrique** (1252, and still very solid) (open Mon–Fri). The church of **Jesús del Gran Poder S** (the powerful Jésus) (open daily, closed 1.30–6pm) has an unusual feature in its image of Christ carrying the cross on the altar; worshippers file behind the altar to kiss or touch the image's heel to help speed their beseeching prayers.

Fine Arts

Standing in the western side of the city is the **Museo de Bellas Artes T** (Fine Arts Museum) (Plaza del Museo, open Tues 3–9pm, Wed–Sat 9am–8pm, Sun

BELOW: piratical exploits at the Isla Mágica.

9am–3pm, closed Mon; admision charge). The museum is housed in the former Convento de la Merced, and recent restorations have included the former main baroque chapel, which itself is worth visiting. The museum is undoubtedly one of the city's best. It has a fine collection of Seville ceramics and works by Andalucían artists as well as El Greco, Goya, Murillo and Velázquez. There is also a collection of religious paintings and sculptures from the city's abundant and wealthy convents, monasteries and hospitals.

Map, page 142

La Cartuja

The **Isla de la Cartuja ⓤ**, on the western bank of the Guadalquivir, was a swampy wasteland for years, but it was transformed for the Expo '92 universal exposition, commemorating the 500th anniversary of the discovery of America. Modern bridges were built connecting the "island" to the rest of Seville, the area was landscaped, and among the permanent buildings erected was a brand new outdoor auditorium.

Once the party was over, part of La Cartuja became a technological park. One of the most popular attractions in Expo 92, the Navigation Pavilion (Pabellón de la Navegación), has been kept as a permanent exhibition on the history of seafaring. It is part of the **Puerta de Triana** recreational area, which includes the **Imax Space Theatre** (open Tues–Sun; closed Mon; admission charge).

Another section of La Cartuja became **Isla Mágica**, the largest theme park in southern Spain (open daily March–October; admission charge). This 35-hectare (86-acre) fantasy land has 14 rides, including the hair-raising Jaguar roller coaster, and live shows with actors dressed in period costume.

The island is named after the 15th-century **Carthusian monastery**, Santa

ABOVE AND BELOW: more amusements on the magic isle.

María de las Cuevas, at its centre. Columbus was a regular visitor during his life, and was temporarily buried here after he died. In the 19th century, the monastery was turned into the Charles Pickman factory, where the prized Cartuja china was made, and it functioned as such until 1982. The monastery was completely restored for Expo '92, and now makes an interesting visit (open Tues–Sun; admission charge).

Celebrations

In the early part of the year, before the heat becomes intolerable, Seville hosts two very important and exhilarating fiestas in swift succession, Semana Santa and the Feria. The **Feria** (mid-April) started as a livestock market but has developed into an exuberant celebration of the arrival of spring, with dancing, drinking, displays of horsemanship, fireworks, bullfighting competitions and more, over the course of a week. A vast area of the Los Remedios district is transformed into a gaudy kaleidoscope of fairground attractions bordered by rows of striped drinking tents, while, dressed in their best, *sevillana* ladies drive by in their carriages.

ABOVE AND BELOW: at the April Feria, a week-long party featuring food and wine, singing and dancing, horse parades and bullfights.

Semana Santa (Easter) has a more religious origin and features processions of more than 100 floats carried by 57 hooded brotherhoods who each have their own image of Christ or of the Virgin; from the crowd come passionate songs of devotion, called *saetas* (literally arrows).

Both celebrations attract large numbers of people to the city. This inevitably pushes up prices and makes accommodation almost impossible to find. If you can be in Seville for either or both, it is likely to be an experience you won't forget (*for more information on festivals, see pages 66–67*).

The province

The industrial and residential influence of Seville extends some way out into the countryside, but there are no further towns of any real size in the province. To the north lies the Sierra Morena, a vast belt of hills covered with rough woodland; to the south lie agricultural flatlands dominated by the river; to the west is the province of Huelva; and to the east the soft rolling agricultural land, the Campiña, extends down a chain of ancient settlements.

A traveller heading due south in the winter may find the minor roads frustrating; a combination of heavy rain and high tides can mean that many a route is cut by swollen streams. The central town to these flatlands is **Los Palacios**, a quiet, rural place and the site of an agricultural research station.

Heading west

Roads west of Seville, once across the Guadalquivir, swiftly leave the city behind. Up the far bank of the river to the north is the Roman site of **Itálica ❷**, near Santiponce. Excavations have revealed the amphitheatre and numerous streets with a couple of mosaics. There is also a small museum (open Tues–Sun; admission charge) but much of the more interesting material unearthed in Itálica is in the Archaeological Museum in Seville (*see page 152*).

North of Seville

Roads north from Seville cross the flat river valley and ascend into the **Sierra Morena**, a thinly populated belt of hills which provides the plain with its water. The Sierra's main attraction is its coolness after the heat of the lowlands; in the winter it is a hunting centre, and the towns of **Cazalla** and **Constantina ❸**

Map, page 159

Itálica was the principal Roman city of the region and the birthplace of three emperors, Trajan, Hadrian and Thodosius.

BELOW: statue of Trajan at Itálica.

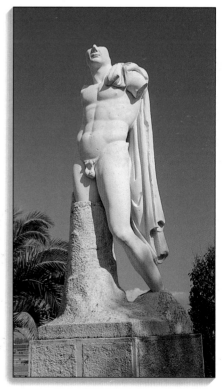

Map, page 159

(the latter surprisingly prosperous, with a dramatic figure of Christ on the hill-side above) are filled with well-dressed young men from Seville swapping stories in the bars. The area is protected as the **Parque Naturel de la Sierra del Norte** nature park, a good place for walks and trout fishing.

East of Seville

Three important historical towns lie east of Seville. **Carmona** ❹, the closest, most interesting and most atmospheric, was an important Roman centre. A Roman amphitheatre and **necropolis** and museum lie on the Seville side of town; the necropolis is well laid out, complete with a crematorium whose walls are still discoloured by the heat of the fire, large numbers of small paupers' tombs and a couple of much grander burial grounds (open Tues–Sun; closed pm on Sat–Sun and in summer; admission charge).

The town itself (ignore anything outside the old walls) commands an extensive view over the plain. The ancient **Córdoba Gate**, well corroded but remarkably intact considering its age (originally 2nd century AD, with Moorish and baroque additions). The other gate, the **Puerta de Sevilla** (on the Seville side of town), is gigantic and features a double entranceway which could turn the town into a fortress. The building incorporates another Alcázar and a museum (open Mon–Sat; closed Sun pm; admission charge). In front, in the newer town, the **church of San Pedro** has one of many imitation Giraldas found around the province.

BELOW: Ecija's Plaza de España. **RIGHT:** in the Sierra Morena.

Écija ❺, some 56 km (34 miles) east, has many such towers. Unlike most Andalucían towns, this is built in a valley bowl rather than on a hill and consequently has no summer breeze to relieve the heat. The town hall promotes Écija as "the city of sun and towers"; however, it is better known as "the frying pan of Spain" because of its relentless summer heat.

The church of **Sta María** (southwest of Plaza Major) has a Mudéjar patio filled with archaeological bits and pieces. The covered market is colourful, and Calle Caballeros (north of the main square) has several rambling and ornate merchants' houses, including the **Palacio de Peñaflor**, with an unusual curved balcony. The town is littered with crumbling church towers, all of which echo Seville's Giralda in some shape or form.

South of Écija is **Osuna** ❻, again with a large collection of merchants' houses. Here the Giralda imitation is built into a grand facade on the **Calle San Pedro** (next door is the cream-cake Palacio Gomera). The Arab tower on the hill has a small archaeological museum (open Tues–Sun; closed 1.30–3.30pm and Mon; admission charge). On the hill is the turreted **Old University** (visits by guided tour only) and the **Collegiate Church of Sta María** (open Tues–Sun; closed 1.30–4pm and Mon; admission charge), big and bare inside. Below the church is the **Convent of La Encarnación** (open daily; closed 1.30–4pm; admission charge), now a museum of religious art.

From Osuna the road, much improved thanks to Expo'92, makes for the heights of the Sierra Nevada and the city of Granada. ❑

FROM LA PILETA TO PICASSO

Artistic treasures abound in Andalucía's churches, and museums, and in the 17th century Seville was the centre of Spain's Golden Age of Art

Pablo Picasso was born in Málaga in 1881 and, although his family moved north when he was only 10, throughout his life he considered himself first and foremost an Andalucían. Refusing to return to Spain while Franco was alive (the dictator survived the artist by two years), he forever yearned for his southern Spanish home. His heirs recognised as much with the donation of 200 works to the city of Málaga, leading to the creation of a new Picasso Museum in 2000.

Picasso was heir to a formidable artistic legacy, stretching back 25,000 years, when prehistoric man decorated the walls of his caves with paintings in charcoal, red and ochre.

GOLDEN AGE

The Moors leaned more towards decorative arts which adorned their palaces and ceramics. Under the Christians, Andalucía was to see a flourishing in the arts. Seville was the cradle of Spain's Siglo de Oro ("Golden Age") of art during the 17th century: it seems incredible that masters of the stature of Francisco de Zurbarán, Bartolomé Murillo and Diego de Velázquez should have gathered at roughly the same time and in the same city. Recognised artists would eventually gravitate to the court in Madrid, with varying success, but Seville was decisive in their careers.

In the 19th century, the age of romanticism, Andalucían art tended to historical themes and *costumbrista* portrayals of everyday life. One of the most popular Andalucían artists of the day was Julio Romero de Torres, famous for his paintings of Andalucían beauties, demure and provocative at the same time.

△ **THE FIRST ARTISTS** Picture of a pregnant mare in the Cueva de la Pileta near Ronda. The cave's paintings are believed to date from 25,000 BC.

▷ **RELIGIOUS EXPRESSION** *Mater Dolorosa* by Bartolomé Estéban Murillo (1617–1682), the foremost exponent of baroque religious art in his day.

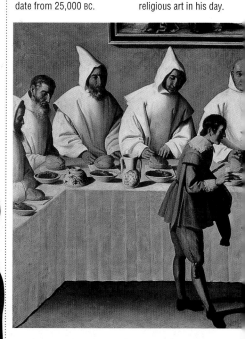

◁ **MASTER CARVER** *Puríysma Concepción* by Alonso Cano (1601–1667), an architect and painter but best known for his carvings.

△ **REALISM AND DRAMA** *St Hugo and the Miracle in the Refectory* by Zurbarán (1598–1664) combines realism with drama.

▽ **ANDALUCÍAN BEAUTY**
Naranjas y Limones
(Oranges and Lemons), a
classic work by Julio
Romero de Torres
(1874–1930)

ANDALUCÍAN IMAGES

▽ **COUNTRY LIFE**
Rural life was rendered in
bold colours by Rafael
Zabaleta (1907–1960).
Popular scenes were a
theme for this artist from
the village of Quesada, near
the Sierra de Cazorla.

One of the most typical
manifestations of
Andalucían art are the
polychrome wood
sculptures of the 17th
century. Unlike northern
European carving, the
general theme was
religious, and churches
were filled with fine
images and carved
altarpieces. The genre was
very popular because the
expressive statues of
virgins and martyred saints
appealed to the Andalucían
sense of drama and
pathos.

Two main schools were
established around the
central figures of Juan
Martínez Montañes (*Cristo
de la Clemencia*, above) in
Seville, and Alonso Cano
(*see the carving picture
bottom far left*) in Granada.
Both artists had numerous
followers, whose work
developed increasingly
exaggerated, baroque
expressiveness.

Many of these priceless
images were destroyed in
the course of various wars
(including the Napoleonic
invasion and the Spanish
Civil War) but others still
survive in the churches of
Andalucía and are well
worth seeking out.

◁ **MALAGA GENIUS**
Homage to the Painter by
Picasso. The genius's 80-
year career encompassed
every genre and medium.

CÓRDOBA AND ITS PROVINCE

Maps:
City 170
Area 175

Capital of al-Andalus, Córdoba is a labyrinth of winding alleyways and Moorish patios. Its supreme monument is La Mezquita, its fabulous mosque

C órdoba ❶, seen in the last rays of the setting sun, glows with an inner light. Huge flocks of birds wheel over the quiet waters of the river Guadalquivir, which shimmers with the city's reflection. At this hour, in this light, it seems as if it were only yesterday that Córdoba was the grandest and most important city in Europe.

The Moors, who swarmed across the Strait of Gibraltar in AD 711, chose Córdoba as the capital of al-Andalus, Islamic Spain. For a while their armies dominated most of the peninsula and even penetrated as far as southern France, before being repelled. Moorish Spain answered to the Damascus caliphate until 756, when Abd-al-Rahman I established an independent emirate ruling al-Andalus from his capital in Córdoba.

The heyday of Córdoba came in the 10th century, under Abd-al-Rahman III the first caliph. While parts of Europe languished in the Dark Ages, Córdoba became a centre of advanced learning in sciences, medicine, philosophy and poetry. Together with Baghdad and Constantinople, it was one of the three greatest cities in the world. Today it has a population of 300,000.

PRECEDING PAGES: arches of La Mezquita.
LEFT: in the streets of the Judería.
BELOW: *mirhab* in La Mezquita.

Monument to the Moors

Powerfully evoking this fabulous epoch is Córdoba's most important monument, the **Mosque ❹**, La Mezquita, the third largest mosque in the world (open daily; admission charge) though it hasn't been used for Islamic rites since the city was conquered by King Ferdinand in 1236. The mosque was begun in 785 by Abd-al-Rahman I on the site of an earlier Visigothic (Christian) church, which itself probably replaced a Roman temple. Its builders recycled a hodge-podge of building materials, taking Roman and Visigothic columns, bases and capitals of many materials, sizes and styles, and topping them with double horseshoe arches, candy-striped in pink and white.

The mosque was enlarged by Abd-al-Rahman II in 833; again in 926 under al-Hakam II, and finally by al-Mansur, chief minister of Hisham II, in 978. Covering 23,400 sq. metres (251,000 sq. ft), it has 856 columns.

The architectural style evolved with each addition, reaching the greatest splendour and technical mastery in what came to be known as the calif style of architecture during the caliphate of al-Hakam. Features to note are great sky-lighted domes for extra interior light and an ingenious engineering system which consists of clustered pillars bearing intersecting lobed arches to support the domes.

The most dazzling part of the mosque is undoubtedly the *mihrab*, the holy sanctuary where the Koran

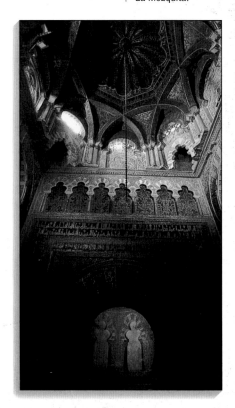

scriptures were kept, which, incidentally, does not quite face Mecca. A scallop-shell dome covers this sanctum, which is richly decorated with mosaics of coloured and gilded tiles glittering in the magical light. Koranic scriptures border the *mihrab* and carved stucco adorns the upper walls.

After Córdoba fell to the Christian King Ferdinand in 1236, the mosque was reconsecrated as a Christian church and, in 1523, construction began on a **Cathedral** within its walls, requiring the removal of some 60 of the original columns and some of the most beautiful stucco work.

On Sundays and on feast days the cathedral is busy with worshippers who are quite oblivious to the tourists gazing up at the fabled cupolas of the mosque. Here are two quite different, formerly opposing worlds under one harmonious roof, a fitting image for Córdoba which over the centuries has sheltered many cultures.

The cathedral is of Gothic design with later additions in plateresque and baroque styles. Within, it is surprisingly light and intimate. Especially noteworthy are the choir stalls, carved by the Andalucían sculptor Pedro Duque Cornejo; these depict, on either side of the Ascension, the lives of Jesus and the Virgin Mary in life-like detail. The Cathedral treasury (located in the sacristy next to the *mihrab*) displays especially good examples of Córdoban silver and gold artistry.

The town

Across from the mosque (on Calle Torrijos) in a 16th-century hospice is the **Palacio de Congresos**, a convention hall housing the tourism office. From here it is a few steps to the river, crossed by the **Puente Romano ❸** (Roman Bridge),

"Had I known what this was, you would not have done it, for what you are building here can be found anywhere; but what you have destroyed exists nowhere."

—CHARLES V

BELOW: view from La Mezquita.

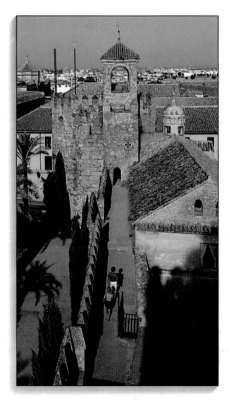

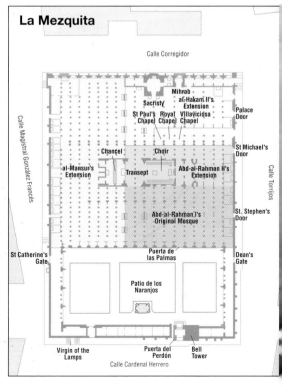

La Mezquita

Calle Corregidor

Mihrab
Sacristy — al-Hakam II's Extension
St Paul's Chapel — Royal Chapel — Villaviciosa Chapel
Palace Door

Calle Magistral González Francés

Chancel — Choir
al-Mansur's Extension — Transept — Abd-al-Rahman II's Extension
St Michael's Door

Calle Torrijos

Abd-al-Rahman I's Original Mosque
St. Stephen's Door

St Catherine's Gate
Puerta de las Palmas
Dean's Gate

Patio de los Naranjos

Virgin of the Lamps — Puerta del Perdón — Bell Tower
Calle Cardenal Herrero

the best place to be at sunset. On the bridge is one of many images of Córdoba's patron, the Archangel Raphael, candles burning at his feet.

In the river bottom, overgrown with rushes where ducks paddle, are the remains of three Arabic mills (**Molinos Arabes**).

Across the bridge is the **Torre de Calahorra** ❻ (open daily; closed Sun pm and 2–5.30pm in summer; admission), a 14th-century watchtower, which houses a museum depicting the glories of al-Andalus, Moorish Spain, with wax figures and a 50-minute diorama, with headphones in several languages.

A few blocks downriver from the mosque is the **Alcázar de los Reyes Cristianos** ❼, a palace built by the Christian kings in 1327 (open Tues–Sun; closed 2–4.30pm and Mon; admission charge). This is supposedly where Queen Isabella told Columbus she would back his harebrained scheme to sail off the edge of the known universe. The views from the tower of gardens and city are worth the climb – for the nimble. Ancient steps are not in the best repair.

Pretty patios

The area around the mosque, Córdoba's old quarter, is best visited on foot or by horse carriage. Many of the streets are hardly more than narrow alleyways which cars can't enter. Whitewashed houses present a blank facade to the street, broken only by an entryway closed by a *cancela*, a wrought-iron gate. Through this gate is glimpsed a *patio*, shaded by a palm, furnished with ferns, perfumed with jasmine, air-conditioned by a bubbling fountain.

Whether intimate heart of private homes or elegant courtyards of great buildings, the *patio* was developed as a survival technique, a cool oasis in the long hot summers. Calle Albucasis and Calle Manriquez are two streets with espe-

ABOVE: corner of one of Córdoba's many *patios*.
BELOW: the Puente Romano, the best place to be at sunset.

Atop the Puerta de Almodóvar

The expulsion order on the Jews was officially rescinded only in 1968; the Spanish Constitution of 1978 further guarantees religious freedom.

cially beautiful *patios*. Córdoba celebrates its courtyards during the first half of May, when many private *patios* are opened to the public.

Within a gentle stroll of the mosque is Córdoba's medieval Jewish quarter, **La Judería** 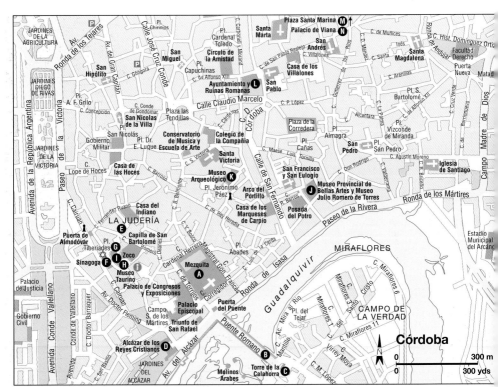, also entered through the **Puerta de Almodóvar**, one of the city's ancient gates. Monumental Córdoba is golden, but its *barrios* or neighbourhoods are usually pristine white, kept lime-washed by house-proud owners.

Jewish influence

If Córdoba is known for the splendour of its 10th-century achievements in art, architecture and science, a part of its glory is attributed to the Sephardim community, the Spanish Jews who settled here during the time of the Roman emperors, when they were allowed the same rights as other inhabitants of Baetica, Roman Spain.

After the fall of the Roman Empire, under the Visigoths, Jews were persecuted so severely that they welcomed the Muslim invaders. In exchange, they enjoyed long periods of peaceful coexistence and a flowering of Sephardim culture during which many achieved rare heights in diplomacy, medicine, commerce and crafts.

Sepharad simply means Spain in Hebrew. Five hundred years after King Ferdinand and Queen Isabella decreed their expulsion in 1492, Spanish Jews, dispersed throughout the world, still speak an archaic Spanish dialect. Were Columbus to come back to life today, he would find it easier to converse with the Sephardic Jews in, say, Istanbul than with modern *madrileños*.

The Jewish **Synagoga** ❼ (Sinagogue) (open Tues–Sun; closed 2–3.30pm, Sun pm and Mon; admission charge) in Córdoba is one of only three medieval

synagogues remaining in Spain, where once there were hundreds (the other two are in Toledo). Córdoba itself had 26 synagogues between the 10th and 15th centuries. This survivor, built in 1315, is entered from the narrow Calle Judíos, through a patio. Segments of Hebraic inscriptions and family history remain on the walls. The upper gallery, where women were seated, and the niche where the Torah was kept are still intact.

Many Córdoban Sephardim achieved high status, either at the Muslim court or within the Jewish community. One was Maimonides, one of the greatest philosophers of Jewish history. A rabbi and Talmudic scholar with an Aristotelian bent, Maimonides was born in Córdoba, in 1135. By this time, fanatic Berber sects, the Almohads, had changed the political landscape, initiating a period of unrest and repression. To escape the repression Maimonides's family fled to Morocco and he eventually settled in Egypt. But Córdoba still claims him as a native son.

Near the Synagogue, in the **Plaza Tiberiades ❿**, under the bower of an enormous jasmine vine, is a statue of Maimonides, dedicated in 1965. He presides over the tiny square with kindly dignity, his slipper rubbed shiny by thousands of passers-by, possibly hoping some of his great wisdom might rub off on them.

Bullfighting memorabilia

In the plaza named for Maimonides is a different sort of monument. Opening off a beautiful *patio*, in the house said to have belonged to Maimonides's family, is the municipal **Museo Taurino ❿** (Bullfight Museum) (open Tues–Sun;

Map, page 170

ABOVE: statue of Maimonides.
BELOW: exhibit in the Bullfight Museum.

Cordoba's craft tradition dates from the Moors. It is still evident in fine leather work and ceramics.

BELOW:
craftsman at work.

closed 1.30–5pm, Sun pm and Mon; admission charge) displaying posters, swords, capes and *trajes de luz*, the "suit of lights" worn by matadors. Córdoba is a famous town for bullfighters and home of two all-time greats, Lagartijo and Manolete.

Craft quarter

Behind the museum, again on Calle Judíos, is the **Zoco ❶**, a group of craft workshops around a central courtyard. Here artisans work in both traditional and modern styles, in silver filigree (for which Córdoba is famous), leather, wood carving and ceramics. Nearby, on Calle Tomás Conde 3, the street leading into Plaza Maimonides, is **Artesanía Andaluza**, in a 16th-century house, featuring an excellent selection of Córdoban crafts, particularly ceramics. One of the exhibition rooms off the central patio has an ancient well.

The **Meryan** exposition rooms contain a pretty patio and leather workshops, run by two brothers whose family has carried on the leather crafting tradition for generations, on **Calleja de las Flores**, the much photographed "Street of Flowers" with its picturesque view of the mosque tower. The shop shows hand-tooled leather handbags, briefcases, mirror frames, and studded coffers and polychromed leather work, called *guadameciles*, which are especially attractive as wall hangings.

Near the Alcázar, at Calle Enmedio 13, **Joyería La Milagrosa** carries on the traditional Córdoban crafts of silver and goldsmithing. Before the holiday of Los Reyes, 6 January, when, instead of Father Christmas, the Three Kings come from Bethlehem bearing gifts, clients throng this elegant shop where salesmen unwrap velvet rolls to reveal gleaming gold trinkets.

Art collections

An easy walk from the mosque, along **Ronda de Isasa** (the avenue bordering the river), is the **Plaza del Potro**, which Cervantes mentions in *Don Quixote*. It is named after a small statue of a colt on top of a 16th-century fountain where two ducks paddle. The inn on one side of the plaza, where Cervantes once stayed, houses a municipal arts and crafts centre. Modern paintings hang where horses and mules were stabled. The plaza opens towards the river and the far bank is open countryside.

On one side of the Plaza del Potro a 16th-century hospice with leaded glass windows houses the **Museo Provincial de Bellas Artes ❶** (Fine Arts Museum) (open Tues–Sun; closed 1.30–5pm, Sun pm and Mon; admission charge), entered through a courtyard, elegantly tiled on one side. The collection may be small but it is wide-ranging: a haunting head of Christ, dating from 1389; several paintings by Antonio del Castillo Saavedra (1616–68); Pedro Duque Cornejo's clay sketches for his carving of the Ascension in Córdoba Cathedral; a wonderful painting by Joaquín Sorolla of a woman with downcast eyes and a red hat, and a whole section devoted to Córdoban sculptor Mateo Inurria, including a life-size sculpture of the Roman philosopher Seneca, another Córdoban, looking wise and wizened.

Sharing the same courtyard is the **Julio Romero de Torres Museum** (open Tues–Sun; closed 1.30–6pm, Sun pm and Mon; admission charge), dedicated to the work of this Córdoban painter who depicted popular scenes and "poster girls" early in the 20th century. The gallery has been recently restored, as has the **Museo Arqueológico ❿** (Archaeological Museum) (open Tues–Sun; closed 2–6pm, Sun pm and Mon; admission charge for non-EU visitors), Plaza Jerón-

Map, page 170

BELOW: eastern legacy – spices in the early morning market.

imo Páez, with impressive displays of artefacts from the Bronze Age through Roman and Moorish times.

Córdoba restored and spring-cleaned quite a few of its buildings for 1992, when this city shared some of the limelight with nearby Seville. Another place to get a facelift (and an underground car park) was the **Plaza de la Corredera**, a 17th-century arcaded plaza with brick facades and wrought-iron balconies. Once the site of bullfights and other public spectacles, the plaza now encloses a lively morning street market, with stalls selling everything from live rabbits, pigeons and chicks to cheap shoes and clothing, used tyres, dubious antiques and junk jewellery. The building with a clock-tower houses a municipal market.

A few blocks up from this plaza, on Calle Capitulares, is a curious architectural landmark, Córdoba's **Ayuntamiento ❶** (town hall), built in the late 1980s in very modern style, incorporating the ruins of a Roman amphitheatre in its foundations. Beside it rise the columns of a Roman temple.

Across from the town hall is the **church of San Pablo**, a beautiful Romanesque building fronted with spiral columns.

Bulls and convents

Another special *barrio*, or neighbourhood, of Córdoba is **La Marina**, named for the beautiful Gothic church of **Santa Marina ⓜ**. This is the *barrio* of bullfighters and here is an extravagant homage to Manolete. Around the corner from the church, in the **Convent of Santa Isabel**, the Clarisa nuns keep up an old Andalucían tradition, confecting pastries to sell to the public.

Near the Marina church (along Calle Morales) is the **Palacio de Viana ⓝ** (open Thurs–Tues; closed Wed and 1–4pm and Sun pm in winter; admission

charge), a 15th-century palace which belonged to the Marquis of Viana. Finding it difficult to maintain such a large establishment, the family advertised the palace for sale in a French newspaper. A Córdoban bank rescued the landmark and opened it to the public in 1980.

The palace presents an austere white facade to the street. Inside, it is a dreamworld, enclosing 12 courtyards, each with different plantings, and interior halls, salons, bedrooms and bathrooms, which still have a lived-in look. Furnishings are a mixed bag and great art shares wall space with the fairly ordinary. There are exceptional displays of ceramic tiles dating from the 13th century; old sabres and muskets; Córdoban polychrome leather wall hangings; china and porcelain; Baccarat crystal chandeliers; and some fabulous carpets.

R & R in Córdoba

Córdoba has a lively custom of the *tapeo*, stopping at one or several *tabernas*, neighbourhood bars, for a *copa* of dry Montilla wine, a *fino*, and a selection of *tapas*, small plates of appetisers, both hot and cold.

It is also known as a flamenco town. The best dancing and singing take place at popular fairs and special flamenco festivals. **El Cardenal** (closed Sundays and Mondays; tel: 957 483112), on Calle Cardenal Herrero, facing the mosque, has a good *tablao* (flamenco show). The town also hosts international guitar festivals and has orchestral, theatrical and operatic seasons.

In the hills

A few miles to the west of Córdoba, on gentle hills above the river plain, is Medina Azahara ❷, the city that, when it was begun in AD 936 under the rule

Maps
City 170
Area 175

of Abd-al-Rahman III, was intended to become the new capital of al-Andalus. Intensive building went on for 25 years, creating a sublime city, with a golden-domed great hall, exquisite mosque, gardens and pools filled with quicksilver. The caliphal court moved here in 945. However, it had hardly been built when, in 1010, swarms of rebellious Berbers began to destroy it again.

Excavation and restoration of the city began in 1911. Master craftsmen still carry on the work, restoring traditional plasterwork, mosaics and columns, and the whole **site** is open to the public (open Tues–Sun; closed 2–6pm in summer and 2–4pm in winter, Sun pm and Mon; admission charge).

Continuing west, the Córdoba to Seville river road (C431) passes through a rich agricultural region of fruit and citrus orchards, wheat, sugar beets and cotton. After the autumn cotton harvest, fluffs of cotton border the road like snow drifts.

At **Almodóvar del Río**, on a hill dominating the river valley, is a picture-book castle, built by the Moors and later embellished. Halfway between Córdoba and Seville, on the Guadalquivir river, is **Palma del Río ❸**, famed for its citrus groves and as the birthplace of the popular bullfighter, El Córdobes. The 15th-century **convent of San Francisco** in Palma was the jumping-off point for missionaries to the New World, such as Fray Junipero Serra, who established California's missions. The monastery has been converted into a small hotel and restaurant where, in season, the menu features venison and boar taken in the nearby **Sierra Morena**.

This mountainous region, happy hunting ground of the aristocracy, has become very popular for its *monterias*, formalised hunts, where on a single good day some hundred deer are shot.

ABOVE: mounted trophy. **BELOW:** Priego de Córdoba.

Map page 175

Wine and oil

South of the capital (main road to Málaga, N331) is Córdoba's wine region, centred on the towns of **Montilla ❹** and **Moriles**, where wine has been made since the 8th century BC. Comparisons with sherry are inevitable, for Montilla wines are produced by the *solera* system of blending in the same way as the more widely marketed Jerez wines.

One winery open for visits is **Bodegas Alvear** in Montilla (tours weekdays at 10am, noon and 4pm; tel: 957-650100). Others are open by appointment only. The region celebrates its wine harvest festival in the last week of August, with some honest grape stomping.

Other towns in the region worth a visit are **La Rambla ❺**, with more than 50 ceramic workshops; **Cabra ❻**, with the 13th-century sanctuary of the Virgin of the Sierra; and **Lucena ❼**, which was a totally Jewish town in the califal epoch, specialising in trade and crafts. Lucena is still a centre for copper, brass and bronze workshops. Outside the town are many furniture factories where newlyweds from all over Andalucía come to furnish their homes at factory prices.

Adjoining the vineyards is Córdoba's important olive oil region, centred on **Baena ❽** (main road to Granada, N432), dominated by its Moorish fortress and surrounded by undulating hills tufted with olive trees. Beyond Baena the terrain becomes more craggy, with villages such as **Luque**, built against a grey rock, and **Zuheros**, with a church on the edge of an escarpment.

ABOVE: a glass or two of Montilla. **BELOW:** country *venta.*

Prime site

The jewel of the province is the town of **Priego de Córdoba ❾** situated on a bluff above the Rio Salado, a salt-water river. Known as the capital of 18th-century Andalucían baroque architecture, Priego has several beautiful churches in this style, notably La Asunción, with a white-and-gold dome in the Sagrario chapel, and La Aurora, where the altar is garlanded with jasmine flowers strung on threads. The Fuente del Rey is a monumental baroque fountain with natural springs. Locals say when the water level is high enough to cover the private parts of Neptune, whose image presides over the spring, there will be sufficient water for the crops.

In the 18th century Priego's thriving silk industry, brought wealth to the town. The fine buildings, including a number of noble mansions with handsome wrought-iron balconies and window grilles, date from that time. The old quarter of town, where passageways are no more than an arm's breadth, dates from Moorish times. Here, neighbours keep up the curious custom of carrying an image of a favourite saint, complete with tiny altar in a carry-case, from house to house. A complex schedule allows each family to keep it one day.

South from Priego, almost to the Málaga and Granada borders, is Córdoba's lake region, stretching from **Iznájar** and all along the tributaries of the Río Genil Here numerous species of wildlife are sheltered, including some that are threatened with extinction. Among the rarer examples is one of Europe's last colonies of white-headed ducks. ❑

THEY CAME, THEY SAW, THEY PLANTED

From the intimacy of the patios to the spectacular gardens of the Generalife in Granada, Andalucía is a magnet for gardeners from all over the world

Fertile soil and abundant sunshine make Andalucía a gardener's paradise, and the region is home to some outstanding gardens including Seville's María Luisa Park and the gardens of the Generalife in Granada.

For the Moors, gardens were intimate places which aimed to appeal to all the senses. Aromatic plants such as mint and basil were key elements, as was the soothing sound of running water. Moorish homes were arranged around interior courtyards which provided a scented refuge from the heat, of which the *patios* of Córdoba are a living example. After the Moors departed, the reigning style was the Italian garden of the Renaissance, designed to impress with proportioned layout, manicured aspect, statues and fountains. The Generalife gardens we see today owe more to this style than to the Moors.

COLOURFUL IMPORTS

Each subsequent lot of settlers brought with them their preferred plants. The Phoenicians, Greeks and Romans introduced olive trees, date palms and grape vines. The Moors brought orange trees and a great many herbs and flowers native to Asia. Explorations of new continents added to this botanical wealth. Geraniums, for instance, came from southern Africa, while mimosas are originally from Australia, wisteria from Asia and bougainvillea from South America.

◁ **MODEL LION**
A statue in the Jardín de los Leones (Lions' Garden) in Seville's María Luisa Park recalls the famous Patio of the Lions in the Alhambra, which served as the model.

△ **TILED FEATURES**
Pigeons congregate around a tiled fountain in the María Luisa Park's Plaza de América. This Seville park was donated to the city by Princess María Luisa de Orleans in 1893.

◁ MOORISH LEGACY

The gardens of El Partal in the Alhambra. Moorish gardens were designed to appeal to all the senses, and pools and channels of water were key ingredients.

▽ ITALIAN INFLUENCE

The Generalife in Granada is Spain's most famous garden. Originally a Moorish royal summer residence, its present layout owes more to Italian influences.

THE WONDER OF WATER

Thanks to their talent as engineers, the Romans tapped Andalucía's water resources, and their canals and aqueducts turned the region into the breadbasket of the empire. But it was the Moors who, adapting and improving on the Roman irrigation system, regarded water as an aesthetic element as well. Fountains, pools and elaborate channels, such as the "water stairway" in the Generalife gardens, filled the air with soothing sound and helped keep summer temperatures down. Water had a symbolic significance for the Moors. Gardens were divided into four sections separated by channels of water representing the four Rivers of Life.

Taking a leaf from the Moors' gardening book, Christian landscapers capitalised on water's use for dramatic visual effect, especially with exquisite fountains, such as in the Patio de la Madama in the 17th-century Palacio de Viana in Córdoba (*above*).

▽ COOL OASIS

Potted flowers adorn a patio in Córdoba. These cool, intimate spaces are a legacy of Moorish times. The Moors, coming as they did from the desert, were especially fond of gardens.

△ NATURALISATION

Geraniums are often considered the quintessential Andalucían flower. Yet, like so many of Andalucía's plants, it is an introduced variety; it was originally from South Africa.

△ EXOTICA

Cupola in La Concepción botanical gardens in Málaga. The garden has a unique collection of palm trees and other exotica.

GRANADA

The last city to fall to the Reconquest, Granada epitomises the refined culture of Moorish Spain. Its exquisite Alhambra is the most impressive medieval Arab palace in the world

Legend has it that, when the Arabs were finally ousted from the Kingdom of Granada in 1492, their defeated king, Boabdil, could not contain his tears as he looked back at the magnificent city his ancestors had forged over nearly seven centuries and which he was now obliged to surrender to the Spanish monarchs. The site of this legendary moment of sadness is 13 km (8 miles) south of Granada, a pass in the hills which is called *El Suspiro del Moro*, the Moor's Sigh.

The modern visitor to Granada will have cause to sigh, too – with wonder at the Moorish conquerors' good taste: the sheer aesthetics of Granada, the beauty of its setting between the everlasting snows of the **Sierra Nevada** and the tranquillity of the extensive fertile *vega* or plain, seem to belong to the world of Japanese art.

For the first-time visitor to **Granada ❶**, a warning and a few words of advice. The centre of the city is noisy, the narrow streets being simply incapable of coping with the volume of traffic which churns through at all hours of the day and night. The visitor who arrives by car may well find himself swept through and out the other side without either having recognised the centre of the town or seen a trace of its much-vaunted monuments. Unlike some other famous Spanish towns, Granada does not keep all its historic jewels neatly in one place, nor does it have a clearly recognisable centre.

Grand views

Granada's hilly situation offers many excellent vantage points from which to get a first overall view. The most obvious is the Alhambra itself, from whose ramparts and towers one can look down on the Albaicín, across to Sacromonte and southwestwards over the town to the Vega.

From the terrace of the **Hotel Alhambra Palace**, built in 1910 when Granada was enjoying a prosperous period thanks to its booming sugar industry, one can contemplate Granada old and new and see how the *vega*, "a blooming wilderness of grove and garden and teeming orchard", as the American writer Washington Irving described it in 1829, is being relentlessly eaten into by the advancing army of high-rise buildings. Kitsch enthusiasts should not miss a visit to this hotel to look at its sumptuous Moorish-inspired decoration.

The **Mirador de San Cristóbal ❹**, on the road which winds up and out of Granada in the direction of Murcia (No 7 bus from the city centre), provides the best view of all and an excellent starting place for the newcomer to Granada. Across the valley of the Darro river the fortress and palace of the Alhambra seem to

PRECEDING PAGES: the Alhambra. **LEFT:** Patio de los Leones. **BELOW:** gypsy welcome.

grow out of the burnt sienna rock and the dark green vegetation, asymmetrically in harmony with the natural landscape. Behind the fortress, the snowcapped peaks of Sierra Nevada; at one's feet the Albaicín.

Hub of the old city

When Granada became an independent Arab kingdom at the beginning of the 11th century the royal court was in the **Albaicín ⓑ**, only to be transferred to the Alhambra on the opposite hill 250 years later. Today it is still easy to imagine what the Albaicín must have been like when it was the hub of Moorish Granada with its 30 mosques, its potters and weavers, veiled women fetching water from the *aljibes* or public water tanks (still used as recently as the 1960s), and then disappearing into the privacy of their walled garden or *carmen*.

To enter the Albaicín, which one should first do without any formal list of places to see, is to enter a world where the smells of jasmine, of damp, of heat or of cooking take over from car fumes, where the dominant sound is burbling water and where mules are still used to carry bricks and bags of cement, not by courtesy of the tourist board but simply because they are the only means of transport suitable for the narrow, steep streets.

Sadly, little trace of Arabic architecture remains in the Albaicín, where churches and convents – of which there are 22 enclosed orders, many famous for the sweets and pastries they produce – rapidly supplanted the mosques after the reconquest of Granada by the Catholic Monarchs, Ferdinand and Isabella.

The 11th-century Arab baths, **El Bañuelo ⓒ**, on the Carrera del Darro, on the left shortly after the bridge where the Darro river disappears underground, are an exception. Entering through a leafy patio, full of peace and birdsong, the

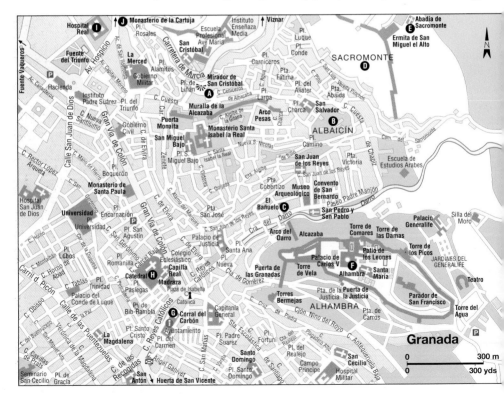

Granada

baths are perfectly restored with sunlight playing through the stars and octagon shapes of its roof (open Tues–Sat am only). The palace of **Dar al-Horra** or **Queen's House** (Callejón de las Monjas), built for King Boabdil's mother in the mid-15th century, is another survivor of the reconquest. It is behind the convent of **Santa Isabel la Real**, also formerly an important Moorish palace.

Map, page 184

The Holy Hill

Up the hill north of the Albaicín is **Sacromonte ⊙**, literally, "the holy hill". Until recently the best-known part of Granada along with the Alhambra, the Sacromonte of caves and gypsies has practically disappeared today. Severe floods in 1962 made many of the gypsies' caves uninhabitable and the occupants were rehoused in a high-rise complex west of Granada, bringing about not only the death of Sacromonte but the break-up of the strong gypsy community there, with the consequent weakening of traditions.

Only three caves still offer *zambras,* gypsy fiestas of flamenco music and dance. Enrique el Canastero, owner of one of these and son of the late and famous gypsy dancer Maria la Canastera, laments that, whereas he absorbed the rhythm of flamenco from the day he was born, parked in a wickerwork playpen (*canastero* means basket-maker) at the mouth of his mother's cave when neighbours came in to dance and sing or play the guitar, his own children show little interest in the art. They have been brought up amongst cars, colour television and a fragmented community.

Further up the road, past the caves, is the **Abadía de Sacromonte ⊖** (open Tues–Sun; closed 1.30–4pm and Mon), which has been recently reopened to the public following the restoration of five fascinating subterranean chapels.

ABOVE: flamenco flourishes in Sacromonte.
BELOW: view over the Albaicín.

Founded at the end of the 16th century on the site where the remains of four Christian martyrs were discovered, including the patron saint of Granada, San Cecilio, the Abadía is at present struggling for survival. Here, on the last Sunday of the month, the gypsy community comes to hold a special mass around their own Christ, El Cristo del Consuelo, a statue by José Risueño, the 18th-century Granada sculptor.

Across the valley from the car park of the Abadía, horizontal streaks are visible on the hill opposite, traces of the elaborate irrigation system devised by the Moorish monarchs to bring water from the mountains to the Alhambra and Generalife gardens.

The Alhambra

Probably no other monument in Europe has exerted such fascination over travellers and historians over the centuries as the **Alhambra** ❻ (open Mon–Sat 9am–5.45pm Oct–Mar, and 9am–7.45pm Apr–Sept; Sun year round, 9am–5pm. The ticket office, located next to the car park, opens 8am until one hour before the Alhambra closes). Nor any other place inspired so many poets, composers, painters and writers. It is a miracle that the palace, its gardens and the summer residence, the Generalife, can still be termed "the best preserved medieval Arab palace in the world".

In 1626 Emperor Charles V decided to built a palace in the confines of the Alhambra and 50 years later the Moorish mosque was knocked down to make way for the Church of Santa María. Other events joined with the general abandonment of the royal city to threaten its survival: an earthquake in 1522; the rebellion of the *Moriscos* (Muslim converts to Christianity) in 1570; an explo-

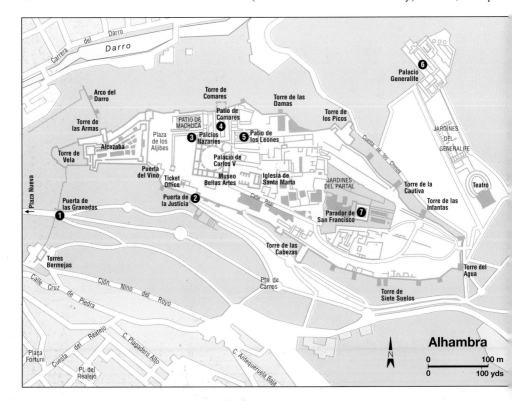

Alhambra

sion of gunpowder in 1590; the partial destruction of the ramparts by Napoleonic troops, who used the Alhambra as their garrison, in 1812.

It is largely thanks to the "discovery" of the Alhambra by 19th-century writers and artists that the monument was at last recognised as unique. Merimée, Chateaubriand, Gustave Doré and Victor Hugo were all profoundly influenced by their stay in Granada, while Washington Irving (*see below*), Théophile Gautier and Richard Ford enjoyed the extraordinary privilege of lodging within the Alhambra itself in the quarters where Charles V spent his honeymoon.

In 1870 the Alhambra was declared a national monument and restoration started, although the first efforts were more geared to creating the ideal image of a fairytale castle as envisioned by the romantics of the day. It wasn't until the 1920s that a measure of historical rigour was applied to the restoration, a painstaking process which continues to this day, carried out by a permanent staff of architects and craftsmen.

Map,
page
186

Form and function

The Alhambra is made up of three parts: the Royal Palace; the Alcazaba or fortress; and the Medina where up to 2,000 members of the royal household lived. There is little left to see of the Medina, and gardens now cover the foundations of the houses. Further up the hills stand the remains of another palace, the Generalife.

When in 1238 Muhammad Ben Nasr founded the Nasrid dynasty that was to rule Granada until 1492, he held court in a castle where today's Alcazaba stands. It wasn't until his descendant Yussuf I became king 100 years later that building on the new palace began. The reign of this Nasrid king, and that of his son

ABOVE: view on the world in the higgledy-piggledy streets of Granada.
BELOW: revealing the secrets behind the Alhambra walls.

ALHAMBRA TALES

Washington Irving, more than anyone else, helped put Granada on the map with his *Tales of the Alhambra*, written following a visit in 1829 when the American author was travelling through Spain as a diplomat. Although the monument had been maintained by the Spanish rulers following the conquest, the Bourbon dynasty which acceded to the Spanish throne in the early 18th century were less attached to it, and it fell into disrepair.

By the time Irving rolled into town and set up headquarters in the Alhambra, the palace had become home to a colourful bunch of squatters. Ironically, it is thanks to the fact it was inhabited that the monument survived, even if it was the worse for wear, rather than being dismantled and carted away piecemeal for building materials.

Irving's fanciful tales of lovesick princesses and hidden Moorish treasure captivated the imagination of bourgeois society when it was first published in 1832, and the many visitors who followed in the author's wake to see for themselves this magical place soon made the authorities aware that it was a major attraction that needed to be preserved.

Mohamed V, which together stretched from 1333 to 1391, saw the construction of all the most important elements of the royal palace as we know them today.

The core of the Alhambra is the Royal Palace (the Casa Real or Palacios Nazaries), a fantasy of delicate arches, intricate carving and trickling fountains. Unlike the self-confident grandeur of the mosque in Córdoba, or the restrained elegance of the Almohads' Giralda in Seville, the Alhambra has an almost ephemeral quality and, indeed, the carved patterns and inscriptions on plaster which are the most striking decorative feature were regarded as no more permanent than today's wall-paper; successive rulers would remove the work of their predecessors and have it replaced with inscriptions more to their liking. Built with clay bricks, mortar and wood, the whole palace is the architectural expression of a race living the last of its twilight years, when the Moors' once formidable military might had been replaced by the intense, if relatively brief, cultural flowering of Nasrid Granada. The intrigues which unfolded in the rooms of the Royal Palace, pitting the sultan Mulay Hassan and his favourite concubine, the Christian-born Zoraya, against his wife Aixa and their luckless son Boabdil, would spark a civil war and precipitate Granada's eventual downfall (*see page 40*).

Visiting the Alhambra

Your ticket will show a 30-minute time slot during which you can enter the Royal Palace. During busy times, you may have to wait several hours, but you can visit other parts of the monument in the interim (the order in which the sights are covered in this guide assumes you visit the Alcazaba while waiting).

You can also reserve your ticket by fax, up to one week before your intended

BELOW: view from the bell-tower.

visit. Specify the number of people in your group, and preferred date and time to visit, and provide a contact (preferably a fax number) so that the ticket office can send you confirmation. (The fax number for the Alhambra is 958-210584; for information, tel: 958 220912; both numbers can often be overloaded, so patience is called for.)

One last word of warning: because of constant restoration works, sections of the monument might be closed when you visit, or the itinerary might change.

Approaching on foot

If your legs and lungs are up to it, it is well worth starting out from the Plaza Nueva, at the foot of the Alhambra hill in central Granada, and walking up the shaded Cuesta de Gomerez and through the **Puerta de las Granadas ❶** (Gate of the Pomegranates), built on Charles V's orders in 1536. It is decorated with three pomegranates, symbol of the city (the Spanish word for pomegranate is *granada*, although the city's name has a different origin; it comes from the name given to the city by its sizeable Jewish population during Visigoth days, Garnatha).

As you approach the Alhambra, to the left you'll see the impressive **Puerta de la Justicia ❷** (Gate of Justice or Bib Xari'a), one of the main entrances to the palace, on which are engraved the Islamic symbols of a hand and a key. As every tour guide will tell you, the Moorish legend had it that Christians would never enter this gate until the hand reached down to grasp the key.

Visitors arriving by bus or car follow a new road coming from the opposite direction, which avoids the traffic-clogged city centre. They will join pedestrian visitors in the queue outside the ticket office, at the bottom of the car park.

TIP

If you have your own car, be warned that the rates charged at the car park are extortionate. You might prefer to take a taxi or the special bus service which runs from Plaza Nueva in the centre of the city every 15 minutes.

BELOW LEFT AND RIGHT: visiting the Alhambra.

Map, page 186

With nearly two million visitors a year, the Alhambra is the most popular monument in Spain. In order to ensure a modicum of crowd control, only 400 visitors are admitted every half hour into the royal palace, although there is no restriction on how long you can stay once you're inside, while the Alcazaba, Generalife and Palacio de Carlos V can be viewed at any time. Your ticket will show a half-hour slot during which you can enter the palace, and usually you'll have an hour or so to spare, though there are plenty of options to fill that time.

Museums, views and the Alcazaba

You can stroll along the garden pathway, following the signs to *Palacios Nazaries*, until you reach the imposing structure of Charles V's Italianate palace. Although glaringly out of place here, the **Palacio de Carlos V** is one of the most outstanding examples of Renaissance architecture in Spain, with its unique circle-within-a-square layout. Off the spacious central courtyard is the new **Museo de la Alhambra** (entrance free) which has well-arranged exhibits of Spanish Islamic art, including coins, tapestries, tiles, latticework, and other Moorish artefacts. Upstairs in the palace is Granada's **Museo Bellas Artes** (Museum of Fine Art).

Leaving the palace, you reach the **Plaza de los Aljibes**. This square commands the first of many magnificent views, over the Albaicín and Sacromonte. If you have a half hour before your allotted time to visit the royal palace, this is the best time to tour the **Alcazaba** (if you visit later, its stark military aspect will come as an anticlimax after the splendour of the Nasrid palaces). The massive fortress juts out like the prow of a ship on the Alhambra hill, commanding a view of the Granada *vega*. Make your way across the Plaza de Armas, where

BELOW:
the Alcazaba from
the Torre de Vela.

you can view the foundations of the houses where the soldiery were quartered, and climb up to the **Torre de Vela**. Isabella had a bell installed on this tower after the fall of Granada to symbolise the Christian triumph (bells are banned under Islam).

For one last stop before the Nasrid palaces, across from the entrance to the palaces is the **Sala de Presentación**, in a Moorish *aljibe (*water cistern) under the Palace of Charles V. This introduction to the background of the monument, from its history to the building techniques and materials used, is interesting, provided you can read Spanish, as the information panels have no translation.

The Royal Palace

The **Royal Palace ❸** (Palacios Nazaries), the highlight of the visit, is composed of three distinct parts. These lead from the most public areas to the most private of quarters, ending up with a visit to the baths of *hammam*. Inside the entrance to the palace is the *mexuar* where citizens of Granada were received and justice was meted out; from here, one enters the *serail* where official, diplomatic life took place; and finally, the *harem*, the monarch's private quarters.

The *mexuar* is the least well preserved part of the Royal Palace, having been converted into a chapel shortly after the expulsion of the Moorish court and also damaged by the 1590 explosion. At the end of the main room is an oratory with a glimpse of the intricate geometrical motifs so prolific elsewhere.

From here a small courtyard (Patio del Mexuar) leads to a room which served as a waiting room for those to be received by the king; this is the **Golden Room** (Cuarto Dorado).

The entrance to the *serail*, through the left-hand door at the end of the patio,

Map, page 186

On 2 January, the anniversary of the Moors' surrender, girls of marriageable age are allowed to ring the 12-ton bell in the Torre de Vela, for it is meant to bring good luck in finding a suitor.

BELOW: the Palace of Charles V.

follows a zig-zag route, thus protecting its access. Within this part of the palace diplomatic life was intense, especially in the later half of the 14th century when the power of the Moors in Spain was being so relentlessly sapped. Central to this part of the Alhambra is the **Patio de Comares** ❹ (also called Patio de los Arrayanes/Courtyard of the Myrtles), which, with the reflection of the buildings in the water of the pond, constitutes an amazing example of the symmetry of pure Arab art. Critics refer to this as "the Parthenon of Arab art in Spain".

Towering at one end of this patio is the **Torre de Comares**, in the ground floor of which is the majestic **Ambassadors' Room**, probably the room which leaves the most lasting impression on the visitor. The domed ceiling, reaching a height of over 15 metres (50 ft), is made of inlaid cedar wood and represents the firmament. The monarch used to sit with his back to the light, facing the entering visitors, thus keeping a clear advantage over them.

From the Courtyard of the Myrtles one passes into the *harem*, built around the **Patio de los Leones** ❺ (the Lions' Courtyard). Here the sultan and his wives lived, as did the Queen Mother, a key figure in Moorish court life.

When visiting the rooms leading off the central courtyard (the **King's Room**; the **Abencerrages' Room**; the **Room of the Two Sisters**; the **Room of the Sultana**), you should bear in mind that the occupants of the rooms – servants excepted – spent their time in a reclining position; the whole design reflects this perspective.

Amid the overwhelming richness of the *harem* as a whole, several architectural and decorative features are distinctive. First there is the anti-earthquake device, a lead plate inserted at the top of the 124 white marble pillars. Next, the 12 lions themselves, surrounding the central fountain. According to one theory,

ABOVE: a lion looks on in the Patio de los Leones.
BELOW: Moorish details – stucco, calligraphy and ceramics.

the lions represent the Twelve Tribes of Israel and the two marked with an equi-lateral triangle on the forehead, the Chosen Tribes.

The paintings on leather in the King's Room, where human figures appear, were probably done by Castilian artists who found refuge in the Moorish king-dom from the reign of terror of Pedro the Cruel. Look for the traces of "blood" in the fountain in the Abencerrages' Room, "proof" of the veracity of the leg-end which tells of how 36 members of the Abencerrages family were beheaded one by one as they entered, a king's revenge for his mistress's infidelity.

The Generalife

The itinerary continues through an open garden area, flanked by the **Palacio del Partal** (the oldest part of the complex) and unrestored parts of the exterior walls, as you head for the Nasrids' summer palace, the **Generalife ❻**, whose gardens are perhaps the most magnificent in Spain. The sound of running water is particularly soothing for anyone who has had enough of heat and monu-ments, although it is questionable whether the Italianate layout of the present gardens owes anything to the Moors, who were more interested in roses, aro-matic herbs and fruits and vegetables than in trimmed cypress hedges.

The gardens and adjoining palace are all that remain of what was once a much larger estate. The likeliest explanation for the name Generalife is that it derives from the Arabic *Gennet al-Arif* ("architect's garden"). The river Darro was diverted 18 km (11 miles) to feed this oasis of fountains and waterfalls. Only a part of the old summer palace remains, including the **Patio de la Acequia**, with its long and narrow central pond flanked by water spouts, and the **Patio de los Cipreses** (Courtyard of the Cypresses). Today, there are no cypress trees grow-

ABOVE: bloom in the Generalife.
BELOW: soothing shade and lily ponds.

For a different experience of the Royal Palace and Alhambra gardens, you can take a night-time tour. The lighting is tenuous and the details of the palace are less visible, so the result is more atmospheric than informative. Night tours are on Sat (8pm–9.40 pm) from Oct–Mar, and Tues, Wed, Thurs and Sat (10pm–11.40 pm) from Apr–Sept.

BELOW: Granada's Cathedral.

ing there, just the enormous, venerable trunk of a dead cypress which, the plaque informs us, was witness to the illicit encounters between Zoraya, the sultan's concubine, and her Abencerrage lover. You can leave the palace by the **Escalera de Agua**, a stairway whose banisters hold channels of rushing water.

Perfectly placed parador

Nestling between the Generalife and the Alhambra is the 15th-century **Monastery of San Francisco** ❼, today one of the most desirable establishments in the Spanish parador network (Parador de San Francisco). It requires booking months in advance to secure a room (and they're not cheap), but there is nothing to stop you from enjoying a drink on the outdoor terrace of its café.

Packed centre

Granada is more than the Alhambra and Albaicín. Many of its other worthwhile sights are scattered around the centre of the city, and the only effective way to visit them is on foot. The best place to start a tour is the **Corral del Carbón** ❼, where a branch of the tourist office is located, providing maps, brochures and information (Calle Reyes Católicos; tel: 958-224550; closed Sat pm and Sun). The Corral is one of the oldest Moorish buildings in Granada, dating back to the 14th century, and was at first an inn. Later it was an outdoor theatre (hence the name, *corral*) and at one time was used for storing coal (thus the *carbón* part).

Trapped in the hubbub of the centre are the **Cathedral** ❼ (Catedral) (open Mon–Sun; closed 1–4pm and Sun pm; admission charge), built wilfully on the site of the main mosque of Granada and considered the most important example of Renaissance architecture in Spain, and the **Royal Chapel** (Capilla Real)

Map, page 184

(open daily; closed 1–4pm; admission charge) housing the tombs of the engineers of the unification of Spain in the 15th century, the Catholic Monarchs.

The warmth of the colour of the stone used for the exterior of these buildings contrasts with the bleak austerity of the interiors, especially the Cathedral. Don't miss the collection of Dutch paintings in the sacristy of the Royal Chapel.

Across the way from the Cathedral is what remains of the **Madraza**, the Arab university founded in the 14th century by Yussuf I. This used to be one of Granada's most impressive buildings but today only the oratory remains (across the patio on the left); its intricate Arabic decoration was covered over for centuries, only to be rediscovered under a layer of plaster in 1893.

It is well worth nosing around and behind the Cathedral: not just in the souk-like streets, but also the **Plaza Bibrambla** with its flower stalls and old ladies selling plants and the **Plaza Pescadería**, where you can buy cottage cheese from the Sierra Nevada or fresh Boletus mushrooms from the Sierra Cazorla.

The old **University of Granada,** founded by Charles V in 1526, opens on to Plaza Universidad at the end of the Calle Jeronimo. Today the building houses the law faculty. The university library is housed in the imposing building of the **Hospital Real ❶**, situated above the **Triunfo** garden. Built at the beginning of the 16th century, this hospital is now the administrative headquarters of Granada University. Not far from the Hospital Real is the **Monasterio de la Cartuja ❶** (open Mon–Sun; closed 1–4pm, Sun pm and Mon; admission charge), another product of the Catholic construction boom after the expulsion of the Moors in 1492, this time a brilliant example of Spanish baroque.

The poetry of Federico García Lorca, born near Granada in 1899, was inspired by the gypsies of the area.

The famous revisited

Three Granada locations are inextricably connected with the life and death of the poet **Federico García Lorca**, shot dead by General Franco's Nationalists on 19 August 1936. The first is his birthplace in **Fuentevaqueros**, a village 16 km (10 miles) to the west of the city, today a museum (open Tues–Sun; closed 1–4pm and Mon; admission charge).

The second, **Huerta de San Vicente**, was bought by Lorca's father as a summer house where the poet spent many summers from 1925 onwards, and which he remembered with fondness when absent from Granada. This house, 50 years ago a cool country home with a splendid view of the Alhambra, is being swallowed by the city. The surrounding fields have been saved from the speculators and transformed into a park, and the house is a **Lorca museum** (open Tues-–Sun; closed 1–4pm and Mon; admission charge).

The third place is **Viznar**, a village 8 km (5 miles) north of Granada, where the poet was taken and shot at the start of the Spanish Civil War.

Manuel de Falla, the composer of *El Amor Brujo* and *El Sombrero de Tres Picos,* was *granadino* by adoption only. He lived here from 1919 until the Civil War precipitated his departure in 1939 to Argentina, where he died in 1946. His house in Granada is now a **museum** (open Tues–Sun; closed 1–4pm and Mon; admission charge), in the district of Antequeruela, in the shadow of the Alhambra. ❑

BELOW: fiesta procession.

AROUND GRANADA

From Granada you can climb into the foothills of the Sierra Nevada and the Alpujarras to visit remote mountain villages, trek along ancient mule tracks or go skiing

Map, page 201

The N342 leaves **Granada ❶** down what in pre-Roman times was a vitally strategic route linking Antequera with Cartagena and Málaga with Murcia and where the Romans laid the Via Herculea. Much improved, the road is high, rarely falling below around 1,000 metres (3,000 ft) and winds through astonishing landscapes where barren hillocks and escarpments are interrupted from time to time by pockets of green, with mountain peaks always somewhere on the horizon.

The town of **Guadix ❷** has many excellent historical monuments. Like so many other Andalucían towns, the splendour of the Christian development here after the Reconquest seems to have been in direct ratio to the former importance of the town as an Arab stronghold. But the real fascination of Guadix and the surrounding region is its caves. The troglodyte population of Guadix has been put as high as 40 percent of the town's inhabitants, representing some 2,000 inhabited caves, not to mention a further 4,000 or so in outlying villages such as Purullena. Visitors can see for themselves what it is like living in a cave. In Guadix, there is an 18-suite cave hotel (Cuevas Pedro Antonio de Alarcón; tel: 958 664986) and "holiday" caves can be rented in the village at **Galera** (Casas Cuevas, tel: 958 739068). (*For more information on cave living, see page 225.*)

PRECEDING PAGES: high summer in the Sierra Nevada. **LEFT:** winter on the ski slopes. **BELOW:** in the streets of Bubíon.

Mountains

The **Sierra Nevada** provides excellent skiing from December to March or April. In addition, this 88-km (55-mile) range, with peaks reaching 3,000 metres (10,000 ft), has been called "the botanist's paradise".

Las Alpujarras, one of Spain's most fascinating corners, deserves a visit all to itself. Some of Europe's highest inhabited villages are so remote, yet each has its own story to tell, and the roads are so slow that it is difficult to combine a visit to this mountainous region, tucked between the Sierra Nevada and the coast, with that of any other part.

Many parts of inland Andalucía are excellent for walking but no part is better than the Sierra Nevada, Europe's second highest mountain range after the Alps. Here some people rock-climb or mountain-walk, but for amateurs who do not want to use more equipment than just good boots, the Alpujarras are ideal. This sensationally beautiful group of mountain valleys runs east and west some 30 km (19 miles) southeast of Granada, between the small towns of **Orgiva ❸** and **Ugíjar ❹**. The main centre of the Alpujarras is **Bubión**, which has become a popular holiday destination and has acquired its fair share of hotels, restaurants and souvenir shops, although it has been spared the excesses of the coastal villages.

It was in the Alpujarras that some 60,000 *Moriscos*

(Muslims nominally converted to Christianity) continued to live when the Kingdom of Granada fell to the Christians in 1492. But after their revolt of 1570 they were forcibly resettled throughout Spain. As a result, the Alpujarras is now only the home of about a tenth as many people as it once was. They live in little white villages dotted about the valley sides.

Two twisting mountain roads connect Orgiva and Ugíjar, dipping and rising to call at most of these villages. Fortunately for walkers, the villages are also still the centres of networks of mule and donkey tracks, often centuries old and paved with stone though little more than a metre wide.

The climate, too, is delightful. Although the whole area is high, it is possible for the hardy walker to bed down in a sleeping bag on an open hillside as late as mid-October. But not, be warned, in a river bed: during a storm these can quickly become terrifying torrents. The owner of an abandoned farm near Los Tablones remembers one storm a few years ago when it was impossible to make conversation because of the continuous crashing together of boulders in the Rio Guadalfeo, even though the river was 200 metres away.

There is anyway no need to sleep rough. The region has a growing number of small hotels in the area, and even the smallest village will have a simple but clean *fonda* (inn).

How to prepare

A map of not less than 1:50,000 is essential, but some of the mule tracks are hard to follow. Starting boldly from a village, they tend to disappear after one or two kilometres, and there will be a gap before the fringe of the next village's network becomes clear. Asking the way is easy with only a little Spanish (you

BELOW: mule market in the Alpujarras.

won't find much else spoken) but the lazy Andalucían dialect is even lazier in the Alpujarras, and understanding the answers is difficult.

A good plan is to start at Orgiva and move eastwards, ultimately reaching Ugíjar, but weave north and south to stop at particular villages. One not to miss is **Yegen ❺**, both for its charm and because it was here that Gerald Brenan, the British author noted for his insights into Spain and its history, lived between the two world wars. Today his house carries a plaque commemorating him.

Also not to be missed is **Trevélez ❻**, which stands some way up the subsidiary valley of the Rio Trevélez and claims to be the highest village in Spain. From here the energetic can climb north to the Puerto de Trevélez, though the route is none too easy to find. It crosses many of the irrigation channels constructed by the Moriscos which are still such a feature of the Alpujarras and will sometimes be found so high up a valley side that it seems the water must flow uphill to reach them. The view from the pass, of another 13 little white villages dotted about the vast landscape, then more and more ranges of mountain, is reward for the effort of getting there.

The first half of October is an ideal time for exploring the Alpujarras on foot. The weather is cooler and this is the time of fiestas, which move eastwards up the valley. Free wine flows from the Fuente de Vino at Cádiar, and at Ugíjar two Spanish passions – for religious processions and for explosive fireworks – reach a fine climax.

From the top of the Veleta ski lift at the resort of Sierra Nevada you can usually see the Mediterranean. On a good day, or so they say, you can even see the distant coast of North Africa. But most people come up to this delightful resort of the Sierra Nevada not for the views but for the skiing.

ABOVE: some of the region's best hams are produced in Trevélez.
BELOW: Yegen, where writer Gerald Brenan lived between the wars.

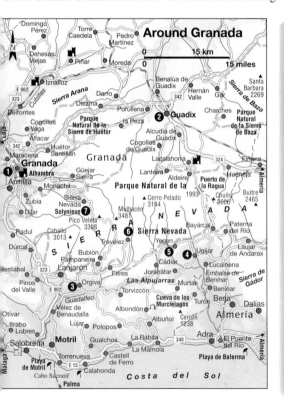

Map, page 201

Champion resort

Sierra Nevada is the southernmost ski resort in Europe, and also the highest, with *pistes* at 2,100 metres (6,890 ft) to 3,282 metres (10,767 ft) altitude. About 32 km (20 miles) southeast of Granada, it has reliable snow cover from December until April and sometimes May, plus a system of snow cannons to cover any bare patches.

Being largely above the tree line, it is not as scenically spectacular as more northerly ski resorts, and its two stations – Pradollano at 2,100 metres (6,890 ft) and Borreguiles at 2,645 metres (8,677 ft) – aren't likely to win any beauty contests. But it makes up for that with modern installations and, above all, a cosmopolitan atmosphere which combines snow sports and the lively, carefree ambience of a Costa del Sol resort.

Food and drink

The après-ski in **Solynieve** ❼ is based on a large number of bars (28 at the last count) catering for all tastes, including piano bars and discos as well as restaurants and cafés.

Finally, to add a touch of difference to this ski resort, it has access to the other attractions of Andalucía, none of which is rendered unattractive by the winter. If you are here on a skiing package, the most rewarding excursion is just down the mountain to Granada, to see the gardens of the Generalife and the Alhambra Palace, as well as the old city (*see pages 186 and 184*). The transfer time from the airport at Málaga is two hours – a great drive through superb mountain scenery, unlikely to be disrupted by the massive traffic queues which spoil many a European skiing week. ❑

BELOW: black widows back from the bakery.
RIGHT: gentle *sierra* living.

IMPROVED FACILITIES

Following a big expansion for the 1996 World Alpine Ski Championships, the Sierra Nevada facilities have improved considerably. Access to the resort from Granada has been upgraded (this is the highest road in Europe), pistes remodelled, cross-country ski routes developed and hotel accommodation increased to 9,000 beds. The skiing is first class, with 19 lifts (including two cabin lifts) and more than 60 km (40 miles) of prepared pistes, from challenging black runs to wide, gentle slopes for beginners, as well as two off-piste routes.

This was the first Spanish ski resort to welcome snowboarders. More than 300 instructors are on hand during the season and there is a special ski school for children aged from six to 12. Because of the southern latitude, you can expect brilliant sunshine: in fact, it is doubly important to use adequate skin protection and sun goggles.

Prices in the resort are sub-Alpine and the food is good. There are excellent restaurants in Solynieve's main hotels, the Melià Sierra and the Nevada, and at the parador, set high on the Veleta. There are also some good *tapas* bars and small, snug, friendly restaurants where you can enjoy convivial après-ski.

JAÉN AND ITS PROVINCE

Map, page 208

The towns of Ubeda and Baeza in Jaén prospered during the 15th and 16th centuries and contain a wealth of renaissance palaces and churches

A massive, undulating sea of 150 million olive trees, Jaén province, 13,498 sq. km (5,212 sq. miles), has always suffered from being labelled as a place of transit.

Named *Giyen* (caravan route) by the Arabs and the gateway of Andalucía for the armies of the Christian Reconquest, trudged through by armies and saints and traders over the centuries, it still tends to be thought of as somewhere to drive through rather than somewhere in which to stop.

In this sense, Jaén's character has been moulded around the natural crossroads carved through the centre by the tributaries of the Guadalquivir. Now only freight trains and chains of lorries criss-cross the plains and slowly roll up the motorway loop to Despeñaperros, the precipitous pass leading to the central sierras.

But under the surface and in cultural terms Jaén remains a border province: Castile and Andalucía meet in the architecture, regional dishes and local temperament, said to be both more receptive and more self-contained than that of the deep south.

Main routes

From the main roads, the geometry of the silvery olive trees imposed on the blotchy cream and rust hills gives the countryside a deceptive rural uniformity. But after a day or two of slower exploration, when the mesmerising effect of the *olivares* has worn off, you begin to notice the changes of landscape in the sierras framing the province and the surprising richness of the historic towns built along the crossroads of power.

The north-south artery (N323) which brings you into the province encapsulates the province's embattled frontier history. Here, on flat plains spiked by the old lead mining chimneys, three key battles, turning points in Spanish history, were fought within a few miles of each other: Beacula, at Castulo (now Linares) where the Romans defeated the Carthaginians; Navas de Tolosa, the first great victory of the Andalucían *reconquista*; and finally, the battle of Bailén, where the tide turned against Napoleon in 1808.

There is little to see at either **Bailén** or **Linares** – an industrial town now known largely for its bars, bullring and most famous son, composer Andrés Segovia – but the trophies taken at Navas are kept in the church at nearby **Vilches**. Also, splendid ruined castles have survived from the century of the Reconquest: **Baños de la Encina**, won and lost again six times by the Christians; **Alcaudete**, a dusty olive town above a sea of olive trees still owned by only five families,

PRECEDING PAGES: olive trees by the thousand.
LEFT: Ubeda's Casa de las Cadenas.
BELOW: Jabalquinto Palace, Baeza.

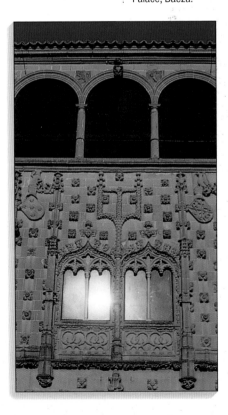

and, in the far south, **Alcalá la Real**, where the later church dropped into the fortress has a strangely post-modern effect.

Bases of beauty: Baeza and Ubeda

The real architectural gems, however, are the small towns of Baeza and Ubeda, which lie a stone's throw apart on the old road running east to Levante. Both were key military bases of the *reconquista*, which grew from hotbeds of aristocratic squabbling into cultured cities stuffed with Gothic, Renaissance and baroque architecture.

Crest in Baeza.

Their astounding richness gives the lie to guidebooks which suggest that there is little of architectural interest in Andalucía outside the great Moorish cities. "*Borrachera espléndida de romanticismo!*" (What a glut of romanticism) exclaimed Andalucían poet García Lorca, overwhelmed by the melancholy air of Baeza's past grandeur at dusk. These days its honey-coloured palaces, churches and civic buildings, dating largely from the peaceful, wealthy 15th to 17th centuries, have a cherished air.

Star features in **Baeza ❶** include the studded **Palacio de Jabalquinto** (currently housing one of the best restoration schools in Spain), the **Convento de San Francisco** (ruined and controversially restored), the austere seminary with its faded antique graffiti on the walls – graduating students' names written in bull's blood – and the **Plaza de los Leones**. But there is so much to see here that you need at least a half-day to explore properly.

Less historic, but compulsory for many Spaniards, is a quick look at the house where the great 20th-century poet Antonio Machado wrote some of his best work, and a more leisurely visit to **Casa Juanito**, the welcoming roadhouse

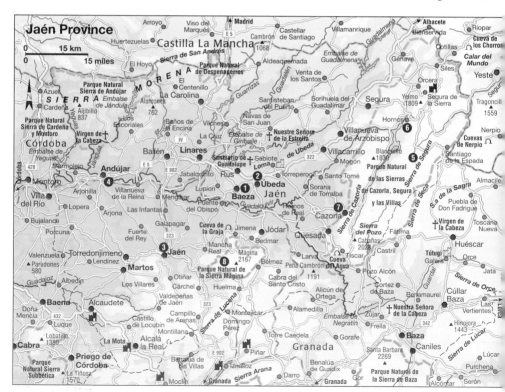

restaurant on the outskirts of town which serves excellent regional cooking.

Ubeda ❷ cannot match up to its smaller sister town for general mood since its past has been absorbed into the fabric of a larger place. But it does have the unmissable **Plaza de Vázquez de Molino**, an architectural set-piece in a class of its own. The rectangular plaza, widening at one end, runs down from the stunningly rich domed chapel of **El Salvador** (built as a family pantheon and still privately owned by the Duques de Medinaceli) past a balanced, beautifully proportioned sequence of austere palaces unbroken by modern additions, considered by many to be the purest architectural expression of the Renaissance in Spain.

At the far end, the **Palacio de las Cadenas** faces the church of **Sta María Alcázar de los Reales**, a church built on the site of the old mosque. The overall effect of monumental calm – kept from being museum-like by the parador and the Hogar de Pensionistas where old dears chat and play cards – deserves hours of long and slow contemplation.

The 50 or so other sights spread around the rest of Ubeda – palaces, churches, seigneurial and modernist houses – are best attacked with the help of the tourist office's walking itinerary; even if your energy flags, don't miss **San Pablo**, the facades in the **Calle del Horno Contador** and **Calle Real**, or Vandelvira's **Hospital de Santiago**, sometimes compared to the Escorial for its severity (its modern conversion into a cultural centre is also a good example of the Spaniards' special knack for putting new wine in old bottles).

On the edge of town, the long-established craft workshops making ceramics and *ubedies* (ornamental straw mats) are not cheap, but for once they offer genuine craftsmanship.

Map, page 208

ABOVE: carving on the Hospital de Santiago, Ubeda.
BELOW: a serious game of dominoes.

To the east of Ubeda stretch the best of the province's olive groves. Despite terrible inequalities of wealth, they have kept the worst of southern poverty at bay, giving the stone towns and villages a solid, contented feel. As a local proverb puts it: "*A quién Dios quiso bien, casa le dio en Jaén.*" (Whomever God wished well, he gave a house in Jaén.) Lovely mansion houses, castles and churches, often given a good sacking in the Civil War, are scattered here in the smaller villages such as Sabiote, Ibros, Rus and Torreperogil.

Provincial centre

After such concentrated architectural beauty, **Jaén ❸** city, perched above the western plain with its back to the sierras, seems surprisingly thin on monuments. But what it lacks in quantity – it was repeatedly stripped by war-time sackings and is now largely a modern business and services capital – it makes up for in scale.

The Cathedral is a massive pile built over three centuries, with a wonderful mish-mash of Gothic to baroque styles; the **Arab baths** (open Tues–Sun; closed Sat–Sun pm), superbly excavated and restored over 14 years, are among the largest and best preserved in Spain; within its walls the museum has one of the best collections of prehistoric Iberian material in the world.

ABOVE: view from the Castillo de Santa Catalina, Jaén.
BELOW: Plaza de los Leones, Baeza.

Equally, the streets, both the wide avenues of the commercial zone and the alleys of the old town stacked against the curving hillside on a series of *cantones*, or terrace walls, have the zip and energy you find only in such self-possessed Spanish provincial cities. The animated bars and taverns in San Juan and the 19th-century balconied streets around the Cathedral make for a good evening's drinking and conversation.

Higher up the hill in La Magdalena, the old up-and-down Moorish quarter with the castle of **Santa Catalina** looming above it, family life spills out on to the steep pebbled alleys, and the soaring Gothic vaulting of its church, the oldest in town, is like a refreshing drink of water after all the rich visual decoration elsewhere.

Map, page 208

In the hills

Each of the three main sierras framing the province has a distinct personality. The western **Sierra Morena**, where Castilian severity meets Andalucían light, is the emptiest, left largely to cows and deer, except in late April when some 500,000 pilgrims flood through on foot, horseback and by car to pay homage to the diminutive Virgin in the sanctuary of **Nuestra Señora de la Cabeza**.

Outside the church stands one of the most moving elegies of modern war, capturing both the idealism and futile sacrifice it inspires; a simple stone tablet tells in detail how Capitán Cortes, leading 250 Nationalist troops and a handful of local villagers, defended the sanctuary against eight months of Republican onslaught until he was finally killed and the enemy burst in to find only 30 starving men.

On the plain below, **Andújar ❹**, once a great walled city and evangelical centre with 48 towers and 12 gates, is now dominated by a sunflower oil refinery. A fine El Greco is kept in the church of Santa María la Mayor.

It also makes a livelier base for exploring the northwest than **Marmolejo**, a small spa-town, or **La Carolina**, which was laid out as a grid by Charles III, the enlightened despot who drew up grandiose plans for settling the sierras in the 18th century.

ABOVE: sunflowers, an alternative source of oil to the ubiquitous olive.
BELOW: baroque sculptures by Pedro Roldan on Jaén Cathedral.

Map, page 208

Olive cultivation reached its zenith in Spain in the early 16th century. Today, the country is the world's largest producer of olive oil, with 11 percent of all cultivated lands planted in olives, supporting more than 600,000 families.

BELOW: hillside town of Cazorla.

Park land

To the east, the more obviously beautiful alpine scenery of **Segura** **❺** has changed dramatically in the past 20 years. The once isolated mountains and remote valleys, famous for their shepherds and the province's best olive oil, are now part of a nature park visited by 500,000 people every year.

The transition has not been easy: the flood of visitors makes fire a real hazard in summer, restrictions on industry have aggravated unemployment and traditional occupations – logging, herding, seasonal work in the olive groves – continue to decline while a stronger tourist economy would clash with the ecological balance.

The olive oil industry has also seen many changes. The thrust now is to replace ancient trees with new, high-yield plantings, to extend mechanisation as far as possible and to emphasise quality. But until someone invents an effective olive-picking machine the fruit is still hand-picked, mainly by day labourers working on the vast estates.

Increasingly, small growers and olive mill owners are forming cooperatives, to pool resources and cut production costs. Only in this way can they hope to win a place in the important international market – with the government's promotional help.

Village life

Meanwhile, the villages remain quietly beautiful, especially hilltop **Segura de la Sierra** (the massive keys to the Arab castle and baths are kept at the Casino café) and **Hornos** **❻**, where the panoramic view from the village square is better than any Hollywood special effect.

To the south, the main town of **Cazorla** **❼**, in recent years swollen by people moving down from the sierras to take up work in the town, is still pleasantly higgledy-piggledy and rural despite its grand ruined cathedral and castle; there is an interesting market where you can buy produce brought down from the sierras on Mondays and Saturdays, and a clutch of restaurants which serve the hearty local dishes such as game sausages or, for those who will brave the unromantic realities of peasant cooking, roast lamb's head and feet.

Off the beaten track

The southern sierras, **Mágina** and **Pandera**, which are gentler around the great central massif, are also now on the tourist map as the **Parque Natural de la Sierra Mágina** **❽**. Attractions here may sound a curious mixed bag: two churches like small cathedrals at **Huelma** and **Cabra** (ask for the keys at the priests' houses), the picturesque village of **Cambil**, which is squeezed into its narrow gorge like a plump woman into a corset, neolithic cave drawings above **Jimena**, a tumbledown spa at **Jabalcuz** and ghostly pictures on a stone floor in **Bélmez** (a natural phenomenon which has been baffling scientists for several decades). But, as in so much of the province of Jaén, they are made immensely pleasurable by the lack of any commercialisation or crowds. ❑

Olive Oil

The Romans planted olive trees across what is now Jaén, Córdoba and Seville above the River Guadalquivir. After milling the oil was transported down river to the sea, to be shipped to Rome. The Moors extended the cultivation of the olive across much of the peninsula. They called it *az-zait*, "juice of the olive". From this derives the Spanish *aceite*, the generic word for oil. The tree in Spanish is *olivo*, from the Latin, but the fruit, *aceituna*, is from the Arabic.

These days a mechanical vibrator is used to shake the trees and plastic crates are used instead of baskets to collect the fallen olives; a tractor rather than a mule hauls the olives to the mill, and great stainless steel vats have replaced the clay amphoras of the Romans. Olive oil is extracted by purely mechanical means and, unlike other vegetable oils, can be consumed without further refining and purification. At the mill, the *almazara*, the olives are thoroughly washed, then crushed to release the oil. Modern methods have brought a dramatic improvement in the finished product. The old-fashioned *almazaras* may have presented a romantic image, with their mule-driven stone presses, but the process was slow, the olives often bruised and rotted in the sun while awaiting their turn, and the oil was more often than not rancid and highly acidic. Today's continuous presses and temperature controls ensure a much higher and consistent quality.

The oil is filtered into a series of settling tanks. The oil rises to the top and is drawn off, while the sediment and water content settle to the bottom. The resulting product is pure virgin olive oil, first pressing.

The quality of that oil depends on several factors, such as variety of olive, soil and climate, but, most importantly, how the olives were picked, transported, stored and milled. The best oil, labelled "extra virgin" or "fine virgin", comes from olives which are picked ripe and milled immediately. Its colour can vary from pale gold to amber to greenish-yellow, depending on the type of olive. It is usually completely clear after filtration. New oil has a

slight bitterness, appreciated by many people, which disappears with a few months' maturation. Two and even three pressings might be made from the same olive pulp.

The product is used extensively in Andalucía. In a typical village home the housewife serves the midday meal. The fish, croquettes, pork and potatoes are all fried in olive oil. The salad is dressed with olive oil. For breakfast, toasted slabs of bread are dipped in a bowl of olive oil.

Everything from glowing complexions (before commercial moisturisers, Spanish women used olive oil and water whipped together) to strong hearts and good digestion has been attributed to olive oil. To encourage production of the highest quality oil, a control board authorises a few select *denominación de origen* labels, or "guarantee of origin", for virgin oils. So far, there are six in Spain, four of which are in Andalucía: Sierra de Segura and Sierra Mágina in Jaén, where olives mix with pines on steep hillsides, and Baena and Priego in Córdoba, where olive groves meet vineyards. ❏

RIGHT: harvesting the olive crop

ALMERÍA AND ITS PROVINCE

Map, page 218

The stark landscapes of Andalucia's easternmost province are hauntingly beautiful, with unspoiled bays, weird rock formations and Europe's only real desert

For much of this century, Almería's harsh landscape of sun-scorched sierras and rocky plains, savagely beautiful in some areas but bleakly featureless and dusty in others, was jokingly dismissed by Spaniards as a forgotten corner. Even British writer Gerald Brenan, sentimentally protective as he felt about his own province, found it hard to disagree when somebody called it *el culo de España*, the backside of Spain.

Not that Almería (8,774 sq. km/3,386 sq. miles), lacks a history of wealth and glory. Under Arab rule, the city of the same name grew from an important port and arsenal to become the seat of one of the most powerful 11th-century *taífas*, or splinter kingdoms, ruling much of Murcia and Andalucía. An industrial city with a population of 200,000, it was famed for its silks and trade with the East, said by chroniclers to be outshone in splendour only by Córdoba, Baghdad and Alexandria.

The fall and rise

Today the ruined castles strategically scattered around the province are all that remain of its former power; piracy, the Reconquest, invasion by the Turks and earthquakes exacerbated the struggle with the heat and aridity to pitch Almería into centuries of rural poverty.

But in the past 30 years the *almerienses*, known to be tenaciously hardworking and independent, have turned all that around by finding gold in their liabilities. Now the desert-like climate powers a massive hothouse agriculture business spreading over more than 20,000 hectares (49,400 acres) of the coastal plain and is also the main prop of a buoyant (and growing) year-round tourist industry that takes advantage of the excellent beaches.

Together, these new areas of economic growth have hauled the average per capita income up from the lowest in the country to one of the highest, bringing with them new social and environmental problems: a steadily falling water table, high suicide rates, a major shift from the interior of the province to the coast and tensions over immigration, particularly from North Africa. According to locals it has also eradicated a fatalistic streak considered inherent in the *almeriense* character.

Nonetheless, nearly half of Almería's population still lives in villages of fewer then 2,000 people in the quiet, little known interior. Here the old extremes remain, the landscape either magnificently raw in the sierras which slice from east to west across the province, or painstakingly tamed around the strings and pockets of *cortijos* and villages following the contours of the valleys.

PRECEDING PAGES: arid Almería. **LEFT:** the castle in Almería city. **BELOW:** fixing up a boat.

Spectacular driving

The mountain roads, which are said to have as many turns as a local *bolero* or *fandango*, make for spectacular driving, snaking up to high passes where the sierras seem to drop away into rumpled folds, then swooping back down to the *ramblas*, or dusty dried-up river beds, which are the most characteristic feature of the countryside

The coast

So far, tourism, which has developed largely since the early 1980s, has left much of Almería's coastline untouched. To the west, the **Campo de Dalias**, now locally better known as the **Costa del Plástico**, is temporarily preserved by the vast plastic greenhouses, or *invernaderos*, nursing tomatoes, which are closely packed between the foot of the mountains and the beach; at good moments, with the sun glinting on the opaque green plastic roofs, the sea seems to have flooded the plain, but on the whole they make an unromantic, semi-industrial backdrop for sunbathing.

In the centre sits **El Ejido**, a boom town that was unmarked on most maps until recently, but now, with a population of over 40,000, ranks second in size in the province. Sprawling along the dead straight highway and clogged with fruit lorries emblazoned with images of the Virgin Mary, it is an Andalucían variation on an American truckers' town.

Just down the road are the province's two high-rise resorts, **Roquetas del Mar** and **Aguadulce**, both pleasantly spacious and sedate by comparison with the hard-core Costa del Sol. Nonetheless, there are more attractive bases within reach of both the beaches and the inland valleys, such as **Enix**, a flowery hill-

ABOVE: marking a nautical past and present.
BELOW: view from the Alcazaba in Almería city.

side splash of white with a 17th-century church plus a good hotel outside the walled village, or **Berja**, a larger market town with shady squares and seigneurial houses.

East of Almería

The coast to the east of Almería could hardly be a greater contrast. Marshland and working salt-beds with a colony of flamingoes run south to the dramatic, volcanic headland of the **Cabo de Gata** ❶, protected as natural parkland since 1980 for its flora, fauna and underwater life, said to be some of the best in the Mediterranean.

Abandoned squat windmills, watchtowers and the atmospheric red-rock ghost town at **Rodalquilar**, once Spain's only gold mine, give a quiet, mournful beauty to the scrubby headlands, while the coast itself swings north through wonderfully unspoiled bays like the **Playa de los Genoveses**, once the crater of a volcano, and the shingly, black-beached fishing hamlet at **Las Negras**.

Either San José or La Isleta provide quiet villa accommodation or, a short drive inland, there is **Níjar**, famous in Spain as the setting for the real-life tale of passion and revenge which inspired Lorca to write the play *Blood Wedding*. Sloping down the foot of a *sierra* from the cramped old town, it has more life of its own than the coastal hamlets and has good shops for buying pottery and cotton rugs.

Further north, beyond **Carboneras**, where plumes of smoke belch out from a large cement works, there is more spectacular scenery as well as the long, fine beach of Algarrobico before a ribbon of low-level development runs towards the town of **Mojácar**.

Map, page 218

TIP

For more information on the wildlife of the Cabo de Gata, *see page 125.*

BELOW: Almería has some superb beaches; most of them are less crowded than those on the Costa del Sol.

Until the 1960s, this was a quiet white village with labyrinthine alleys inherited from the Arabs and everyday traces of the ancient Indalo culture, most famously in the women's custom of half-covering their faces with *cobijas*, triangular shawls. Now, like so many other small places which are discovered and colonised, it has become a chintzy resort where it is hard to pick out the interesting architecture and history amongst the boutiques and bars, many of them British-owned.

Neighbouring **Garrucha** is plainer but less precious by far, with some excellent fish restaurants down by the port and, to the north, long golden beaches with Spain's first official naturist (nudist) hotel.

City centre

At the centre of the southern coast sits **Almería ❷** city, the Moorish "mirror of the sea", still dominated by the massive walls of its 11th-century well-preserved **Alcazaba** (open daily; closed 1–4pm) looming protectively over the old town and broad double bay.

In the past 50 years the city has grown from "a bucket of whitewash thrown down at the foot of a bare, greyish mountain", as Brenan described it in 1939, to a modern provincial capital with characterless commercial and industrial zones which have gobbled up the green *huertas* (gardens). But the new is neatly sectioned off from the palmy, old town by the **Rambla del Obispo**, which runs down to the port, and the *almerienses'* easy-going warmth keeps the friendly atmosphere of quieter, slower times; they like to say that here, "*nadie se siente extraño*". (Nobody feels like a stranger.)

From the Alcazaba – by far the most impressive monument of the province,

BELOW: the battlements of the Alcazaba.

with its magnificently severe Moorish fortress architecture overlaid by the more grandiose Catholic upper courtyard – you can first breathe in the atmosphere and scale of the city. Open to the sea and fenced in at the back by the mountains, the old town, or *barrio monumental*, runs east from the fishing port and hillside gypsy **Chanca** quarter – often described by the guidebooks as "colourful" but more realistically also as desperately poor – gradually smartening towards the broad, shady 19th-century **Paseo de Almería**.

At the back, you look out over the remaining stretch of the ramparted city walls, rebuilt by Charles V, which once ran down to the sea.

Down below, the 16th-century **Cathedral** (open daily, closed 2–4.30pm and Sat pm; admission charge) is another reminder that long after the Reconquest Almería remained a vulnerable defensive outpost; its bulky golden exterior, built as much against piracy as for worship, belies the graceful vaulting and superb wood carving on the *coro* (choir) inside.

Elsewhere in the network of narrow one-way streets, there are large and small tree-shaded squares, a handful of small churches and all kinds of small shops. At night the bars and cafés take over, turning the alleys between the Cathedral and the Paseo into a fashionable crush.

Inland attractions

As the province's main road junction, Almería is also the best access point to the sierras and valleys of the interior. On the main roads to Murcia and Granada there is little of interest except for the arid moonscape west of **Tabernas**, uninhabited but curiously familiar as the film-set of classic spaghetti westerns and epics like *Lawrence of Arabia* and *Indiana Jones and the Last Crusade*, and

Map, page 218

BELOW: a mini-Hollywood adds to the air of unreality in this region.

worth a detour to visit the gloriously tacky old film-sets with piped music and dust eddying across from the Indian reservation to the gallows.

Back in the real world, a few miles further on, **Sorbas** has galleried houses hanging out over the kitchen gardens in the river valley and is one of the few places where the rough local pottery is still made and sold. Apart from this, the smaller roads that wind along the two main valleys, named after their rivers, the Andarax and Almanzora, are more satisfying.

River valleys

The **Andarax** valley, abruptly lush below the harsh sierras, prospers on orange trees and vines producing the famed sweet white Ohanes grapes that have been exported around the world since the middle of the 19th century. It is easy to see why the Moors, drawn by the watery greenness, came here to retreat from the coastal heat. They named the village of **Alhama** after its thermal waters and the last Moorish ruler Boabdil "The Unlucky" chose **Laujar**, on the fringes of the Alpujarras, as his last home in Spain after he was run out of Granada; today Alhama has an old-fashioned spa hotel and Laujar remains a favourite destination for Sunday outings.

Initially, the **Almanzora** valley seems less appealing. Filmed with dust around the ugly marble quarries of Macael and elsewhere sleepily impoverished by the closure of iron mines and the railway, it is less obviously picturesque. But at the top of the valley there are two lovely villages: **Purchena ❸**, which is sometimes fancifully described as a miniature Granada for its dramatic setting slapped right up against a rock face (ask where you can find the key to the fine 17th-century church), and **Serón ❹**, attractively clumped below a ruined cas-

BELOW: Almería's coast is Europe's winter garden.

tle on a dome-shaped hill – from where you explore the dramatically beautiful, little-explored **Sierra de los Filabres** with the help of the provincial map of the Instituto Geográfico Nacional (the best large-scale reference map of the area).

Map, page 218

The best of the winding roads leads from **Cantoria** to the villages around **Cóbdar**, a world of their own at the bottom of a precipitous valley. As if to make the point, **Líjar**, a village with more bars than shops, proudly displays the plaque commemorating peace with France after a private hundred years' war declared by the mayor in 1883 (*for details, see page 62*). Another good route is the track from **Serón** which leads up past a picturesque abandoned mining village, to the highest point of the province, **Calar Alto**, 2,168 metres (6,937 ft), where there is an astronomical observatory with the most powerful telescope in Europe and a stunningly empty panorama.

Scattered cortijos

To the north of the Almanzora, there are only scattered *cortijos* and the **Santuario de la Saliente** (which has a good bar and restaurant) in the "burnt, cactus-sharp, breathless sprawl" of hills, as Rose Macaulay described them. In the valley beyond, sliced through by the Autovía del Mediterraneo, are the "two Vélezes" – named after the marquises who owned huge tracts of the surrounding countryside – which have been emptied by emigration.

Nobody is sure how these *pueblos* got their second names. **Vélez Rubio ❺** (Blonde), the larger of the two, carries their aristocratic imprint in a series of churches, convents and mansions; but the restored ruins of the 16th-century castle at **Vélez Blanco ❻** (White), the small sister village, are more impressive for their scale and setting, with a splendid view over Murcia ❑

BELOW LEFT: prickly pears used to be the main crop.
BELOW RIGHT: face of experience.

CAVES AND CAVE LIVING

Parts of Andalucía are riddled with caves, some adorned with prehistoric art, some packed with stalagtites and stalagmites, and some that have been turned into comfortable homes

Twenty thousand years ago, human beings dipped their fingers in ochre and traced the outlines of fish and deer on cave walls in southern Spain. Today, evidence of these early cave-dwellers is still coming to light. Meanwhile, to the astonishment of travellers, more than 30,000 people still live underground in Andalucía. This is not so much due to backwardness as to convenience. Many of the caves are comfortably fitted out with all modern conveniences and their inhabitants prefer them to concrete apartment blocks.

Living quarters

In 1985 the Junta de Andalucía, the regional government, recognised this fact and began a programme to improve the caves. Of 9,500 caves in the region, 8,600 were found to be inhabited permanently.

The rehabilitation programme began with 31 caves in La Chanca, in the shadow of Almería's Arab fortress. This zone, notorious for its poverty, is mainly inhabited by gypsies, as the Sacromonte cave area of Granada used to be. However, after a storm caused caves to collapse, many of Sacromonte's gypsies moved to apartment blocks. By night a number return to their former homes to offer flamenco entertainment to visiting tourists.

Most cave-dwellers are not gypsies and there is no stigma attached to living as they do. Indeed, they have a special pride in their homes. Some work in offices and factories. Many are small farmers or landless labourers who keep their mules or goats – and sometimes their cars – in adjacent caves.

Troglodytes are to be found in the valleys of the Andarax and Almanzora rivers of Almería province, but the greatest number are in communities in and around Guadix, in Granada province. In the latter region, they inhabit an area of harsh eroded hills where the compact, impermeable clay is ideal for excavating waterproof caves. Bars, a church and shops can all be found wholly or partly underground.

In-cave conveniences

Far from being dank and inhospitable, man-made caves are often as comfortable as any conventional dwelling and are usually immaculately whitewashed. They have several rooms. The outer wall, pierced by one or two windows, may be of rock or of bricks. For ventilation, a chimney thrusts up to the surface. Washing machines, refrigerators and other modern appliances are also common. Proper drainage and sewage may be installed. Some caves even have telephones.

The inhabitants like the tranquillity of their homes compared to modern apartments, which act as echo chambers to noise. They also point out that the tem-

LEFT: cave house at Purullena.
BELOW: outside the family cave.

It is believed that the Moriscos, fleeing from persecution in the 16th century, took refuge underground, but people have inhabited caves continuously in the Guadix-Baza region since early times.

perature rarely varies from 16–18° C (62–68° F), summer or winter. Caves have title deeds like normal dwellings, but they are cheaper. A reasonable one may cost only a million *pesetas.*

Old caves and new finds

Traces of prehistoric man's campfires, paintings and ceramics have been found in many parts of Andalucía. Indeed, archaeologists have a difficult time keeping up with the past. Almost daily, a plough or a bulldozer uncovers traces of early human endeavour. Often by the time anybody in authority arrives, Bronze Age tools, Phoenician pots or Roman scarabs have disappeared, buried in concrete or sold for a few *pesetas* to the first comer. Many a home holds an artefact that would be coveted by museums.

New finds throw light on prehistoric man and his customs along the Mediterranean. One discovery occurred in the cave of the Boquete de Zafarraya, on the border of Málaga and Granada provinces, where investigators' torches revealed the large bones and lower jawbone of a Neanderthal man, possibly dating back 85,000 years. Other traces of Neanderthal occupation have turned up in caves at Piñar (Granada), Vera (Almería) and in the Gibraltar area.

There are abundant indications that, as the last Ice Age receded (around 40,000 years ago), Cro-Magnon man took up residence in Andalucían caves. Regarded as our direct ancestor, he was an artist, used tools and was skilled in hunting. Arrow and spear heads and other evidence of his presence have been found in the Almerían caves of Zájara at Vera, and Ambrosio at Vélez-Blanco. In the Doña Trinidad cave, near Ardales, in the mountains behind Málaga, a drawing of a horse is believed to date from the Upper Palaeolithic period.

BELOW: Guadix inhabitants.

Evidence of fertility cults and religious rites are common. Near Vélez Blanco in Almería province, the Cueva de los Letreros shelters prehistoric inscriptions which include the Indalo, depicting a man holding an arc over his head. This symbol was long believed to ward off the "evil eye" and it has been chosen by Almería's artists to represent their movement.

Biggest and best

One of the most significant discoveries occurred on 12 January 1959, when five boys playing on a hillside near the hamlet of Maro, in Málaga province, came across the entrance to an immense grotto. Investigators found evidence that it was inhabited at least 15,000 years ago and that it had also been used as a burial chamber.

Remains of shellfish and the bones of goats and rabbits have been found in these caves, as well as wall paintings depicting deer, horses and fishes. Drawings representing a female deity and red-painted pebbles indicated that religious rites had taken place.

Known as the Cueva de Nerja, the series of chambers with their impressive stalactites and stalagmites has since become a tourist attraction and music and special lighting has been added.

Visitors to La Pileta cave in the mountains near Ronda find their way along limestone galleries by the light of oil lamps. Scoured out millennia ago by an

underground river, the caverns provided shelter for man as long ago as the Upper Palaeolithic period when he daubed the image of a stag's head on a wall.

La Pileta was discovered in 1905 when José Bullón Lobato, whose family still owns the cave, was searching for *guano* (bird droppings) to fertilise his land. Seeing a large hole, he let himself down 30 metres (100 ft) by rope into a chamber. Its walls were sooty from fires and ceramic shards were scattered. Penetrating further, he noted human remains and wall paintings. Later exploration turned up human skeletons, silex, bones, polished stone tools and ceramics from the Neolithic period.

Numerous mysterious symbols adorn the walls of La Pileta and there are suggestions of a fertility cult, particularly in the painting of a pregnant mare.

Buried treasure

The existence of some caves has been known for centuries, but for one reason or another they have not been fully explored. This was the case with the Aracena cave in the sierras of Huelva province. It was flooded until early this century. Then the water was pumped out, to reveal a dazzling array of stalactite and stalagmite formations. Now known as the *Gruta de las Maravillas* (the Grotto of the Marvels), it attracts large numbers of visitors.

Somewhere in the Alpujarras region another cave awaits discovery. In this mountainous terrain, Aben Humeya, the last king of the Moriscos, defied the Christian armies. However, he reigned for only 10 months. His own followers schemed against him and strangled him. According to legend, he possessed a great treasure, which he had hidden in a cave near the village of Trevélez.

Four hundred years have passed. Many have sought Aben Humeya's treasure in vain. Perhaps, one day, another group of boys playing hide-and-seek on an Andalucían mountainside will stumble across an opening. ❑

BELOW: Cueva de Menga at Antequera.

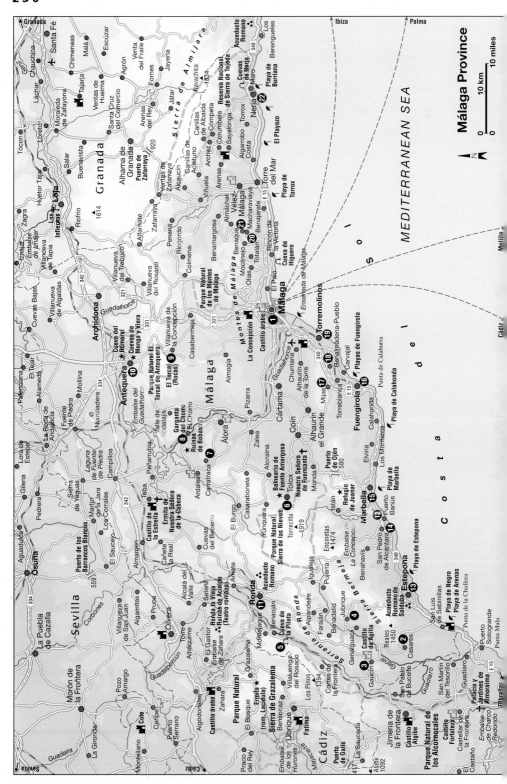

Málaga Province

MÁLAGA AND ITS PROVINCE

Malaga's main draw may be its coast, but its spectacular interior is crammed with interesting attractions, from sleepy pueblos blancos to impressive caves and delightful spa towns

Map, page 230

O f the millions of visitors who flock annually to Málaga province, very few stray more than a couple of miles from the beach. But the province has a lot more to offer than its famous coast.

Any exploration of Málaga province should start – though it probably won't – with **Málaga ❶** itself. Originally Phoenician, it sided briefly with Carthage before becoming a Roman *municipium* (a town governed by its own laws). In 711 it fell to the Moors within a year of their invasion of Spain and was the port of the Kingdom of Granada until 1487, when it was taken by the Christians after a four-month siege followed by brutal burnings.

Since then, too often for its own good, it has been a place of revolution. It was on Málaga's San Andrés beach that the rebel General Torrijos and his 52 companions were shot in 1831. In revolt against the repressive government of Ferdinand VII, this young Spanish general landed on today's Costa del Sol, encouraged by an invented story that the Málaga garrison would join him. Instead it surrounded and captured him.

In 1931, and again at the start of the Civil War five years later, left-wing citizens burned Málaga's churches and convents, and it held out against General Franco's Nationalists until 1937. When it finally fell, its refugees were murderously bombed and shelled as they escaped up the coast road towards Almería.

PRECEDING PAGES: Laguna de Fuente Piedra in Málaga Province. **BELOW:** Málaga's Alcazaba.

Main sights

Málaga's historical ruins can be found mainly on the high ground at the eastern end of the city. First comes the Moorish palace or **Alcazaba ❹**, a maze of pretty little gardens and courts, and at its foot a partially excavated Roman theatre. Connecting the Alcazaba with the Gibralfaro Castle, formidable double walls and great square turrets ascend the hill, while a rocky path climbs beside them. At one point a mirador gives a view over the harbour and down on to Málaga's **Plaza de Toros ❺** (bullring) – where Théophile Gautier, enthusiast for romantic Spain, saw 24 bulls killed in three days and 96 horses left dead on the sand – and he thoroughly approved of the carnage.

At the top of the climb you will discover that you could have driven up from behind the hill after all. **Castillo de Gibralfaro ❻** (Gibralfaro Castle), which has been restored, lies there as a reward.

The great dry river bed which cuts the city in two is also part of Málaga's history. Until 1927, when the Rio Guadalmedina was dammed in the hills above, this would regularly flood; in the disastrous flood of 23 September 1628 well over 400 people were drowned. Unusually heavy rains in 1989 brought another flood disaster, prompting big public works to

safeguard the city. Beneath the dam is the **Jardin-Botanico La Concepcíon** 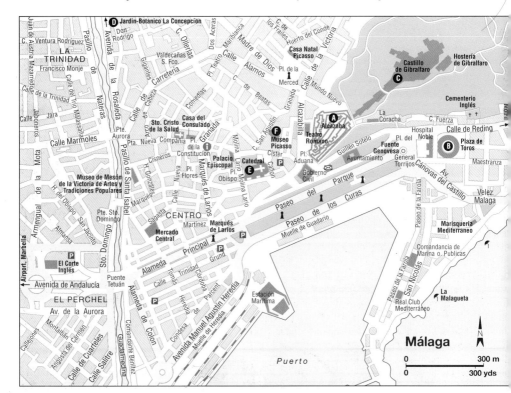, a garden started 150 years ago (open Tues–Sun; closed Mon; guided tour; admission charge).

Today Málaga has become a city of careering traffic, in which only brave foreigners drive on weekdays and only the suicidal on a Saturday night. For a peaceful place away from this frenetic speeding, go to the English Cemetery, which lies beyond the bullring, approached along avenues of orange trees. Founded in 1830, it was Spain's first Protestant cemetery, and Captain Robert Boyd, the Englishman who financed Torrijos's revolt and died with him, was one of its first customers. Before then Málaga's Protestants were buried on the beach below high-water mark, where not only did the sea wash their bones out of the sand but the fishermen were afraid that the bodies of these heretics might infect their fish. In a little walled enclosure near the cemetery's summit are the tiny shell-covered graves of a dozen children. Málaga was not a healthy place for northerners in the mid-19th century.

Málaga's most prominent landmark is the **Catedral** (Cathedral) (open daily). Its construction took place in fits and starts between 1528 and 1782, and it is still unfinished, as one of its twin towers is missing.

Birthplace of Picasso

Málaga is also the birthplace of Pablo Picasso, who spent his childhood here. The family home on Plaza de la Merced has been restored and functions as a study centre devoted to the artist. The city's former art museum, on Calle San Agustin, is to house a new Picasso Museum (**Museo Picasso**), scheduled to open in 2000, with works donated by the artist's daughter-in-law Christine.

For a long time the city had no decent **beach**, but a massive programme involving the pumping of millions of tonnes of sand and the removal of unsightly shacks has vastly improved both Málaga's beaches and all those along the coast. Beaches have been doubled in width and breakwaters constructed to protect them from storms, while a series of promenades have been built at mighty cost. Great efforts are made to maintain the beaches in tip-top condition. *Málagueños* flock to the city beaches and those to the east at **El Palo, Cala** and **Rincón de la Victoria**.

There is not much to choose between these places, with each offering a bewildering choice of beach restaurants, the usual sunbeds and sandy beaches. At Rincón the main road has at least been built a few metres further inland, but tall blocks of flats line an otherwise more attractive shallow bay.

Maps:
City 232
Area 230

Sample the White Towns

Málaga province, all of it that lies inland, has more to offer today that is genuinely Spanish or historically interesting than its coast. Typical are the so-called White Towns of the west of the province near Estepona, and a simple circuit includes two of the best known, Casares and Gaucín (*for more extensive circuits, see The White Towns, pages 261–266*).

To reach **Casares ❷**, take the Gaucín road (the MA539) from the coastal highway, passing by Manilva. Casares surges dramatically into view. Its two or three hundred white-walled, red-roofed houses, rising up the far side of a deep rocky gorge, seem so closely packed together that if one was taken away the rest would tumble. At the top, in earthy red brick, stand the shell of its ruined church

ABOVE: fun in the sun. **BELOW:** inside Málaga cathedral.

A WINE TOUR

Tasting the famous wine of Málaga can start in Málaga city at Antigua Casa Guardia, close to Paseo del Parque, where 21 big barrels line the back wall and every variety can be tried. Before the 1870s Málaga wine was known all over Europe. Though unfortified, it was strong, often 18° proof (typical table wine is 11° proof), as it was made from sweet raisins. Then two things happened. In just a few years the vines of Europe were destroyed by the phylloxera bug. In other countries they were regrown, grafted on to American rootstock which is immune, but this did not happen in Málaga. Perhaps the world was already losing its taste for sweet wines, and this was ultimately the most disastrous blow to Málaga wine. But some is still made, even a so-called *seco*, to cater for modern tastes.

However, it is better to accept that the real thing should be sweet and set out on a tasting tour. Every little *pueblo* will claim that its own is the best. Climb from the coast at Torre del Mar to Vélez Málaga, the market town for the eastern half of the province. Then turn northeast and circle through Arenas, Corumbela, Archez, Cómpeta and back to Torrox. The wine of Cómpeta is considered the finest, but there are less raisin-flavoured varieties which taste like pure liquified muscatel grapes.

Cork, used in the wine and sherry industry, being transported to Cádiz.

BELOW LEFT: bull-raising country lies west of Gaucín on the way to Cádiz. **BELOW RIGHT:** cork is an important industry north of Estepona.

and all that now remains of its Moorish fort. The town has been discovered, but not spoiled: menus have English translations but the food is still Spanish. On any summer evening the central plaza and narrow surrounding streets will echo with that special Spanish roar, created by most of the town's male population talking to each other at the tops of their voices. From Casares's summit there are splendid views to the peaks of the **Sierra Bermeja** and, in the opposite direction, to the valley of the **Río Genal**.

Gaucín ❸ lies in the sierra beyond, and a first view is equally dramatic though, unlike Casares, it sits high up, spread across a saddle between rocky peaks. Gaucín, with its long narrow streets, remains even more Spanish in character – loaded mules and donkeys are common and piles of fodder stand at street corners – but it was discovered long before Casares.

Its Fonda Nacional, hiding behind a roller blind like most houses in Gaucín, has been catering for British visitors since about 1800, and was once known as El Hotel Inglés. Today it is only open for meals but the owner will show two ancient visitors' books with entries, mainly in English, from the 1870s onwards. Most entries are enthusiastic about the stabling, food, cheap prices and absence of bed bugs, though a few complain about the temper of Don Pedro Reales, the host of the time, who was always quarrelling with his wife. The British stopped at the *fonda* when riding between Gibraltar and Ronda.

Gaucín also has a well restored Moorish castle, perched high above the town. From here you can see Gibraltar and the coast on a clear day, but the gates will be chained unless you find the ancient custodian before you climb. Up here died that great hero of Spanish history, Guzmán the Good, who, besieged by Moors at Tarifa, sacrificed his son rather than surrender.

Into the hills

Map, page 230

For a more adventurous circuit take the little-used but perfectly serviceable MA557 due north from Estepona and climb by some 50 hairpin bends to **Puerto de Peñas Blancas**. This is a beautiful route, through terraced hillsides of red earth and rock, newly planted with bright green pines, past occasional cork oaks, looking, with their bare chocolate trunks and bushy tops, like clipped poodles. Piles of harvested cork lie by the roadside. The pass itself, at 980 metres (3,266 ft), has a magnificent view of the coast far below.

To the north the view includes four White Towns, dotted here and there on the wooded mountain sides. Each has its charm, and **Jubrique ❹**, the first the road descends to (by another long succession of hairpin bends), is one of the most delightful. It climbs almost vertically up the side of a gorge with steps in its main streets. Chain curtains hide a few tiny bars, one of them optimistically called a discotheque, skinny cats slink round corners, bougainvillaea cascades from balconies, and everywhere there are the smells of fresh white paint or – in season – jasmine. Where are the men of the village, for you see mainly women? Most have gone to work at the coast; profitably, judging by the new houses being built on Jubrique's fringes.

Any circuit north from here will include 10 or more similar White Towns and villages. They can be enjoyed for what they are, since few have exceptional architectural features, though there is a fine castle at Benadalid, also kept locked, now housing the cemetery.

North again, on the steep western side of the valley of the Rio Guadiaro, is the remarkable **Cueva de la Pileta ❺**, discovered in 1905 by a local farmer who was looking for *guano* (bird droppings) to manure his fields. "CALL" says a no-

ABOVE: country character. **BELOW:** the slow way home.

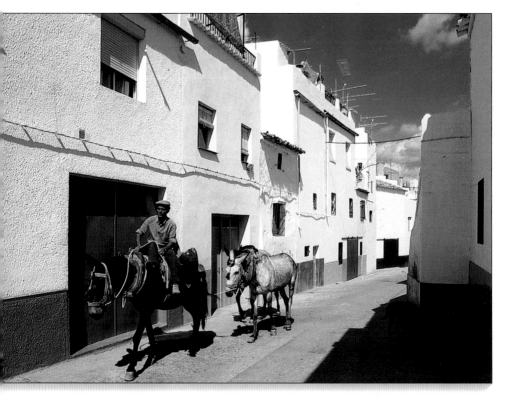

tice where the steps to the cave mouth begin. Sometimes the present owner, grandson of the discoverer, will emerge with his previous handful of visitors; sometimes he will come trudging up the hill from his farm below.

Inside are prehistoric wall paintings and magic symbols (the most impressive a huge fish which seems to have swallowed a small seal).

Frontier land

The cave lies in the **Sierra de Grazalema**, a national park of more than 47,000 hectares (16,135 acres). The formidable bare grey mountains of this park make one of the most impressive landscapes of southern Spain and conserve much wildlife – 136 bird and 40 mammal species. It is a splendid area to explore on foot, and can be sampled near **Cortes de la Frontera**.

Descend 5 km (3 miles) from Cortes to the Rio Guadiaro, ignore local discouragement and drive south down a dirt lane until the valley narrows and the track ends at a small reservoir. From here it is possible to walk and scramble down the fine **Angosturo del Guadiaro** (Guadiaro Gorge). The railway shares the gorge with the river, but often retreats into tunnels.

A short hop from Marbella

Another circuit of the hills starts from Marbella (*see page 254*), up the C337. After 12 km (7 miles) a side road leads high into the Sierra Bermeja to the **Refugio de Juanar**, orginally a parador until the Spanish government sold it to the workers for the symbolic sum of one *peseta*. A pleasantly simple place, decorated with animal horns, it is patronised by hunters who come to shoot the Spanish wild goat, a sport which these days is organised on a strict quota sys-

The Abies pinsapo, a species of prehistoric fir found in the Sierra de Grazalema grows nowhere else in Europe.

BELOW: views from Grazalema.

Map, page 230

tem. The animals are otherwise protected and can be seen at dawn or dusk. A couple of miles further up a dirt road is the **Mirador de Puerto Rico**. Its view is restricted but dramatic since it looks down directly on to Marbella.

Water therapy

The C337 goes to Monda, then minor roads lead to the pretty town of **Tolox** ❻, filling the end of its valley. At the valley's head, the 19th-century hydro was until the mid-1980s a ruin of rusting cisterns and broken windows. Today the cisterns are silver-bright and the hydro building a fresh yellow with green tiled roof. Here on any day in summer 50 or 60 patients, mainly Spanish, sit at little tables breathing the fumes of the water, to which they are connected by transparent plastic tubes with plastic mouthpieces, as if whispering their problems to the spirit of the spring. White-coated nurses attend, sell glasses of the water to drink, or help other patients to bathe their eyes.

Tolox is not the only revived hydro of Málaga province. North from Fuengirola, past the sprawling but prospering mountain town of Alhaurín el Grande – where the British writer Gerald Brenan made his third Spanish home up the fertile Guadalhorce valley – a mountain road of many bends and alarming precipices leads to **Carratraca** ❼.

The first odd thing a stranger notes about this small village is a surprising smell of sulphur permeating its narrow back streets. The smell comes from behind the tall stone walls of the *balneario*, where a spring of sulphurous water flows from the mountainside at a rate of 700 litres (185 gallons) a minute. The baths are Roman in their splendour. Two magnificent oval ones are surrounded by columns and a connecting architrave, their enclosing walls set with brilliant

Carratraca is said to have been discovered by Juan Camisón – so-called because he wore a long shirt to cover his sores – who seeing a goatherd bathing his goats with the spring's water, successfully tried some on himself.

BELOW: Tolox.

TIP

The spa at Carratraca is open from 15 June–15 October. The waters are said to benefit rheumatism, circulation, the nervous system, skin conditions and gynaecological problems.

BELOW: landscape near the Garganta del Chorro.

blue and yellow tiles. They are open to the sky and the scrubby mountainside rises directly behind. The coolish waters (18°C/67°F as they emerge) are heated to body temperature for the comfort of bathers. Rows of 19th-century bathrooms, a pump for drinking from and a doctor's surgery complete the complex.

Lakeland splendour

North from Carratraca lies what has been described as Andalucía's Lake District, though the phrase gives little idea of these opaque blue reservoirs with their sandy beaches, lying at the bottom of steep pine-clad valleys. They are slowly being discovered by visitors to the coast. Here the rich can dine well and the poor picnic, camp and fish.

The return to the coast leads down the **Garganta del Chorro ❽**, an astonishing gorge (*pictured on page 241*) with walls 180 metres (600 ft) high. When the reservoirs were opened by King Alfonso XIII in 1921 the King's Path (El Camino del Rey) was also inaugurated. This narrow pathway is attached to the vertical face of the gorge. No doubt it was in good condition when King Alfonso walked it but today its hand rail is missing from long sections and sometimes the path itself has gaps. Spanish youths, ignoring warning signs and obsessively flirting with death, venture out on the path.

Moors and vultures

High up to the west of the gorge, in a remote and once barely accessible area known as Mesas de Villaverde, there is a storage reservoir to which winter water is pumped for use in summer. Here, around the year 900, Umar Ibn Hafsun is said to have set up a kingdom in defiance of the Caliph of Córdoba, with

a capital town by the name of Bobastro. Little can be seen today except the ruins of a mosque built into the hillside.

At the village of El Chorro (from which the Camino del Rey is reached) take a dirt road in the opposite direction to Valle de Abdalajís and, a couple of miles before reaching it, look up left to another rock face. Circling high above you may see some of Andalucía's surviving vultures. There are not so many as there used to be, because fewer herds of goats and sheep wander the mountains and fewer of these are left for dead, but the vultures have been saved by feeding them occasional unwanted carcasses. They are not pretty birds, well described as flying mattresses with escaping feathers. Now they are joined by multi-coloured paragliders, for Valle del Abjulajís has become a popular gliding venue.

Limestone heights

The ancient city of Antequera, third in importance of the province, is most easily approached from Málaga by the N331, but another approach, via the MA 423 and C3310, passes the most remarkable of the province's natural phenomena: **El Torcal ❾**. Photographs show the towering shapes of some of its spectacular limestone pillars, sculpted by wind and rain to look like piled-up heaps of limestone sandwiches; but these images do not reveal their extent, or their situation, high up in the Sierra de Chimenea, where they will frequently be lapped in cloud blown up from the distant coast.

El Torcal has been saved from exploiters, who would have liked to quarry it, and is now a *paraje natural* (nature park) though a regrettably intrusive restaurant/café has been allowed at its centre. Fortunately you can quickly lose sight of this and wander undisturbed in one of the weirdest of natural landscapes.

Map, page 230

As well as the Egyptian vulture (pictured here), one of Europe's last colonies of griffon vultures is found in Andalucía.

BELOW: climbing at El Torcal.

Map, page 230

Prehistoric man lived in this sierra some 6,000 years ago and his remains have been found in the caves.

Crossroads of history

The abrupt descent from El Torcal to Antequera leads down the Boca del Asno (Ass's Mouth Gorge), site of one of the many battles fought around here between Moors and Christians, this one a Christian victory, during the period when Antequera was an almost isolated outpost of Moorish Granada. Its history is far older, and it too has its share of prehistoric caves, even if they date from about 2,000 years after the Cave of the Bull.

For good views in Antequera climb up to the Giant's Arch leading to the Moorish Castle at the top of the town.

Two of the most remarkable, **Cuevas de Menga** and **Viera** (open Tues–Sun; closed Mon and 1–4pm), lie just outside the town on the Granada road; look for a filling station named Los Dolmenes. The caves are set in a once-elegant but now shabby public garden of cypress trees and stone benches. Though nothing remains inside these huge caverns, their horizontal roof stones are quite sufficient to wonder at. One alone is estimated to weigh 180 tonnes, and they make the stones of such northern European burial chambers as the long barrows of England's Salisbury Plain look like pebbles.

A little further out of town **El Romeral** dolmen is smaller but more interesting, its domed chambers supposedly influenced by the famous Treasury of Atreus at Mycenae. From here, indeed from almost anywhere in Antequera, there is a good view of the oddly shaped rock which sticks up from the plain to the east and is known as La Peña de los Enamorados (Lovers' Rock), because the imaginative can see it as two entangled lovers. One legend makes their story a Romeo and Juliet tragedy, the young man a Christian, his girl a Moor. The pair threw themselves into the valley below. To the more prosaic admirer, the rock looks like a large misshapen nose.

BELOW: in Antequera.
RIGHT: the King's Path crosses El Chorro Gorge.

Antequera

The Romans settled in **Antequera** ❿, both in the city itself and in the newly discovered settlement at *Singilia Barba* to the west. There is a fine 1st-century AD bronze, the Antequera Ephebus, in the city **museum** (open Tues–Sun mornings; closed Mon and pm; admission charge). But religion, and above all Christianity, gives the city its overriding character today. Nowhere can there be so many churches (about 24 in all) for such a small town, nor such an odd assortment of belfries.

For a close impression of a few of them, stand in the Plaza de Guerrero Muñoz, which the city museum, an 18th-century palace, also faces. For an aerial view, climb to the Moorish castle, a fine ruin, approached through the formidable Giant's Arch (1585), which also leads to the large church of Santa María. The castle fell to the Christians in 1410 after a siege lasting five months.

Local legend says that, far below it, passages run underground to emerge at two places in today's city. Because the defenders needed water? No. Partly so that they could take the besiegers in the rear, but more importantly because they needed women. ❑

RONDA

Map, page 246

Nothing can detract from Ronda's incomparable setting, perched above the Tajo gorge. It also has fine architecture, one of the oldest bullrings in Spain and Moorish and Roman remains

Seville
Ronda

Encircled by mountains, riven by the deep fissure of the Tajo, **Ronda ⑪** (*see map on page 230*) was one of the first small Spanish cities (with 35,000 inhabitants today) to earn a place on the tourist map. Mentioned by geographers and travellers from Strabo and Pliny through Ibn Batuta to the Baron de Bourgoing, it received its most enthusiastic write-up from Richard Ford, in his *Hand-Book for Travellers in Spain* (first edition 1845): "There is but one Ronda in the world, and this Tajo, cleft as it were by the scimitar of Roldan, forms when the cascade is full... its heart and soul. The scene, its noise and movement, baffle pen and pencil, and, like Wilson at the Falls of Terni, we can only exclaim, 'Well done, rock and water, by Heavens!'"

Ford wrote this lyrical description in the heyday of the Romantic movement, which drew to Andalucía Scottish artists David Wilkie and David Roberts, French men of letters Théophile Gautier and Alexandre Dumas *fils*, the great lithographer Gustave Doré, and a succession of writers hardly less ecstatic about Ronda than was Ford.

In 1906 the Hotel Reina Victoria on the edge of the inland cliff was completed and immediately became popular as a hill station and retreat for the officers of the Gibraltar garrison. In 1913 the poet Rainer Maria Rilke stayed here for several weeks and wrote his *Spanish Trilogy*, including the eulogistic lines on observing a shepherd tending his flock on the hillside: "Even today a god might secretly enter that form and not be diminished."

Later came swashbuckling Ernest Hemingway and Orson Welles to hobnob with the leading matador Antonio Ordóñez, a son of Ronda, and painter David Bomberg, who brought his intensely Jewish determination to reveal the soul of the landscape.

The face of change

With such a legacy of international interest, Ronda has a lot to live up to and is probably the repository of too many expectations. The inevitable has happened. Urban sprawl, an industrial estate and bleak municipal housing have occupied the commanding heights; unfortunately there was nowhere else for these necessary developments to go.

It is wise to approach Ronda today with circumspection. The best routes in, yielding the best views of the old city, are from Algeciras and from San Pedro de Alcántara. If you enter from Seville or from Granada, take the new ring-road round the town, as if aiming for San Pedro, and then double back into Ronda on the unblemished flank.

From this side, you first encounter the Barrio de San Francisco, which is rather like a small mountain *pueblo* picked up and deposited under the city walls.

PRECEDING PAGES: Tajo gorge in morning mist. **LEFT:** the Tajo bridge. **BELOW:** savages on Salvatierra palace.

Reception at the Hotel Reina Victoria, which despite more modern rivals, remains a good place to stay.

Here there is a lively market every Sunday and an important animal fair early in October, held in the oblong square surrounded by village houses. The most striking building, reached through the Moorish Almocobar gate, is the fortress-like church of the **Espíritu Santo** (open daily; admission charge), the first one built after the recapture of Ronda from the Moors in 1485.

Winding up the hill into the old city, past the small but interesting **Museum of Bandits** (open daily; admission charge), the first motorable turn on the left leads into the **Plaza de la Duquesa de Parcent A**, a charming square with cypresses and medlars and river-bred oleanders in the neat flower-beds inside low box hedges. The square is flanked by an early 18th-century barracks, now the town hall; by a 19th-century boys' school on the site of the Moorish fortress (left ruinous after the Peninsular War); by the convents of the Poor Clares and of the Little Sisters of the Cross; by the main church of **Santa María la Mayor** (open daily; admission charge); and by the law courts.

The church, under a great barnlike roof, has interesting features: a late Gothic nave, baroque choir stalls, High Renaissance east end and sanctuary, and a tower whose lower stages belonged to a minaret. Facing the square is an arcade supporting a gallery from which priests and notables would watch bullfights. The permanent bullring was built later.

Arab style

Not far from the Plaza de la Ciudad is the **Palacio de Mondragón B** (open daily; closed Sat and Sun pm; admission charge). This is a grand town house with a stone Renaissance facade, cobbled porch with mounting block, front patio of about 1570 and rear *patio arabe*, which is really *mudéjar* (post-

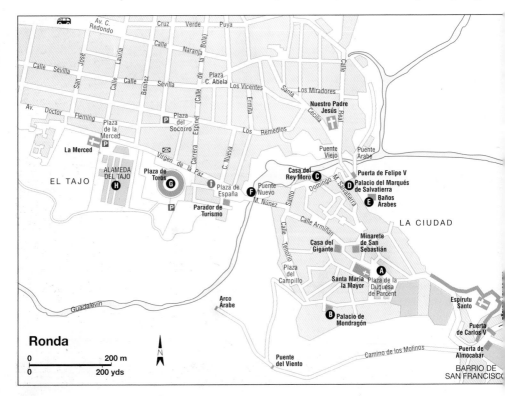

Ronda

0   200 m
0   200 yds

N

Map, page 246

Reconquest in the Arab style). There are few remaining examples of domestic building to show for nearly eight centuries of Moorish occupation, but the nearby Casa del Gigante has a patio with 14th century arabesque stucco work.

An alley leads from the Plaza de Mondragón into the Plaza del Campillo, which is open on one side to the mountains. Here stood one of the three Moorish gates into the city. Halfway down a steep slope are the remnants of an outer wall and gateway, through which winds a track down to the market gardens and abandoned water mills in the valley.

From the Plaza del Campillo, Calle Tenorio leads back to the main road which bisects the old city. The steep Cuesta de Santo Domingo then leads down past the Casa del Marqués de Santa Pola (with basements preserving some traces of Moorish wall-painting) to the so-called **Casa del Rey Moro ❻**. This is a 19th-century pastiche with dark hanging gardens, from which the Mina de Ronda, a staircase cut inside the rock, descends to the river bed. During times of siege, it was manned by a live chain of Christian captives passing up pitchers of water to supply their masters in the citadel, "whose fierce king" – according to a romantic travel book of 1923 – "drank only from the skulls of enemies; cutting off their heads and making them into goblets inlaid with splendid jewels". The house is being converted into a hotel, scheduled to open in 2000. The gardens and Mina can be visited (open daily; admission charge).

Next comes the **Palacio del Marqués de Salvatierra ❼** (open daily; closed 2–4pm and Thur and Sun pm; guided tour; admission charge) with an interesting facade showing colonial influence. Just below this the **Roman Bridge**, rebuilt in 1616, crosses the gorge.

Lower down yet is the **Arab Bridge**, also completely rebuilt. It is adjacent to

ABOVE: family frills at Ronda's *feria*.
BELOW: afternoon airing.

the crumbling **Baños Arabes** (Arab Baths), which form an outpost of the town thrusting out into the fields. They are still being excavated. From this point, a rough pebbled track leads up under the Salvatierra palace to the third city gate of medieval times.

Beyond bridges

The old city is an agreeable architectural hotchpotch based on a Moorish groundplan, but not all of it in good repair: the whole is greater than the sum of the parts. The **Puente Nuevo** (New Bridge) crosses the gorge at its deepest and narrowest point and is a uniquely assertive feat of engineering, more like a solid causeway with apertures than an aerial span over the abyss. Begun in 1755, after a previous effort collapsed, it seems to have been first opened for transit in 1784; its architect José Martin de Aldehuela fell to his death inspecting the structure shortly before its completion. Once it was open, tightly corseted Ronda spilled out on to the tableland known as the Mercadillo, which was used until then mainly for markets and fairs.

The **Plaza de Toros** (open daily; closed on days when there are fights: admission charge) which claims to be the oldest bull-ring in the country, opened its doors on 11 May 1784 and played a leading role in the development of the modern bullfight under the determined guidance of Pedro Romero (1754–1839), the foremost matador of his age. An annual *corrida goyesca* in dress of the period is held every year in his memory during the September fair, so-called because suits worn by the fighters – and many members of the audience – are based on those shown in Goya's series of etchings, *The Tauromachia*.

A little higher up than the Plaza de Toros on the same side of the street is the

BELOW: Ronda's famous bullring.

Alameda de Tajo , a shady public promenade dating from 1806, which ends in a balustrade on the brink of a sheer drop. "The view," says Ford, "from this eminence over the depths below, and the mountain panorama, is one of the finest in the world." Few will accuse him of hyperbole.

It is not necessary to go beyond the Alameda (or the neighbouring church of La Merced, which once housed the arm of Santa Teresa of Avila) other than to reach the Hotel Reina Victoria on the highest point of the new town. With the coming of coach tours, this has lost some of its Edwardian atmosphere. It is worth visiting to see the room where the poet Rilke stayed, preserved with some mementoes, and for a drink on the terrace at sunset. Other possibilities for lodging include the comfortable Hotel Polo, near the Alameda, or the parador on the edge of the gorge.

Paseo places

Despite its claim to an aristocratic and warlike past, and its delight in legends of brigands and smugglers, Ronda has for long been a lively commercial centre for almost 30 smaller towns and villages. This is borne out in the **Calle de la Bola**, a traffic-free shopping street running from the bull-ring due east for more than half a mile. Ronda's answer to Las Ramblas of Barcelona or Calle Sierpes in Seville, it is packed both before lunch and for the evening *paseo*. Modern times have brought tourists pink as prawns, buskers and trinket stalls recognisable from any international city.

But almost all the traditional elements are there, too: the agricultural brokers and livestock dealers with their caps and canes and muddied boots, gypsies tugging at the sleeve, blind lottery sellers crying out the winning number, bourgeois couples perambulating on tiny well-shod feet, and children dressed up as brides or sailors for their first communion. The old culture is not beaten yet and Ronda has managed its modernisation not quite as romantics would desire but with a solid feeling for its role as Capital de la Serranía.

Nearby Nature

The **Parque Natural Sierra de las Nieves** south of Ronda and stretching almost to Marbella, has been protected since 1919. It is famous for a rare species of prehistoric fir, the *pinsapo*, which grows only above the 1,000 metre (3,200 ft) line, and for the *Capra pyrenaica* or ibex; some pairs of golden eagles also survive. Access by jeep trail via the *pueblos* of El Burgo, Yunquera or Tolox is relatively unrestricted, though shooting is limited.

West of Ronda the **Parque Natural de Grazalema** (*see also pages 278–79*) covers an area of nearly 50,000 hectares (120,000 acres), including 13 villages, mainly in the province of Cádiz. The flora and fauna on this side are more varied but access is more strictly controlled and some of the routes in the *pinsapares* (which also exist here) are closed during the summer months as a precaution against forest fires. The park office is in the small town of **El Bosque** en route from Grazalema to Jerez. ❑

Map, page 246

TIP

Ronda, worth a day or two for itself, is also the best centre for excursions to the White Towns; to the Cueva de la Pileta; and to Roman Acinipo. It is also a great springboard for hiking and horse trekking.

BELOW: the Serranía de Ronda.

THE COSTA DEL SOL

The Costa del Sol's resorts range from glamorous Marbella to brash Torremolinos, from family-focused Fuengirola to exclusive Puerto Banús and laid-back Tarifa

I t is impossible to write about the Costa del Sol without regret. What a lovely coast it must have been, with its small sandy bays and fishing villages, connected to each other by no more than dirt roads, backed from end to end by a dramatic line of sierras which, as well as being beautiful, made it almost frost-free at any season. Even in 1957, when the first two hotels had arrived at Castell de Ferro (between Málaga and Almería), the owner of the smaller, a cunning Catalan, was heard to offer to exchange it for "three Leyland lorries" so that he could return to his home province and make real money. How things change.

But if the Costa is scenically and ecologically a disaster it can still be fun. The climate remains delightful, the sea is warm and the sandy beaches are still there, even if it is difficult to see them for the sunbeds. Some of the new building is architecturally exciting; a place like Torremolinos is a curiosity, to say the least, and little-spoiled mountain villages are never far away.

West end

The least changed section lies closest to Gibraltar, where the main highway runs a few miles inland. Here, belatedly, the Spanish authorities are trying to prevent building on the very edge of the waves. Where the road returns to the coast, near the mouth of the Rio Guadiaro, the artificial harbour, **Puerto Sotogrande**, has been built. There are 11 yacht harbours in the 200 km (125 miles) between Sotogrande and Almunecar, on the Granada coast. The best known of these, **Puerto Banús** ⓬, close to Marbella, acquired a reputation in the 1970s as the playground of the rich and wicked. They are still there, judging by the huge yachts, so huge that they seem to overhang the jetty, but for most visitors Puerto Banús consists of arcades of fish restaurants and boutiques. You can dine well here, if at a price. Architecturally, it is a bizarre but attractive recreation of the traditional Andalucían style, decorated with mock minarets and Moorish arches, its jetties fringed with palm trees.

The *puertos* which have been built since are similar, though smaller, and because they have failed to achieve Puerto Banús's notoriety, have more charm. **Puerto Duquesa**, 10 km (6 miles) northeast of Puerto Sotogrande, is a good example. At **Puerto Benalmádena**, just outside Torremolinos, architectural pastiche reaches a climax, its maze of cool white courtyards with Moorish decorations topped by roof-lines which have igloo curves, the whole suggesting that some inspired Arabian chef has been let loose with a million tonnes of icing sugar.

Estepona ⓭, most westerly of the Costa's swollen fishing villages, now a largish town, has so far avoided

PRECEDING PAGES: eggbox living. **LEFT:** promo girl brushing up the Costa image. **BELOW:** Puerto Banús.

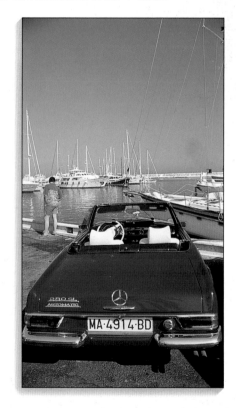

The ultimate Costa accessory – a yacht.

too many high-rises and remains Spanish, with an old quarter of narrow streets and bars. Originally Phoenician, then Roman – the remains of Salduba aqueduct are nearby – Estepona also has one of the little round towers built in times when Barbary pirates regularly threatened the coast. The long esplanade has a pre-World War I elegance. The town also has several 18-hole golf courses – Nairobi was once said to have more of these per head of (white) population than anywhere else in the world, but the Costa del Sol must now easily hold the record.

San Pedro de Alcántara ⓮ maintains its Spanishness for another reason: it stands more than a mile from the sea. It was to San Pedro that the early British and American settlers escaped when Marbella swelled out of recognition, and they still meet at bars in the "English Arcade" to read English newspapers, borrow English books, talk of "home" – and experience the added excitement that some customer may be a notorious English fugitive. For the moment the seaside area remains a Sunday picnic spot for extended Spanish families who set up tables and eat vast spreads of pre-cooked paellas and tortillas. San Pedro was also Roman, and the Costa road itself was the Roman Via Augusta, leading eventually all the way to Rome itself.

Beyond the facade

Another 11 km (7 miles) east, **Marbella ⓯** may be swollen out of all recognition, its main street a jam of east-west traffic, but at its centre an old town survives, of narrow white traffic-free lanes. At the centre of this is its showpiece, the Plaza de los Naranjos, planted with orange trees and overlooked by the 16th-century Casa del Corregidor, one of the town's few old buildings. On a hot

summer night this plaza, set from side to side with dining tables, lit by an orange glow, becomes one vast open-air restaurant, and can delight even hardened Costa-watchers.

Just outside **Fuengirola** ⓖ – 27 km (17 miles) east of Marbella – Sohail Castle was intended for defence. Standing on a lumpy hill, with views up and down the coast, it was originally built in 956, some 250 years after the Moorish conquest of Spain, by Abd-al-Rahman III, the best known of the Umayyad Caliphs. Fuengirola grew up under its protection. Even after the Christian conquest of the Kingdom of Granada it survived for a few years and was not finally captured and levelled until 1497. The present castle was built in 1730, to prevent trade with Gibraltar which the British had occupied in 1704.

Eighty years later, in 1810, it was connected with one of the more shameful (from a British point of view) episodes of the Peninsular War. A British expedition of 800 men under General Blayney landed here and advanced on Mijas, but found the country too difficult and retreated to the castle. Here Blayney disposed his troops "with the utmost contempt of military rules" and as a result was forced to surrender to 150 Polish troops who were fighting for the French.

Tourist retreats

The mountain villages of Mijas, 8 km (5 miles) above Fuengirola, and Benalmádena, 9 km (5 miles) above Torremolinos, now have more connection with the Costa than with inland Spain. Everywhere in **Mijas** ⓗ are shops selling sheepskin jackets, local pottery and tourist junk. You can take a ride in a four-wheeled carriage under a huge striped umbrella, ride a *burro* taxi, or visit a mobile museum to see the 2,000 most curious things in the world. Despite all this, there is

Map, page 230

ABOVE: Fuengirola's Tuesday market is one of the best on the Coast.
BELOW: Aquapark at Mijas.

fresher air up here and fine views from both villages down on to the coast. With their clean white houses and green shutters, they are good examples of the Spanish genius for giving even tourist traps a certain enchantment.

The village of **Benalmádena-Pueblo** , a few kilometres inland from the coast, is much more unspoilt, and is home to a surprisingly good Museum of Pre-Columbian American Art (open Mon–Fri; closed 2–4pm and Sat–Sun; admission charge).

But **Benalmádena-Costa**, on the coast road, is merely an extension of Torremolinos. It is in **Torremolinos** ⓲ that the Costa's excesses froth over into self-parody. The grotesquely overgrown village, with its hundreds of bars, lush vegetation and overhead walkways is like some Hollywood director's concept of what a Spanish resort should be. At night there are discos, homosexual bars and just about every other sort of entertainment.

Further east lies the provincial capital of Málaga (*see page 231*).

Inland

For a completely different world, head inland at Torre de Benagalbón and climb past the emerald-green fairways of yet another golf course to the tiny villages of Benaque and Macharaviaya. They first appear far below the road, delightfully set against the stern grey peaks of the Sierra de Tejeda: just a couple of straggles of white houses. More immediately below, on the steep valley sides, are their vineyards.

Macharaviaya ⓴ is the smaller and more charming, with cobbled streets and a huge dilapidated church. How could such a tiny place need a church of this size, you may wonder, but in the 18th century it had a factory and an important

TIP

Just west of Torremolinos, the fishing quarter of La Carihuela retains a certain Spanish feel, and is famous for its fish restaurants – all of which are good.

BELOW: Virgen del Carmen fiesta, Nerja.

industry: the making of playing cards, with a monopoly for supplying them to the Americas. In the church's crypt are memorials to the Gálvez family, the local landowners who brought the village its prosperity. They were powerful Spanish colonialists, who extended Spanish influence up the west coast of America as far as San Francisco Bay. Alas for Macharaviaya, the Gálvez family died, its monopoly lapsed and the factory closed.

Benaque ㉑, slightly larger, is no more prosperous. At the end of a road to nowhere, you may still see the local housewives outside its one grocery shop, haggling about the prices of trousers with a peddler who has brought them on a bicycle. Peering into the dark doorways of its white houses, you will see villagers sieving and packing raisins; raisin production is its only industry.

Map, page 230

Sea view

At Nerja ㉒, 52 km (32 miles) east of Málaga, the famous Balcony of Europe does not run parallel to the sea, as its name suggests, but is a marble-paved projection above a headland, set with palms and decorated with a couple of cannon recovered from the sea. The Spanish king Alfonso XII gave it this appropriate name in 1885 – there is nothing ahead but the Mediterranean, with Africa somewhere beyond the horizon. He was here to comfort the people after the devastating earthquake of the previous Christmas Day.

Tucked below the balcony to the east is a small sandy cove with fishing boats, while, beyond, the coast curves away in a big crescent of cliffs backed by mountains. Maro, 3 km (2 miles) round this curving bay, has its own balcony, a palm walk above surrounding market gardening slopes, with fine views east. While Maro is still relatively unexploited, there is no pleasanter place than Casa Maro (facing west) to sit with a glass of wine as the evening sun sinks behind the mountains beyond Málaga.

The Cuevas de Nerja first opened to the public in June 1960, when a French ballet company presented "Swan Lake" there.

Journey to Middle Earth

Turn away from the coast for the other explanation for Nerja's explosive growth: here, in 1959, five young Spanish boys went on a bat-hunting expedition, felt warm air coming from a crack in the rocks and discovered the Cueva de Nerja (Nerja caves) (open daily; closed 2–4pm; admission charge).

Today, dozens of busloads of tourists come daily to see these astonishing underground caverns. Needless to say, one has been fitted out as an auditorium where ballets are performed, and all are paved with walks and are well-lit, while soft music, not the squeak of bats, echoes above among the stalactites.

The caves remain a staggering sight, if only for their immense size. Prehistoric man used them 20,000 years ago, and a typical skeleton is displayed in a glass case. It is of a woman who apparently died of mastoid infection.

Beyond Maro, where the Sierra de Tejeda comes down to the sea, Málaga province's section of the Costa ends as it began, still more or less unexploited, though with an entirely different character. Steep, stony hillsides protect small rocky coves, and if you climb down you can still bathe alone beside some local farmer's avocado plantation. ❏

BELOW: fun on the beach in Nerja.

EXPLORING THE WHITE TOWNS

Map, page 262

A route linking a selection of the so-called White Towns is an excellent way of sampling the hilly hinterland behind the Costa del Sol. The higher you go, the whiter and prettier they get

The lowlands of Andalucía are characterised by large whitewashed agricultural villages from which hosts of landless labourers used to go out to till the big arable farms of the river plains. Though certainly "white", these villages are bleak and functional; not all members of the White Town species are charming or pretty. But the higher you climb into the sierras, with their more rugged terrain, the smaller and more picturesque the towns and villages (both can be called *pueblos*) become.

In the hills large monocultures give way to smallholdings, herding and forest crops such as chestnut and cork. Glimpsed from the road or railway, whether framed in forest green or tucked under some vertiginous fang of rock, the mountain *pueblos* fuel nostalgia and inspire the hope that they will be as unspoiled on closer acquaintance.

The various tourist organs have striven mightily to establish these White Towns as the great attraction of the Andalucían interior. Some *pueblos* bear the official sign Ruta de los Pueblos Blancos; others, no less attractive, do not. The major promotion is concentrated on the province of Cádiz and the western half of the province of Málaga. As some 50 or 60 *pueblos* are commended in a number of leaflets, a little inside knowledge may help.

PRECEDING PAGES: Grazalema. **LEFT:** Setenil. **BELOW:** brightening the white.

Regional differences

Some of the *pueblos* netted in the official trawl belong to the Atlantic coast (as opposed to the foreign-dominated Costa del Sol), which runs from the Bay of Cádiz to the Straits of Gibraltar. They are not dealt with here – faultlessly iron-grilled and flower-potted though most of them are – because tourism, albeit national rather than international, is a large part of their economy and they are not representative of the modes of survival in the hinterland.

A few miles inland all this changes, because the effect of tourism, though not absent, is much less direct. There is large-scale migration of labour to Madrid, Barcelona or the coasts; the remaining townsfolk or villagers pursue a traditional pattern of life and the odd stranger remains a rarity.

Though the mountain roads have improved vastly, virtually all the other elements of tourist infrastructure are still absent. There are few beds, although official encouragement and private enterprise are increasing the number. The best way of exploring the *pueblos blancos* (other than for genuine campers, who are well catered for) is to set up base camp in Ronda, Arcos de la Frontera or Olvera.

The white-washed villages must make the most of abrupt terrain and fend off summer heat. Hollow clay roof tiles channel rainwater and improve ventilation. Interior courtyards provide privacy as well as a welcome refuge from heat, while exterior windows are kept small to keep out the summer glare. Thick walls of stone and mortar provide insulation. The yearly application of limewash not only reflects the sun's rays, but also serves as a disinfectant.

Key routes

Running on a spine between the Rio Guadiaro and its tributary the Genal, the Ronda-Algeciras road whets the appetite of the White Town addict, though a minority of the 15 or so *pueblos* of the Genal valley fall within the official designation. All are small. **Gaucín** ❶, on the main road with roughly 2,500 inhabitants, is the largest; most have in the region of 1,000; Alpandeire has shrunk to 210. Perched on steep wooded slopes (the chestnut is the main crop), they have names – Atajate, Alpandeire, Benarrabá, Benalauría, Benadalid, Farajan, Jubrique, Genalguacil – that speak eloquently of their Berber past.

After the Reconquest of 1492 and their nominal Christianisation, these towns-people all joined the Morisco (converted Muslim) rebellion of 1570. Resentment smouldered on for centuries and bred a wary, sometimes violent race, whose villages were accessible only by steep mule track. The greatest revolution in their lives has been the recent construction of well-engineered roads. Now their populations increase markedly in the summer months with migrant workers returning to stay with elderly relatives for the holidays and fairs, and in some cases to rebuild and modernise their family homes.

A good example is **Genalguacil** ❷, with a population of just over 1,000 in the heart of the area. Its name means "Vizier's Garden" and it exhibits a certain hill-station gaiety, exemplified by the fine municipal swimming pool, packed with young people. This local renaissance is essentially Spanish; there is no special provision for foreign tourists and no hotel. But there is a shady camp site down by the bridge over the Rio Genal between Algatocín and Jubrique, and there is a direct link from Jubrique to Estepona on the coast.

The Rio Guadiaro (joined lower down by the Genal) rises above Ronda to

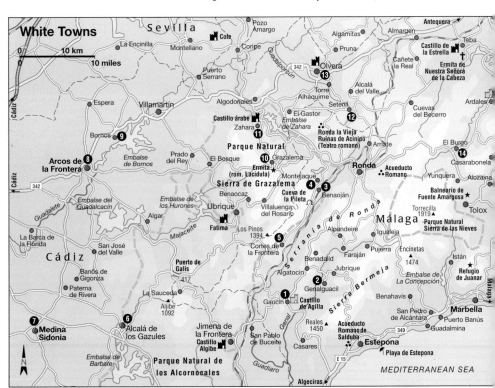

debouch in the Mediterranean a little north of Gibraltar. The railway hugs it closely much of the way; a minor road (MA501) also follows it in a switchback fashion, rising to the White Towns of **Benaoján ❸** and **Montejaque ❹**, renowned for their *embutidos* (tinned pork products) and mountain-cured hams; then plunging down to the station of Jimera de Líbar before rising again to **Cortes de la Frontera ❺**.

Cortes is a pleasant, medium-sized *pueblo* (population just under 5,000) on a high shelf above the Guadiaro: it is clad in standard dazzling white, with the exception of its distinguished stone town hall from the period of that enlightened despot Charles III (1759–88); it also boasts a proper bullring of masonry and a fine *alameda* or public promenade.

Cortes derives its relative wealth from the cork forests which stretch for over 30 miles (48 km) to the west. With these advantages, it exudes confidence. From Cortes, the road winds westwards through the forest with only occasional clearings for a smallholding with witch-like cottage, to the remote crossroads of **Puerto de Galis**.

Eminent places

From Galis, a bumpy road (CA511) descends towards the undulating arable farms and bull-breeding pastures of the province of Cádiz. The towns become larger. Alcalá de los Gazules, Medina Sidonia and Arcos de la Frontera (all on eminences above the plain) are approved White Towns. All three were strongholds of Moorish tribes until the Reconquest, when they passed into the hands of Spanish nobles who then abandoned them in favour of the larger cities.

Alcalá de los Gazules ❻, with several wayside restaurants on the Cádiz

Map, page 262

Pata negra is derived from a breed of black-footed Iberian pigs which roam semi-wild and feed on acorns.

BELOW: Lunes del Tor fiesta, Grazalema.

road, is the seediest and its flat-topped houses climbing up to the church and fort are the most Moorish. **Medina Sidonia** ❼, bearing the name of the Armada's admiral, excites some expectations: it is a windswept place on top of a conical mound ánd its monuments are mostly ruinous, although it has a fine main square.

Arcos de la Frontera ❽, on its inland cliff above the Guadalete (giving it a certain family resemblance to Ronda) is the most spectacular and probably the best base camp for the area. But it has an ancient reputation for witchcraft, sorcery and incest, which has not been entirely deodorised by the luxurious parador and the tourist propaganda; the whiff of it lingers in the tortuous streets.

Yet the strangest atmosphere of all is to be found in low-lying **Bornos** ❾ on the shores of a reservoir squeezed out of the waters of the Guadalete. White-washed walls are the backdrop for a pullulating street life marked by gypsies, squatting or cross-legged, playing cards on the pavements which they share with a large population of evil-looking hounds. Above this picaresque scene rise the remnants of the palace-castle of the Riberas and other grand but gutted buildings. From the desiccated lakeside beach with its *chiringuitos* (shanty bars) there is a superb view of the Sierra de Grazalema. With its decayed grandeur and raffish character, Bornos makes a perfect foil for the purity of the mountains rising across the glassy water.

The cities of the plain, intriguing in their way, do not quite live up to the *beau idéal* of the White Town. For this we must return to the mountains where the whiteness of the walls is matched by a simpler, sturdier character in the people. In this category **Grazalema** ❿ (some 32 km/20 miles west of Ronda) must rank high. Grazalema was once more populous, as is testified by its three

ABOVE: popular afternoon entertainment in the town bars.
BELOW: Church of Santa María, Arcos de la Frontera.

handsome parish churches, one gutted in the Civil War (1936–39) and still a shell today. When its wool trade collapsed in the 19th century, the town shrank and some houses on the rim crumbled back to nature or became byres for beasts.

If there is any criticism, it is that Grazalema is just a little too sanitised. **Zahara ⓫** on the other side of the spectacular pass of Las Palomas (over 1,200 metres/4,000 ft) is equally picturesque and less self-conscious.

One of the most publicised sights in the region is **Setenil ⓬**, a small White Town set in the ravine of the Rio Guadalporcun, 20 km (12 miles) to the north of Ronda. It has two or three streets of semi-cave houses whose roofs are formed by overhanging rock, giving their neat white facades the appearance of mushroom stems under a spreading fungoid crown.

Passing under the walls of **Torre Alháquime** (a little hilltop village which has endowed itself with a post-modern promenade) you come to Olvera, White Town par excellence.

King of them all

With around 12,000 inhabitants **Olvera ⓭** is a larger place than its immediate neighbours. Its silhouette is almost outrageously dramatic with Moorish keep and Christian basilica soaring above the tightly packed slopes of blindingly white houses under biscuit-coloured tiles, running down to a clear perimeter, where the countryside begins. Famous as the refuge of outlaws and murderers in the 19th century, Olvera today has a reputation for religiosity. A monument to the Sacred Heart of Jesus on a natural outcrop of rock dominates the lower town and people have been known to crawl for miles on their hands and knees, in fulfilment of a vow, to the popular sanctuary of the Virgen de los Remedios.

Map, page 262

Grazalema is plastered like a martlet-nest on the rocky hill, and can only be approached by a narrow ledge...The wild women, as they wash their parti-coloured garments in the bubbling stream, eye the traveller as if a perquisite of their worthy mates.

– RICHARD FORD
A Handbook for Travellers in Spain 1855

BELOW: Olvera.

Map, page 262

Olvera's streets are neat and somewhat stern. The handsome facades make few concessions to the floral trimmings beloved of the brochures. But the local fair, late in August, is among the most lavish in the region – and is also one of the lengthiest: five nights until 5am or later of stalls, sideshows, bars, attractions, spectacles of song and dance and private club enclosures; during the day there are football matches, clay-pigeon contests and two or three novice bullfights held in a portable ring.

Community centres

TIP

When touring the White Towns, take your swimming costume with you. The municipal pools are open to all and some make very agreeable oases on a hot-day's sightseeing.

BELOW: pool in Grazalema.
RIGHT: white turns blue as night falls.

The survival kit of the mountain *pueblo* is made up of migrant labour, some jobs in agriculture, some in building, social security for the old and a strong belief that the *pueblo* is the natural unit of society. Tourism plays no part except to provide work on the coast in catering or construction. Although less closed than before, the White Town still remains a very self-contained unit. The cafés and bars are patronised almost exclusively by men; they are more like clubs, though the stranger will be served with perfect courtesy.

Beds are not plentiful. Olvera, a large *pueblo* by mountain standards, has one *pension* in the town and a new *hostal* on the outskirts; most of the smaller *pueblos* have no lodgings.

There are two new institutions of great importance to contemporary *pueblo* life: the municipal swimming pool and the discotheque. Both are for the young. It is the firm belief of local government that without them the young folk of the *pueblo* would vote with their feet for the cities. The discos may not seem exactly what you came for but there are some amazingly plush examples (Ronda, Cortes, El Burgo) which you may well be shown with pride.

At **El Burgo** ⓮, on the road from Ronda to Málaga via Coín, an unremarkable bar front is the gateway to a vast cork-lined cavern of a disco decorated with tropical love scenes in black silhouette on gold panels. According to the owner, all the youth of the *pueblo*, including young married couples, flock in on Saturday nights. All behave impeccably. If they transgress, they are banned for good and their social life is ruined. That sums up the White Town attitude to the law. The sanctions of the *pueblo* are stronger than those of the authorities.

The summer fairs might be thought of as a way into White Town life and it is true that local people let their hair down and talk more freely in the bars at fairtime. But especially in the smaller *pueblos* (under 3,000 inhabitants) the annual fair is really no more than an extended family party lasting several nights and usually timed to allow villagers who have emigrated to return and join in the fun. With the exception of brilliant fireworks against flawless night skies, specific attractions are usually few and not particularly traditional.

The young dictate the choice of music: there is a brand of modernised flamenco, but genuine *cante jondo* is hard to find. As at all parties, they are little fun if you don't know anybody, but if you go with a Spanish family or a knowledgeable friend you can have a whale of a time. ❏

CÁDIZ AND ITS PROVINCE

An illustrious seafaring history, a centuries-old wine and sherry industry and a proud equestrian tradition make the province of Cadiz a fascinating place to visit

Maps:
City 273
Area 276

W hen the English author Laurie Lee described **Cádiz ❶** in *As I Walked Out One Midsummer Morning*, his lyrical account of a walk he made through Spain in 1934, he recalled "Cadiz from a distance, was a city of sharp incandescence, a scribble of white on a sheet of blue glass… sparkling with African light. In fact it was a shut-in city, a kind of Levantine ghetto almost entirely surrounded by sea – a heap of squat cubist hovels enclosed by medieval ramparts and joined to the mainland by a dirty thread of sand."

Today Cádiz has changed in substance but not in its essence. The dirty thread of sand has been replaced by a thick, black hawser of tarmac and the town is now moored to its province by another asphalt cable arching across the bay to Puerto Real. Within the ramparts – not medieval but mainly 17th- and 18th-century – Cádiz is still a Levantine ghetto, but made up of four- and five-storey tenements packed tight behind the defences and the roadway that encircles the historic city.

Frontier town

Ghetto Cádiz is a walled enclave of humanity, a frontier town, founded as an outpost of the Phoenician trading empire on what was once an offshore island. Gadir, the defended place, they called it then.

The Phoenician patron of the city, the god Melkart, was Hercules to the Romans, and the twin bronze-clad columns of his temple became a man-made marker beyond which man did not dare travel. This was the frontier of land and ocean, of Europe and Africa, of Old World and New.

During the wars between Carthage and Rome, when dominion of the classical world was at stake, Gadir was the Carthaginian gateway into Europe. Here, in the temple of Melkart, Hannibal swore his undying hatred of Rome. Then when the Roman legionaries turned Gadir into Gades, they transformed the city into Europe's gateway to Carthaginian Africa, building a lighthouse on the present Punta de San Sebastián. The 90-metre (290-ft) tower with its gilt bronze statue survived, so they say, until the Moors came in the 8th century.

The Frontera

In 1263 Moorish Cádiz and western al-Andalus fell to the Christian king Alfonso the Wise. Cádiz, repopulated by Christian Spaniards, became part of the Frontera, which gives its name to so many towns and villages in the province of Cádiz. Nothing remains of Alfonso's castle except the arches of two postern gates across alleyways landward of the Cathedral: **Arco de los Blancos** and **Arco de la Rosa**.

PRECEDING PAGES: Columbus monument on the Río Odiel. **LEFT:** old city gate in Cádiz. **BELOW:** girl of Cádiz.

Wrecks and Wreckers

At the entrance to the Bay of Cádiz, just beyond the fortified island of San Sebastián, lies the *Bucentaure*, flagship of the French fleet at the Battle of Trafalgar (1805).

The *Bucentaure* was seized by the British Admiral Nelson as a prize of war. Badly damaged, she was taken under tow towards Gibraltar, but the storm that wrecked so many of the Trafalgar warships broke her tow-rope and nearly sent her to the bottom. The Frenchmen on board managed to turn her about and they made for Cádiz. There, near the La Olla rock, she went down. All those aboard were taken off by the *Indomptable*, but shortly after, overloaded with 500 sailors and marines, the *Indomptable* also went down in a storm.

The *Bucentaure* was not the first ship to go down in the Bay of Cádiz. Nor was the *Indomptable* the last. As the mud and silt of

the Guadalquivir shifts slowly beneath the waters of Cádiz bay, evidence of shipwrecks is uncovered: a handful of shards of Phoenician or Greek pottery, a Roman amphora, a medieval stone anchor or just the rotting ribs of a fishing smack.

The first ships known to have gone down on this coast foundered in November 1473. What type of vessels they were, their cargoes or the names of their masters or crews were of no interest to the medieval scribe who recorded the loss. All he tells us is that the three vessels belonged to one man, Anton Bernal, and that they were sunk by the Portuguese fleet as it chased the French pirate Coulom. Other pirates roamed the coast in historic times. The great Barbarossa (Redbeard), raided all along the Gulf of Cádiz and east through the Straits of Gibraltar into the Mediterranean. Many of those crews which escaped his clutches came to grief running for the safety of Cádiz Bay.

For some, though, the Bay was not protection enough. In 1587, Sir Francis Drake attacked the growing Spanish Armada as it lay peacefully at anchor in the bay. Drake fired some 16 or 17 ships, seized six more packed with supplies and razed the town before standing off to spread terror up and down the coast. In less than three months during that summer, ranging from Cádiz to Lisbon, he captured or sent to the bottom some 60 fishing vessels and 40 coasters laden with materials for the Spanish fleet.

After Drakes' death the English didn't leave Cádiz alone: within six months it was a smoking ruin again. If Drake had "singed the King of Spain's beard", the new fleet under its leaders Essex and Howard was responsible for severe facial burns. They fell on the port with a force of some 80 English and Dutch men-o'-war. The Spanish were obliged to burn the galleons of the Indies fleet in the Bay to prevent their "sumless treasuries" falling into Anglo-Dutch hands.

Today little of this violent period of maritime history survives – just a few naval cannon built into house walls in Cádiz town. But historians, archaeologists and divers still keep their eyes out for the sites of possible treasures from the age of Philip II. ❑

LEFT: old seafarer.

Wayward heart

Cádiz meant much to Alfonso. It gave him a haven from which to launch his ill-fated attack on Salé, in the Moroccan heartland of the Infidel. He wanted to be buried in Cádiz, but his wishes were not carried out. His body now lies in Seville Cathedral; his heart was removed to the monastery of Santa María de las Huertas in Murcia.

The dismembered Alfonso no doubt turned in his several graves as his successors spent the next two centuries reducing the rump of al-Andalus, the Kingdom of Granada. Cádiz remained the seaward end of Christian Spain's frontier until Granada fell and Columbus stumbled across America. With the opening up of the New World, Cádiz entered its own Golden Age.

But the promise of easy pickings attracted pirates – a roughish alley behind the Cathedral (the Calle Piratas) records their passing. And yet, despite the presence of Barbary corsairs, the desperate pleas of the town's *Corregidores* (Governors) for new defences were ignored. The old castle crumbled while the Catholic Monarchs chatted with their fashionable Italian military engineers.

Eventually the massive Anglo-Dutch raid of 1596 (*see page 272*) spurred the Spanish Crown to act. The half-built circuit wall and the projecting gun platforms were quickly finished off, and the Puerta de Tierra replaced the already obsolete Muro.

Old gate

The **Puerta de Tierra Ⓐ**, which took on its present form in the mid-18th century, marks the entrance to the old town. Vandalised in the late 1940s, when two breaches were made in it for the benefit of motorists, the central gate tower is

Map, page 273

BELOW: Santa María de Sanlúcar de Barrameda.

Spain's best known composer, Manuel de Falla, was born in Cádiz. This portrait of him hangs near his grave in Cádiz's Cathedral.

BELOW: declaration of Spain's first constitution, in 1812.

now all but cut off from its protective flanking bastions. The twin lions that defend the white stone escutcheon above the old gate stare out over pretty fountains set within an oval enclave of grass and flowers.

Inside the gate, Cádiz is a jewel of military architecture, defaced only by the railway to the north and by the conflicting Spanish passions either to glorify or to deride history. Right behind the gate itself are 18th-century barrack blocks and arsenals, some still in military hands and others taken over by the fire brigade. Beyond, the town wall is lost beneath tarmac and a not unattractive townscape until it reaches the **Murallas de San Carlos** and the **San Felipe Battery** which are on the far side of the **Plaza de España B**.

In the centre of the plaza stands the **Monument to the Cortes** (Parliament) of 1812. Built for the centenary of its short-lived liberal constitution, the monument commemorates the first, brief, democratic interlude in Spanish history, when most of the country was in fact occupied by Napoleon's troops. It was this Cádiz assembly and its resolutions that gave the word "liberalism" to the world.

From San Carlos the walls form a broad esplanade looking out to sea, though the bastions of Candelaria, Santa Barbara and San Carlos are off limits. Between Santa Catalina and the causeway reaching out to the fortified and still military islet of San Sebastián is the **Caleta**, a crescent-shaped beach dominated by the crumbling arms of the Balneario (bathing resort) de la Palma, built in 1925.

Among the rocks of the causeway, the poor of Cádiz still collect crabs as they did when Benito Pérez Galdós, Spain's Dickens, visited in the 19th century – and as Gabriel, hero of his book *Trafalgar*, did in the previous century. In the back streets by the Cathedral, they still sell the tiny, slime-green crabs to hardy gaditanos and to reckless visitors.

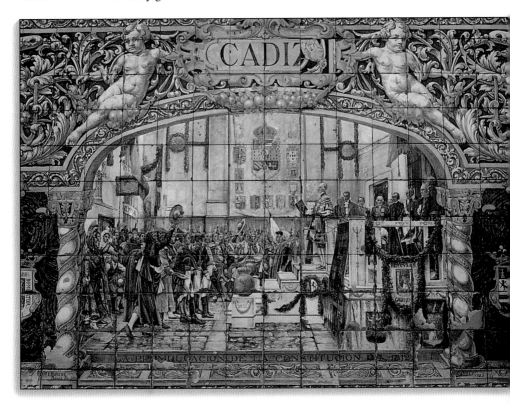

Bird's-eye view

The old city of Cádiz is dotted with churches and monuments. For an initial overview of the sights, make your way to the **Torre Tavira** ● (open daily; admission charge) in the heart of a maze of side streets on Calle Marqués del Real Tesoro. At 46 metres (150 ft) above sea level, this is the tallest of the many towers atop former shipping magnates' town houses, from which lookouts kept an eye on arriving ships in the 18th century. Today it houses a *camera obscura*, from which you can enjoy a 360 degree bird's-eye view of the city thanks to an ingenious system of mirrors and lenses.

Map, page 273

The first building to grab your attention is the **New Cathedral** ● (Catedral) (open mornings Tues-Sat; closed Sun, Mon; admission charge), so called because it replaced the "old" cathedral next door, now officially renamed the church of Santa Cruz (dating from the 13th century, it was destroyed when the British sacked the city in 1592 and had to be rebuilt). The 18th-century New Cathedral's exterior, with its Byzantine-style dome, is more interesting than the interior, although it is the last resting place of one of Spain's best composers, Cádiz-born Manuel de Falla, who died in 1946.

The long history of Cádiz can be traced at the rather modest **Museo Histórico Municipal** ●, (open Tues–Sun; closed 1–4pm and Sat–Sun pm) which contains a remarkable model of Cádiz as it was in 1777, and the more ambitious **Museo Provincial** ● (open mornings Tues–Sun) on the Plaza Mina, which is well worth visiting for its impressive archaeological collections from throughout the province, most notably two Phoenician sarcophagi. The museum's collection is the result of the merging of the former archaeological and fine arts museums, the latter containing a number of works by Zurbaran and Murillo. Across

Visitors in the crypt of the New Cathedral.

BELOW: on horseback in Jerez.

the square from the museum is the **tourist office**, where you can pick up a map to guide you around old Cádiz's complicated maze of narrow streets.

Among the sights are the recently restored 18th-century **Oratorio de la Santa Cueva**  (open Mon–Fri 10am–1pm; admission charge), an oval-shaped chapel with frescoes by Goya, and **Oratorio de San Felipe Neri** ❶ (visits by guided tour only), considered a shrine of Spanish liberalism as it was here that the first *cortes*, or parliament, convened in 1812.

Sherry country

North of Cádiz, over the swing bridge across the bay and past Puerto Real, is the motorway to Seville; there's a stiff toll. Better is the old road through **El Puerto de Santa María** ❷ and **Jerez de la Frontera** ❸, both ringed by the *bodegas* (wine warehouses) of Harvey, Terry, Tío Pepe and Domecq.

The Puerto is a pleasant town with a castle half-hidden by houses and decorated with religious-patriotic slogans in Latin on its tiled towers. Around the town, tourist "attractions" have been built – the Puerto Sherry marina and apartment complex, and the **Aguasherry** sun-and-fun *parque acuático*. Puerto is best known for its **Ribera del Marisco** (shellfish shore), a seafront street lined with restaurants and bars serving fresh seafood.

Jerez has grown rich on the wine trade. Nowadays it is a posh Andalucían city suburb – genteel self-satisfied and pricey. For most visitors, Jerez means sherry-tasting and watching the prancing stallions at the **Real Escuela Andaluza del Arte Ecuestre** (the Royal Andalucían School of Equestrian Art) (shows Thurs 11am; rehearsals other weekdays 11am; admission charge).

West of Jerez, across rolling brown and black claylands, is the fishing port of

ABOVE: one of many famous names.

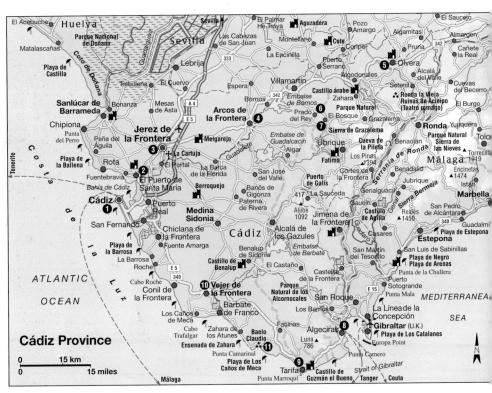

Cádiz Province

0   15 km
0   15 miles

Sanlúcar, once the outport of Seville but now a sprawling, laid-back place, a complete contrast to Jerez. The town looks out across the mouth of the Guadalquivir river to the marshlands of Doñana National Park and an excursion boat takes visitors to stops on the futher shore. To the north, half buried in the dunes, is the castle of **Bonanza**.

Maps:
City 273
Area 276

Windy shore

The coast here is golden sand from Sanlúcar to Rota and, as it faces into the Atlantic winds, a paradise for windsurfers. An unexciting resort of second homes for the middle-class of Cádiz and Seville has grown up at **Chipiona**, once a fishing port and still a market gardening centre. Between Chipiona and Rota a few surviving stone and thatched cottages are crumbling into ruins, to be replaced by flat-roofed cubes. **Rota** is a Spanish naval base with a big US presence, attached to a little fishing port with some surviving medieval defences. To get back to El Puerto and Jerez, the road makes a long detour round the base.

To Rome for bulls,
for tobacco to
Gibraltar,
to Sanlúcar for
sherry
and for salt Cádiz
– POPULAR REFRAIN

White Town territory

East of Jerez, the countryside is more innocent and the wine is rougher. The roads rise gently towards the sierras marking the boundary between the provinces of Cádiz and Málaga. The tourist board's Ruta de los Pueblos Blancos (White Towns route) and the Ruta del Toro (Bullfight route) open up. (For a fuller description of the region, see Exploring the White Towns, *page 261*.)

Twenty-four kilometres (15 miles) out of Jerez de la Frontera along the N342, is the first of the White Towns, **Arcos de la Frontera ❹**. Like the better known and more spectacular town of Ronda, over the border in Málaga province, Arcos

BELOW: fishing in the old *salinas*.

FROM SALT TO FISH

Not so long ago, the marshes around Cádiz and west of Huelva were dotted with snow-white heaps of drying sea-salt. But over the past couple of decades the number of working *salinas* (salt-works) has dropped dramatically, leaving only a handful still in operation for their orginal purpose (the largest is in Puerto de Santa María). They are part of an industry that dates back to pre-Roman times.

Until the 1950s the marshes would have seemed little different from those of 2,000 years ago: the trapped sea water evaporating in the summer heat, the crystalline salts being scooped out to dry by weather-beaten peasants; the salt stored in white heaps before being shipped inland, or being used on the spot to cure hides and salt beef provided by the cattle brought down to the marshes for summer grazing. Salted fish paste, known as *garum* to the Romans, was a valued item of trade. Roman amphoras, made in southern Spain for the transport of *garum*, preceded the legions to the Celtic city of Colchester in remote Britannia. Nowadays the abandoned saltings of the island of Saltés, where the Odiel and Tinto rivers meet the sea, are a recognised sanctuary to migrating water fowl.

Placenames that include the word "Frontera", of which there are several, date from the two and a half centuries before 1492 when the area was indeed the frontier between Christian Spain and the surviving Kingdom of Granada.

sits on a knife-edge of rock. The main street narrows to less than a car's width (or so it seems) as it rises towards the old town centre and the parador in the **Casa del Corregidor**. The plaza in front of the parador is a crowded visitors car park ringed with ancient buildings. From here there are views out over the broad valley of the Guadalete and along the cliff to the church of San Pedro.

The parador is an ideal stop for coffee in luxurious surroundings, but the local cafés down the hill offer the real atmosphere of Andalucía and, for breakfast, home-made orange marmalade on thick-cut toast.

A road staggers down the north face of the Arcos rock to the Bornos reservoir and the Grazalema road, but there are more White Towns on and off the N342. The small town of **Olvera** ❺ lies 68 km (42 miles) to the east. Its narrow streets of white houses are spread over the foot of a steep rock on which stands the Arab castle of Almedina. Further on is **Setenil**, a curious village hacked out of the living rock; the houses and bars are rock-roofed and in places the streets are shaded by threatening overhangs.

North of the Arcos to Grazalema road is **Prado del Rey** ❻ (the King's Field), a White Town with a difference. Founded by King Charles III in 1768 in an attempt to stimulate agricultural reform in Andalucía, this town is something of an early Spanish garden city with wide streets and leafy squares.

Sierra watching

BELOW LEFT AND RIGHT: young stick and old sticks pause for thought.

In **El Bosque** ❼ a small information centre beside the river offers self-guided tours of the **Parque Natural de Sierra de Grazalema**. Set up in 1984 to protect the limestone scenery along the border between Cádiz and Málaga, the park extends from El Bosque to **Benaoján** in the east and **Cortes de la Fron-**

tera to the south. Much of the ancient Mediterranean forest of holm oak and Montpelier maple still survives, but in places the activities of man have converted the forest to open ranges or brush. Here mountain goats can still be seen, with a superb range of birds of prey, including buzzards, griffon vultures and Bonelli's, booted and short-toed eagles.

The towns and villages of the park and its adjacent hills record the area's frontier history. A string of de la Frontera towns runs from Morón to Arcos, Jimena and Castellar, with Cortes probing the Moorish heartland. Throughout the sierra itself the villages have still kept their Moorish names: Benmahoma, Grazalema (once Ben-Zalema), Benaocaz, Ubrique and Zahara, and the line of Ben villages on the Jimena to Ronda road.

Coming down from the sierra to the coast, there are glimpses of the **Rock of Gibraltar**, more impressive from the hills than from the ugly industrial chaos around the Bay of Algeciras. **Algeciras** ❽ itself is best avoided but is almost unavoidable. It is the main Spanish ferry port for the North African destinations of Ceuta and Tangier. Once a town "entirely free of malice" where "even the worst of its crooks were so untrained that no-one was expected to take them seriously", Algeciras has been changed, partly by pressure of constant traffic, partly from doing time under Franco.

Capital surf

On the road for Cádiz, Europe's southernmost town of **Tarifa** ❾ is a "bit of washed-up Africa" which is losing its African-ness to become the windsurfing capital of Spain. Atlantic winds constantly maltreat the length of this shoreline, but at Tarifa, trapped between Europe and Africa, they can be maniacal.

This "Most Noble, Most Loyal and Heroic City" takes its name from Tarif ibn Malluk, who headed a reconnaissance mission here in 710; his enthusiastic report led to the Muslim invasion of Spain in 711. The earliest surviving part of Tarifa's castle is 10th-century, and its fall in 1292 to Christian Spain gave the place its nobility. But it was Alonso de Guzmán's defence of the town two years later that earned it the other titles and the epithet "el bueno" (the good).

Well into the 20th century, the women of Tarifa and nearby Vejer wore the severe, black cobijada – a full-length skirt with a burnous-type cloak which was attached to the waistband. Only the Spanish Civil War really caused the demise of this Moorish-style traditional costume, which was too useful for smuggling arms and supplies to Republican guerrillas behind Franco's lines and was accordingly outlawed.

Vejer de la Frontera ❿ is a White Town of narrow streets, high on a hill with artificial Berber caves at its foot. Between Vejer and Tarifa is the Roman city of **Baelo Claudia** ⓫ (now Bolonia), under restoration. Founded in 171 BC, it has survived remarkably well. Cattle trample the grassy banks of the unexcavated area. Visits are by guided tour (Tues–Sun; closed Sun pm and Mon; admission charge).

On the coast nearby is Cape Trafalgar, beyond which Nelson defeated the combined French and Spanish fleet in 1805. ❏

Map, page 276

Laid-back Tarifa is totally different from the resorts further east: characterful, low-key and, above all, uncommercial.

BELOW: where life's a breeze.

HUELVA AND THE COTO DE DOÑANA

Map, page 284

Huelva's sleepy towns, marshy estuaries and mudflats create an ethereal beauty that belies its powerful past as the centre of the Tartessos civilisation

For most Spaniards, Huelva is just another name to be learnt by rote in a geography class. For most Andalucíans Huelva means the town of Lepe, nationally famous for slow wits and strawberries. For the Portuguese, Huelva is on the way to somewhere else, and for the rest of the world it is somewhere else – but where?

Yet the province of Huelva was once the centre of the powerful Tartessos civilisation; its mines at Rio Tinto were, and are, internationally renowned, and it was from the mouth of the Rio Tinto that Columbus first set sail for the Indies. Perhaps it is the uninspiring, gentle landscape alongside the N431 from Seville that puts people off exploring Huelva province.

PRECEDING PAGES: Coto Doñana Wildlife Park. **LEFT:** a closer look at the park's wildlife **BELOW:** Isla Cristina.

Main stops

The tedious A49 *autopista* is even more discouraging, for it avoids the blood-red walls of **Niebla ❶**. This town stands on the west bank of the Rio Tinto, the coloured river, which stumbles over its rocky bed, a natural kaleidoscope of yellow, orange and red. Once the centre of a wealthy Moorish kingdom, Niebla fell to the Christians in the early 13th century. It was during the siege of Niebla that gunpowder was reputedly first used in European warfare.

Beyond Moorish Niebla and its Roman bridge is the city of **Huelva ❷**, the provincial capital. Founded over 3,000 years ago by Phoenician traders, the early port of trade spread over several *cabezos* (low hills) between the marshy estuaries of the Rio Tinto and the Odiel. Onuba, as the classical world knew Huelva, was an outlet for the Rio Tinto mines, and here Tartessans mingled with Phoenicians, Greeks, Carthaginians and finally Romans. The people of Huelva are now known as *onubenses*.

Huelva is a small town spoilt by industry which has been developed with a callous disregard for the place and its setting. Nevertheless, a refreshingly innocent small-town atmosphere has survived along Huelva's Gran Via.

The town owes much to the last wave of foreign traders attracted by its mineral riches. The English-style "company village", the Reina Victoria *barrio*, built in the 1920s to house the Rio Tinto Company's employees, is one surviving vestige of British commercial colonialism. The local football club, now in the second division with the other "British" teams, was the first to be set up in Spain.

The golf club was another British introduction, and **Punta Umbría** beyond it was founded as the seaside

A stalking heron, just one of many different varieties of birds that inhabit the marsh-lands and mudflats at the mouth of the Odiel river.

resort of Rio Tinto's expat community, who made the trip from Huelva to the Casas de los Ingleses in a tiny paddle steamer. Now Punta Umbría is reached by road and the last "English Houses" were demolished in the 1960s. It remains a mercifully small holiday resort of discos, bars and night-clubs.

Behind Punta Umbría are the **Marismas del Odiel**, the marshlands at the mouth of the Odiel. The flats, from the Isle of Saltés to Gibraleón, have been declared a Paisaje de Interés Nacional (Landscape of National Interest) and include two breeding reserves of special importance for herons and spoonbills.

On **Punta del Sebo**, the tip of land where the Tinto and the Odiel meet, stands a colossal statue to Christopher Columbus, the Spirit of Exploration, sculpted by American Gertrude Whitney, staring out to sea with blind determination and affected heroism.

Monkish enterprise

Over the Rio Tinto are the real monuments to the "Enterprise of the Indies". A complete contrast to the industry around it, **La Rábida monastery** (Tues–Sat; closed 1–4 pm; donation encouraged) is a haven of contemplative peace set in formal gardens. Dedicated in the 13th century soon after the fall of Moorish Huelva, this Franciscan monastery holds a special place in history. Here Columbus met the Friars Antonio de Marchena and Juan Pérez, who took his case to Queen Isabella and persuaded her to back the venture.

The monastery is centred on a Moorish courtyard, converted to a monkish cloister. The Friars provide a guided tour for a small contribution.

Just inside are the Columbus murals, painted by Vázquez Díaz in 1930 and giving a simplified picture history of the "Discovery" of America. Beyond is the

BELOW: horse and rider on the Playa de Doñana.

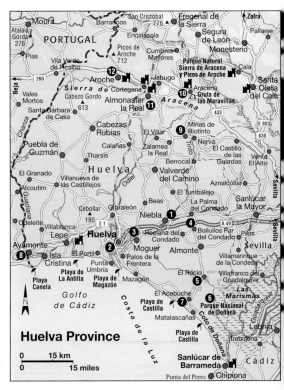

Huelva Province

0 — 15 km
0 — 15 miles

church, built in the early 15th century, with traces of original wall paintings.

Upstairs, above the refectory, is the Sala Capitular (Chapter House) which, but for the modern paintings of Ferdinand and Isabella, is spartanly appointed with heavy Castilian furniture of the Columbus period. The ceiling is a fine piece of Spanish carpentry. Also on the upper floor is the Sala de Banderas, the Flag Room. Something of a place of pilgrimage for South American students attending the University summer schools at La Rábida, the room contains the flags of the South American nations and a casket of soil from each.

Columbus sails again

On the banks of the river 1 km (½ mile) from the monastery is the **Muelle de las Carabelas** (Quay of the Caravels), a reproduction of a 15th-century harbour which opened to visitors in 1994 (open Tues–Sun; closed 2–5pm in summer and Sun; admission charge). The most interesting features of the attraction are the full-scale replicas of Columbus's flotilla, the *Niña, Pinta* and *Santa María*, constructed using the ship-building methods of the time. You can clamber aboard and wonder at how his crew made the two-and-a-half month voyage in such cramped quarters.

Inland from La Rábida is **Palos de la Frontera**. In the plaza, outside the church of San Jorge, the royal order giving the go-ahead to the "Enterprise of the Indies" was read out to the assembled seamen of the town in May 1492. In August that year Columbus's tiny fleet of three caravels set sail from Palos, then an important sea port. The harbour Columbus used now lies beneath dark clayey fields between the present river and the Fontanilla (the Moorish well by San Jorge) from which Columbus provisioned his vessels.

Map, page 284

BELOW: wedding in the grounds of La Rábida Monastery.

The tower of the church of Nuestra Señora de la Granada in Moguer.

BELOW: Jiménez statue in Moguer..

From rhyme to wine

Further upstream again is the town of **Moguer ❸**, the birthplace of poet and writer Juan Ramón Jiménez; his house in the Calle Nueva has been turned into a museum and library (**Casa-Museo Juan Ramón Jiménez**; open daily ; closed 2–5pm and Sun pm; admission charge). Jiménez is perhaps best known for his children's story, *Platero y Yo*, but his poetry eventually won him the 1956 Nobel Prize for Literature.

A poet of the 1927 generation, like García Lorca from the opposite end of Andalucía, Jiménez was able to escape Franco's bully boys – unlike Lorca – and became the Republican government's cultural attaché in the United States. Walking round the Jiménez Casa-Museo (home-cum-museum) is uncomfortably like prying into the private grief of someone else's family. But it does give a remarkable insight into the man's creative genius.

Behind Moguer are the wine-growing lands of the Condado (county) de Niebla – the triangle of gently rolling farmland marked by Niebla itself, Palma del Condado and Almonte. The main *bodegas* are to be found in the three del Condado towns – **La Palma, Rociana** and **Bollullos ❹**, the last being the centre of the largest wine producing cooperative in Andalucía.

The typical wines from here are the amber-coloured, nutty *olorosos*, similar to dark sherry but, living in the shadow of mighty Jerez, Huelva wines never earned much recognition. These days, thanks to modern wine-making techniques which prevent the fussy local grape, the Zalema, from oxidising and turning dark, wine-makers are switching to young, fruity white wines which go well with the local seafood. The best time to check out both the old-fashioned *vino del Condado* and the new-style whites is September, when Bollullos holds

its Feria Agrícola y Artesana (Farm and Craft Fair) and its Día del Vino (Wine Day). At the same time La Palma celebrates its Fiesta de la Vendimia (Grape Harvest Festival), a fruitful fiesta in honour of Nuestra Señora de la Guía which is accompanied by "battles of flowers".

But the area sees more visitors in May for the Romería del Rocío. For most of the year the village of **El Rocío ❺** is a sleepy sprawl of low white houses set around vast red-earth plazas as if it were auditioning for a part as a Mexican backwater in a western movie. Then at Whitsun El Rocío suddenly becomes the most popular spot in Andalucía – full of Spanish beauties dressed in brilliant flounced flamenco dresses and their menfolk in black velvet and frilled white shirts. By day, cries of *"Viva la Virgen"* and the creaking sway of flower-bedecked carts; by night *cante* and guitars, and the unsteady sway of wine-drenched *romeros*.

Wild terrain

El Rocío stands on the edge of the **Parque Nacional de Doñana ❻**, Spain's biggest, and an absolute must for any visitor – no business schedule to western Andalucía is so tightly packed that a day cannot be set aside for Doñana.

Most of the park is a special reserve but guided trips in four-wheel-drive buses start from the visitors' centre (open daily 8am–7pm) at **El Acebuche ❼**. These five-hour excursions leave twice every day. It is prudent to book them up in advance (tel: (955-430432). They are pricey but worth it.

The convoys of three or four green *todoterrenos* (all-terrain vehicles) enter the park through **Matalascañas**, a mini-Benidorm on Huelva's Costa de la Luz. Built in 1965, Matalascañas is on land that should have formed part of the park

Map, page 284

The Coto Doñana is associated with one of Goya's most famous paintings. While staying in the old Coto palace, the artist allegedly painted "The Naked Maja", using as a model his lover, the Duchess of Alba.

BELOW: watching wildlife in the Parque Nacional de Doñana.

The eagle has landed.

– but then the park is still not safe from those with money and *enchufe* (contacts) in high places.

In the park the route follows the beach, where oystercatchers, dunlins and sanderlings scurry officiously among the broken waves and sandwich terns and black-backed gulls swoop low across the cream sands. Once it has reached the Guadalquivir estuary the convoy then swings towards the centre of the park, through pine forest and Mediterranean brush, past the former hunting lodge, the **Palacio de los Marismillas,** and the neolithic *chozas* – reed and pine branch huts – of the charcoal burners. In among the trees stands a wary red deer stag; a fallow deer flicks a contemptuous white rump at humanity, and a black and bristly boar saunters across the track. From time to time a shy lynx shows itself.

Along the edge of the **Lucio del Membrillo** – almost solid land in summer, almost a lake in winter – the convoy stops at the deserted **Casa del Cerro del Trigo.** Here, in the right season, flock pink flamingos, grey-lags, spoonbills and all sorts of ducks, and at any time of the year the rare imperial eagle surveys his empire from the topmost branches of a pine.

The vehicles turn back toward the ocean again, through more pines, to the dunes; these moving mountains of sand are slowly but surely burying part of the pine wood. And over the crest of a dune, the sea appears again and the drivers swap the lead so their passengers always have a chance to be the first to spot a new species. Visitors can only explore on foot the outskirts of the park around the El Acebuche centre and the smaller centre at La Rocina.

BELOW:
the Río Tinto
("coloured river").

Outside the Doñana Park, the stretch of coast from Matalascañas to the outskirts of Huelva is one long beach, backed by dunes and pines – a virtually unspoilt windsurfers' paradise with exquisite Atlantic sunsets. The coast beyond

THE RÍO TINTO

Writing in the 4th century, the chronicler Avienus in his *Ora Maritima* noted a Mount Argentario whose "slopes glint and shine in the light when the sun's rays ward the earth's surface. The river Tartesors is ladened with nuggets of ore and washes the precious metal to the very doors of the city." The Greeks and the Phoenicians trekked the length of the Mediterranean to get that ore, and the local Iberian tribesmen founded the Tartessos civilisation on the back of the profits they made. But it was Roman engineers that developed the potential of Río Tinto's resources. The Roman miners – first slaves, then free men – worked in galleries 1 metre (3 ft) in diameter, their only light coming from tiny oil lamps placed in wall niches. The problem of flooding was solved with waterwheels (*norias*) that lifted the water from one level to another. The mines survived the fall of Rome and the town of Niebla grew into a powerful Moorish enclave through its control of Río Tinto. Later, the easy pickings that were to be had in the Americas almost put an end to the mines. They were finally bought in 1873 by a consortium of British and German bankers. Today, the mines are the property of the miners themselves, who continue to extract copper, as well as smaller amounts of gold and silver.

Huelva is similar in many ways, though behind the dunes there are lagoons and wild or drained marshland. Huelva produces most of Spain's strawberries and the fields around **Lepe** are carpeted with this fruit. **Isla Cristina** and **Isla Canela** have become popular holiday resorts.

The so-called coastal road, 5 km (3 miles) back from the shore, heads towards Portugal but first reaches **Ayamonte ❽**, and its parador, on the banks of the Rio Guadiana, which forms the border between the two countries. A bridge now spans the river, giving easy access to the Algarve coast.

Northern Jewels

Some of Huelva's best but least known sights are in the north of the province. The **Sierra de Aracena** is, perhaps, the real jewel of Huelva. The road out of Huelva climbs steadily through the fields of Trigueros and Valverde until the mountains begin before Zalamea. A diversion to **Minas de Rio Tinto ❾** reveals an otherworldly landscape of purple and vermilion near the vast open-air mines.

Throughout Spain the town of Lepe is famous for its strawberries

The mines used to be owned by the British-owned Rio Tinto Company, which built a railway between the mines and the port of Huelva. Now the miners themselves own the mines, and have started well-organised tours, taking in the **Museo Minero** (Mining Museum), with interesting displays of archaeological artifacts, old mining gear, and historical railway cars; visits to Corta Atalaya, one of the largest open-pit mines in the world, and to the English-style Barrio de Bellavista where the mining company's head honchos lived; and a train trip along 20 km (12 miles) of the old miners' railway (open mornings Tues–Sun; miners' train runs daily Jul–Aug, weekends rest of year; admission charge).

BELOW: Ayamonte on the Guadiana.

Heading north, you reach the wooded hills that lead to **Aracena ❿**, the main town in the Sierra de Aracena nature park. Aracena is a huddle of white walls and Spanish tiles around the Moorish castle. Tacked on to it is the massive, parapeted church built by the Knights Templar. But its great attraction is below ground – the **Gruta de las Maravillas** (the Grotto of the Marvels) (open daily; visits by guided tour only) – a complex of caves over 2 km (1 mile) in length and furnished with curtains and pillars of petrified water. At the entrance is a collection of minerals from throughout the world.

From Aracena towards Portugal the wooded sierra is dotted with villages famous for their *jamón serrano* (cured ham). The best hams reputedly come from **Jabugo**, but villages like Fuenteheridos, Alájar, Castaño del Robledo and Cortegana are prettier and their hams just as good.

At **Almonaster la Real ⓫** is another Moorish castle. The castle church is a converted mosque with its internal brick pillars still intact after over a millennium; Almonaster is the common man's Córdoba. A bullring hangs suspended from the castle walls.

Halfway to Portugal is **Aroche ⓬**, which has a Moorish castle, cobbled African streets and working medieval tile kilns. If Huelva is Andalucía's Cinderella, Aroche is Huelva's; nothing much has happened here since a lost detachment of Christian knights stumbled across it in the 13th century and replaced the Moorish lord with a Castilian one. ❑

Map, page 284

GIBRALTAR

Map, page 294

This massive lump of limestone, known as the Rock, stands at a point where Africa and Europe almost touch and the Atlantic and Mediterranean almost merge – at a crossroads of civilisations

Anyone who lands at Gibraltar airport confronts at once a significant fragment of Gibraltar's history. There, high up on the north face of the rock, which rises ahead like a great grey canine tooth, are the embrasures through which British cannon shot down on the Spanish during the Great Siege of Gibraltar, just one in a long history of wars which focused on this commanding lump of stone.

Siege upon siege

This particular siege lasted from 18 June 1779 to 30 January 1783 and was part of the American War of Independence, when Spain and France – to simplify a complex story – saw Britain losing her American colonies and ganged up to capture British possessions which they coveted. For Spain this meant Gibraltar above all.

General Eliot, in charge of the British defenders of the Rock, had other ideas. It was across the flat isthmus which separates Gibraltar from Spain and now supports the airport runway that Eliot's troops sallied out from at 2.45am on 27 November 1781 in one of his most successful defensive actions. The British overran the three closest Spanish batteries, spiked their guns, set fire to their timber emplacements and blew up their powder magazines. Conveniently, the captured Spanish duty officer had the magazines' keys in his pocket and their replicas can be seen in Gibraltar's museum – the originals are in the British Army Museum, London.

The airfield's runway belongs to the history of a different struggle: World War II. It was built in the early 1940s, and, because the isthmus was narrow, had to be extended by the mining and dumping of a million tonnes of limestone into Gibraltar bay. It still seems none too long to air travellers who are liable to giggle with relief when the roar of their plane's reversed engines halts it just short of the Mediterranean.

The siege of 1779–83 was the 14th the Rock had survived. Immediately on the Spanish side of the airport's terminal building are the Spanish frontier gates, a reminder of what is now called the 15th siege, though this was a bloodless one. These gates were shut to Gibraltarians on 6 May 1968 on Franco's orders and a year later to Spaniards as well. Soon afterwards the ferry to Algeciras across Gibraltar bay was suspended and telephone connections to Spain were cut. For 11 years the Rock was totally isolated.

The most dramatic effect was that Gibraltar, deprived of the 4,666 Spanish who used to cross from Spain every day, was forced to recruit some 3,000 Moroccans to do not just the more menial jobs but also to staff banks and offices. This partly explains

PRECEDING PAGES: bobby on Main Street. **LEFT:** Gibraltar Marina. **BELOW:** the Moorish Castle.

the Arab costumes in Gibraltar's streets today. Water was shipped in tankers daily to the Rock from Tangier.

Also prominent at the north end of the Rock are relics of Gibraltar's earlier sieges, in particular the solid and square Moorish castle and the Moorish wall zig-zagging up to it. Gibraltar, like the rest of Spain, formed part of the Roman Empire, and subsequently fell under Visigothic control when the empire collapsed. But for 740 years from AD 711, apart from one brief interval, it was Moorish.

Gibraltar's name comes from the Moorish commander Tarik ibn Zyad (Jebel Tarik – Mountain of Tarik), who, historians now guess, landed on the Rock's east coast, perhaps as far north as Punta Mala.

British conquest

The Moors were finally driven from Gibraltar in 1462 as part of the Christian Reconquest of Spain. For another 250 years the Rock was Spanish, and it was not till 1704 that the British first hoisted the Union Jack on the Moorish castle where it has flown ever since. In 1704 General Rooke was not actually claiming Gibraltar for Britain, but merely occupying it on behalf of one of several contenders for the Spanish throne. In 1714, however, by the Treaty of Utrecht, the Rock officially became British.

Between the Moorish castle and the shore stand the defensive walls and gun batteries which the British then started to build. The old town which these were defending has gone, so badly damaged in 1727 during a Spanish attempt to recapture it (the 13th siege) that it was demolished and the area levelled to form Casemates Square. Here twice a year the ceremony of the keys is re-enacted, when at sunset the Governor of Gibraltar, in full dress uniform with white topee, is handed the keys by the Port Sergeant after he has locked various of Gibraltar's gates, just as General Eliot was handed them nightly during the Great

BELOW: fighting old battles in the museum.

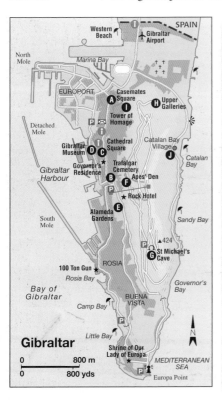

Siege. "God Save the Queen" is played and loyal Gibraltarians clap. Most are loyal: in 1967, 12,138 voted to remain British and just 44 for return to Spain.

Map, page 294

Landmarks

From **Casemates Square** Ⓐ there are several ways to explore today's town, which extends southwards and can be pictured as a frill to the Rock's tall skirt. Still narrow, the town is today creeping up the Rock, as engineers manage to find footing for more houses on the steep slopes above. More land has also been created by filling in the old harbour.

The conventional route south leads along **Main Street**, among jostling tourists, past fish and chip shops, pubs claiming to have been serving fine ales since the 18th century and innumerable window displays of duty-free cameras and watches. Here, too, is the **Governor's Residence**, once a Franciscan convent, the back side of the **Cathedral** and a re-erected church archway, one of the few fragments saved from the old town.

At the southern end, beyond a defensive wall built in 1540 after the pirate Barbarossa had attacked Gibraltar and taken many of its people to sell as slaves, in a little triangular depression is the so-called **Trafalgar Cemetery** Ⓑ. In fact, it was a cemetery from 1708 to 1835 and was used for the burial of English seamen who died from wounds received at three naval battles besides Trafalgar.

It was to Gibraltar that Nelson's ship the *Victory* was towed back, Nelson's body on board in a barrel of brandy. One tradition says that the body was brought ashore and placed in Vincent House, Rosia Bay, but others claim that the seamen of the *Victory* would never have parted with it. Certainly they insisted on sailing it home themselves in their temporarily repaired ship.

Intermarriage of different waves of immigrants means that Gibraltar has an amazing genetic mix. It includes Spaniards, Britons, Maltese, Portuguese, Sephardic Jews and Genoans. There are churches of every description, plus Jewish synagogues, a Hindu temple and the King Fahd mosque.

BELOW: the Key Ceremony.

Rock Talk

Thirty thousand years ago, a primitive people were living the final years of their race in the caves of Gibraltar. Today, archaeologists from Gibraltar, the United Kingdom and Spain are painstakingly trying to reconstruct the way they lived. Gorham's Cave, a grotto discovered in 1907 by a British Army captain, could hold the clue to the mysterious disappearance of an entire race.

By one of those quirks of history, we know him as Neanderthal Man, but he should more correctly be called *Homo calpensis*, "Gibraltar Man". In 1848, the skull of a woman was discovered at the foot of the northern face of the Rock. No one paid much attention to it until a similar skull was found eight years later in the Neander valley, Germany, and scientists discovered it belonged to a hitherto unknown race of men. The world was theirs for hundreds of thousands of years, yet they suddenly disappeared, perhaps killed off or crowded out by our own ancestors. Gibraltar

was to be the scene of the final confrontation – the Rock's first siege.

Gibraltar is a place where things happen. This 426-metre (1,398-ft) rock stands at the point where Africa and Europe almost touch. It has always been in the path of great historical events, fought over since the dawn of history. Even today, it continues to inspire heated debate and give headaches to politicians in far-off capitals, as Spain continues to claim Gibraltar as part of Spanish territory.

All efforts to engage Gibraltarians in topics other than their uneasy relationship with the government in Madrid end in failure, for sooner or later the conversation turns to "The Frontier". Ever since the English snatched Gibraltar during the War of Spanish Succession, Spain has been trying to get it back

Gibraltar receives around five million visitors a year, the majority day trippers, British residents in Spain on shopping sprees to Safeways, Spaniards visiting to see what all the fuss is about and to load up on cigarettes, whisky and cheap petrol. First-time visitors to the Rock usually find something completely different from what they expected. Spaniards from the north, hoping to meet people in bowler hats speaking Oxford English, are instead confronted with a Mediterranean people conversing in thick Andalucían Spanish. English tourists likewise fail to find the little piece of England they expected.

Around every corner there is something to confuse the issue. Double-decker buses, red phone booths and more than 40 English-style pubs notwithstanding, this is an undoubtedly Mediterranean town. For every Union Jack, there is Gibraltar's own proud symbol, the Key and the Fortress – a coat of arms conveyed on them by a Spanish Queen, Isabella La Católica. The Trafalgar Tavern is headquarters for the local Barcelona Football Club fans, while across the street at the Piccadilly Tavern Gibraltarians queue up for their morning *churros*. *Pesetas* are just as welcome in local shops as sterling, and the locals switch between Spanish and English in mid-sentence. They even have words that don't exist in other languages, like *manolo* for manhole and *marchapie* for pavement. ❏

LEFT: the *Gibraltar Chronicle*, founded in 1801, is one of the oldest newspapers in the world.

Cannon quarters

A route south with as much history and less tourism begins with the Wall Road and runs just within the great stone ramparts that protected the town from attack by sea. Here, in **Cathedral Square** ⓒ, the most impressive of Gibraltar's cannon, a row of nine, faces out into the bay. Gibraltar must have more cannon per square metre than anywhere else in the world and these nine were no doubt among those which fired red-hot balls during the most famous of all engagements of the Great Siege.

On 13 September 1782 D'Arcon's 10 bombarding vessels, specially constructed with double hulls in between which were sandwiched layers of cork, tow (hemp fibre) and sand, specially shaped so that the enemies' cannon balls would roll off into the sea, sailed into the bay. At first they seemed invincible, but gradually the red-hot balls imbedded in their timbers set them alight. By the end of the next day, nine had exploded or burned to the waterline and the tenth been abandoned and destroyed. More than 2,000 of their 5,000 crew members died and the planned landing was abandoned.

Close to Cathedral Square stands Gibraltar's admirable small **museum** ⓓ (open Mon–Sat; closed Sat pm and Sun). As everywhere in Gibraltar, military history predominates, but the building incorporates the well-preserved 14th-century **Moorish Baths**.

Beyond the southern end of the town lie the **Alameda Gardens** ⓔ, a pleasant spot though the effort of maintaining something so bosky in Gibraltar's climate is apparent, and Eliot's Memorial, his bust with its great hooked nose topping a column surrounded, inevitably, by four small cannon. A short climb leads to Gibraltar's best-known inn, the Rock Hotel, with its fine views across

Map, page 294

ABOVE: Spanish hats strike a paradoxical note in the shops.
BELOW: Bar girls in Irish town.

Although at first glance it may seem barren, the Rock in fact is home to 530 plant species, including three that are unique to Gibraltar.

the bay to Algeciras. Next to it is Gibraltar's small but lively gambling casino.

Gibraltar's other curiosities are sited high up on the western face of the rock, a steep slope naturally coated with dense scrub and the home for a surprising amount of wildlife, from rabbits and partridges to the famous apes, but now laced with paths and small roads. The energetic will gain more by walking these (though a full circuit will fill most of a day) than by taking a rock tour in a minibus or taxi, or by being swept to the top in today's **cable car** (every 15 minutes 9.30am–5.15pm; fare includes admission to Apes' Den and St Michael's Cave: *see below*), where a restaurant of the baked-beans-and-chips variety perches on the very edge of the Rock's vertical eastern face.

Here there was once a signal station, but it was eventually abandoned because its view was so often spoiled by the Levanter, the easterly wind which is forced up by the Rock to form a cloud over its summit. Beyond the lip, where wisps of cloud continually form, there is a view vertically down to the great concrete catchment area at the bottom. Water has always been one of Gibraltar's problems, and patches of the western face of the Rock have now also been concreted to collect more.

Apes and caves

Close by stands another of Gibraltar's defensive walls, this one built by Philip II, husband of Britain's Queen Mary. Steps lead down behind it directly to the **Apes' Den ❻** (open 9.30am–7pm). According to tradition, Britain will lose Gibraltar only when the apes go. During the last world war, Winston Churchill, hearing the numbers were getting low, signalled that they must be preserved. As a result, the army took charge and the Apes' Den was built.

BELOW: the cable car climbs the Rock.

They are friendly creatures, a lot smaller than postcards suggest, and will pose for the camera, obligingly rattle the branches of a dead olive tree and even sit on your shoulders – though if you make a sudden noise or movement they may run off with your handbag, wallet or spectacles. The apes of a less tame pack roam the Middle Rock area.

The apes (actually tail-less monkeys) were probably brought to Gibraltar by the Moors – there is a similar species in the Atlas Mountains – but according to another tradition they came across the Straits by underground tunnel. No doubt the supposedly bottomless **St Michael's Cave** ➌ (open 9.30am–7pm) is the origin of this story. In 1840 two British officers who descended into these caves never returned and no subsequent expedition has found their bones.

The entrance to the cave – one of 140 that exist on the Rock – is further south on the same rock face, an easy walk from the Apes' Den. At once you step down into a vast cavern with such good acoustics that it is used today as a concert hall. More remarkable are the smaller caves beyond, where there are fewer coloured lights and the vast curtains of stalactites are left to make their own impression. This section can only be visited with a guide.

Vital tunnel

At the northern end of the Rock's western face is the entrance to the **Upper Galleries** ➍ (open 9.30am–7pm), leading to those embrasures from which the British shot down on the Spanish during the Great Siege. When inspecting his troops one day Eliot was heard to say, "I will give 1,000 dollars to anyone who can suggest how I can get a flanking fire upon the enemy."

One of his officers, Sergeant Major Ince, at once suggested tunnelling through

Map, page 294

ABOVE a private investigator.
BELOW: Catalan Bay is Gibraltar's best beach.

Map,
page
294

TIP

The price of many goods is cheaper on Gibraltar than in Spain. Good buys include electronics, watches, jewellery, spirits, tobacco and cashmere.

BELOW: St Michael's Cave. **RIGHT:** cheeky monkey.

the rock to make a way for cannon to be hauled up to the Notch, a projection high on the Rock's north face. After five weeks, using sledgehammers and blasting powder, the miners had made a 2.4 metre (8 ft) square tunnels 25 metres (82 ft) long. At this point they decided to blow a side hole for ventilation. When the dust had cleared it was obvious that this hole already provided a perfect point from which to fire down on the isthmus. One of Lt Koelher's "depression guns", used to fire downhill, can be seen today in Casemates Square.

When the Great Siege ended and the commander of the French and Spanish forces, the Duc de Crillon, was shown the galleries he commented that the works were worthy of the Romans. Once the embrasures had been opened the miners were under fire from Spanish guns and, to protect themselves, employed two members of the Soldier Artificer Company with good eyesight to shout out when a shot was fired by the enemy and where the ball was coming from.

The galleries were continued for another couple of years after the siege was lifted and now lead to St George's Hall, a hollow under the Notch large enough to house a seven-gun battery .

This was by no means the end of tunnelling on the Rock. During World War II the Royal Engineers built another 48 km (30 miles) of tunnel, which can be seen by arrangement. The Tunnelling Company of the last war could tunnel 55 metres (181 ft) a week.

Older remains

Towards the northern end of the Rock stands the Moorish castle. Known as the **Tower of Homage ❶** (open 9.30am–7pm), the present castle is by no means the first to be built on or near the site, but dates from the middle of the 14th century. Massive and solid, it has little interior to see except four small upper rooms. In these rooms, the Spanish governor of Gibraltar held out in a siege for five weeks in 1467 against the Duke of Medina Sidonia who had already captured the rest of Gibraltar for his Queen, Isabella.

Beside the seaside

To indulge in seaside pleasures, leave Gibraltar town, go round the northern end of the Rock and reach the Mediterranean just south of the airport runway. Here there is a bleak sandy beach. Continue south along a rocky shore to the charming settlement of **Catalan Bay ❷** founded by Genoese shipbuilders. Ignore the monstrous hotel on the point, which could as easily stand on any other beach from Bali to the Bahamas, and eat delicious fish at one of the little Anglo-Spanish pub-cafés down by the shore.

It was to Catalan Bay, in 1811, that the inhabitants of San Roque, then the first town across the Spanish border, fled when the French army approached in an attempt to stop the supplies which Wellington's army was receiving from Gibraltar.

Finally, for a view of Africa through a telescope, go to Gibraltar's southern tip, Europa Point, a barren area of old military foundations. From Mediterranean Step Morocco's shore rests like a two-humped camel on the horizon. ❏

GOING TO MOROCCO

The ferry ride from Spain to Morocco is one of the most dramatic short journeys a traveller can make. It is well worth venturing across the Strait, particularly if you have never visited North Africa

Map, page 306

The legendary Pillars of Hercules – the Rock of Gibraltar paired with Ceuta's Monte Hacho on the African coast – formed a colossal entrance to the classical world. Modern travellers veer past this Mediterranean gateway and touch the face of Africa, only 16 km (10 miles) away from Spain at the narrowest point, so close that there has even been talk of a bridge. It is a short journey that takes the traveller straight into the perplexities of Africa. Spain's North African enclaves, Ceuta and Melilla, may ease the transition into a thoroughly different world, while entry direct into Morocco at Tangier or Tetouan will be abrupt, and bound to be either thrilling or frightening or both.

Getting there

The usual port of embarkation for Morocco is Algeciras. Ferries leave regularly for the 90-minute voyage to Ceuta (Sebta in Arabic) or 2½ hours to Tangier. Although often a glorious daytrip, with dolphins trailing in the ferry's wake, the crossing can be miserable. Sometimes it is fraught with delays and tedious passport formalities, and in July and August mobs of exhausted Moroccan migrant workers compete for seats and car spaces, sleeping rough at the quayside to keep their place in the queue.

In clear weather, the Transtour hydrofoils will speed travel without increasing the price much; but they don't run on Sundays or when the Straits are choppy.

The trip to Tangier from Algeciras or Gibraltar takes an hour, but with only one departure a day. In summer three hydrofoils a day leave from Tarifa, the windsurfing mecca west of Algeciras, for a quick half-hour run to Tangier, but the service can be erratic. In August, a ferry runs between Málaga and Tangier, a four-hour trip.

Gibraltar can be a quick escape-hatch, and is underused by Moroccans, even though the frontier with Spain has long been reopened. In high season, there is a convenient hydrofoil link from Gibraltar to Mdiq, north of Tetouan, which takes a little more than an hour. Book early for this, because Costa del Sol tour groups can easily fill all seats. In addition, GibAir has reasonable flights to Tangier and Casablanca.

To reach Melilla, Spain's eastern Moroccan enclave, takes considerably longer. Trasmediterranea ferries travel during the day from Málaga (an 8½-hour trip) or from Almería through the night (also 8½ hours). Dreadful crowds are a hazard in August. If time is a priority, there are regular air connections from Málaga or Almería as well. For the most complete advice on crossing the Straits of Gibraltar, contact Turafrica, who are based in Fuengirola (tel: 952-471899 or 461452).

PRECEDING PAGES: leaving Europe behind. **LEFT:** parador in Spanish Morocco. **BELOW:** you can step into Africa at several points, including Tangier's port.

There are plenty of exotic experiences in store – some designed specially for tourists.

Cautionary words

Without your own set of wheels, you must expect some harassment at bus stations and taxi ranks on the Moroccan side. Speakers of French or Spanish will be able to negotiate reasonable fares for communal Gran Taxis. These are battered Mercedes which make routine trips between main Moroccan towns. Anyone who has visited Israel should apply for a duplicate passport, as Arab League guidelines make it possible for Moroccan border officials to bar any tourist who has an Israeli visa.

Save exchange slips, for after 48 hours you may legally convert only half of your money back from *dirhams*. In Tangier and Tetouan some shops will take *pesetas* or American dollars.

Today's Morocco is surprisingly dense with people, and there is virtually no solitude. Even if you think you are alone, you will be watched intently, so any sense of privacy vanishes. The meek might prefer to go herded in a tour group, but do remember that all those hustlers are only the most brazen face of Morocco. There is generous hospitality and frank curiosity here.

The usual advice is to travel south as quickly as possible to escape threatening border towns like Tangier or Tetouan. If you have time to delve deep, do press on to Fez, to Marrakesh and eventually to the Berber villages in the Atlas valleys. Even the most fleeting encounter with the Moors will enhance your understanding of Andalucía.

Garrison town

Those who enter Africa at **Ceuta ❶** (Sebta) won't need to contend with such stresses, for they haven't technically left Spain. Ceuta is a dusty garrison town

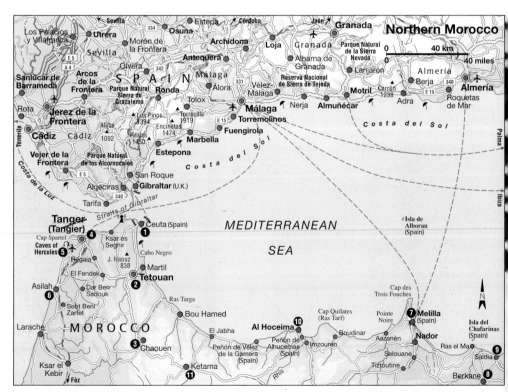

with the dubious appeal of duty-free shops. Row after row of digital watches, portable radios, cigarettes, booze, batteries and bootleg cassettes are on sale.

Most tourists hurry through to the border at **Fnideq** where they can change their money and enter Morocco. However, it is worth dawdling in Ceuta to climb up to the Hermitage of San Antonio atop Monte Hacho, just to look across to Gibraltar. The mythological moment of standing atop a Pillar of Hercules is marred for some by a grandiose monument to General Franco, who in July 1936 crossed over from Ceuta with Nationalist troops at the beginning of the Spanish Civil War. The Spanish Foreign Legion museum is rather meagre, but the Cathedral of Our Lady of Africa is a proud assertion of Catholicism.

Ceuta was first snatched from the Moors in 1415 by the Portuguese and now bears few Arab traces. Strategic towers survey the Campo de Moros (Field of Moors), and the Spaniards hold on to this outpost with as much patriotic tenacity as the Britons show towards Gibraltar.

Tetouan first stop

After the rather Frenchified resorts on the coast (**Smir-Restinga**, **Cabo Negro** and **Martil**), **Tetouan ❷** itself may be overpowering. Clusters of insistent multilingual youths lie in wait for first-time tourists. Each promises protection against the other seedy types loitering nearby, with no motive other than friendship (plus, of course, an appropriate fee and a commission on any purchases). Their clamouring can become oppressive, along with the constant offers of hashish. Don't be tempted to shop until you've become more familiar with your surroundings. You needn't stick to the new town, even though the *medina* or city centre, with its main entrance off Place Hassan II, can be confusing at first.

Map, page 306

Cactus fruit (also known as prickly pear and Barbary fig) is a common cure for upset stomachs.

BELOW: pottery for sale near Chaouen.

The Berber name of Tetouan translates as "Open your Eyes", and a new arrival will be blinking in wonder after the first quick turn around the souk. This warren of vendors hawking pottery, brass, leather slippers and textiles is not as confusing as it seems, for each item is assigned its own area.

Tetouan's *medina* is not so immense that you need worry about never re-emerging. Since it backs up on a hill, you can climb up and survey the walls for an exit. The city ladies here are clad in tailored *djellabas* and sheer veils squared off below the chin, accentuating their kohl-lined eyes.

Turbulent history

More than almost any other place in Morocco, Tetouan is a true Andalucían town, built by Spanish Jews and Muslims fleeing persecution in the 15th century. Before that, it was a Barbary pirates' lair and a base for raiding Portuguese Ceuta. In contrast to imperial Moroccan cities where the architecture harkens back to the Almohad extravagance of 8th-century Spain, the tile trim and dainty wrought-iron balconies on Tetouan's white houses would fit into the popular quarters of Córdoba or Seville.

When Spaniards feared a menace to their stronghold at Ceuta in 1859, they seized the city for three years. Spanish soldiers came again in 1913, using Tetouan as a base for forays into the Rif. There is little sign of the prolonged aerial bombardment Tetouan suffered from the Republicans at the start of the Spanish Civil War.

Many who used to live in Tetouan's old Jewish quarter, the Mellah el Bali, have emigrated to Israel or moved to the "new" quarter along the Rue Msallah, which is a mere 300 years old. The name mellah is derived from the Arabic for salt, and has come to be the generic term for an old Jewish neighbourhood. In the past, Jews were called on to salt the decapitated heads of criminals or enemies as a means of preservation for what went on to be a grisly display on the ramparts.

Mountain retreat

A highland village south of Tetouan, **Chaouen** ❸ may draw its share of visitors, but the Berber inhabitants stay unperturbed. Stone houses teeter over steep cobbled streets. Around many unscreened windows, some hand has brushed paint of an ethereal blue, believed to repel flies and the evil eye.

Until the Spanish marched on it in 1920, Chaouen had deliberately been kept isolated. Only four Europeans had laid eyes on the place, a sacrosanct pilgrimage site containing the *marabout* or shrine of Moulay Abdessalam ben Mchich.

As a hidden base founded to attack the Portuguese in Ceuta, the town attracted Marranos, refugees who were banished from Spain after the fall of Granada, and soon became rabidly hostile to all Europeans. Four centuries later, in 1921, the Spanish were driven out with a loss of 10,000 lives. The attitude towards foreign visitors has changed considerably since then. There is now a growing number of hotels, including a Spanish-style parador with swimming pool, at the top of the *medina*.

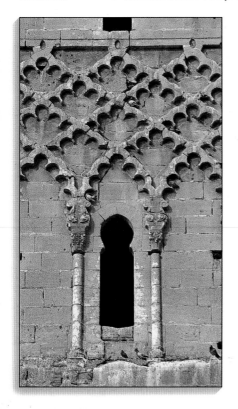

BELOW: the Tour Hassan in Morocco's capital, Rabat, is one of three such minarets built by the Almohads. The other two are in Seville (the Giralda: *see page 146*) and Marrakesh.

Chaouen is a gentle interlude in Morocco. It has an elaborate women's steam-bath (*hammam*) in the *medina*, and a separate one for men. Buses run daily to the border at Ceuta, just two hours away.

Map, page 306

African perdition

The decadent, deviant image of **Tangier ❹** is sometimes traced to its louche days as a neutral International Zone, from 1923–56, when a free-living cosmopolitan community was governed by a council of seven European nations plus a committee of Jews and Muslims. But American humorist Mark Twain had already dismissed "that African perdition called Tangier" years before. Successions of Phoenicians, Carthaginians, Romans, Moors, Portuguese and English who ruled this port city doubtlessly complained about the wily con-men and flagrant brothels they found.

Today, it's quite obvious that some of the locals are descended from Vandals and pirates. Nevertheless, if you keep your wits about you, pleasant adventures await in the wide boulevards of the Ville Nouvelle, the cafés of the Petit Socco or the Place de France, the broad beaches and the narrow alleys of the *medina*. The old bullring has been fashioned into flats, but local guides will prefer pointing out villas owned by millionaire celebrities, including Sidi Hosni which once belonged to the flamboyant Woolworth heiress Barbara Hutton and one that belonged to the late Malcolm Forbes, the American tycoon.

To see what talented Moorish artisans can produce, visit the Dar el Makhzen, the former sultan's palace, for its displays of regional arts, especially the exquisite ceramics and some Delacroix sketches of 19th-century Tangier. The Café Detroit just below the palace is a relaxing spot for a glass of mint tea. This

The indigenous Tangier aroma, compounded of flowers, spices, hashish and Arab drains, is infiltrated by the pungent smell of typewriter ribbon from the overheated portables of best-selling London and New York novelists

– KENNETH ALLSOP

The Daily Mail 1959

BELOW: collecting water near Al Hoceima.

In the autumn, melons are sold by the roadside in abundance, especially along the Atlantic Coast.

ubiquitous drink – more mint than tea and more sugar than either – was unknown until the British introduced tea here in the 18th century.

The British imperial presence is still felt at St Andrew's, an odd Anglican church which grafts a simple English graveyard on to an Arabesque fantasy, built in 1894. The old American Legation, the earliest US diplomatic residence, dates from 1777 when the Sultan Moulay ben Abdallah was the first sovereign to recognise American independence. The sultan's historic letter to George Washington is on display in the library.

Just outside Tangier, at **Cap Spartel**, are the **Caves of Hercules** ❺. These seaside grottoes are worthwhile if you don't have time for the 29-km (18-mile) journey along the Atlantic coast to the fortified town of **Asilah** ❻, a former Portuguese settlement and now a trendy artists' colony.

Melilla

Spain's smaller and quieter enclave, **Melilla** ❼, is a dreary duty-free port and centre of black market currency exchange. Spanish colonial buildings, few dating back as far as the first occupation in 1497, give its narrow hilly streets almost the look of a Latin American *pueblo*. Fittingly enough, the rebel forces that launched the Spanish Civil War started their campaign from this plaza on 17 July 1936.

Palms shade the Plaza Mayor where a zodiac is laid out in the stones. The *pueblo*'s fortifications are almost over-restored, with drawbridges and the vestiges of moats. Moroccan merchants stride around in pointed slippers that match the yellow of the market melons. With a small community of Indian traders, the town is more cosmopolitan than ones in more typical Spanish provinces.

BELOW: Melilla

Down the only road, which means that passing through town is unavoidable, **Nador** is truly the nadir of northern Morocco. The Spaniards deserted it in 1957 and now this bleak place lacks most amenities you'd expect in a provincial capital. Move on quickly if you can.

Kariet Arkmane, out past the airport, is an estuary favoured by flamingos. Further east, the road goes through the sheer **Zegzel Gorge** and up into the mountains. One cavern near Taforalt has an odd stalactite shaped like a camel. **Berkane ❽** is the market town for the terraced orchards which the road climbs through, and the only semblance of a resort is over on the Algerian border. The sandy beach at **Saidia ❾** extends for 14 km (9 miles), with a fringe of woods and a town for a change of pace.

Floating on the horizon are the **Islas Chafarinas**, a cluster of three small Spanish islands. The biggest one is **Congreso**, home to fishing eagles, cormorants, gulls and endangered monk seals which live nowhere else in Iberia. It is almost wilderness, aside from a tidy Spanish plaza and a lighthouse. Transport to the Chafarinas is by private launch, which may draw undue suspicion in this smuggling zone. Sporadic road checks for drugs and arms are common on all roads leading from Nador and Melilla.

Travelling west from Nador, the road passes a turn-off to a pretty valley cut through the foothills of the Rif Mountains by the Nekor river. Beyond lies **Al Hoceima ❿**, a rather bland Euro-resort built around a wide bay. It offers calm beaches and a good respite from the gruelling roads ahead in the Rif. On the landmark Peñon de Alhucemas, a fortress church has been converted to a mosque, the reverse of what has happened in most hilltop towns in Andalucía.

Map, page 306

TIP

It is vital to keep all documents relating to your hire car with you at all times while travelling in Morocco. You should also keep your passport with you. Road checks are common throughout the country but especially in the Rif region. If you can't show your papers you may be detained.

BELOW: back street in Melilla.

Kif in the Rif

The stony soil in the Rif region is poor, but can sustain terraced fields of cannabis. This crop was condoned by the Spanish Protectorate which figured that smoking kif would keep the tribes pacified. Puffing clay pipefuls of cannabis cut with harsh black tobacco was long tolerated as a harmless peasant custom, one that eased a hardscrabble existence.

But when an enterprising American drug dealer introduced the Lebanese technique of pressing plant resin into blocks of hashish, underworld greed overwhelmed these isolated heights.

The heart of the Moroccan hashish business is **Ketama ⓫**, best avoided by anyone who wants tranquil travel. Bands of Riffian ruffians stop tourists and have been known to make deals at knife-point. Corruption is rife and the police not necessarily reliable. Simply driving innocently through this area may be grounds for suspicion in the eyes of officials.

Bridge too far

After exposure to Ketama, you may want to flee in the opposite direction, back to the relative calm of Andalucía. An enormous bridge may someday link the continents, if occasional discussions are to be taken seriously. The engineering is feasible, but such a bridge is historically dubious. It would require a tremendous suspension of grudges on both sides. ❑

Insight Guides
Travel Tips

Simply travelling safely

American Express Travellers Cheques

- are recognised as one of the safest and most convenient ways to protect your money when travelling abroad

- are more widely accepted than any other travellers cheque brand

- are available in eleven currencies

- are supported by a 24 hour worldwide refund service and

- a 24 hour Express Helpline service provides assistance and information when travelling abroad

- are accepted in millions of shops, hotels and restaurants throughout the world

Travellers Cheques

CONTENTS

Getting Acquainted

The Place 314
Climate 314
The People 314
Government/Economy 314

Planning the Trip

What to Bring 315
Photography 315
Electrical Goods 315
Visas and Passports 316
Animal Quarantine 316
Mapping the Route 316
Health 316
Money 316
Festivals 317
Getting There 318
Public Holidays 318
Student Travel 319

Practical Tips

Business Hours 320
Weights and Measures 320
Media 320
Postal Services 320
International Calls 321
Information Offices 321
Consulates 322
Emergencies 322

Getting Around

On Arrival 323
Public Transport 323
Private Transport 324
Hire Car Numbers 324

Where to Stay

Choosing a Hotel 324
Hotels in Almería 325
Hotels in Cádiz 326
Hotels in Córdoba 327
Hotels in Granada 328
Hotels in Huelva 329
Hotels in Jaén 329

Hotels in Málaga 330
Hotels in Seville 331
Campgrounds 332
Youth Hostels 333

Where to Eat

Listings by Province 334

Culture and Attractions

Theatre and Music 340
Spas 340

Nightlife

Bars 341
Flamenco Venues 341
Nightclubs 342
Casinos 342

Sport

Fishing 342
Golf 342
Horse-riding/Trekking 343
Marinas 344
Skiing 345
Tennis 345
Watersports 345
Bullfighting 345

Shopping

What to Buy 345
Shopping Areas 346

Gibraltar

The Basics 347
Planning the Trip 347
Getting Around 349
Where to Stay 349
Where to Eat 349

Language

Words and Phrases 350

Further Reading

Recommended Books 354
Other Insight Guides 355

Getting Acquainted

The Place

Andalucía covers 87,000 sq. km (34,700 sq. miles), 17 percent of Spain's total area. Most of the 7 million inhabitants live on the coast or along the **Guadalquivir river valley**. The 660-km (410-mile) long Guadalquivir is the backbone of the region, draining a vast basin and providing water for power, irrigation and drinking. The alluvial sediments bordering the river provide fertile soil for a variety of crops.

North of the Guadalquivir, the hills of the Sierra Morena are a barrier to easy communication between Andalucía and the rest of Spain. To the south, the Cordillera Bética runs from Gibraltar to Murcia, forming another higher barrier between the Guadalquivir basin and the Mediterranean coast. Mulhacén in the Sierra Nevada is the peninsula's highest mountain at 11,402 ft (3,478 metres) and the ranges bristle with dramatic crags. These sierras shield the coasts of Almería, Granada and Málaga from frost and snow.

Time Zones Andalucía and the rest of Spain, except the Canary Islands, follow Continental time. They are one hour ahead of the Canaries and Britain. Clocks go forward one hour in March and back in October.

Climate

Andalucía's position at the southern edge of Europe gives it a privileged climate. Summers are hot and winters generally mild. However, there are considerable variations due to the size of the region, its mountainous character and the fact

that it is bordered by both the Atlantic and Mediterranean. Summers can be extremely hot in the interior with temperatures rising to 45°C (113°F) and even higher in the provinces of Seville and Córdoba. Almería has an extremely arid, desert-like climate. Snow covers the Sierra Nevada from November to June and frost is common in upland areas.

Weather in coastal areas is moderated by the sea and offshore breezes so that neither extremes of heat nor cold are experienced, except for a few weeks at the height of summer. Strawberries ripen in Huelva and Málaga in early February. Tropical fruits can be grown along the Mediterranean without the aid of greenhouses. The Levante wind has considerable influence, often blowing hard for several days on the Cádiz coast and creating a persistent cloud over the Rock of Gibraltar. June to October are usually dry, except for sporadic torrential downpours. Heavy rain in the winter months is usually interspersed with brilliant sunshine.

The best months to tour the region are in spring and autumn, when there are no climatic extremes.

The People

Isolated from the mainstream of European culture, differing in climate and temperament from the rest of Spain, conquered by a succession of invaders, Andalucía is unique in many ways, although the 20th century has brought sharp changes.

Moorish, Oriental and **Mediterranean** influences, overlaid by Castilian and church domination, are clear in the people's character and customs. Worship of the Virgin reaches ecstatic heights in the hundreds of fiestas that mark the Andalucían year. Ancient customs and superstitions linger on in rural areas.

In business and social life, personal relationships are all-important. Andalucíans love to talk at all hours, in bars, cafés and restaurants. This is where you will

Fact finder

- **Language** Spanish.
- **Religion** Roman Catholic.
- **Time zone** Central European Time.
- **Currency** Spanish peseta.
- **Weights and measures** Metric.
- **Electricity** 220 volts.
- **International dialling code** 34.

meet them. Home is for the family. Although more emphasis is put these days on punctuality, the *mañana* philosophy has far from disappeared. Faster-moving European ways are bringing changes, but in the summer heat the siesta remains understandably popular.

Andalucíans tend to rise late and eat late, compared to North Europeans. Lunch is usually at 2pm or later and dinner can be any time after 9pm. Andalucían executives can be difficult to contact, perhaps because some follow a rigorous schedule on the lines of: 10am, coffee time in the bar next to the office; 11am, breakfast; noon, in conference; 1pm, taking a pre-lunch *aperitivo*; 2pm, time for tapas; 3–5pm, lunch; from 5pm, at the bullfight.

Government/Economy

Since 1982, when it elected its own parliament for the first time, Andalucía has enjoyed a considerable degree of self-government as one of Spain's 17 autonomous regions. The **Socialist Party** dominates the regional government, known as the Junta de Andalucía. The 109 members of parliament, which sits in Seville, are elected for a four-year period.

Madrid retains overall control of such sectors as taxation, customs, defence, security and the judiciary, while Andalucía exerts important influence in agriculture, consumer protection, environment, health, urban planning, industry, roads, and tourism promotion. The region is split into eight provinces, each of

which has a *diputación*, a provincial council composed of representatives of the municipalities. The Andalucían flag has three horizontal stripes, green, white and green.

Andalucía is Spain's most important agricultural region and agriculture continues to play a vital part in the economy. **Traditional products** such as olive oil, cereals and grapes have been joined by new crops and new methods. Irrigation has been extended to new areas. Cotton, olives, sunflowers, citrus fruits, sugar beet and rice are major crops. Strawberries have become a money-spinning export from Huelva and along the sheltered Mediterranean coast avocados, sweet potatoes, kiwi fruit and custard apples flourish. Fish-farming is also an expanding industry.

Mining of copper, lead, silver and gold, which dates from ancient times, is declining but service industries are growing and the regional authorities are striving to attract high-tech industry into the area.

Since 1960 there has been phenomenal growth in **tourism**, which has brought undreamed-of wealth to one of Spain's poorest areas. Thousands of Andalucíans depend directly or indirectly on this industry, particularly on the Costa del Sol in Málaga province. Apart from the annual influx of package-tour visitors, several hundred thousand North Europeans have permanent or semi-permanent residences on or near the Mediterranean coast. Foreigners have invested heavily in hotels and thousands of apartments and villas. The Atlantic coast and inland areas have also been affected by the tourist avalanche.

Planning the Trip

What to Bring

Bring a sun hat (especially if you are fair-complexioned), health insurance, first aid kit, needle and thread, sunglasses, spare spectacles, anti-diarrhoea tablets, insect repellent (particularly if camping), phrasebook and/or dictionary, essential contact numbers at home (bank, doctor, relatives), towel and soap.

Bring your own English-language books. Though available in tourist spots, books are expensive. Pack a plug adaptor if you are bringing electrical appliances, such as electric razor.

If you are driving your own vehicle, remember the car documents, international insurance and a bail bond in case of accident, a red warning triangle, spare car light bulbs, fanbelt etc.

What to Wear

Although Andalucíans like to dress stylishly, they do not demand the same of visitors, and **informal** (as opposed to sloppy) **dress** is acceptable almost everywhere, although it should not be too garish or too scanty when visiting cathedrals and religious sites, and men should not go bare-chested anywhere but the beach or poolside.

More **formal clothing** is called for in gambling casinos and elegant dining spots.

Light clothing is fine for much of the year on the coast, with perhaps a light sweater or jacket for the occasional cool evening. In winter take a heavy sweater and raincoat or umbrella.

Photography

With its wide variety of landscapes and people, Andalucía is highly photogenic. Some museums and monuments ban photography; others allow it for tourists, but not for professional photographers (professionals should try and look as much like a holiday maker as possible – a tripod is a dead giveaway). Most Andalucíans are very obliging if you wish to capture their image, but where possible ask permission and establish a relationship first. Nobody likes a camera thrust into their face by a stranger. **Gypsies** may be hostile and demand payment.

Unless you are using an all-automatic camera, double check exposure times with a good meter. The sub-tropical light is surprisingly strong and can lead to over-exposed pictures. Outdoors, you will seldom need fast film. Watch those whitewashed walls. They can confuse your meter. Avoid attempting portraits in mid-day sun as this gives a subject nasty shadows under eyes and chin, unless you use fill-in flash. Flash and tripods are often banned from churches and art galleries, unless you obtain special permission before your visit.

Most types of film are obtainable. Airport X-ray machines are claimed not to affect film, but ask security officials to hand-check film if it is particularly important to you. Don't put film in baggage intended for the hold. Processing colour negative film is more costly than in Britain.

Professionals should have a list of all equipment ready to show customs. Film crews usually have to obtain permission to work in public places and sometimes pay a fee.

Electrical Goods

British plugs do not fit Spanish sockets so British visitors should bring an adaptor. Wall sockets for shavers etc take plugs with two round pins. If you are taking 110V appliances on your trip, you will need a transformer.

Visas & Passports

As requirements change, always check before leaving your home country. Border restrictions have been removed with the creation of a **Single Market**, allowing visitors from European Union countries to enter and leave freely. However, they are still required to carry a passport or national identity card. If EU citizens stay six months or more in any calendar year, they are required to obtain a residence permit. North Americans can stay three months without visas, after which they can request an extension for a further three months. Visitors from Australia and South Africa require visas and New Zealanders need visas if staying more than three months. Stays cannot be extended beyond the length of the visas, which must be obtained before coming to Spain.

Extensions of Stay

EU citizens wishing to extend their stay should apply for a *Tarjeta de Residente Communitario* available from the *Oficina de Extranjeros* (Foreigners Office) or police station. Further information from Ministerio del Interior, tel: 900-150-000.

United States citizens can stay for three months in a calendar year which can be extended to six months providing the request is made before the first three months expire. After six months you can apply for a *residencia* which requires a visa which should have been requested prior to leaving the United States.

If you know before travelling that you will be staying longer than the permitted time, it can save trouble to apply for the necessary visa at a Spanish consulate in your home country. Otherwise you are required to tangle with Spanish bureaucracy. You must visit a police station, where you will be required to show your passport, provide photos, and give evidence that you have the necessary funds to live without working in Spain.

Animal Quarantine

You can import your cat or dog into Spain on presentation of relevant health certificates, but check first whether you can take it freely back to your home country – Britain, for example, has stringent quarantine laws. Regulations require a health certificate and, depending on age of animal, proof of rabies vaccination.

Mapping the Route

Michelin map 446, on a scale of 1:400,000 (1 centimetre to 4 kilometres), is the clearest road map of Andalucía. **Guía Campsa** includes maps, as well as details of sights, hotels and restaurants. **Firestone T-29**, 1:200,000, provides greater detail of the Costa del Sol and inland areas. Hikers and horse-trekkers will find most useful the military maps, scale 1:50,000, produced by Spain's **Servicio Geográfico del Ejército**. A handy map of the Sierra Nevada, 1:50,000, is published by the **Federación Española de Montañismo**.

Customs

Spanish customs officials are usually polite and unlikely to hassle travellers unless they have reason to believe they are wrongdoers. They are particularly on the lookout for drug smugglers at such ports as Algeciras and Málaga.

EU nationals are not restricted in what they can import, but anybody moving products in commercial quantities may require appropriate licences.

Non-EU nationals can import 200 cigarettes or 50 cigars or 250 grammes of tobacco products, 1 litre of alcohol over 20 percent proof or 2 litres up to 22 percent and 2 litres of other wines, one-quarter litre of eau-de-cologne and 50 grammes of perfume. Irrespective of nationality you can also bring in duty free: two still cameras with 10 rolls of film each, one movie or video camera, a portable radio, a tape-recorder, a typewriter, golf clubs, tennis rackets, fishing gear, a bicycle, skis and two hunting weapons with 100 cartridges each.

Health

Common sense is the best preventative medicine. Don't over-expose yourself to the sun, which can be surprisingly fierce – remember that you are close to Africa. Don't drink too many iced drinks and beware of excessive alcohol. The latter can produce devastating effects on your stomach, especially when eating unaccustomed food, which is often fried in olive oil and includes liberal doses of garlic and peppers. Take it easy until your body has become accustomed to changes in climate and diet. You are particularly warned to partake sparingly of cheap wine, as this is almost certain to give you a headache or worse, and is foolish in a country where superb wines can be enjoyed for a few pesetas more.

Bottled water is the best bet for visitors. Tap water is generally safe to drink, although it may taste strongly of chlorine. Local stomachs are used to it, but those of newcomers may initially revolt. However, it is not necessary to clean your teeth in *vino blanco* as some visitors appear to believe. Drink only packaged, pasteurised milk and beware of home-made cheese as Maltese fever is common in rural areas. Do not go barefoot in gardens and fields as scorpions can give very painful bites.

Money

Although as of January 1 1999 Spain's official currency is the **Euro**, all monetary transactions in Spain are still carried out in **pesetas** (until the year 2002). Coins are in circulation to the value of 1, 5, 10, 25, 50, 100, 200 and 500. Duros (five-peseta pieces) are common but the 1, 10, 50 and 200-peseta coins are little seen. Check your change carefully as some of

Festivals

Diary of Events: The following is a list of some of the more important or interesting festivals and events in the region. As dates vary each year, it is advisable to check with local tourist offices for exact details of each year's edition.

THROUGHOUT ANDALUCÍA

January New Year is greeted at midnight by eating twelve grapes, one for each chime of the clock; Three Kings Parades, on the eve of the Epiphany (Jan 5).
February carnival celebrations in most towns.
March/April Semana Santa processions, from Palm Sunday to Easter Sunday.
June *Noche de San Juan*, midsummer bonfires lit at midnight June 23 in many Andalucían towns.
July *Virgen del Carmen*, patroness of fishermen, honoured with seaborne processions in fishing communities along the coast in mid-July.
November Día de los Difuntos (Nov 1), when Andalucíans honour their dead.
December Spaniards celebrate *Nochebuena* (the Good Night), on Christmas Eve, with a family meal followed by the *Misa del Gallo* (Mass of the Cockerel – Midnight Mass); the *Día de los Inocentes* (Day of the Innocents) on December 28 is the Spanish equivalent of All Fools' Day.

CÁDIZ

February The city of Cádiz hosts one of Spain's best-known carnival celebrations.
March/April coinciding with Holy Week, running of bulls in Vejer de la Frontera and Arcos de la Frontera.
May Jerez, World Motorcycling

Championship at Jerez race track.
May Jerez, Jerez Horse Fair. Display of horses and horsemanship.
August Sanlucar de Barrameda. Horse races along the beach.
August Sotogrande, International Polo Competition. Matches throughout the month.
September/October Jerez, Fiesta de Otoño (Autumn Festival), including sherry harvest festival.

CÓRDOBA

May Córdoba, *Festival of the Patios* (first week of month) and annual fair (last week of month).
June *Romeria de los Gitanos* – pilgrimage of the gypsies – in Cabra.
July International Guitar Festival at the Gran Teatro in Córdoba.

GRANADA

January Granada celebrates the Día de la Toma (Jan 2) to commemorate the city's capture from the Moors.
March Espárrago Rock, Andalusia's biggest outdoor rock festival, in Granada.
May Día de la Cruz festival in Granada.
May/June Corpus Christi marks Granada's annual fair.
June/July Granada, International Festival of Music and Dance. One of Spain's leading festivals offers a varied programme of music and dance by national and international companies. Concerts in the Auditorio Manuel de Falla and the Palacio Carlos V in the Alhambra, dance in the Generalife.
August pilgrimage sets out from village of Trevelez and heads for the peak of La Veleta in the Sierra Nevada (Aug 5).
November Granada International Jazz Festival (particularly modern).

HUELVA

May *Romeria del Rocío*, Spain's biggest pilgrimage, to the shrine of the Virgin in El Rocio (Doñana).

JAÉN

February International chess tournament in Linares.
April *Romeria de la Virgen de la Cabeza*, a major pilgrimage in Andújar.

MÁLAGA

July International Music and Dance Festival in the Caves of Nerja.
August Málaga fair, the second biggest in Andalucía; the village of Cómpeta celebrates in *Noche del Vino* (Night of Wine), on August 15.
September Goyesca Fair in Ronda, with carriage displays and bullfight.
October Fuengirola, Fiesta del Rosario, the Costa del Sol's biggest annual fair.
December Festival of Verdiales, a primitive mountain music (Dec 28).

SEVILLE

April Seville, Spring Fair or Feria. The biggest Andalucían festival and most magnificent.
Seville, Antiques fair. Exhibitors from all over Spain.
May/June Corpus Christi celebrations in Seville, including performance of the medieval dance, Los Seises, in the cathedral.
July Italica, International Festival of Theatre and Dance. Contemporary dance and classical ballet by prestigious international companies. Held in the Roman amphitheatre.
September Biannual Flamenco Festival. Held every two years (1998, 2000, etc). Lasts throughout the month and represents the best in flamenco.

the coins are easy to confuse. Bills for 1,000, 2,000, 5,000, and 10,000 pesetas are in circulation. Try to keep some small change about you, as it can be difficult to change large-denomination notes.

Visitors bringing in or taking out cash worth more than 1,000,000 pesetas must declare it.

Credit cards are widely used in Spain and even smaller towns have cashpoint facilities, where you should be able to use your bank card. Although most major cards are known, the most widely-used and accepted is Visa. Smaller establishments may be unwilling to take your Diner's or Amex card.

Travellers' cheques remain one of the safest ways of transporting your cash and **Eurocheques** are

also widely accepted. Travel agencies and hotels will change currency as well as banks but it is worth checking rates – and commissions charged. You may often find that the savings banks (*cajas de ahorros*) offer a better deal than the big commercial banks. To get the most favourable rate, avoid changing small amounts at a time.

Banks have varied hours. Normal opening times are: Monday to Friday, 9am–2pm, Saturday 9am–1pm. During summer trading (June–September) banks do not open on Saturday. Some banks now stay open until 4pm on one or more days a week.

Important note: Unless you are importing very large sums of money, it is best to avoid transferring cash via banks. Many tourists have been left stranded for weeks, waiting for cash that inexplicably got lost in the pipeline. Even telexed cash can take days or weeks.

Internet

On-line information about Andalucía and Spain:

http://www.andalucia.org – official website of the Andalucían Tourist Office.
http://www.andalucia.com – private site devoted to information about Andalucía.
http://www.tourspain.es – home page for the Spanish Tourist Office. Includes an extensive data base of hotels.
http://www.okspain.org – put out by the Spanish Tourist Office in New York.
http://www.DocuWeb.ca/SiSpain (mirror site: **http://www.fundesco. es/SiSpain**) – sponsored by the Spanish Embassy in Canada, one of the most complete Internet sources of information about Spain.
http://www.parador.es – home page for the Parador network.
http://www.renfe.es – home page of the Spanish national railway company.
http://www.iberia.com – official site for the Spanish national airline.

Getting There

Tour operators offer hundreds of possibilities for all-in holidays in Andalucía, usually based on the Costa del Sol. From the coast, numerous excursions are possible, taking in the better-known sights of the region. Day trips include Granada, Seville, Ronda and Tangier. Two-day trips to the natural splendours of the Alpujarras, Cazorla, Doñana, Grazalema, Serrania de Ronda, Aracena and the Subbetica Cordobesa are also available.

A train ride in the grand style of the **Orient Express** is offered by the Al-Andalus. Operating April–October, this deluxe train visits Seville, Córdoba, Granada, Ronda and Jerez (from 210,000 pesetas). Information from Iberrail, tel: 915 715 815, 915 716 692. *See Sport* for details of horse-trekking tours.

Tour guides: tourist information offices can put you in touch with official guides.

If you are travelling at peak periods, i.e. Christmas, Easter, July–August, and at long weekends, it is advisable to reserve seats and hotel accommodation well in advance. Within Spain fully-booked flights can delay you for a week, especially at the end of July and the end of August when half the country

Public Holidays

There are a lot of public holidays. Apart from national holidays, every region and every community has its own celebrations which usually fall on the most inconvenient day for a visitor. Remember also that if a holiday falls, for example, on a Thursday, Spaniards like to make a *puente* (bridge), meaning that they take Friday off too to create a long weekend. Many factories and offices, some restaurants and shops close during August when most of Spain is on holiday, including the government. It is a month to be avoided if you intend to do much more than lie on a beach.

Holidays Throughout Andalucía
January 1 New Year's Day (*Año Nuevo*)
January 6 Twelfth Night (*Día de los Reyes*)

February 28 Andalucía Day (*Día de Andalucía*)
Holy Thursday (*Jueves Santo*), moveable feast, March or April.
Good Friday (*Viernes Santo*), moveable feast, March or April.
May 1 Labour Day (*Fiesta del Trabajo*)
August 15 Assumption of the Virgin (*Fiesta de la Asunción*)
October 12 Columbus Day (*Día de la Hispanidad*)
November 1 All Saints' Day (*Todos los Santos*)
December 6 Constitution Day (*Día de la Constitución*)
December 8 Immaculate Conception (*Inmaculada Concepción*)
December 25 Christmas Day (*Navidad*)

Local Holidays
Each town has two extra fiesta days when all businesses are closed. It is also likely you will encounter half-day opening only during Holy Week, particularly in Seville and Málaga, and during the major ferias, especially those of Córdoba, Jerez, Seville and Málaga.

Almería 25 August, 26 December.
Cádiz Monday after Carnival week, 7 October.
Córdoba 8 September, 24 October
Granada 2 January, 1 February, Corpus Christi
Huelva 3 August, 8 September
Jaén 11 June, 18 October.
Málaga 19 August, 8 September
Estepona 15 May, 16 July
Fuengirola 16 July, 7 October
Marbella 11 June, 19 October.
Mijas 8 September, 15 October.
Nerja 15 May, 24 June
Torremolinos 16 July, 29 September
Seville 30 May, Corpus Christi

appears to be on the move. This is also a bad time to attempt the Algeciras–Ceuta and Tangier crossing, as thousands of Moroccan immigrants will be queuing for the ferries.

BY AIR

Southern Spain has frequent air links with the rest of Europe and North Africa. It is within two-and-a-half hours' flying time of London. Most transatlantic flights are via Madrid. Málaga and Seville airports have daily scheduled connections with **international destinations**, but in addition large numbers of visitors arrive by charter flights. Jerez and Gibraltar are also important entry points.

The colossal growth of the Costa del Sol tourist industry has converted Málaga into Spain's sixth busiest airport, with five million passenger arrivals annually. Scheduled services are available from the major airlines, including Iberia, British Airways, KLM, Lufthansa, Sabena, SAS, Air France, Swissair and Royal Air Maroc. Málaga airport has undergone a major expansion programme, as has Seville. Airport porters have set charges, often displayed, for handling baggage. Trolleys are available in bigger airports. Only more expensive hotels have porters available to carry your bags to your room.

BY SEA

Few liners call at Southern Spain ports, apart from those on cruises. **Trasmediterranea vessels**, carrying passengers and vehicles, ply between Almería, Málaga, Algeciras, and Cádiz and ports on the African coast and on the Canary Islands.

There are frequent services across the Straits of Gibraltar, both by ferries and hydrofoils, from Algeciras to Ceuta and Tangier.

BY RAIL

AVE, the high-speed rail service, links Seville to Madrid. The new trains have halved travel time between these two cities, to two and a half hours. The special AVE

track is also used on other services, such as the Madrid-Malaga Talgo, which has brought a considerable saving on travelling time. The most comfortable way to travel south is by Talgo trains, smooth-running expresses which run from Madrid to major Andalucían cities.

● Some of the main bus and train stations have coin-operated lockers or left-luggage offices.

BY ROAD

Road access to Andalucía has improved dramatically in recent years. It is now possible to drive on four-lane highways virtually all the

Student Travel

Under-26s can obtain reduced rates on rail travel with the InterRail card which is valid for travel throughout Europe. The system divides Europe into five zones, Spain and Portugal representing one of those zones. For students holding an **International Student Identity Card** discounts are available on bus and rail travel, KLM and selected Iberia flights, accommodation, as well as entrance to museums, monuments and sports and cultural events.

Information can be obtained from **Interjoven**, Calle Miño 24, Seville, tel. 954 558 293.

way from the French border at La Junquera to Seville (a toll is payable on the section from France to Alicante).

An alternative for those travelling from Britain is the **ferry service** from Portsmouth or Plymouth to Bilbao or Santander on the northern Spanish coast, then south via Madrid. Four-lane *autovías* link Granada, Córdoba, Málaga, Seville, Cádiz and Huelva. The *Autovía de Andalucía*, from Madrid to Córdoba and Seville, has slashed driving times and the age-old bottleneck created by the Despeñaperros Pass, which cuts through the Sierra

Morena, has been removed.

Entry from Portugal's southern coast – served by Faro airport – has been smoothed with the opening of a bridge across the Guadíana river at Ayamonte, thus cutting out the time-consuming ferry.

Comfortable **bus services** offer economic travel from Northern Europe to many of the major Spanish cities. Fares sometimes include meals and overnight hotel stops. There are daily bus services to the region from Barcelona and Madrid (one-way fares to Málaga from Barcelona start at around 8,500 pesetas, and from Madrid 4,500 pesetas).

When driving through Spain, travellers should try to avoid peak holiday times, as the country has one of Europe's worst accident records. Easter and the first weekend of August are particularly black periods.

Practical Tips

Business Hours

Shops usually open 9.30am or 10am–1.30pm, opening again from 5–7.30pm or 8pm. Large **department stores** and hypermarkets stay open from 10am–9pm or 10pm.

Shops are closed on Sunday although newsagents are open on Sunday mornings. In tourist areas, some stores open on Sunday during summer. Government offices are usually open to the public between 9am and 1pm.

Weights & Measures

Spain has followed the **metric system** since 1971. Rainfall is measured by the number of litres falling per square metre. One inch of rain is 25.4 litres per square metre. Land is calculated in square metres and hectares. One hectare equals 10,000 sq. metres or approximately 2.5 acres.

Some traditional Spanish weights and measures are still in popular use. These include: *fanega* (6,460 sq. metres or 1.59 acres); *arroba* (11.5 kg); *quintal* (4 *arrobas* or 46 kg). Farmers sell wine and olive oil by the *arroba*, referring to a wine container with a capacity of 15 to 16 litres.

Religious Services

In tourist areas, especially the Costa del Sol, there are churches and synagogues serving resident and visiting non-Catholics. There are also several mosques.

Media

Newspapers National papers published in Madrid are available every morning. Dailies such as *El País*, *El Mundo* and *ABC* have special Andalucían editions printed in Seville. At least one local daily is published in each of Andalucía's provincial capitals. They can be very useful for finding out what events are scheduled locally and usually include emergency telephone numbers and transport information.

European newspapers are readily available on the Costa del Sol and in larger cities. Some UK dailies print editions in Spain and are distributed in the morning. Otherwise, foreign newspapers are available at midday or early afternoon.

A number of English-language publications serve the large number of expatriates living along the Mediterranean coast.

Of the **magazines**, the longest established and most respected is *Lookout*, a glossy, Fuengirola-based monthly featuring sound, practical information, current affairs and well-researched articles about life and life-styles in Spain. *Absolute Marbella* is a glossy monthly devoted to the lifestyle of the rich and famous of the resort.

Several free papers come out weekly, with details of events in the expatriate community. They include *Sur* in English and *The Entertainer*. German publications include the monthly *Aktuelle,* and the monthly *Solkysten* caters for Scandinavians. **Television & Radio** Andalucía is served by the two national state-run television channels, two Andalucían channels, several private networks which started functioning in 1990, and local television in many towns and villages. Satellites allow the beaming in of foreign programmes in English, Italian and other languages. Sky and Super Channel are among these.

Most communities have their own FM radio stations in Spanish. Several radio stations on the Costa del Sol broadcast in English. The best is OCI (*Onda Cero International*), based in Marbella (FM 101.6).

Postal Services

Post Offices Usual opening times for the *Correos* (post office) are from 9am–2pm, Monday to Friday, and 9am–1pm, Saturday. In larger cities, main post offices have longer business hours. More often than not, there are long queues at the stamp counters, but stamps can also be bought in *estancos* (they advertise themselves with a "Tobacos" sign in yellow and brown). Within Europe all letters go by air. *Aerogramas* (special airmail letters) are also available at post offices. The general information number for the postal service is 902 197 197.

You can receive mail at post offices if it is addressed to *Lista de Correos* (equivalent to Poste Restante), followed by the place name. Remember that Spaniards usually have two surnames, that of their father first with their mother's tagged on after it. This can lead to confusion with foreign names. Thus, if a letter is addressed, for example, to James Robertson Justice, it will probably be filed under "R" rather "J".

Postboxes are bright yellow but you may also come across red postboxes; these are for express mail.

Telecoms Telex and fax facilities are available in main post offices. Telephone boxes (*cabinas*) take five, 25, 50 and 100 peseta coins. There are also card-operated telephones which work with *Telefónica* phone cards, available from *estancos* and many newsstands. You cannot make reverse charge calls from a *cabina*, nor receive calls.

All Spanish phone numbers have nine digits.

In tourist areas in season you will find glass Portacabin structures housing small exchanges. These are handy for long-distance calls as instead of fumbling with change you pay the operator afterwards and have the added advantage of being able to pay by credit card. Bars also have telephones but make a surcharge. Restrict your calls from hotels as they often treble the charge.

International Calls

Dial 07, wait for the high-pitched tone, dial the international code for the country you require, e.g. to Britain: 07-44 + area code + number; to the United States: 07-1 + area code + number. (Please note that the Spanish telephone system is changing to adapt to European standards; the international access code is to be change to 00, followed directly by the country and area code, without waiting for a second dial tone.)

You can make a reversed charge call through the Spanish operator – 1008 for Europe, 1005 for rest of world – or by dialling the operator of your home country directly:

BT 900 990 044
Mercury 900 990 944

ATT 900 990 011
MCI 900 990 014
Sprint 900 990 013

Canada 900 990 015
Ireland 900 990 353
New Zealand 900 990 064

Digital cellular phones, European GSM standard, can be used if the "roam" feature is activated.

Information Offices

Almería
Tourist information Parque Nicolás Salmerón, tel: 950 274 355.
Airport 8 km (5 miles) from centre, tel: 950 221 954.
Iberia Paseo de Almería, 44. Information, tel: 950 230 933.
RENFE train station: tel: 25 11 35. Information: Alcalde Muñoz, 1, tel: 950 231 822.
Bus station Plaza de Barcelona, tel: 950 210 029.
Boats to Melilla
Transmediterranea, Parque Nicolas Salmerón 26, tel: 950 236 155.
Post office Plaza San Juan Casinello, tel: 23 72 07.

Cádiz
Tourist information Calderón de la Barca, 1, tel: 956 211 313.
RENFE train station Plaza de Sevilla, tel: 956 254 301.
Bus station Plaza de la Hispanidad, 1, tel: 956 224 271. Los Amarillos, Avenida Ramón de Carranza, 31, tel: 956 285 852.
Teletaxi, tel: 956 286 969.
Post office Plaza de Topete, tel: 956 213 945.

Algeciras
Tourist information Juan de la Cierva s/n, tel: 965 572 636.
Bus stations Portillo (for Costa del Sol), Avenida Virgen del Carmen, 15, tel: 956 651 055; Comes (for Cádiz, Seville), Plaza Hispanidad, 1, tel: 956 227 811.
RENFE train station, tel: 956 630 202.
Boats to North Africa
Transmediterranea, Recinto del Puerto, tel: 956 663 850.
Radio taxis, tel: 956 654 343.
Post office Ruiz Zorrilla, tel: 956 663 648.

Jeréz de la Frontera
Tourist information, Alameda Cristina 7, tel: 33 11 50.
Airport 17 km (4 miles) from centre, tel: 956 150 000.
Bus station Madre de Dios.
RENFE train station Plaza de la Estación, tel: 956 342 319.
Post office El Cerrón 2, tel: 956 342 295.

El Puerto de Santa María
Tourist information, Guadalete s/n, tel: 956 542 475.
Ferry to Cádiz, summer service from San Ignacio Pier, Plaza de las Galeras Reales, tel: 956 870 270.

Córdoba
Tourist office Plaza de Juda Levi, Judería, tel: 957 200 522. Torrijos 10 (Palacio de Congresos), tel: 957 471 235.
RENFE train station, tel: 957 478 221. Reservations: Ronda de los Tejares, 10, tel: 957 490 202.
Buses Alsina Graells (for Málaga, Granada, Badajóz), Avenida de Medina Azahara, 29, tel: 957 236 474. **Ureña (for Jaén, Seville)**, Avenida Cervantes, 22, tel: 957 472 352.
Taxi stands Tendillas, tel: 957 470 291; Gran Capitán, tel: 957 415 153; Plaza de Colón, tel: 957 471 306.
Post office Cruz Conde, 15, tel: 957 478 267.

Granada
Tourist office Corral del Carbón, tel: 958 225 990; also Plaza Mariana Pineda 10, bajo, tel: 958 226 688.
Airport 11 miles (18 km) from centre, tel: 958 245 200.
Iberia Pl Isabel la Católica, 2, tel: 958 221 452, 958 227 592.
Buses Alsina Graells (services to Andalucían cities), Ctra. de Jaén, tel: 958 185 010; Bacoma (services to Madrid, Alicante, Valencia and Barcelona), Avenida de Andaluces, 10, tel: 958 284 251. Bus to Sierra Nevada: daily at 9am from Puerta Real. Returning at 5pm. Autocares: Bonal, tel: 958 273 100.
RENFE train station Avenida de Andalucía, tel: 958 271 272.
Radio Taxi 958 151 461.
Post office Puerta Real, tel: 958 224 853.

Huelva
Tourist office Avenida de Alemania, 12, tel: 959 257 403.
RENFE train station Avenida de Italia, tel: 959 246 666.
Bus station Avenida de Portugal, 9, tel: 959 256 900.
Teletaxi, tel: 959 250 022.
Post office Avenida de Italia, tel: 959 249 184.

Jaén
Tourist information Arquitecto Berges, 1, Jaén, tel: 953 222 737.
Train station Jaén, tel: 953 255 607.
Bus station Jaén, Plaza Coca de la Piñera, tel 953 255 014.

Málaga
Tourist information Pasaje de Chinitas, 4, tel: 952 213 445; Paseo del Parque, tel: 952 604 410. Also at airport, tel: 952 240 000.
Airport 8 km (5 miles): tel. 952 048 804.

Iberia and flight information, tel: 952 136 166. Iberia city office, Molina Lario, 13, tel: 952 136 147.
British Airways (airport), tel: 952 048 170.
RENFE train station Esplanada de la Estación, tel: 952 360 202; information & tickets, Strachan, 2, tel: 952 214 127.
Bus station Paseo de los Tilos, tel: 952 350 061.
Radio taxis, tel: 952 320 000.
Post Office Avenida de Andalucía, tel: 952 359 008.

Antequera
Tourist information, Palacio de Najera, tel: 952 841 427.
RENFE train station La Bobadilla, tel: 952 720 022.
Post Office Najera, 26, tel: 952 842 083.

Benalmádena-Costa
Tourist information Avda Antonio Machado, tel: 952 242 494.

Estepona
Tourist information Paseo Maritimo Pedro Manrique s/n, tel: 952 800 913.
Bus station Avenida de España, tel: 952 802 954.
Taxi tel: 952 802 900.
Post office Calle Málaga 82, tel: 952 800 537.

Consulates

MÁLAGA
Canada Edificio Horizonte, Plaza de la Malagueta, 3, tel: 952 223 346.
Great Britain Duquesa de Parcent, 8, tel: 952 217 571.
Ireland Avenida de los Boliches, Fuengirola, tel: 952 475 108.
United States Centro Comercial Las Rampas, phase 2,1, Fuengirola, tel: 952 474 891.

SEVILLE
Canada Avenida de la Constitución, 30, tel: 954 229 413.
Great Britain Plaza Nueva, 8, tel: 954 228 875.
United States Paseo de las Delicias, 7, tel: 954 231 885.

Fuengirola
Tourist information Avenida Jesús Santos Rein (near Mercacentro), tel: 952 467 457.
Bus station Avenida Ramón y Cajal, tel: 952 475 066.
Trains to Málaga every 30 minutes.
Taxis, tel: 952 471 000.
Post office Plaza de los Chinoros, tel: 952 474 384.

Marbella
Tourist information Glorieta de la Fontanilla, tel: 952 822 818.
Bus station Avenida del Trapiche, tel: 952 764 400.
Radio taxis tel: 952 774 488.
Post office Notario Luis Oliver, tel: 952 772 898.

Nerja
Tourist information Puerta del Mar, 4, Nerja, tel: 952 521 531.
Bus station Avda Pescia, tel: 952 521 504.
Taxi rank, tel: 952 520 537.
Post office Almirante Ferrandiz, 6, tel: 952 521 749.

Ronda
Tourist information Plaza de España,1, tel: 952 871 272.
Bus station Plaza Concepción García Redondon s/n, tel: 952 872 262.
Train station tel: 958 71 673.
Post office Infantes 11, tel: 952 872 557.

Torre del Mar
Tourist information Avenida de Andalucía, 92-A, tel: 952 541 104.
Bus station Calle del Mar, tel: 952 540 936.
Post office Paseo Larios, 12, tel: 952 540 665.

Torremolinos
Tourist information Plaza Pablo Picasso, tel: 952 371 159.
Bus station Calle Hoyo, tel: 952 382 419.
Trains regular services along coast and to airport from town centre.
Taxis, tel: 952 381 030.
Post office Avenida Palma de Mallorca, tel: 952 384 518.

Vélez-Málaga
Bus station Avda Vivar Tellez, tel: 952 501 731.
Taxi rank, tel: 952 500 088.
Post office Pl. San Roque, tel: 952 500 143.

Seville
Tourist office Avenida de la Constitución, 21, tel: 954 221 404; Paseo de las Delicias, tel: 954 234 465. Also at airport, tel: 954 255 046.
Airport 7 miles (12 km), tel. 954 449 000
Iberia Almirante Lobo, 1. Information, tel: 954 228 901.
Buses Prado de San Sebastian station, Manuel Vazquez Sagastizabal, tel: 954 417 111; Plaza de Armas station, Plaza de Armas, tel: 954 908 040.
Train Station Santa Justa, 954 414 700
RENFE office Zaragoza, 29. Information, tel: 954 414 111; Information ave, tel: 954 541 444.
Radio taxis, tel: 954 580 000.
Teletaxi, tel: 954 622 222.
Post office Avenida de la Constitución, 32, tel: 954 216 476

Emergencies

Security & Crime
Thefts from tourists and their cars have become common in recent years. Common sense precautions should prevent your holiday being spoiled in this way.

Cities, particularly Málaga and Seville, are black spots. Never leave anything of value in your car, including when parking near a beach. Don't leave cash or valuables unattended while you are swimming. When staying overnight, take all baggage into the hotel. If possible, park your car in a garage or a guarded car-park.

Particularly when driving into Seville, do not leave anything of value within sight. A favourite trick is to smash the windows of cars stopping at traffic lights, seize handbags and cameras and then take off on a motocycle.

When walking, women should keep shoulder bags out of view if

Insight Guides portray destinations in depth, providing the complete picture and the top photography

Insight Pocket Guides *focus on the best choices for places to see and things to do and include large fold-out maps*

Insight Compact Guides *'portability makes them the perfect books to carry with you for on-the-spot reference*

Three types of guide for all types of travel

INSIGHT GUIDES Different people need different kinds of information. Some want *background information* to help them prepare for the trip. Others seek *personal recommendations* from someone who knows the destination well. And others look for *compactly presented data* for on-the-spot reference. With three carefully designed series, Insight Guides offer readers the perfect choice. Insight Guides will turn your visit into an experience.

The world's largest collection of visual travel guides

When you're

bitten by the travel bug,

make sure you're protected.

Check into a British Airways Travel Clinic.

British Airways Travel Clinics provide travellers with:
- A complete vaccination service and essential travel health-care items
- Up-dated travel health information and advice

Call **01276 685040** for details of your nearest Travel Clinic.

**BRITISH AIRWAYS
TRAVEL CLINICS**

possible. Avoid badly-lit back streets at night. A sensible precaution is to carry photocopies of your passport and other documents and leave the originals in the hotel safe.

If you are confronted do not resist, as thieves often carry knives. If robbed, remember that thieves usually want easily disposable cash. Check the nearest gutters, rubbish containers, toilets for your personal possessions; thieves swiftly toss away what they don't want.

Municipal police, who generally have limited powers and are mostly seen controlling traffic, wear blue uniforms and peaked caps. **National police** wear dark blue uniforms and caps. Both will assist you, but it is the national police who will take details of an offence and conduct any investigation. In smaller towns and rural areas, **Civil Guards** – in olive-green uniforms, but without the distinctive triocorn hat, recently excluded except for ceremonials – perform these duties. Few policemen speak anything but Spanish, but many national police stations (*comisarías*) now have report forms in several European languages to aid tourists.

Loss of Belongings

If you lose anything, report it to the municipal police who will issue a certificate for any insurance claim. Lost property offices (*Oficina de Objetos Perdidos*) are usually located in town halls (*ayuntamiento*) and railway stations (*estación de tren*). **Lost passports** should be reported to the nearest consulate. If you lose or have credit cards or travellers' cheques stolen go to the nearest bank, or phone the emergency number issued with travellers' cheques.

Emergency Numbers

National Police: 091
Local Police: 092
Medical emergencies: 061
Fire brigade: 080

Medical Services

Private clinics offering a range of medical services – some open 24 hours a day – are located in most towns of any size. Emergency services are also provided by *ambulatorios*, national health clinics run by Spain's Seguridad Social (social security system).

Free medical attention is available if you are from EU countries, which have reciprocal arrangements with Spain. Before leaving home, it is worth inquiring about this at your local government health department. As Seguridad Social facilities are often over-stretched, visitors are also advised to take out private health insurance.

Farmácias (chemists) are well-stocked. They display lists of the duty chemists at night and on weekends.

The Cruz Roja (Red Cross) offers first aid services. Posts are along major highways.

Getting Around

On Arrival

Cheap bus services run from main airports to city centres and taxi drivers are authorised only to charge fixed rates. Málaga airport is also served by a good train service, which runs between the provincial capital and Torremolinos and Fuengirola.

Public Transport

The main Andalucían cities are linked by rail, although this can be a rather slow means of transportation and is often more expensive than using buses. **Overnight trains**, with sleeping compartments and *couchettes*, run between Algeciras, Málaga and Madrid.

Train fares are reasonable, but you pay supplements to travel at peak times. Saturday is generally the cheapest day to travel and Friday and Sunday the most expensive. Discounts available include: *Tarjeta dorada* for over-60s (foreigners must be resident in Spain) and *Tarjeta turística* for non-residents, issued for 3, 5 or 10 days.

There are also a variety of passes for rail travel in Europe including Spain: *Tarjeta InterRail* for **under-26s** and *Euro Domino* for **over 26s**. New fare structuring divides Europe into five zones, Spain and Portugal together being one of those zones.

Regular bus services run between Andalucía's cities and towns and this is a cheap, and generally comfortable way to travel. Ask for the *Estación de Autobuses*.

Taxis are readily available in major centres and fares are reasonable. Fares are officially controlled; in urban areas fares are by metre, outside towns fixed rates apply.

Private Transport

Hire Cars: Remember your international driving licence. Scores of car hire companies offer their services. Such international chains as **Avis**, **Europcar** and **Hertz** have airport offices, and offer collect and deliver service. As a guide to rates from a major international car rental firm (1998): a small car, one week, unlimited mileage, 45,000 pesetas. Rate per day, 15,000 pesetas. Smaller local companies are much cheaper and will arrange to meet you on arrival if you book beforehand.

Hire Car Numbers

Avis airport offices:
● Almería tel: 950 224 126.
● Granada: tel: 958 446 455.
● Jerez de la Frontera, Cádiz: tel: 956 150 005.
● Málaga: tel: 952 048 483.
● Seville: tel: 954 449 121.
Europcar airport offices:
● Almería: tel: 950 292 934.
● Granada: tel: 958 245 275.
● Jerez de la Frontera: tel: 956 150 098.
● Málaga: tel: 952 048 518.
● Seville: tel: 954 254 298.
Hertz airport offices:
● Almería: tel: 950 292 500.
● Córdoba (railway station): tel: 957 402 060.
● Granada: tel: 958 252 419.
● Jerez de la Frontera: Tel: 956 150 038.
● Málaga: tel: 952 233 086.
● Seville: tel: 954 449 125.

Advice for Drivers
Driving in Spain is on the right, but often – on the part of Spanish drivers – in the centre of the road. The best advice is: be prepared to take evasive action at all times in the face of local devil-may-care attitudes. Civil Guard motorcycle patrols, out in force on holiday weekends, brook no nonsense and can administer heavy, **on-the-spot fines** for driving offences. Radar traps are common. Secondary roads have been much improved and can be much pleasanter to use

than main highways, which are often clogged with heavy transport.

Seat belts are obligatory. Traffic from the right has priority except on roundabouts or unless otherwise signalled. The speed limit in built-up areas is 50 kph (30 mph), 90 kph (55 mph) on roads and 120 kph (75 mph) on motorways. Keep your eyes open at night for plodding mules and motorcycles without lights.

Mopeds, low-powered **motorcycles**, can be hired in main centres. They are ideal for short excursions, but make sure you are fully covered by insurance.

Cycling: Intense heat and precipitous mountain roads make cycling a means of transport reserved for the fit. Drivers do not give you much room as you pedal along. However, this is an ideal way to enjoy the beauty of Andalucía's scenery. Be warned that you cannot take bicycles onto trains.

On Foot: The sierras of the region are crisscrossed with forestry roads, footpaths and muletracks. With a good map, you can walk from village to village, camping or spending the night in inns far away from the usual tourist beat. Spring and autumn are the best times for hiking. In summer the heat strikes like a hammer and in winter heavy rain and snow can make progress impossible or at least uncomfortable. Some of the most striking mountain scenery is in the national park of Cazorla (Jaén) and in the sierras of Granada, Málaga and Cádiz provinces.

Hitchhiking: It may not be difficult to get lifts along the coastal highways, but off the track you can be stranded for days. Hitching was never easy, but the increase in crime has made Spanish drivers more reluctant to pick up strangers, particularly travel-stained back-packers. Women are strongly advised to travel in male company.

On Departure

Booking out time is noon in most hotels, but they will usually look after your luggage if your transport does not leave until later.

Where to Stay

Choosing a Hotel

Spain may no longer be the bargain it once was but accommodation still offers **good value**. Hotels are officially rated from one to five stars. Five-star establishments are in the luxury category with all the comforts one would expect in a first-class hotel. Bear in mind that the rating has more to do with the amenities offered than the quality of the service.

The ratings do not take into account charm or friendly atmosphere. Small, **family-run** places in the lower categories can be more comfortable than large soulless establishments with gilded fittings and marble halls. Some amenities offered by large hotels may be a positive disadvantage – do you want a *discoteca* or bingo hall under your window or a rooftop night-club above your bed? Independent travellers can find it disagreeable to stay in a hotel packed with tour groups.

Hotel prices are posted at the reception desk and behind your room door. **IVA** (value added tax) goes on top. There is a maximum and minimum price, but often the maximum rate is applied year round. Hotels in Seville are more expensive than the equivalent elsewhere in Andalucía, and a **hefty premium** is charged during Holy Week and the April Fair. There is no obligation to take breakfast or other meals, except at boarding houses. In any case, breakfast in smaller hotels often consists of little more than coffee, bread and jam, and better value can be obtained in the nearest bar.

If the **blue plaque** at an establishment's door carries the

sign "**Hs**", this signifies that it is a *hostal*. These also have star ratings but offer fewer facilities and are worth seeking out if you are on a tight budget. "**HR**" and "**HsR**" signify *hotel residencia* and *hostal residencia*, meaning there is no restaurant or meal service.

At the bottom of the market are the *pensión* (boarding house), the *fonda* (inn) and *the casa de huéspedes* (guesthouse). These are small and spartan, but usually clean. They may not run to carpets or hot water and the beds may sag alarmingly. But most are perfectly adequate considering the low price.

Paradors are state-run hotels. Sometimes the service can be a little glum, but they are usually located in unrivalled positions, sometimes in modern buildings but often in old castles, palaces and convents.

Motels are not common in Spain, but you will find some on main highways. Thousands of apartments have been built in tourist areas and if you are planning to stay more than a few days it is worth renting one. In summer they are usually fully booked, but off-season it should be possible to negotiate a reasonable price.

A recent introduction offers hotel vouchers, books of five or 10, which are exchanged for accommodation at participating hotels of three–five stars. The system offers a considerable saving on normal rates. Schemes on offer include: Bancotel, Ibercheque, Hotel Color, Talonario 10, all of which are available at travel agents. El Corte Inglés have their Bono Hotel, available from their in-house travel agency.

The Red Andaluza de Alojamientos Rurales (RAAR) publishes a catalogue in several languages listing members' accommodation available in rural areas and has a reservation service, tel: 950 265 018, fax 950 270 431. To obtain the catalogue, send two international reply coupons to RAAR, Apartado 2035, 04080 Almería.

Prices: In a *pensión*, expect to pay about 2,000 pesetas for a double room. In one and two-star *hostals*, prices will range from 4,000 to 6,000 pesetas. Hotel prices run roughly from 4,000 pesetas for a one-star establishment to 16,000 for a four-star. A double in a five-star hotel is usually in the 17,000 to 25,000-peseta bracket. *Paradors* charge 10,000 to 22,000 pesetas a double room.

● **Hotels Note:** s/n in an address signifies *sin número* (no number); ctra means *carretera* (highway). Hotel names are in bold print.

Price Guide

All the prices are for a double room:
$$$$ = Over 20,000 pesetas
$$$ = 15–20,000 pesetas
$$ = 8–15,000 pesetas
$ = Under 8,000 pesetas

ALMERÍA
Gran Hotel Almería
Avda Reina Regente, 8.
Tel: 950 238 011.
Almería's class hotel, with views over the harbour and bay. **$$$**
Torreluz II
Plaza Flores, 1.
Tel: 950 234 799.
The middle-range hotel in one of a series of hostelries of different categories and restaurants of the same name, centred on the Plaza Flores. The location is convenient, the rooms are clean and modern, the price reasonable. **$$**

North of Almería
Hotel San Nicolás
Calle Baños, s/n, Alhama de Almería.
Tel: 950 641 361.
Old-fashioned spa hotel next to hot springs in the foothills of the Sierra de Gádor, near the Tabernas desert, 24 km (15 miles) from Almería. **$**
Sierra Alhamilla
Pechina.
Tel: 950 317 413.
A pleasant small hotel in Pechina, 10 km (6miles) north of Almería, built over old Moorish baths, next to a thermal spring. **$**

West of Almería
Golf Hotel Almerimar
Urb Almerimar.
Tel: 950 497 050.
Modern and comfortable resort hotel in a holiday complex with golf course and yachting marina. **$$$**
Melia Almerimar
Urb Almerimar.
Tel: 950 497 007.
New hotel in the Almerimar holiday complex, large, modern and with all the amenities, convenient to the golf course. **$$$**
Playacapricho
Urb Playa Serena, Roquetas de Mar.
Tel: 950 333 100.
Modern 330-room resort hotel next to the beach. The first impression is of the enormous glassed-in area containing the lobby, tropical garden and indoor pool. The outdoor pool is 2,500 sq m (26,850 sq ft). **$$$$**
Playasol
Urb Playa Serena, Roquetas de Mar.
Tel: 950 333 802.
Totally renovated in 1998, one of the first hotels to open in the burgeoning holiday resort of Playa Serena, near Roquetas de Mar. Next to the beach, and with a spectacular pool. **$$**

Mojácar and Environs
Parador Reyes Católicos
Playa de Mojácar.
Tel: 950 478 250.
A splendid beachside location is the main attraction of this modern parador. **$$$**
El Moresco
Avda Encamp, Mojácar.
Tel: 950 478 025.
A good choice for those who want to stay in Mojácar itself, rather than on the beach 3 km (2 miles) below the village, with good views of the surrounding countryside. **$$**
Mamabels
Calle Embajadores, 3, Mojácar.
Tel: 950 472 448.
Down a staircase in Mojácar, teetering at the very edge of the village, arty and reasonably priced six-room hostelry, with good views of the coast. **$**
El Puntazo
Paseo del Mediterraneo, Mojácar.
Tel: 950 478 265.

Bright, modern and next to the beach, a comfortable and reasonably-priced option if you want to be close to the seashore. **$**

Finca Listonero
Cortijo Grande, Turre.
Tel: 950 479 094.
Inland from Mojácar, on the edge of the Tabernas desert, gourmet food and tasteful decor in a converted Andalucían farmhouse turned five-room hotel. **$$**

Vera Playa Club
Ctra Garrucha-Villaricos km 1, Vera.
Tel: 950 467 475.
The only nudist hotel in southern Spain, next to the beach 15 km (9 miles) north of Mojácar, with a wholesome, family atmosphere. Clothing is allowed only in the restaurant and reception area. Closed November–April. **$$$**

Cabo de Gata and Environs
Hotel San José
Calle Correos, San José.
Tel: 950 380 116.
Small hotel with eight large rooms overlooking a secluded cove in the relatively unspoilt Cabo de Gata. Closed: November–January. **$$$**

Mikasa
Ctra Carboneras, Agua Amarga.
Tel: 950 138 073
More like a private home than a hotel, in a modern building, with 12 artfully decorated rooms, convenient for the beaches of the Cabo de Gata nature park. **$$$**

CÁDIZ
Atlántico
Avenida Duque de Nájera, 9.
Tel: 956 226 905.
State-run hotel in a modern but stylish building, the best bet in its category if you want to stay in the picturesque old part of the city. **$$$**

Algeciras
Reina Cristina
Paseo de la Conferencia.
Tel: 956 602 622.
Surrounded by luxuriant gardens, this British-style, stately turn-of-the-century hotel is a classic, its ambience recalling days gone by. **$$$$**

Arcos de la Frontera
Parador Casa del Corregidor
Plaza de España, s/n.
Tel: 956 700 500.
The splendid views from this hotel, perched on a cliff at the very top of the village, are worth a visit in their own right. The rooms are very large, furnished in typical parador style. The best ones look over the cliff. **$$$**

El Convento
Maldonado, 2.
Tel: 956 702 333.
Tiny 8-room hotel occupying part of a former convent. It's right around the corner from the Parador, and some rooms enjoy the same views, at half the price. **$$**

Los Olivos
Paseo Boliches, 30.
Tel: 956 700 811.
Small hotel in an old Andalucían town house, its rooms arranged around a courtyard. Good value. **$$**

Cortijo Fain
Ctra de Algar km 3.
Tel: (956) 70 11 67.
Two miles from the village of Arcos, installed in a rambling 17th-century country manor in the middle of an olive grove. **$$$**

Hacienda El Santiscal
Avda El Santiscal, 129.
Tel: 956 708 313.
Rustic hotel in a renovated 15th-century country manor with central courtyard, next to the Arcos reservoir. Good base for horse-riding holidays. **$$**

El Puerto de Santa María
Monasterio de San Miguel
Larga, 27.
Tel: 956 540 440.
Tasteful and comfortable, installed in a former 18th-century monastery which still retains the original cloisters, chapel and enclosed garden. **$$$**

Grazalema and environs
Villa Turística de Grazalema
El Olivar, Grazalema.
Tel: 956 132 136.
Part of the Andalucían "Villa Turística" network, with self-catering units (perfect for small groups), in addition to a small hotel. **$$**

Las Truchas
Avda de la Diputación, s/n, El Bosque.
Tel: 956 716 061.
Simple and comfortable hotel at the entrance to the small village of El Bosque, one of the entry points to the Grazalema park. "Trucha" means trout, and there is a trout stream next to the hotel. **$**

Cortijo Huerta Dorotea
Ctra Villamartín-Ubrique km 12, Prado del Rey.
Tel: 956 724 291.
Accommodation is split between eight rooms in a traditional Andalucían farmhouse, and in Finnish log-cabins (originally imported for Seville's Expo 92), each with two bedrooms. There is also a horse-riding centre. **$**

Jerez de la Frontera
Jerez
Avda Alvaro Domecq, 35.
Tel: 956 300 600.
In the pleasant, leafy residential part of town, the classic Jerez hotel, recently renovated. Swimming pool and tennis courts. **$$$$**

Montecastillo Hotel and Golf Resort
Ctra de Arcos.
Tel: 956 151 200.
A few kilometres outside Jerez, near the motor-racing track, a sprawling and luxurious neo-Moorish palace adjoining a top class golf course designed by Jack Nicklaus. **$$$$**

Avenida Jerez
Avda Alvaro Domecq, 10.
Tel: 956 347 411.
Modern, comfortable and functional, and at a good address on Jerez's wide Alvaro Domecq boulevard. **$$$**

Hotel Torres
Arcos, 29.
Tel: 956 323 400.
Centrally located, perhaps the best budget-option in a town short on lower-priced hotels. **$**

Jimena de la Frontera and environs
Hostal El Anón
Calle Consuelo, 34, Jimena de la Frontera.
Tel: 956 640 113.

Delightfully haphazard in its distribution, the result of joining several village houses, this is a long-time favourite rural inn, a good base for excursions into the spectacular surrounding countryside. **$**

Casa Convento La Almoraima
Finca La Almoraima, Castellar de la Frontera.
Tel: 956 693 002.
Set in the middle of a 40,000-acre hunting estate cloaked in cork oaks, a 17th-century convent restored as a 17-room country hotel offering tranquil, though basic, lodgings. **$$**

San Roque
Suites Hotel
San Roque Club, N340 km 126.5.
Tel: 956 613 030.
Luxury accommodation, bungalow-style, next to golf course, with full sports facilities including horse-riding centre. **$$$$**

Hotel Sotogrande
Ctra N-340 km 131.
Tel: 956 794 387.
Light and airy, and a favourite with golfers, this hotel is next door to the legendary Valderrama golf course, and on the edge of a cork oak forest. **$$$**

Casa Señorial La Solana
N340 km 116, Torreguadiaro.
Tel: 956 780 236.
An atmosphere of faded elegance, in an 18-room country hostelry in a tastefully restored 18th-century mansion surrounded by a large garden. **$$**

Sanlúcar de Barrameda
Los Helechos
Plaza de la Madre de Dios, 9.
Tel: 956 367 655.
Friendly atmosphere in a classic Andalucían setting, around a central courtyard with colourful potted plants in the centre of the town. **$**

Posada del Palacio
Caballeros, 11.
Tel: 956 364 840.
Welcoming ambience in an 18th-century aristocratic town house, with rooms arranged around a central patio. Closed January–February. **$**

Tarifa and environs
Dos Mares
Ctra Cádiz–Málaga, km 79.5, Tarifa.
Tel: 68 40 35.
Cheerful, recently renovated hotel located right on the windsurfing beach of Los Lances. Closed January–March. **$$$**

Hurricane Hotel
Ctra Cádiz-Málaga km 77, Tarifa.
Tel. 956 684 919.
Near the windswept Tarifa beach, popular with the wind-surf set and horse-trekkers (there are stables and horses for hire on the premises), with a fun, laid-back ambience. **$$**

Convento de San Francisco
La Plazuela, s/n, Vejer de la Frontera.
Tel: 956 451 001.
Basic but comfortable, 25 rooms in a restored 17th-century convent in the spectacular hilltop village of Vejer, overlooking the coast. Meals are served in the former refectory. **$$**

Price Guide

All the prices are for a double room:
$$$$ = Over 20,000 pesetas
$$$ = 15–20,000 pesetas
$$ = 8–15,000 pesetas
$ = Under 8,000 pesetas

CÓRDOBA
Amistad Córdoba
Plaza de Maimónides, 3.
Tel: 957 420 335.
One of the best options in its range if you want to be close to the sights. Comfortable rooms in two former mansions looking over the Plaza Maimónides. **$$$**

Parador de Turismo La Arruzafa
Avda de la Arruzafa, 33.
Tel: 957 275 900.
Modern establishment in the parador network offers fine views from a hill on the outskirts of the city. **$$$**

Maimonides
Torrijos, 4.
Tel: 957 471 500.
Close to the Mosque, medium-sized hotel with a pretty Andalucían patio. **$$**

Albucasis
Buen Pastor, 11.
Tel: 957 478 625.
Family-run establishment offering good value and clean, comfortable lodgings around a central courtyard in the heart of the old town. **$$**

Gonzalez
Manriquez, 3.
Tel: 957 479 819.
Simple but comfortably appointed hotel in the heart of the old Jewish quarter of Córdoba, installed in a converted 16th-century palace. Very convenient for sight seeing. **$$**

Los Omeyas
Calle Encarnación, 17.
Tel: 957 492 267.
In the Judería, this new 27-room hotel, built in traditional style, offers more amenities than you'd expect of this category. **$**

Marisa
Cardenal Herrero, 6.
Tel: 957 473 142.
Comfortable and friendly, a good budget option, facing the Córdoba mosque. **$**

Lucena
Santo Domingo
El Agua, 11.
Tel: 957 511 100.
Opened in 1997, in a former 17th-century convent, 30 rooms arranged around central cloisters. **$$**

Montilla
Don Gonzalo
Ctra Madrid–Málaga km 447.
Tel: 957 650 658.
Convenient, modern highway hotel on the outskirts of Montilla, in the heart of Córdoba's wine country. **$$**

Bellido
Enfermería, 57.
Tel: 957 651 915.
Inexpensive pension in the centre of town, basic but clean and comfortable. The bar dispenses local wine from its own stock of barrels. **$**

Palma del Río
Hospedería San Francisco
Avda Pío X11, 35.
Tel: 957 710 183.
This hotel, also renowned for its fine food, is installed in a former 15th-century Franciscan monastery. **$$**

Priego de Córdoba
Villa Turística de Priego
Aldea de Zagrilla.
Tel: 957 703 503.
This holiday complex of self-catering units, part of the Andalucían "Villas Turísticas" chain, is located in the countryside a few kilometres from the town of Priego. **$$**

Zuheros
Zuhayra
Calle Mirador 10.
Tel: 957 694 693.
Simple but comfortable, with good restaurant, in the pretty village of Zuheros at the northern entrance to the Subbética nature park. **$**

GRANADA
Parador de Turismo de San Francisco
Real de la Alhambra.
Tel: 958 221 440.
Reservations are essential to get into the most sought-after rooms in the parador network, in a converted 15th-century Francisco monastery within the Alhambra gardens themselves. **$$$$**
Alhambra Palace
Peña Partida, 2.
Tel: 958 221 468.
At the foot of the Alhambra walls, an ochre-coloured neo-Moorish fantasy with good views over the city. The hotel bar and terrace is a popular meeting place. **$$$$**
Triunfo
Plaza del Triunfo, 19.
Off the main thoroughfare of Granada, the Gran Vía de Colón, a small and comfortably-appointed hotel, convenient for shopping and sights in the centre of the city. **$$$**
Hostal América
Real de la Alhambra, 53.
Tel: 958 227 471.
A small and intimate family-run hotel in an enviable location within Alhambra grounds. Closed November–February. **$$$**
Victoria
Puerta Real, 3.
Tel: 958 257 700.
Old-world charm prevails in this classic hotel in the centre of Granada. **$$**

Juan Miguel
Acera del Darro, 24.
Tel: 958 521 111.
Reasonably-priced, comfortable option in the busy central district of Granada. **$$**
Reina Cristina
Tablas, 4.
Tel: 958 253 211.
Comfortable and reasonably priced, in the heart of the city in what was once home of poet Luis Rosales, now completely modernised. **$$**
Hostal Suecia
Calle Molinos, 8.
Tel. 958 225 044.
In a tranquil location at the southern foot of the Alhambra, seven rooms in a traditional villa with a leafy garden, offering excellent value for money. **$**

Price Guide

All the prices are for a double room:
$$$$ = Over 20,000 pesetas
$$$ = 15–20,000 pesetas
$$ = 8–15,000 pesetas
$ = Under 8,000 pesetas

Almuñecar
Los Fenicios
Paseo de Andrés Segovia,
La Herradura.
Tel: 958 827 900.
A bright, modern hotel right on the beach in the quiet fishing village of La Herradura, next to Almuñecar, with good views of the coast. **$$$**
Casablanca
Plaza San Cristobal, 4.
Tel: 958 635 575.
With its camp-Moorish façade, the mood in this colourful 15-room hotel in the centre of Almuñecar has more to do with Casablanca the movie than Casablanca the Moroccan city. Eclectically-furnished rooms are large and airy. **$$**
La Tartana
Ctra de Málaga km 308, La Herradura.
Tel: 958 640 535.
Resembling an Andalucían-style doll's house, the charm of this delightful five-room hostelry more than makes up for its inconvenient

location on the wrong side of the highway from the town and beach of La Herradura. **$**

Alpujarras area
Villa Turística de Bubión
Barrio Alto, Bubión.
Tel: 958 763 111.
The first, and still the best, of the Andalucían regional "Villas Turisticas" network, with modern self-catering apartments of various sizes, built in the traditional Alpujarras style. **$$**
Las Terrazas
Plaza del Sol, 7, Bubión.
Tel: 958 763 252.
Simple but tasteful, and excellent value for money, a favourite with trekkers and bikers as a base to explore the Alpujarras. **$**
Alcazaba de Busquistar
Ctra Orgiva-Laujar km 37, Busquístar.
Tel: 958 858 687.
Not far from Trevelez, the highest village in Spain, a rural holiday complex of 47 self-catering units. **$$**
Alquería de Morayma
Ctra Cádiar-Torvizon, Cádiar.
Tel: 958 342 221.
Rooms are in a group of five small houses with adjoining shrine and farmhouse which evoke Moorish Andalucían atmosphere in a pristine rural setting. **$**

Guadix
Comercio
Calle Mira de Amezcua, 3.
Tel: 958 660 500.
Early 20th-century charm still permeates this family-run hotel, built in 1905, in spite of complete renovation in 1998. The common areas feature art exhibitions and live music concerts, and the restaurant serves the best food in town. **$**

Loja
La Bobadilla
Ctra Loja–Seville.
Tel: 958 321 861.
Super-deluxe hotel resort, built in Andalucían country palace style, standing on its own estate in the heart of the countryside. Top-rated restaurant, champagne for breakfast, and prices to match. **$$$$**

Sierra Nevada
Melia Rumaykiyya
Dehesa de San Jerónimo.
Tel: 958 481 400.
Comfortable modern hotel offering good services to skiers. **$$$**
Ziryab
Plaza Andalucía.
Tel: 958 480 512.
Conveniently close to the ski lifts and reasonably priced, the newest hotel in Granada's ski resort. **$$**

HUELVA
Tartessos
Avda Martín Alonso Pinzón, 13.
Tel: 959 282 711.
Good location in a quiet residential area of the city. **$$**

Aracena
Sierra de Aracena
Gran Vía, 21.
Tel: 959 126 175.
Family-run hotel in the centre of the town, with a neo-Mudejar façade and 42 simply furnished but comfortable rooms. **$**

Ayamonte and environs
Parador Costa de la Luz
El Castillito.
Tel: 959 320 700.
Modern parador in a superb situation on a hill overlooking the village of Ayamonte, the Guadiana river, and Portugal on the farther shore. **$$$**
Riu Canela
Paseo de los Gavilanes, Playa Isla Canela.
Tel: 959 477 124.
Large hotel, near the beach and surrounded by gardens. **$$**
Confortel Islantilla
Ctra La Antilla-Isla Cristina km 3, Isla Cristina.
Tel: 959 486 017.
Large, modern beach front hotel on a wide sandy beach, near a new golf course. **$$$**

Palos de la Frontera and environs
Parador Cristobal Colón
Ctra Matalascañas, Mazagón.
Tel: 959 536 300.
A modern parador in a tranquil, pine-shaded spot overlooking a sandy beach, with rooms opening out onto a garden. **$$$$**
Hostería de la Rábida
La Rábida.
Tel: 959 350 312.
Five-room hostelry, simple but comfortable, next door to the 15th-century Monastery of La Rábida. **$**
La Pinta
Rábida, 75, Palos de la Frontera.
Tel: 959 350 511.
Unpretentious, friendly 30-room hotel in the centre of the town of Palos. The restaurant serves simple but tasty fare. **$$**

Matalascañas
Tierra Mar
Matalascañas Parc, 120 Sector M.
Tel: 959 440 300.
Matalascañas, a grossly overbuilt beach resort, has little to recommend it... except that it is next to Doñana. This beachside hotel is a good base for exploring the national park. **$$**

JAÉN
Parador Castillo de Santa Catalina
Tel: 953 230 000.
On a hill overlooking the city, right next to Jaén's Moorish castle and built in the same style, with magnificent views of the sierra. **$$$**

Andujar
Don Pedro
Gabriel Zamora, 5.
Tel: 953 501 274.
Modest two-star hotel in the centre of the town, and a good place to sample reasonably-priced local specialities. **$**

Baeza
Casa Juanito
Avda Arca del Agua, s/n.
Tel: 953 740 040.
Simply appointed and inexpensive, on the main road out of town, a central position for the province. The restaurant is considered one of Jaén province's best. **$$**
Fuentenueva Hospedería
Paseo Arca del Agua.
Tel: 953 743 100.
Friendly, tastefully decorated small hotel installed in what used to be the town's women's prison. **$**

Cazorla and environs
Parador El Adelantado
Sacedo (26 km/16 miles from Cazorla).
Tel: 953 727 075.
In the heart of the sierra, a modern parador which is a good base from which to explore the wilderness of Cazorla park. **$$$**
Sierra de Cazorla
Carretera Sierra de Cazorla, La Iruela.
Tel: 953 720 015.
Functional but comfortable small hotel just outside the village of La Iruela, at the main entrance to the Cazorla park. **$**
Refugio Montaña Riogazas
Ctra Iruela-El Chorro, La Iruela.
Tel: 953 124 035.
10-room hotel, on its own at the northern edge of the Cazorla park. Open daily July–September, weekends only from October–June. **$**
La Hortizuela
Ctra del Tranco km 18, Santiago de la Espada.
Tel: 953 713 150.
In the heart of the Cazorla nature park, 27-room country inn in a former game warden's cottage. **$**

Ubeda
Parador Condestable Dávalos
Plaza Vázquez Molina, 1.
Tel: 953 750 345.
One of the oldest hotels in the parador chain, installed in a 16th-century palace in the centre of Ubeda's old Renaissance section, with large rooms. **$$$**
Palacio de la Rambla
Plaza del Marqués, 1.
Tel: 953 750 196.
This 16th-century palace continues to be the part-time residence of the Marquesa de la Rambla, but eight rooms – large, furnished with antiques, surrounding an ivy-covered central patio – have been opened to guests. **$$$**
La Paz
Andalucía, 1.
Tel: 953 750 848.
In the modern section of Ubeda but within walking distance of the

sights, a simple, comfortable budget option. **$**

MÁLAGA AND THE COSTA DEL SOL

Antequera
Parador de Antequera
Paseo García del Olmo, s/n.
Tel: 952 840 261.
Airy, spacious modern parador with good views of the sweeping plain of Antequera. **$$$**

Benaoján
El Molino del Santo
Barriada Estación.
Tel: 952 167 151.
English-run, 14-room country inn next to a rushing stream in the mountains near Ronda, not far from the Cueva de la Pileta and the Grazalema nature park. Restaurant serves good food. **$$**

Benalmádena
Alay
Puerto Deportivo, Benalmádena-Costa.
Tel: 952 446 000.
A modern hotel situated right next to the lively Benalmádena yacht harbour, one of the nightlife centres of the Costa del Sol. **$$$**
La Fonda
Calle Santo Domingo, 7, Benalmádena-Pueblo.
Tel: 952 568 273.
Small hotel in the middle of the surprisingly unspoiled village of Benalmádena a few miles inland from the coast. Lunch in the restaurant is prepared by students of the official hotel and catering school. **$$**

Estepona
Las Dunas
La Boladilla Baja, Crta N-340 km 163.
Tel: 952 794 354.
Luxurious spa hotel, split into several Andalucían-style buildings next to the beach east of Estepona, with large, sumptuously-decorated rooms. **$$$$**
El Paraíso
Urb El Paraíso, Ctra N340 km 167.
Tel: 952 883 000.

Modern hotel on a hill east of Estepona, by a golf course with views of the Strait of Gibraltar. **$$$$**
Atalaya Park
Ctra N340 km 163.
Tel: 952 889 000.
Not far from the Puerto Banús end of the Estepona municipality, set amidst gardens adjoining a top rate golf course. **$$$**
Caracas
Avda San Lorenzo, 50.
Tel: 952 800 800.
Comfortable and reasonably priced, a good choice in the centre of the relatively quiet seaside town of Estepona. **$**

Fuengirola
El Puerto
Paseo Marítimo, 32.
Tel: 952 470 100.
Modern high-rise hotel overlooking the fishing port of Fuengirola, on the busy seafront promenade. **$$**
Florida
Paseo Marítimo.
Tel: 952 476 100.
Comfortable and unostentatious lodgings on the seafront, close to the main shopping and nightlife spots in the town, with a pleasant leafy garden and pool, and convenient to the beach. **$$**

Malaga
Parador de Turismo Gibralfaro
Monte de Gibralfaro.
Tel: 952 221 903.
Recently renovated, this small parador is on the hill overlooking the city, next to an old Moorish fortress. Not convenient for those without a car. Reserve. **$$$**
Larios
Marqués de Larios, 2.
Tel: 952 222 200.
Modern hotel in the centre of the city, in a restored old building. **$$$$**
Don Curro
Sancha de Lara, 7.
Tel: 952 227 200.
A classic Málaga hostelry, with an old-fashioned atmosphere, on a quiet side street off central Málaga's main shopping district. **$$$**
Las Vegas
Paseo de Sancha, 22.
Tel: 952 217 712.

Near the Málaga bullring and next to the city's seafront promenade, with a pool and a large garden. **$$**
Hostal Derby
San Juan de Dios, 1.
Tel: 952 221 301.
Small, friendly hostal in a good central location just off the Plaza de la Marina. **$**

Marbella
El Fuerte
Avda El Fuerte.
Tel: 952 861 500.
Among the most professionally-run establishments on the Costa del Sol, and the best option in the centre of Marbella, at the end of the town's seafront promenade, with a tropical garden and rooms with views of the sea. **$$$**
Los Monteros
Ctra N340 km 187.
Tel: 952 771 700.
Exclusive luxury resort hotel adjoining a golf course near the beach 5 km (3 miles) east of Marbella. **$$$$**
Meliá Don Pepe
José Melia.
Tel: 277 0300.
Deluxe hotel on the western end of the town surrounded by a large tropical garden. **$$$$**
Puente Romano
Ctra N340 km 176,7.
Tel: 952 820 900.
A landmark on the "Golden Mile" west of the town, a palatial hotel designed like a Moorish-Andalucían pueblo, with gardens and trickling fountains and, within, marble and carpeted sumptuousness. **$$$$**
Marbella Club
Ctra N340 km 1178,2.
Tel: 952 822 211.
This classy 1950s hotel was the birthplace of the Marbella legend. Bungalow-style accommodation set among gardens which spread down to the beach. **$$$$**

Nerja
Parador de Nerja
Almuñécar, 8.
Tel: 952 520 050.
Modern parador on a cliff, overlooking beach, with rooms arranged around a pleasant garden. **$$$**

Monica
Playa Torrecilla.
Tel: 952 521 100.
Large, white Moorish style hotel
with good views of the sea. **$$$**
Paraíso del Mar
Calle Prolongación del Carabeo, 22.
Tel: 952 521 621.
Tranquil location on the edge of a
cliff, near the Parador, 12 rooms,
some with breathtaking views. **$$**
Casa Maro
Carmen 2, Maro.
Tel: 952 529 552.
Cosy small rustic 8-room German-
run hostelry on the sea-facing side
of the village of Maro, east of Nerja.
Its 5-table dining room advertises
itself as "the smallest gourmet
restaurant in the world". **$$**

Mijas
Hotel Mijas
Urb. Tamisa.
Tel: 952 485 800.
Modern, airy hotel with ample
gardens at the entrance to the
postcard village of Mijas, offering
fine views of the coast. **$$$**
Byblos Andaluz
Urb. Mijas Golf (near Fuengirola).
Tel: 952 473 050.
A super-deluxe spa hotel adjoining a
golf course 5 km (3 miles) inland
from Fuengirola. Top class restaurant
and stylish atmosphere. **$$$$**

Monda
Castillo de Monda
El Castillo.
Tel. 952 457 142.
Overlooking the village of Monda, a
castle-like 16-room hotel incorpora-
ting the ruins of a Moorish fortress.
Stylish and comfortable. **$$$**

Ojen
Refugio El Juanar
Sierra Blanca.
Tel: 952 881 000.
Standing in the middle of a forest in
the Sierra just inland from Marbella,
this was once a royal hunting lodge
and later part of the Parador chain.
Twenty-three rooms, and restaurant
serving game dishes in season. **$$**

Ronda
Parador de Ronda
Plaza de España.
Tel: 952 877 500.
The newest of Spain's paradors,
spectacularly perched on a cliff in
the best possible position next to
the famous gorge, the restored
façade of an old building concealing
a striking modern interior. **$$$$**
Polo
Mariano Souvirón, 8.
Tel: 952 872 447.
Comfortable with a pleasant atmos-
phere, in the centre of the town. **$**
Reina Victoria
Jerez, 25.
Tel: 952 871 240.
This grand old hotel built in 1906
could do with some renovation, but
the views over the cliff are still
unbeatable. **$$$**

Price Guide

All the prices are for a double
room:
$$$$ = Over 20,000 pesetas
$$$ = 15–20,000 pesetas
$$ = 8–15,000 pesetas
$ = Under 8,000 pesetas

Villanueva de la Concepción
La Posada del Torcal
Ctra La Joya.
Tel: 952 031 177.
Stylish hilltop hostelry built in the
style of a traditional Andalucían
farm manor, with 8 rooms, at the
foot of the Torcal nature area. **$$$**

Torremolinos
Aloha Puerto
Salvador Allende, 45, Montemar.
Tel: 952 387 066.
Large and modern, in a good
location next to the beach. **$$$**
Cervantes
Las Mercedes.
Tel: 952 384 033.
Large, modern hotel, the best option
for those who want to stay close to
the centre of Torremolinos. **$$$**
Tropicana
Trópico, 6.
Tel: 952 386 600.
Good choice right on the beach at
western end of Torremolinos's

popular fish-restaurant quarter, La
Carihuela, with fun atmosphere. **$$$**
Miami
Aladino, 14.
Tel: 952 385 255.
Inexpensive, informal small family-
run hotel in a traditional Spanish
villa next to the Carihuela beach.
They don't take credit cards. **$$$**

SEVILLE
Alfonso XIII
San Fernando, 2.
Tel: 954 222 850.
Old-style elegance in this all-time
classic hotel of Seville, built in Neo-
Mudéjar style in the 1920s. **$$$$**
Hotel Casa Imperial
Imperial, 29.
Tel: 954 500 300.
One of Seville's newest hostelries
in a restored 16th-century palace
behind the Casa de Pilatos, with
four inner patios. Twenty four
suites, each decorated differently,
with enormous bathrooms. **$$$$**
Inglaterra
Plaza Nueva, 7.
Tel: 954 224 970.
Comfortable and friendly, overlooking
the Plaza Nueva, a convenient
location for touring the city. **$$$$**
Las Casas del Rey de Baeza
Plaza Cristo de la Redención, 2.
Tel: 954 561 496.
Tucked away on a small square
near the Casa de Pilatos, 44 rooms
in a renovated town house. **$$$**
Las Casas de la Judería
Callejón de Dos Hermanas.
Tel: 954 415 150.
Three old palaces in the Santa Cruz
quarter were restored and
converted into this maze-like hotel,
with inner courtyards. **$$$**
Doña María
Don Remondo, 19.
Tel: 952 224 990.
Close to the cathedral, with rooms
of various size, some with antiques,
and a roof-top swimming-pool. **$$$**
Murillo
Lope de Rueda, 7.
Tel: 954 216 095.
Simple but comfortable and
reasonably-priced, with a friendly,
informal atmosphere, in the heart
of Santa Cruz quarter. **$$**

Simon
García de Vinuesa, 19.
Tel: 954 226 660.
One of the best-value choices in the centre of the city, not far from the cathedral, offering pleasant but no-frill lodgings in an 18th-century house around an Andalucían patio. **$**

Internacional
Aguilas, 17.
Tel: 954 213 207.
Inexpensive, family-run hotel in an old building centred around an inner courtyard, not far from the Casa de Pilatos in central Seville. **$**

Near Seville

Oromana
Avda de Portugal, s/n, Alcalá de Guadaira.
Tel: 955 686 400.
Andalucían country manor set among pines, 15 km (9 miles) east of Seville, just off the A-92 motorway. **$$**

Hacienda San Ignacio
Real, 194, Castilleja de la Cuesta.
Tel: 954 160 430.
Installed in a rambling 17th-century Andalucían manor at the edge of this town, just off the motorway to Huelva, just east of Seville. **$$$**

Casa Manolo
Avda Sevilla, 29, Los Palacios.
Tel: 955 811 086.
The prosperous farming town of Palacios doesn't have much to tempt the traveller (unless you're into conversations about farm machinery), but this small, comfortable hotel offers inexpensive lodgings a half an hour from Seville. The restaurant is surprisingly good. **$**

Cortijo El Esparragal
Ctra de Mérida km 21, Gerena.
Tel: 955 782 702.
This is one of a number of working ranches just north of Seville which have been converted for paying guests. Owned by a Marquis, it stands on a 7,500-acre estate. **$$$**

Hacienda Benazuza
Virgen de las Nieves, s/n, Sanlúcar La Mayor.
Tel: 955 703 344.
Built on the site of an old farmhouse, a Moorish fantasy palace, 20 km (12 miles) from Seville. **$$$$**

Carmona

Casa de Carmona
Plaza Lasso, Carmona (33 km/20 miles/east of Seville).
Tel: 954 143 300.
One of Andalucía's most stylish hotels, installed in a 16th-century aristocratic mansion. **$$$$**

Parador Alcázar del Rey Don Pedro
Carmona.
Tel: 954 141 010.
A Mudéjar-style building on a hill overlooking the town, completely renovated in 1998, with spacious rooms. **$$$**

Price Guide

All the prices are for a double room:
$$$$ = Over 20,000 pesetas
$$$ = 15–20,000 pesetas
$$ = 8–15,000 pesetas
$ = Under 8,000 pesetas

Cazalla de la Sierra

La Cartuja de Cazalla
Ctra Cazalla-Constantina, km 55.
Tel: 954 884 516.
This small hotel, a few kilometres from the village, stands within an old Carthusian monastery which was abandoned last century and is now in the process of being restored. **$$**

Pasada del Moro
Paseo del Moro.
Tel: 954 884 858.
In a modern section of the village, gleaming white 15-room hotel offering good value for money, and a restaurant serving interesting local specialities. **$**

Las Navezuelas
Ctra SE196 km 43.
Tel: 954 884 764.
Country hotel in a restored 16th-century olive mill surrounded by a large farm estate, with a cosy, friendly, and informal atmosphere. **$**

Campgrounds

Although there are some campsites in wilderness areas, camping in Spain is seen as a cheaper alternative to hotels, not as a way to get back to nature. Camping outside official sites is not generally allowed, and authorities are especially vigilant by the side of main roads and on the beaches. Independent campers can try and obtain permission to camp on private property, such as a farm, from the owner.

Official camp sites are rated according to facilities as luxury, first, second, or third class. Some have supermarkets and restaurants attached. An **Area de Acampada** indicates something that approximates camping out in the wild. **Campings** (camp-grounds) in main tourist areas are too crowded for comfort in summer.

A full list of campsites is published in the camping guide (*Guía Oficial de Campings*) published by Turespaña (Secretaria General de Turismo), available in most bookshops. Not all sites are open all the year, so it is advisable to phone beforehand.

Below is a selection of camp sites, chosen because of their location in or near nature reserves.

Almería

Naútico La Caleta
Parque Natural Cabo de Gata, Níjar.
Tel: 950 525 237.
Close to the beach.

Rodalquilar
Poblado Minero Rodalquilar, Níjar.
Next to the only gold mine in Spain (no longer in operation), in the Cabo de Cata nature park.

Los Escullos-San José
San José.
Tel: 950 389 811.
Just under one kilometre from the beach, in the Cabo de Gata nature park. Scuba diving centre.

Tau
San José.
Tel: 950 380 166.
In a eucalyptus wood in Cabo de Gata, 270 yds (250 metres). from the sea.

Las Menas
Ctra Seróm-Gergal km 10, Serón. In an abandoned mining town surrounded by pines in the Sierra de Filabres.

Cádiz
Caños de Meca
Barbate.
Tel: 956 437 120.
Near Cape Trafalgar on the Atlantic coast, 656 yrds (600 m). from one of the best beaches in Andalucía.
Los Linares
Parque Natural Sierra de Grazalema, Benamahoma.
Tel: 956 716 275.
In the Grazalema nature park.
La Torrecilla
El Bosque.
Tel: 956 716 095.
In the Sierra de Grazalema nature park.
Tajo Rodillo
Ctra C-344 km 49, Grazalema.
Tel: 956 234 015.
Near the town of Grazalema in the mountains of Cádiz.
Tavizna
Ctra C-3331 km 49, Puente de Tavizna, Ubrique.
Tel: 956 463 011.
On the banks of a river, in the Grazalema nature park.

Córdoba
La Breña
Almodóvar del Río.
Tel: 957 338 333.
Next to a reservoir.
Cortijo Las Palomas
Ctra Carcabuey-Zagrilla km 5
Tel: 957 720 002.
Next to a natural spring in the Sierra Subbética nature park.
Cortijo Los Villares
Ctra Carcabuey-Rute, Priego de Córdoba.
Tel: 957 704 054.
In the Sierra Subbética nature park.

Granada
Orgiva
Valle del Guadalfeo, Orgiva
Tel: 958 784 307.
Close to a river, and near the Poqueira valley in the Alpujarras.
Balcón de Pitres
Ctra Orgiva-Ugíjar km 51, Pago Taruguera, Pitres.
Tel: 958 766 111.
In the Alpujarras region.

Huelva
Aracena Sierra
Marimateo, Aracena.
Tel: 959 501 005.
In the Sierra de Aracena nature park.
Centro de Educación Ambiental Relieve
Ctra N-433 km 118, Cortegana.
Tel: 959 425 468.
Las Cabañas de Cumbres
Cumbres Mayores.
Tel: 959 710 177.
In the Sierra de Aracena nature park.
El Madroñal
Fuenteheridos.
Tel: 959 501 201.
In a chestnut wood in the Sierra de Aracena nature park.

Jáen
San Isicio
Camino San Isicio, Cazorla.
Tel: 953 721 280.
2 km (1 mile) from Cazorla village.
Chopera de Coto Rios
Santiago Pontones, Coto-Ríos.
Tel: 953 713 005.
In the middle of the Cazorla nature park.
Fuente de la Pascuala
Ctra del Tranco km 23, Coto-Ríos.
Tel: 953 713 028.
In the middle of the Cazorla nature park.
Llanos de Arance
Ctra del Tranco km 22, Coto-Ríos.
Tel: 953 713 139.
In the middle of the Cazorla nature park.

Málaga
Parque Ardales
Embalse Conde de Guadalhorce, Ardales.
Tel: 952 458 087.
Surrounded by pines in the lake area, north of Málaga.
Eco Camping Amatista
La Dehesilla, 23, Benaoján.
Tel: 952 114 241.
Next to the Cueva del Gato cave near Ronda.
Mirador de la Axarquía
Las Encinillas, Comares.
Tel: 952 509 209.
In the grape-growing region of the Axarquía east of Málaga.
Presa La Viñuela
Ctra A-356 km 2,4, La Viñuela.

Tel: 952 030 127.
Next to reservoir in the Axarquía region.
Pinsapo Azul
Parque Sierra de las Nieves, La Yunquera.
Tel: 952 482 754.
In the Sierra de las Nieves park, off the old road from Málaga to Ronda.

Seville
Reserva Verde del Huéznar
Ctra Cazalla-San Nicolás, Cazalla de la Sierra.
Tel: 954 884 560.
In the Sierra Norte nature park.
Sierra Brava
Avda de los Lagos, Guillena.
Tel: 954 131 165.
Near Seville, in bull breeding country.

Youth Hostels

It is advisable not to turn up on spec as some youth hostels only open part of the year or may be undergoing restoration. For information and reservations, contact **Interjoven**, Calle Miño 24, Seville, tel: 954 558 293.

Almería
Almería
Isla de Fuerteventura, s/n.
Tel: 950 269 788.
Aguadulce
Campillo del Moro, s/n.
Tel: 950 340 346.

Cadiz
Algeciras
Ctra N-340 km 95,6.
Tel: 956 679 060.
El Bosque
Molino de Enmedio, s/n.
Tel: 956 716 212.
Chipiona
Pinar de Villa, s/n.
Tel: 956 371 480.
Jerez
Avenida Carrero Blanco, 30.
Tel: 956 143 901.

Córdoba
Córdoba
Plaza Juda Levi, s/n.
Tel: 957 290 166.

Granada

Granada
Ramón y Cajal, 2.
Tel: 958 284 306.
Sierra Nevada
Estación de Pradollano.
Tel: 958 480 305.
Viznar
Camino Fuente Grande.
Tel: 958 543 307.

Huelva

Huelva
Avenida Marchena Colombo, 14.
Tel: 959 284 065.
Punta Umbría
Avenida Océano, 13.
Tel: 959 311 650.
Mazagón
Cuesta de la Barca, s/n.
Tel: 959 536 262.

Jaén

Cazorla
Plaza Mauricio Martinez, 6.
Tel: 953 720 329.

Málaga

Málaga
Plaza Pio XII.
Tel: 952 308 500.
Marbella
Trapiche, 2.
Tel: 952 771 491.

Seville

Seville
Isaac Perál, 2.
Tel: 954 613 150.
Constantina
Cuesta Blanca, s/n.
Tel: 955 881 589.

Eating Out

What to Eat

It is not necessary to step into a restaurant to eat well in Andalucía. Fast food was a part of Spanish culture when the hot dog was hardly more than a puppy. **Tapas**, tasty snacks varying from a plateful of olives to stewed tripe and chick peas, are served in thousands of bars. Sometimes they come automatically with the drink. Sometimes you have to order them and pay extra. If you want more, you can ask for a *ración* (plateful), or *media ración* (half plateful). In many bars calling themselves cafeterias, you can order a *combinado*. This is usually a variation on pork chop, fried eggs, ham, salad and chips. Even the smallest village usually has a bar serving *tapas* or a *fonda* (inn) serving simple set meals at budget prices.

But Andalucía also offers a vast range of good restaurant eating to suit all pockets and tastes. Efforts have been made to develop regional dishes and resuscitate Moorish recipes. The greatest variety of restaurants is to be found along the Costa del Sol, where you can try everything from Vietnamese cuisine to Lebanese. Only a brief selection of these eating places is listed here.

Restaurants usually offer a *menú del día*, a three-course meal, including wine, at an economical price. Note also that on the Atlantic and Mediterranean coasts you can eat well on the beaches in restaurants known as *chiringuitos* and *merenderos*. Some of these have become quite sophisticated, with prices to match. Others remain simple.

Opening times: most restaurants open at 1–1.30pm for lunch (last orders around 3.30pm) and 7–8pm for dinner (last orders 10.30–11pm). Restaurants in coastal areas, especially the Costa del Sol, tend to open and close earlier.

Where to Eat

ALMERÍA
Club de Mar
Muelle de las Almadrabillas.
Tel: 950 235 048.
Lunch and dinner. Closed Monday.
Amex, Mastercard, Visa.
Recently moved to a modern new location by the beach, this classic Almería restaurant has built a solid reputation on its fresh seafood dishes. (**$$**)
La Gruta
Ctra N340 km 436.
Tel: 950 239 335.
Dinner only. Closed Sunday and November. Diners, Amex, Mastercard, Visa.
Unusual setting, inside a cave overlooking the sea between Almería and Aguadulce. Grilled meat is the speciality. (**$$**)
Veracruz
Avda Cabo de Gata 199.
Tel: 950 251 220.
Lunch and dinner. Amex, Mastercard, Visa.
Near the beach in Almería, specialising in seafood, with a selection of live fish and shellfish kept in tanks. (**$$**)

Garrucha
El Almejero
Explanada del Puerto, s/n.
Tel: 950 460 405.
Lunch and dinner. Closed Monday, November. Amex, Mastercard, Visa.
Fresh fish and prawns on the terrace overlooking the fishing port where the catch is unloaded, in the fishing town of Garrucha near Mojácar. (**$$**)

Roquetas de Mar
Albaida
Avenida de las Gaviotas, Urb .
Tel: 950 333 821.
Lunch and dinner. Closed Monday, January. Amex, Diners, Visa.
Fresh seafood, including a selection of live fish and shellfish from the restaurant's own tanks. (**$$–$$$**)

Vera
Terraza Carmona
Manuel Giménez 1.
Tel: 950 390 188.
Lunch and dinner. Closed Monday,
Sept 1–15. Amex, Mastercard,
Visa.
Located in the beachside
community of Vera, north of
Mojácar, long-established
restaurant offers a good
combination of local dishes (mainly
fish) and international fare in a
lively atmosphere. (**$$**)

Price Guide

Inexpensive ($) = under 1,500
pesetas per person for a three
course meal, not including wine.
Moderate ($$) = 1,500–4,000
pesetas.
Expensive ($$$) = more than
4,000 pesetas.
Moderate to Expensive
restaurants usually accept at
least one of the credit cards;
Mastercard and Visa are more
widely accepted than Amex or
Diners. Cheaper establishments
prefer cash.

CÁDIZ
El Faro
San Felix, 15.
Tel: 956 211 068.
Lunch and dinner. Amex, Diners,
Mastercard, Visa.
The best-known of Cádiz's
restaurants, located in the crusty old
quarter of town, and justifiably
renowned for its fresh seafood served
in its wood-beamed dining room.
There's also a *tapas* bar. (**$$–$$$**)
Ventorillo del Chato
Ctra de San Fernando km 647.
Tel: 956 250 025.
Lunch and dinner. Closed Sunday.
Amex, Mastercard, Visa.
In an 18th-century inn standing on its
own on the sandy isthmus that joins
Cádiz to the mainland, specialising in
seafood, although good meat dishes
are also offered. (**$$**)
Achuri
Plocia, 15.
Tel: 956 253 613.
Lunch and dinner. No dinner

Sunday, Tuesday, Wednesday.
Mastercard, Visa.
For more than half a century, this
down-to-earth establishment, on a
back street not far from the Puerta
de Tierra in the old part of the city,
has been popular for its
combination of Andalucían and
Basque cuisine. (**$$**)

Arcos de la Frontera
El Convento
Marques de Terresoto, 7.
Tel: 956 703 222.
Lunch and dinner. Amex,
Mastercard, Visa.
Dining area decorated in Seville tiles
and potted plants and arranged
around interior courtyard in a 17th-
century palace on narrow street in
the old part of the village. Menu
features some unusual regional
dishes for the more daring. (**$$**)
El Sombrero de Tres Picos
Avda Sombrero de Tres Picos,
El Santiscal.
Tel: 956 708 017.
Lunch and dinner. Mastercard, Visa.
By the shore of the lake beneath
the village, a pleasant place
(especially when weather allows for
outdoor dining), mainly meat and
sausages. (**$$**)

Barbate
Torres
Ruiz de Alda, 1.
Tel: 956 430 988.
Lunch and dinner. Closed Monday.
Amex, Mastercard, Visa.
On the seafront in the fishing
village, two-storey restaurant
serving fresh seafood caught
locally. (**$$**)

El Puerto de Santa María
Casa Flores
Ribera del Río, 9.
Tel: 956 543 512.
Lunch and dinner.
Small restaurant with an
excellent *tapas* bar and a few
tables, serving fresh seafood near
the town's famous "Ribera del
Marisco"("Shellfish Row"). (**$$**)
La Goleta
Ctra Rota km 0.75.
Tel: 956 854 232.
Lunch and dinner. Closed Monday,

except June, July, August, for
fortnight from first Sunday in
November. Amex, Mastercard, Visa.
A pleasant villa in a residential area
just outside the town, offering good
value in fresh fish dishes. (**$$**)
El Faro de el Puerto
Crta El Puerto-Rota.
Tel: 956 858 003.
Lunch and dinner. Closed Sunday
dinner. Amex, Diner, Mastercard,
Visa.
Sister restaurant to the famous El
Faro of Cádiz, run by young chef-
proprietor Fernando Córdoba, with
equally fresh seafood, but a more
imaginative approach, set in a
pleasant villa outside the town
centre. Best to reserve. (**$$$**)
El Patio
Misericordia, 1.
Tel: 956 540 506.
Lunch and dinner. Amex, Diners,
Mastercard, Visa.
Near El Puerto's legendary Ribera del
Marisco (Shellfish Row), in an old
house with a cool interior courtyard,
serving local seafood in addition to
classic Andalucían meat dishes such
as Rabo de Toro (oxtail). (**$$**)

Jerez de la Frontera
La Mesa Redonda
Manuel de la Quintana, 3.
Tel: 956 340 069.
Lunch and dinner. Closed Sunday,
holidays and August. Amex,
Mastercard, Visa.
Small, eight-table restaurant, serving
impeccable Jerez dishes, most
based on recipes from aristocratic
Sherry families, in a comfortable,
friendly atmosphere. One of the best
restaurants in Andalucía.
Reservations essential. (**$$–$$$**)
Venta Antonio
Ctra Jerez-Sanlúcar km 5.
Tel: 956 140 535. Lunch and
dinner. Amex, Diners, Master, Visa.
Five kilometres outside Jerez on a
country road, Venta Antonio started
out as a modest roadside inn, but
has earned an enviable reputation
for its fresh seafood. A Jerez
favourite. (**$$**)
La Posada
Arboledilla 1–2.
Tel: 956 337 474.
Lunch and dinner. Closed Saturday

dinner and Sunday, and August.
Amex, Mastercard, Visa.
Split into two locales on opposite
sides of the street, popular place
with a short but sweet menu,
mainly traditional meat and fish
dishes. (**$$**)

San Roque
Los Remos
Finca Villa Victoria, Ctra La Linea-
Gibraltar km 2, Campamento San
Roque.
Tel: 956 698 412.
Lunch and dinner. Closed Sunday
night, except July and August.
Amex, Diners, Mastercard, Visa.
Delicious seafood served in style in
a magnificent colonial house
surrounded by gardens. Best to
reserve. (**$$$**)

Sanlúcar de Barrameda
Bigote
Bajo de Guía.
Tel: 956 362 696.
Lunch and dinner. Closed Sunday.
Amex, Diners, Mastercard, Visa.
The Bajo de Guía is a district
outside Sanlúcar, on the banks of
the Guadalquivir river. Every other
house is a restaurant specialising
in the local seafood, such as giant
prawns and fried sole. This is one
of the best. (**$$**)

CÓRDOBA
Almudaina
Jardines de los Santos Martires, 1.
Tel: 957 474 342.
Lunch and dinner. Closed Sunday
lunch (all year), Sunday dinner (15
June–1 September).
Installed in a 15th-century house
near the Alcázar gardens, serving
local recipes based on fresh
produce. Seven different dining
areas, around a central courtyard,
are decorated with antiques. (**$$$**)
El Caballo Rojo
Cardenal Herrero, 28.
Tel: 957 478 001.
Lunch and dinner. Amex, Diners,
Mastercard, Visa.
Near the mosque, the longest
established and best-known of
Córdoba's restaurants is still a
good bet. Aside from traditional

Spanish dishes, the menu
incorporates some unusual Moorish
preparations, based on medieval
recipes, such as Cordero a la Miel
(lamb in honey). Reservations
essential. (**$$$**)
El Churrasco
Romero, 16.
Tel: 957 290 819.
Lunch and dinner. Closed August.
Amex, Diners, Mastercard, Visa.
The name suggests grilled meats (a
speciality here), but there is much
more besides in this restaurant. A
good place to try Salmorejo, a thick
Cordoba version of gazpacho. Also
worth checking is the wine museum
and wine cellar housed in an annex.
Best to reserve. (**$$**)
El Blasón
José Zorrilla, 11.
Tel: 957 480 625.
Lunch and dinner. Amex, Diners,
Mastercard, Visa.
In an old inn in central Córdoba,
with bar downstairs and dining area
upstairs, under the same
management as El Caballo Rojo
(above) with a slightly more modern
menu. (**$$–$$$**)
Bodegas Campos
Los Lineros, 32.
Tel: 957 474 142.
Lunch and dinner. Closed Sunday.
Amex, Diners, Mastercard, Visa.
Colourful restaurant installed in a
former wine cellar near the Julio
Romero de Torres museum,
decorated like an upmarket tavern,
serving variations on classical
Cordoba cuisine. (**$$**)
Federación de Peñas Cordobesas
Conde y Luque, 8.
Tel: 957 476 698.
Lunch and dinner. Closed
Wednesday. Mastercard, Visa.
In the old town, a good budget
option for simple traditional
Andalucían fare, with dining on open
patio in summer. (**$**)

Palma del Río
Hospedería San Francisco
Avenida Pío XII, 35.
Tel: 957 710 183.
Lunch and dinner. Closed Sunday
evening and 1–15 August.
Mastercard, Visa.
Restaurant in the hotel of the same

name, in a restored 17th-century
monastery, famous for its
combination of Basque and
Andalucían flavours. (**$$–$$$**)

Montilla
Las Camachas
Ctra Cordoba-Malaga km 48.
Tel: 957 650 004.
Lunch and dinner. Amex,
Mastercard, Visa.
A rambling old roadside restaurant
where the landed gentry of the wine
district dine out. Sturdy, good food,
and Montilla wines on sale. (**$$**)

Price Guide

Inexpensive ($) = under 1,500
pesetas per person for a three
course meal, not including wine.
Moderate ($$) = 1,500–4,000
pesetas.
Expensive ($$$) = more than
4,000 pesetas.

GRANADA
Sevilla
Oficios, 12.
Tel: 958 221 223.
Lunch and dinner. Closed Sunday
dinner, Monday all day. Amex,
Diners, Mastercard, Visa.
This Granada classic, opened in
1930 and close to the cathedral, is
a good place to sample traditional
dishes from Granada such as
Jamon con Habas (cured ham with
broad beans) or Tortilla Sacromonte
(omelette with lambs brains, ham
and vegetables). (**$$**)
Galatino
Gran Vía, 29.
Tel: 958 800 803.
Lunch and dinner. Amex, Diners,
Mastercard, Visa.
Conveniently located in the centre
of the city, Granada's newest
restaurant (opened 1996) has a
striking modern decor, and its
creative cuisine has already earned
an enviable reputation. Best to
reserve. (**$$$**)
La Mimbre
Avda del Generalife.
Tel: 958 222 276.
Lunch only. Closed Saturday. Amex,
Mastercard, Visa.

Small restaurant in an unbeatable location at the very foot of the Alhambra walls, with outdoor dining on shaded terrace in summer. Traditional Granada dishes. (**$$**)

La Alacena
Plaza del Padre Suarez, 5.
Tel: 958 221 105.
Lunch and dinner. Closed Sunday. Amex, Mastercard, Visa.
Intimate restaurant, location underground, in the cellar of a former 16th-century convent in central Granada, serving variations on regional dishes. (**$$$**)

Los Manueles, Zaragoza, 2,
Tel: 958 223 413.
Lunch and dinner. Amex, Diners, Mastercard, Visa.
Very atmospheric, traditional tiled tavern, serving classic Granadine fare such as Tortilla de Sacromonte. (**$$**)

Cenes de la Vega
Ruta del Veleta
Ctra Sierra Nevada km 5.4
Tel: 958 486 134.
Lunch and dinner. Closed Sunday evening. Amex, Diners, Mastercard, Visa.
On the old road to Sierra Nevada, 5 km (3 miles) from the city, spacious restaurant which has served good food for decades. Spacious, well decorated dining rooms, and a new outdoor terrace for dining al fresco. Classic Spanish food is the speciality. Best to reserve. (**$$$**)

Alpujarras
Teide, Carretera 1, Bubion.
Tel: 958 763 037.
Lunch and dinner. Closed Tuesday and one week in June. Mastercard, Visa.
Straighforward international fare and some regional dishes. (**$$**)

Casa Ibero
Parra, 1, Capileira.
Tel: 958 763 006.
Lunch and dinner. Closed Sunday night and Monday. No cards.
No frills establishment offering local dishes at unbeatable prices. (**$**)

Almuñecar
Jacqui-Cotobro
Edificio Río, Playa Cotobro.

Tel: 958 631 802.
Lunch and dinner. Closed Monday, last week November and first week December. Mastercard, Visa.
The simple dining room with bare brick walls gives little indication that this restaurant by the beach is famous all over Spain for its French cuisine. The best plan is to order the *Menu Degustacion*, including a wide choice of three different courses, plus dessert. Best to reserve. (**$$**)

Loja
La Finca
Hotel La Bobadilla, A95 km 115 (Salinas-Rute turn-off).
Tel: 958 321 861.
Lunch and dinner. Closed lunch June–August. Amex, Diners, Mastercard, Visa.
First-class cuisine in a fairytale setting, the luxurious La Bobadilla hotel. (**$$$**)

Meson Don Isidro
Río Frío.
Tel: 958 321 066.
Lunch and dinner. Mastercard, Visa.
Río Frío, a hamlet next to a trout stream and fish factory, has several simple but good restaurants, serving various preparations of trout as well as other local dishes. This one is the longest established. (**$**)

HUELVA

Las Candelas
Avda Huelva, Aljaraque.
Tel: 959 318 301.
Lunch and dinner. Closed Sunday. Amex, Diners, Mastercard, Visa.
Located 6 km (4 miles) from the centre of the city, Huelva's best-known restaurant offers good value and quality fresh seafood and fish stews. (**$$–$$$**)

Aracena
Jose Vicente
Avda Andalucía, 53.
Tel: 959 128 455.
Lunch and dinner. Closed June 1–15. Amex, Mastercard, Visa.
In an unassuming location on the outskirts of the village, this small restaurant is a true gem in the heart of Huelva's northern Sierra.

The best place to try fresh pork from the prized Iberian pig. (**$$**)

Moguer
La Parrala
Plaza de las Monjas, 22.
Tel: 959 370 452.
Lunch and dinner. No cards.
Pleasant family-run tavern in the centre of the town, serving traditional home cooking. (**$**)

JAÉN

Mesón Vicente
Francisco Martín Mora, 1.
Tel: 953 232 222.
Lunch and dinner. Closed Sunday dinner. Amex, Mastercard, Visa.
Popular family restaurant next to the cathedral, serving traditional Jaén dishes and game in season. There is also a good *meson* (tavern) serving *tapas*. (**$$**)

Andújar
Don Pedro
Gabriel Zamora, 5.
Tel: 953 501 274.
Lunch and dinner. Amex, Diners, Mastercard, Visa.
Regional dishes at good prices, service is friendly and fast. Outdoor dining in summer. (**$$**)

Baeza
Juanito
Paseo Arca del Agua, s/n.
Tel: 953 740 040.
Lunch and dinner. Closed Sunday dinner, Monday dinner. Visa.
Spacious and friendly, one of the best-known restaurants in Andalucía has based its reputation on its owner's missionary zeal in recovering traditional recipes, in most of which (even the desserts) the excellent virgin olive oil of Jaén plays a key role. (**$$**)

Cazorla
Cueva de Juan Pedro
Plaza de Santa María.
Tel: 953 721 225.
Lunch and dinner. No cards.
Literally a hole in the wall, this tiny, informal cave-restaurant specialises in grilled meat. (**$$**)

MÁLAGA AND THE COSTA DEL SOL

Antequera
La Espuela
Plaza de Toros.
Tel: 952 703 424.
Lunch and dinner. Diners,
Mastercard, Visa.
Friendly atmosphere and an
unusual setting, beneath the
grandstand in Antequera's bullring.
The cuisine is Andalucían, with
specialities such as the well-known
Porra antequerana (a thick type of
gazpacho) and rabbit in almond
sauce. (**$$**)

Benalmádena
Ventorillo de la Perra
Avenida de la Constitucíon, s/n,
Arroyo de la Miel.
Tel: 952 441 966.
Lunch and dinner. Closed Monday.
Amex, Diners, Mastercard, Visa.
Installed in a pleasant old roadside
inn on the road between
Torremolinos and Arroyo de la Miel,
serving a mixture of local and
international dishes. (**$$**)
Mar de Alborán
Avenida de Alay.
Tel: 952 446 427.
Lunch and dinner. Closed Sunday
evening and Monday. Amex,
Mastercard, Visa.
Near the lively Benalmadena
marina, serving fish dishes using
local ingredients with a Basque
touch. (**$$$**)
Chef Alonso
Dársena de Levante, 11, Puerto
Marina Benalmádena.
Tel: 952 561 303.
Lunch and dinner. Amex,
Mastercard, Visa.
In the Benalmadena yacht harbour,
a good place for meat dishes as
well as fish, with a spacious terrace
for outdoor dining. (**$$$**)
Casa Fidel
Maestro Ayala, 1, Benalmádena
Pueblo.
Tel: 952 449 165.
Lunch and dinner. Closed
Wednesday evening, all day Tuesday.
Amex, Diners, Mastercard, Visa.
A long-established favourite among
Costa del Sol diners, both Spanish
and foreign, located in the

Price Guide

Inexpensive ($) = under 1,500
pesetas per person for a three
course meal, not including wine.
Moderate ($$) = 1,500–4,000
pesetas.
Expensive ($$$) = more than
4,000 pesetas.

picturesque old village of
Benalmádena. Fish available, but
lamb is the speciality. (**$$**)

Estepona
Costa del Sol
Calle San Roque.
Tel: 952 801 101.
Lunch and dinner. Closed Monday.
Amex, Diners, Mastercard, Visa. A
small French bistro on a side street
near the main bus station in
Estepona, offering excellent value.
The menu of the day is a bargain.
(**$$**)
Alcaría de Ramos
Ctra N340 km 167.
Tel: 952 886 178.
Lunch and dinner. Closed Sunday
dinner. Mastercard, Visa.
Located in an Andalucían-style
house with good views east of the
town, serving very well prepared
classic Spanish dishes. (**$$**)

Fuengirola
El Bote
Paseo Marítimo, Torreblanca del Sol.
Tel: 952 660 296.
Lunch and dinner. Closed
Wednesday. Amex, Mastercard,
Visa.
Spacious and popular, right next to
the beach at the eastern end of
Fuengirola's seafront promenade,
serving fresh fish dishes. (**$$**)
Portofino
Edificio Perla, 1, Paseo Marítimo.
Tel: 952 470 643.
Lunch and dinner; dinner only in
summer. Closed Monday and first
fortnight in July. Amex, Diners,
Mastercard, Visa.
Friendly and lively Italian-owned
restaurant on the seafront in
central Fuengirola, enormously
popular, and serving consistently
good international dishes, with a

few Italian specialities as well. Best
to reserve. (**$$**)
La Langosta
Francisco Cano, 1, Los Boliches.
Tel: 952 475 049.
Dinner only. Closed Sunday.
This small restaurant has been a
popular venue since it opened in
the 1960s. It was the first place on
the southern coast to serve lobster,
still a house speciality. (**$$**)

Málaga
afé de Paris
Velez Málaga, 8.
Tel: 952 225 043.
Lunch and dinner. Closed Sunday.
Amex, Diners, Mastercard, Visa.
On a back street near the
lighthouse, Málaga's most
sophisticated restaurant, serving
imaginative dishes in an elegant
atmosphere. The *Menu Degustacion*
is a good way to try a variety of the
house specialities. Reservations
essential. (**$$$**)
Escuela de Hostelería
Finca La Consula, Churriana.
Tel: 952 622 562.
Lunch only. Closed Saturday and
Sunday. Amex, Mastercard, Visa.
Málaga's official hotel and catering
school, 8 km (5 miles) west of the
city, serves some of the best food
on the coast, in a magnificent
setting adjoining a country mansion,
surrounded by gardens.
Reservations essential. (**$$$**)
El Chinitas
Moreno Monroy, 4.
Tel: 952 210 972.
Lunch and dinner. Amex,
Mastercard, Visa.
Traditional-style Andalucían
restaurant with attached *tapas* bar,
just off the colourful Pasaje de
Chinitas in the old part of city. (**$$**)
Astorga
Gerona, 11.
Tel: 952 346 832.
Lunch and dinner. Closed Sunday.
Amex, Mastercard, Visa.
The food here, both in fish and
meat, has earned this lively, friendly
restaurant the reputation as one of
the city's best, and reservations
are essential. (**$$**)

Casa Pedro
Playa de El Palo.
Tel: 952 290 013.
Lunch and dinner. Closed Monday
night. Amex, Diners, Mastercard,
Visa.
In the fishing district of El Palo at
the eastern end of Málaga, this
beachside restaurant is spacious,
boisterous and informal, a favourite
with local families for its fried fish.
Very crowded on Sunday. (**$$**)

Marbella
Santiago
Paseo Marítimo, 5.
Tel: 952 770 078.
Lunch and dinner. Closed
November. Amex, Diners,
Mastercard, Visa.
Long famous for its super-fresh
seafood, this long-established
restaurant now has an adjoining
Castilian-style *tapas* bar and tavern,
and serves top quality meat dishes
as well. (**$$$**)

La Chêne Liège
La Mairena, Elviria.
Tel: 952 836 092.
Dinner only, closed Tuesday. Amex,
Diners, Mastercard, Visa.
A 10-minute drive into the hills east
of Marbella, through one of the
most luxurious residential areas on
the coast, is rewarded with splendid
views and some of the best French
cuisine you'll find anywhere. (**$$$**)

In Vino
Ctra Cádiz km 176, Río Verde.
Tel: 952 771 211.
Dinner only. Amex, Diners,
Mastercard, Visa.
Fine wine is the central theme in
this restaurant, which has an
impressive selection, in addition to
gourmet food. Especially pleasant
when weather permits dining on the
terrace. (**$$$**)

La Meridiana
Camino de la Cruz, near mosque.
Tel: 952 776 190.
Lunch and dinner. Closed January.
No dinner in summer.
Near the gleaming modern Marbella
mosque, this elegant dining spot is
a favourite among the resort's
famous glitterati. Fresh ingredients
are given imaginative treatment.
Reservations essential. (**$$$**)

La Hacienda
Urb. Las Chapas.
Tel: 952 831 267.
Lunch and dinner. Closed Monday,
Tuesday and mid-Nov–mid-Dec.
Amex, Diners, Mastercard, Visa.
Pleasantly set in a villa in the hills
east of Marbella, this restaurant
which started in the 1970s was
among the first truly top-class
international dining spots on the
Costa del Sol. Its French-Belgian
cuisine adapted to local recipes set
a model for others. Best to
reserve. (**$$$**)

El Rodeito
Ctra de Cádiz km 173.
Tel: 952 810 861.
Open 24 hours a day. Mastercard,
Visa.
Former inn on the main highway
between Marbella and San Pedro de
Alcántara, specialising in Castilian
roast meats, served any time of day
or night. (**$$**)

Mijas
Venta El Higuerón
Málaga-Fuengirola motorway exit 217.
Tel: 952 119 163.
Lunch and dinner. Amex,
Mastercard, Vista.
A roadside inn has stood on this
spot since 1840. Today, this
restaurant, with views over
Fuengirola and the coast, serves a
wide menu of Spanish food,
including a selection of Asturias
specialities. (**$$**)

El Mirlo Blanco
Plaza de la Constitución, 13.
Tel: 952 485 700.
Lunch and dinner. Amex,
Mastercard, Visa.
Overlooking a square in the old part
of Mijas, a long-established
restaurant serving Spanish and
Basque specialities. (**$$**)

Nerja
Casa Luque
Pl. Cavana, 2.
Tel: 952 521 004.
Lunch and dinner. Closed Monday
and November. Amex, Diners,
Mastercard, Visa.
Authentic Spanish food in an old
Andalucían house, near Nerja's
main landmark, the Balcón de

Europa. Pleasant patio for al fresco
dining, and a good selection of
dishes with a northern Spanish
accent. (**$$**)

Pepe Rico
Almirante Ferrandiz, 28.
Tel: 952 520 247.
Lunch and dinner, dinner only
summer. Closed Tuesday, Sunday
lunch, mid-November–mid-
December. Diners, Visa,
Mastercard.
In the centre of Nerja, in an old
Spanish house with cool patio.
International cuisine with a
Scandinavian touch. (**$$**)

Ronda
Parador de Ronda
Plaza de España.
Tel: 952 877 500.
Lunch and dinner. Amex,
Mastercard, Visa.
The restaurant here is considered
one of the best in the parador
chain, serving interesting variations
on traditional dishes. (**$$$**)

Don Miguel
Villanueva, 4.
Tel: 952 871 090.
Lunch and dinner. Closed 15–30
January. Amex, Mastercard, Visa.
Spectacular setting at the edge of
the Ronda gorge, with a pleasant
terrace for al fresco dining, offering
Spanish and international food. (**$$**)

Pedro Romero
Virgen de la Paz, 18.
Tel: 952 871 110.
Lunch and dinner. Amex, Diners,
Mastercard, Visa
Unabashedly touristy, but serving
good traditional Andalucían fare. It
is across from the Ronda bullring,
and is named after the "father of
bullfighting"; the taurine theme
prevails in the decor (bull's heads,
posters) and the menu (Rabo de
Toro is the speciality). (**$$**)

Mesón Santiago
Marina, 3.
Tel: 952 871 559.
Lunch only. Mastercard, Visa.
In an old house one street back
from the bullring, serving traditional
Spanish home cooking. (**$**)

Torremolinos
Frutos
Ctra de Cádiz km 228,5 (next to Los Alamos petrol station).
Tel: 952 381 450.
Lunch and dinner. Closed Sunday dinner. Amex, Mastercard, Visa.
Midway between Torremolinos and the airport, a spacious restaurant which for decades has been known for its hearty helpings of traditional Spanish fare, with excellent meat and fish. **($$–$$$)**

El Roqueo
Carmen, 35, La Carihuela.
Tel: 952 384 946.
Open lunch and dinner. Closed Tuesday and November. Amex, Mastercard, Visa.
In Torremolinos's fishing quarter, La Carihuela, it's hard to go wrong: every other house is a seafood restaurant, and they're all good. This one, facing out onto the seafront promenade, is among the longest established and the best known. **($$)**

Price Guide

Inexpensive ($) = under 1,500 pesetas per person for a three course meal, not including wine.
Moderate ($$) = 1,500–4,000 pesetas.
Expensive ($$$) = more than 4,000 pesetas.

SEVILLE

Don Raimundo
Argote de Molina, 26.
Tel: 954 223 355.
Lunch and dinner. Closed Sunday dinner. Amex, Diners, Mastercard, Visa. Near the cathedral, this large, restaurant offers a classic Sevillano experience. The specialities are meat and game, and the portions are large. **($$)**

Egaña–Oriza
San Fernando, 41.
Tel: 954 227 211.
Lunch and dinner. Closed Saturday lunch, Sunday, August. Amex, Diners, Mastercard, Visa.
The Basque-inspired cuisine of this attractive restaurant, near the Murillo gardens, is among the best in Andalucía. Imaginative food in elegant, modern setting. Best to reserve. **($$$)**

Enrique Becerra
Gamazo, 2.
Tel: 954 213 049.
Lunch and dinner. Closed Sunday. Amex, Diners, Mastercard, Visa.
Small restaurant in an old Seville house, serving Andalucían fare. Has a popular *tapas* bar as well. **($$)**

Casa Robles
Alvarez Quintero, 58.
Tel: 954 563 272.
Lunch and dinner. Amex, Diners, Mastercard, Visa. Typical Seville decor, innovative dishes. **($$)**

La Taberna del Alabardero
Zaragoza, 20.
Tel: 954 562 906.
Lunch and dinner. Closed August. Amex, Diners, Mastercard, Visa.
One of a well-known chain of restaurants, with Spanish/ international cuisine in a typical setting. Adjoining cafeteria for budget travellers. **($$)**

La Albahaca
Pl. Sta Cruz, 12.
Tel: 954 220 714.
Lunch and dinner. Closed Sunday. Amex, Diners, Mastercard, Visa.
A pretty restaurant in the heart of Seville's Barrio Santa Cruz, in a turn-of-the-century town house. The accent is on the decor as well as on the food – an imaginative mixture of Andalucían, French and Basque influences. Best to reserve. **($$$)**

Hostería del Laurel
Plaza de los Venerables, 5.
Tel: 954 220 295.
Lunch and dinner. Amex, Diners, Mastercard, Visa.
On a small square in the Barrio de Santa Cruz, enormously popular, both as a good-value dining spot and a *tapas* venue. Traditional Andalucían cuisine, **($)**

Culture

Theatre & Music

Córdoba
Gran Teatro, Gran Capitán.
Information, tel: 957 480 237.
Regular performances by city orchestra; recitals; theatre; guitar festival in July.

Granada
Auditorio Manuel de Falla, Paseo de los Mártires. Tel: 958 228 288.
Orchestral recitals, performances during International Festival of Music and Dance in June–July.

Málaga
Teatro Miguel de Cervantes, Plaza de Ramos Marín. Tel: 952 220 237.
Theatre; musical concerts.
Teatro Alameda, Calle Cordoba, 13.
Tel: 952 213 412. Theatre.
Salon Varietés Theatre, Calle Emancipación, 30, Fuengirola. Tel. 952 474 542. Theatre in English.

Seville
Teatro de la Maestranza, Plaza de Colón. Tel: 954 223 344. Seville opera house. Orchestra recitals.
Teatro Lope de Vega, Avenida María Luisa, Seville. Tel: 954 234 546.
Drama; flamenco; concerts.

Spas

Andalucía has a number of *balnearios* (spas) where the waters have medicinal properties. These are tranquil spots with doctors on hand to offer advice. Further information can be obtained from the **Asociación de Balnearios de Andalucía**, Calle Nueva de la Virgen 25, Granada, tel: 958 770 811.

Almería
Sierra de Alhamilla, Pechina, tel:

950 317 413. Open all year.
Waters recommended for arthritis,
rheumatism, gout, bronchitis,
asthma, digestive disorders, ulcers,
gastritis, stress.
San Nicolás, Alhama de Almería,
tel: 950 641 361. Open all year.
Digestive disorders, respiratory
ailments, arthritis, sciatica, obesity,
rheumatism, nerves.

Cádiz
Fuente Amarga, Chiclana de la
Frontera, tel: 956 400 520. Open
February–December. Recommended
for rheumatism, arthritis, arthrosis,
skin problems, alopecia, respiratory
problems, gynaecological problems.

Granada
Lanjarón, tel: 958 770 137. Open all
year. Recommended for arthrosis,
rheumatism, lumbago, renal lithiasis,
respiratory ailments, diabetes,
insomnia, stress, kidney infections,
cholesterol.
Alicún de las Torres, Villanueva de
las Torres (32 km/20 miles, from
Guadix), tel: 958 694 022. Open
April–November. For respiratory
problems, allergies, catarrh,
circulation, rheumatic disorders,
digestive system, traumatism.
Alhama de Granada, tel: 958 350 0
11. Open 10 June–10 October.

Recommended for rheumatic
disorders, gout, neuritis, sciatica,
bronchitis, asthma, traumatism,
obesity.
Graena (8 km/5 miles, from
Guadix), tel: 958 670 681. Open
1 June–31 October. Recommended
for rheumatic disorders, sciatica,
bronchitis, allergies, stress,
nervous disorders.

Jaén
San Andres, Canena (10 km/6
miles, from Ubeda), tel: 959 770
209. Open: 1 July–30 October.
Recommended for digestive
system, kidney and urinary
disorders, respiratory system,
rheumatism, traumatism,
circulation, nervous system,
gynaecological problems.

Málaga
Carratraca, tel: 952 458 020.
Open: 15 June–15 October.
Recommended for rheumatism,
circulation, nervous system, skin
problems and gynaecological
ailments.
Tolox, tel: 952 487 091. Open 15
June–15 October. Recommended
for respiratory system, bronchitis,
asthma, pulmonary ephysema,
renal lithiasis, pharyngitis and
rhinitis.

Nightlife

Bars

Spaniards like nothing better than to
drink and talk until the early hours.
All cities have at least one bar area
which comes to life in the evening.
The *tapeo* is an accepted custom, in
which you move between bars,
sampling with every drink a different
tapa, the tasty titbits that can run
from grilled shrimps to stewed tripe.
    In all bars and cafés it is
cheapest to drink at the counter. If
you sit at a table, the price goes up
– and up again on a terrace. Bars
with live music charge extra. Bars
advertising themselves as "pubs"
are usually dimly lit and favoured by
the young and trendy. An "American
bar" is one where the staff is
female or there are hostesses, i.e.
expect to be ripped off.
    Seville has a lively nightlife.
There are numerous *tapas* bars,

Flamenco Favourites

Not all the best performers are
earning millions in New York,
contrary to what you may have
heard. Even so, you will be
fortunate to come across a top-
quality authentic flamenco
performance. Often it is
cheapened to make it more
palatable for popular taste. The
best performances come
spontaneously, when a singer is
moved by emotion rather than
money and that is unlikely to
happen before a crowd of tourists.
    Some of the better flamenco
clubs offer solid entertainment
that fairly closely approximates the
genuine article. The best places to
see flamenco are Seville and the
Santiago district in Jerez. Most

venues open at around 10pm and
stay open until very late.
A few recommended venues:
El Arenal, Calle Rodo 7, Seville.
Tel: 954 216 492.
Tablao Los Gallos, Plaza Santa
Cruz 11, Seville. Tel: 954 228
522.
Peña Antonio Chacón, Calle
Salas, 2, Jerez de la Frontera,
Cádiz. Tel: 956 347 472.
Peña La Buena Gente, Plaza de
San Lucas, 9, Jerez de la Frontera
Cádiz. Tel: 956 338 404.
Meson La Bulería, Calle Pedro
Lopez, 3, Córdoba. Tel: 957 483
839.
Tablao Cardenal, Calle Torrijos,
10, Córdoba. Tel: 957483 112.
Jardines Neptuno, Calle Arabial,

Granada. Tel: 958 251 112.
The best flamenco is to be seen in
the flamenco festivals and
contests held between the end of
June and the middle of September
in small towns and villages –
there's one, or more, every
Saturday, somewhere in Andalusia.
    The best known are the Potaje
in Utrera (Seville) at the end of
June, La Caracolá in Lebrija
(Seville) in mid-July, the festival in
Mairena del Alcor (Seville) at the
beginning of September, and
Fiesta de la Bulería held in the
Jerez bullring in mid-September.
    In true flamenco tradition, these
events never start on time and
they tend to be drawn-out affairs,
lasting far into the early hours.

including El Rinconcillo, considered the city's oldest (founded in 1670). The Santa Cruz area, with its maze of streets and countless bars, is a favourite night-time combat zone for the young set, but many have switched to the newer bars along El Torneo, the street running parallel to the Guadalquivir river, across from La Cartuja.

Lively summer terrace bars include the Babaloo, sometimes featuring live music, and the Barqueta (both near Puente la Barqueta bridge). A few streets in from El Torneo, on Plaza de la Niña de los Peines, is the trendy and not at all expensive XL. There's a good ambience around the Alameda de Hércules square and in La Macarena district.

Seville also has a number of live music bars, the best known of which is Blue Moon (Calle Juan Cavestany), featuring live jazz, and during summer there are free concerts staged at night in the Puerta de Triana.

Granada knows how to fill the evening hours, thanks to its large student population. Students tend to gravitate towards the area around the Plaza del Principe, the maze-like Albaicín district and the Plaza Nueva. In summer, a good place for bars and outdoor action is the poetically misnamed Paseo de los Tristes (Sad People's Promenade), below the Alhambra.

Andalucía's real nightlife centre is the **Costa del Sol**. The best action revolves around the bustling Puerto Banús yacht harbour – the Sinatra bar is the traditional meeting place. Other classic watering holes include Joe's Bar, Crescendo, La Comedia, and Mambo. There are also swank discos nearby, including Regine's (Puente Romano) and the palatial Olivia Valere (Ctra de Istan, near the mosque).

Other nightlife hotspots on Costa del Sol are the old town and the seafront area in Marbella, the seafront in Fuengirola, the marina in Benalmádena, and the legendary town of Torremolinos.

Nightclubs

Fullyfledged nightclubs are few and far between. If you are looking for a Folies Bergeres-type extravaganza, the Sala Fortuna at **Casino Torrequebrada** near Málaga is probably the best bet (*see Casinos below*).

Restaurants and cafes often put on live entertainment. "Sexy shows" usually feature strippers. Remember that a "*sala de fiestas*" may not be a genuine nightclub. Many establishments that use this name are in fact brothels, or otherwise bars where prostitutes make their contacts.

Casinos

Gambling is a national pastime in Spain. People of all ages pour their cash into "tragaperras", the slot machines found in many bars. Every week during the soccer season there is the "Quiniela", football pool. Vast sums are gambled on the frequent lotteries, run by the state or ONCE, the organisation for the blind.

Southern Spain's casinos (in Benalmádena-Costa and Marbella on the Costa del Sol, and in Puerto de Santa María near Cádiz) are elegant night-time venues, offering the full gamut of American and French **roulette**, **black jack** and

other traditional casino games. They all have classy restaurants and top quality night clubs and discotheques, and stay open late.

Formal dress and identification (ID card or passport) are required for admission.

Casino Bahia de Cádiz, Ctra Madrid-Cádiz km 650, Puerto de Santa María, Cádiz. Tel: 956 871 042.
Casino de Torrequebrada, Ctra de Cádiz km 226, Benalmádena-Costa (Málaga). Tel: 952 442 545.
Casino Nueva Andalucia, Urb. Nueva Andalucia, Marbella (Málaga). Tel: 952 780 800.

Sport

Fishing

Offshore fishing: boats can often be hired at marinas. Some excursions are available, particularly for the popular sport of shark fishing. **Inland fishing**: It is possible to catch tench, carp, pike, black bass and trout. Fishing permits can be obtained from branches of the Caja Rural savings bank. Legislation varies from province to province with regards licences, so it is advisable to check details with local tourist offices.

Golf

Southern Spain, particularly the Costa del Sol, is a golfer's paradise, with Europe's biggest concentration of golf courses. Information from the **Andalucían Golf Federation**, Sierra de Grazalema, 33, Málaga, tel: 952 225 590.

Almería
La Envía, Ctra Parador-Enix km 10,3, Vicar, tel. 950 559 641. 18 holes.
Cortijo Grande Golf Club, Cortijo Grande, Turre, tel: 950 479 175. 18 holes.
Golf Playa Serena, Urb. Playa Serena, Roquetas de Mar, tel: 950 333 055. 18 holes.
Golf Almerimar, Urb. Almerimar, El Ejido, tel: 950 497 454. 18 holes

Cádiz
Alcaidesa Links, Cortijo Las Aguzaderas, Ctra N340 km 124,6, San Roque, tel: 956 791 040. 18 holes.
La Cañada, Avenida Profesor Tierno Galván, s/n, Guadiaro, tel: 956 794 100. 9 holes.
San Roque Club, Ctra de Cádiz km

126, 5, San Roque, tel: 956 613 030. 18 holes.

Real Club de Golf Sotogrande, Paseo del Parque, Sotogrande, tel: 956 795 050. 18 + 9 holes.

Club de Golf Valderrama, Avenida de los Cortijos, Sotogrande, tel: 956 795 775. Venue of the 1997 Ryder Cup. 18 holes.

Montecastillo Golf, Ctra de Arcos, Jerez de la Frontera, tel: 956 151 200. 18 holes.

Novo Sancti Petri Golf, Novo Sancti Petri, Chiclana, tel: 956 494 005. 18 + 9 holes.

El Campano Golf, Ctra Cádiz-Malaga km 14,5, Chiclana, tel: 956 230 020. 9 holes.

Vista Hermosa Golf, Casa Grande, Urb. Vista Hermosa, El Puerto de Santa María, tel: 956 541 968. 9 holes.

Córdoba

Club de Golf Pozoblanco, San Gregorio, 2, Pozoblanco, tel: 957 339 003. 9 holes.

Club de Campo Córdoba, Avda de Arruzafa, Córdoba, tel: 957 350 208. 18 holes.

Granada

Granada Golf de Club, Avda Los Corsarios, Las Gabias, Granada, tel: 958 584 436. 18 holes.

Los Moriscos, Urb. Playa Granada, Motril, tel: 958 825 527. 9 holes.

Huelva

Islantilla Golf Club, Ctra Isla Antilla-La Antilla, s/n, Isla Antilla, tel: 959 486 039. 18 + 9 holes.

Club de Golf Bellvista, Ctra Huelva-Aljaraque km 6, Huelva, tel: 959 319 017. 18 holes.

Isla Canela Club de Golf, Paseo de los Gavilanes, Playa de Isla Canela, Ayamonte, tel: 959 477 263. 18 holes.

Málaga

Alhaurín Golf & Country Club, Ctra Fuengirola-Alhaurín el Grande km 15, Alhaurín el Grande, tel: 952 595 970. 18 + 9 holes.

Aloha Golf, Urb. Aloha, Nueva Andalucía, Marbella tel: 952 813 750. 18 + 9 holes.

Añoreta Golf, Urb. Añoreta Golf,

Rincón de la Victoria, tel: 952 400 400. 18 holes.

Atalaya Golf & Country Club, Ctra de Benahavís km 0, 7, Estepona, tel: 952 882 812. 18 + 18 holes.

Club El Candado, Calle Golf, Urb. El Candado, Málaga, tel: 952 299 340. 9 holes.

Club Miraflores, Ctra de Cadiz km 199, Mijas-Costa, tel. 952 837 383. 18 holes

El Coto de la Serena, Ctra de Cadiz km 173, 5, Estepona, tel: 952 804 700. 9 holes.

El Paraíso Golf Club, Ctra de Cadiz km 167, Estepona, tel: 952 883 835. 18 holes.

Estepona Golf, Arroyo Vaquero, Ctra de Cadiz km 150, Estepona, tel: 952 113 081. 18 holes.

Golf Club Las Brisas, Avda del Golf, Nueva Andalucía, Marbella, tel: 952 813 021. 18 holes.

Golf Río Real, Urb. Río Real, Carretera de Cadiz km 185, Marbella, tel. 952 773 886. 18 holes.

Guadalhorce Club de Golf, Ctra de Cártama km 7, Campanillas, tel: 952 179 378. 18 + 9 holes.

Guadalmina Club de Golf, Urb. Guadalmina Alta, San Pedro Alcántara, tel: 952 883 375. 18 + 18 + 9 holes.

La Cala Golf & Country Club, La Cala de Mijas, Mijas-Costa, tel. 952 589 100. 18 + 18 holes.

La Dama de Noche, Camino del Angel, Río Verde, Marbella, tel: 952 818 150. Floodlit course. 9 holes.

La Duquesa Golf & Country Club, Urb. El Hacho, Manilva, tel: 952 890 725. 18 holes.

La Quinta Golf & Country Club, Urb. La Quinta, Benahavís, tel: 952 783 462. 18 + 9 holes.

Lauro Golf, Los Caracolillos, Alhaurín de la Torre, tel: 952 412 767. 18 holes.

La Siesta Golf, Calle José de Orbaneja, Urb. Sitio de Calahonda, Mijas-Costa, tel: 952 836 370. 9 holes.

La Zagaleta, Ctra de Ronda km 38, Benahavís, tel: 952 786 800. 18 holes.

Los Arqueros Golf, Ctra de Ronda km 42, 9, San Pedro Alcántara, tel: 952 784 600. 18 holes.

Los Naranjos Golf Club, Urb. Nueva Andalucía, Marbella, tel: 952 815 206. 18 holes.

Mijas Golf, Camino Viejo de Coín km 3, Urb. Mijas Golf, Mijas-Costa, tel. 952 476 843. 18 + 18 holes.

Montemayor Golf Club, Ctra de Cadiz km 165, 6, Benahavís, tel: 952 113 088. 18 holes.

Real Club de Campo de Málaga, Ctra de Cadiz, Malaga. Tel. 952 238 1255. 18 holes.

Santa María Golf & Country Club, Coto de los Dolores, Ctra de Cadiz km. 192, Urb. Elviria, Marbella, tel: 952 830 388. 18 holes.

The Golf Club Marbella, Ctra de Cadiz km 188, Marbella, tel: 952 830 500. 18 holes.

Torrequebrada Golf, Ctra de Cadiz km 220, Benalmádena-Costa, tel: 952 442 742. 18 holes.

Seville

Real Club Pineda, Avda Jerez, Seville, tel: 954 611 400. 18 holes.

La Rocina Golf and Country Club, Ctra Isla Mayor km 0,8, Aznalcázar, tel: 955 750 806. 9 holes.

Real Club de Golf de Sevilla, Ctra Sevilla-Utrera km 3,2, Seville, tel: 954 124 301. 18 holes.

Club Zaudin, Ctra Bormujos-Mairena km 1,5, Seville, tel: 954 153 344. 18 holes.

Horse-Riding/Trekking

Riding is available for all levels, from instruction for beginners, renting by the hour, to treks through the sierras.

Cádiz

San Roque Club Equestrian Centre, Suites Hotel, San Roque, tel: 956 613 030

Rancho Los Lobos, Estación de Jimena de la Frontera, tel: 956 641 180

Cortijo Las Piñas, Ctra N340 km 74,3, Tarifa, tel: 956 685 136.

Rancho Huerta Dorotea, Ctra Villamartin-Ubrique km 12, Prado del Rey, tel: 956 724 291.

Hurricane Hotel, Ctra N-340 km 77, Tarifa, tel: 956 684 919.

Hacienda Buena Suerte, Ctra

Villamartín-Prado del Rey km 3, Villmartín, tel: 956 231 286.

Córdoba
Actividades Ecuestres de la Subbetica, Plaza Caballos 4–6, Córdoba, tel: 957 700 629.

Granada
Cabalgar-Rutas Alternativas, Bubión, Alpujarras, tel: 958 763 135. One- to 10-day treks in the Alpujarras.
Cortijo Aventura, Orgiva, Alpujarras, tel: 958 785 253.

Málaga
El Ranchito, Ctra N340 km 235, La Colina, Torremolinos, tel: 952 383 063.
Los Monteros Riding School, behind Los Monteros golf course, Marbella, tel: 952 770 675.
Lakeview Equestrian Centre, Pantano Roto, San Pedro de Alcántara, tel: 952 786 934.
Club Hipico Alhaurín, Ctra Fuengirola-Alhaurin el Grande km 15, Alhaurin el Grande, tel: 952 595 970.
Rafael Garrido Equestrian Centre, Calle Jose de Orbaneja, Urb. Sitio de Calahonda, Mijas-Costa, tel: 952 838 124.

Seville
Centro Ecuestre Epona, Ctra Madrid-Cádiz km 519, Carmona, tel: 908 155 359.
Cortijo El Aguila Real, Ctra Guillena-Burguillo km 4, Guillena, tel: 954 798 006.
Equiberia SL, Calle Julio Cesar 2-I D, Seville 954 211 311.
El Vizir, Hacienda El Visir, Espartinas, tel: 955 710 020.
Hípica Puerta Príncipe, Alcalá de Guadaira, tel: 954 860 815.
Las Lumbreras, Fernando IV, 40 1B, Seville, tel: 954 877 246.
Rancho el Rocío, Puebla del Río, tel: 955 571 212.

Marinas

Almería
Garrucha Marina, tel: 950 460 048
San José Marina, Níjar, tel: 950 380 041.

Hunting

You are legally entitled to import two hunting guns with 100 cartridges. It is advisable to contact the **Andalucían Hunting Federation** (Federación Andaluza de Caza), Los Morenos, s/n, Archidona, tel: 952 714 871/952 714 855 for details of licences, restrictions and seasons, as some species are protected and others have a quota ceiling.

For the serious, hunting is available in controlled areas and state-run game parks such as Cazorla in Jaén where it is possible to hunt **wild goat** (*capra hispanica*), **deer** or **wild boar**. Organised parties, known as "monterias", take part in shoots in the Sierra Morena, where deer and boar abound.

Club de Mar, Almería, tel: 950 230 780.
Aguadulce Marina, tel: 950 341 502.
Roquetas de Mar Marina, tel: 950 322 909.
Almerimar Marina, El Ejido, tel: 950 497 350.
Adra Marina, tel: 950 401 417.

Cádiz
Sotogrande Marina, tel: 956 790 000.
Real Club Náutico, Algeciras, tel: 956 601 402.
Club Náutico, Barbate, tel: 956 433 333.
Club Náutico Sancti Petri, Chiclana de la Frontera, tel: 956 495 428.
Real Club Náutico, Cádiz, tel: 956 228 701.
Real Club Náutico, El Puerto de Santa María, tel: 956 852 527.
Puerto Sherry, El Puerto de Santa María, tel: 956 870 303.

Granada
Motril Marina, tel: 958 600 037.
Marina del Este, La Herradura, tel: 958 827 018.

Huelva
Huelva Marina, tel: 959 247 627.
Punta Umbria Marina, tel: 959 311 899.
El Rompido Marina, tel: 959 390 728.

Málaga
La Caleta de Vélez Marina, Torre del Mar, tel: 952 511 390.
El Candado, Málaga, tel: 952 296 097.
Real Club Mediterráneo, Málaga, tel: 952 228 528.
Marina Benalmádena, tel: 952 442 944.
Fuengirola Marina, tel: 952 468 000.
Puerto Cabopino, Marbella, tel: 952 831 975.
Marbella Marina, tel: 952 775 700.
Puerto Banús, Marbella, tel: 952 814 750.
Estepona Marina, tel: 952 801 800.
Puerto de la Duquesa, Manilva, tel: 952 890 100.

Seville
Club Náutico, Auda Tablada, s/n, Seville, tel: 954 454 777.

Scuba/Sub-Aqua Diving

The rocky shoreline around much of the coast offers plenty of scope for **underwater exploring**. Fishing with a spear-gun is permitted only if you dive without bottles. If you swim any distance from the shore, you are required to tow a marker buoy.

There are a number of scuba clubs on the coast, offering courses for beginners and guidance for licensed visiting divers. For details, contact the **Federación Andaluza de Actividades Subacuáticas**, Playa de las Almadrabillas, 10, Almería, tel: 950 270 612.

Best areas for diving are:
Almería: Cabo de Gata, Las Negras, La Isleta, San José and Morrón de los Genoveses, where international underwater fishing competitions have been held.
Cádiz: North of Tarifa, especially for underwater fishing.
Granada: La Herradura and west towards Málaga.
Málaga: from Nerja east towards Granada coast.

Skiing

There is skiing in the **Sierra Nevada** 32 km (20 miles) from Granada, the southernmost ski slope in Europe. The slopes are between 2,100

metres (7,000 ft) and 3,390 metres (11,000 ft) above sea level, with 45 ski runs of varying difficulty and 21 lifts.

Facilities include equipment to rent, instruction, with a special school for children, first aid and rescue service and emergency clinic.

The Sierra Nevada complex offers a variety of accommodation and *après ski* entertainment. **General information**: 958 249 100. **Weather information, snow report** 958 249 119.

Tennis

There are too many tennis clubs in the region to list them all. A number have outstanding facilities, including tuition in some cases by ex-international champions:
Lew Hoad's Tennis Ranch, Ctra Mijas-Fuengirola, Málaga, tel: 952 474 858.
El Madroñal Tennis Club, San Pedro de Alcantara, Marbella, Málaga, tel: 952 780 990.
Los Monteros Tennis Club, Hotel Los Monteros, Ctra N340, Marbella, Málaga, tel: 952 771 700.
Manolo Santana Tennis Club, Hotel Puente Romano, Ctra N340, Marbella, Málaga, tel: 952 770 100.
Don Carlos Tennis Club, Hotel Don Carlos, Urb. Elviria, Marbella, Malaga, tel: 952 831 739.
El Casco Tennis Club, Urb. El Rosario, Marbella, Málaga, tel: 952 837 651.

Bullfighting

Andalucía is the cradle of bullfighting, the controversial struggle between man and beast, and the town of **Ronda** is regarded as the cradle of modern bullfighting. Many of Spain's top matadors come from the region and many of the most respected fighting bulls.

There are occasional charity fights in winter, but the season really gets under way at Easter and with the series of corridas during the Seville Fair in April.

Seville's **Maestranza** bullring is

the most important arena. Daily fights are held during the fairs in other towns, throughout the summer. Six bulls are killed during a corrida, which usually starts at 6pm. **Tickets** are expensive, particularly if you want to be in the shade ("Sombra") and near the barrera, the ringside. Cheaper tickets are sold for "Sol", the seating on the sunny side of the arena. In some communities, bull-runs are held in the streets during local festivities.

Watersports

Facilities for sailing, windsurfing, scuba diving, waterskiing and sub aqua diving are available on the Atlantic and Mediterranean coasts.
Windsurfing: many beaches have schools and rent equipment. The best area is near **Tarifa**, Cádiz. The good winds attract surfers from all over Europe and various competitions are held throughout the year.

Spectator Sports

Soccer and **basketball** are Spain's most popular spectator sports. Andalucía's leading soccer teams are Betis and Sevilla (both of Seville) and Cádiz. Games usually start at 5pm on Sunday. Basketball attracts a fanatical following.

There is a **motor-racing** circuit in Jerez (Cádiz), with occasional car races, but the biggest event is the **Motorcycling Grand Prix**, on the first weekend in May (Circuito de Jerez, tel: 956 151 000).

Horse races are staged at Seville La Pineda hipodrome weekly during January–March; there are horse races on the beach in Sanlúcar de Barrameda (Cádiz), during August, a tradition dating back more than 150 years.

Shopping

Opening Hours

Shops are generally open 9.30–10am to 1–1.30pm and 4.30–5pm to 8–8.30pm Monday to Friday, mornings only on Saturday. The larger department stores such as El Corte Inglés do not usually close at midday.

El Corte Inglés has become a Spanish institution, offering a vast range of products, as well as a service for foreign tourists and export facilities.

What to Buy

Purchases worth making anywhere in Spain include qood-quality leather goods, Havana and Canary Islands cigars, porcelain statuary, cultured pearls, bargain-priced alcohol, virgin olive oil, saffron and craftware.

Andalucía offers a variety of handmade products, including intricate fans, embroidery, finely-tooled leather goods, earthenware pottery, baskets, Seville tiles, silver jewellery, and rugs. Some of the finest **guitars** are made in Granada and Seville.

Exports

Visitors resident in non-EU countries, the Canaries, Ceuta or Melilla can claim back tax (IVA) on purchases, but each item must have a value of over 15,000 pesetas. Shops should have the forms to fill in.

The tax refund will normally be sent to your home address, except for travellers leaving via Málaga airport, who can claim the refund immediately from the office of the Banco de España in the airport terminal.

Shopping Areas

Almería

The commercial centre is around the Paseo de Almería, Puerta de Purchena, Obispo Orbera, and Calle de las Tiendas.

What to buy: principal buys are in **ceramics and pottery** from Albox, Nijar, Sorbas and Vera; **basketwork** from Almería, Alhabia and Nijar; **jarapas**, rugs made with rags and strips of cotton from Nijar, Huercal Overa and Berja; **bedspreads and blankets** from Albox, Berja and Macael; marble **objects** from Macaél.

Cádiz

The main shopping area is in the delightful warren of streets near the cathedral.

What to buy: sherry from Jerez and Puerto de Santa María such as Harveys, Williams and Humbert, Pedro Domecq and Osborne; **dolls** from the doll factory in Chiclana, Fabrica de Muñecas Marin, Rivero 16, tel: 956 400 067; **fine leather** from Ubrique; **carpets** from Arcos de la Frontera; **capes and ponchos** from Grazalema; **guitars** from Algodonales; **wickerwork** from Jerez; **saddlery** from Olvera.

Córdoba

For general shopping the busiest area is between the streets Gondomar, Tendillas and Ronda de los Tejares.

Of the various markets, the most interesting are held on Saturday and Sunday mornings in the **Plaza Corredera**. **Handicrafts** can be bought at the municipal handicrafts market (Zoco Municipal de Artesanía) behind the bullfighting museum.

What to buy: Silver filigree jewellery; **Montilla wines** *(Bodegas* in Montilla, 46 km/28 miles from Córdoba); **anís liquor** from Rute (Anís Machaquito, Anís De Raza); **ceramics**, **Lucena pottery** with geometric green and yellow design, and **botijos** (two-spouted drinking pitchers) from La Rambla; **leatherwork; decorative metalwork** in copper, bronze and brass (from Espejo and Castro del Río).

Granada

The main shopping area is around Recogidas, Acera de Darro, Gran Vía and Reyes Católicos and the maze of surrounding streets. Granada offers some excellent handicrafts, many incorporating techniques and designs handed down from the Arabs. You will find a large range of handmade articles in the Alcaiceria (old Arab silk market), near the cathedral.

What to buy: cured mountain hams from the Alpujarras; **pottery**, most typical is Fajalauza with distinctive blue and green design originally from the Albaicín; **leather**, especially embossed leatherwork; **marquetry** (technique of inlaying wood with bone, ivory, mother of pearl and other woods) **chests**, chess boards, small tables; metal craftwork, **lanterns** made to traditional **Moorish designs; rugs, cushions** and **bedspreads** from the Alpujarras; handmade guitars, several workshops on the Cuesta de Gomerez leading to the Alhambra; **silver filigree jewellery.**

Huelva

What to buy: cured hams from Jabugo; **white wine** from the Condado de Huelva; **pottery** from Aracena and Cortejana; **rugs** from Ecinasola; **embroidery** from Aracena, Alosno and Puebla de Guzmán); **handmade leather boots** (Valverde de Camino.

Complaints

From August 1990 it became a statutory requirement for all businesses dealing with the public (hostelries, garages, transport, shops, etc.) to have a complaints book *(Libro* or *hoja de reclamaciones).* Any complaint is registered in the book and sent to the local authority. Any receipts should be attached to the claim.

You can also take your complaint to the town hall or the Consumer Advice Office *(Oficina de Información al Consumidor)* if one exists.

Jaén

What to buy: glass and ceramics (from Andújar, Bailen and Ubeda); **carpets and wickerwork** (from Ubeda, Jaén and Los Villares); **forged iron objects and lanterns** (Ubeda); **guitars** (Marmolejo).

Málaga

The main shopping area in the city is centred around the streets Larios, Nueva, Granada, Caldereria and adjacent streets, and also around Armengual de la Mota and Avenida de Andalucía where there is an El Corte Ingles.

On the outskirts of Málaga are several hypermarkets and shopping complexes such as **Larios, Los Patios** and **La Rosaleda**.

The towns along the Costa del Sol also offer a wide variety of street markets, colourful and entertaining, they are not necessarily the best place to find a bargain.

Markets: Monday, Marbella; Tuesday, Fuengirola and Nerja; Wednesday, Estepona and Rincón de la Victoria; Thursday, Torremolinos, San Pedro de Alcántara and Torre del Mar; Friday, Arroyo de la Miel and Benalmádena pueblo; Saturday, Coín, Mijas-Costa and Nueva Andalucía; Sunday, Estepona port and Málaga (by the football stadium).

What to buy: leather goods at factory prices; **Málaga wine**; **pottery** and **ceramics** from Málaga, Ronda, Vélez Málaga and Coín; **embossed copper** (Málaga); **castanets** (Alora); **guitars** (Málaga and Ronda); **basketry** (Vélez Málaga, Benamocarra); **rugs** from Mijas (can be made to order).

Seville

For general shopping, go to the area behind the El Salvador church; for clothes, Sierpes, Campana, O'Donnell and Velázquez; department stores around Plaza del Duque, and the streets O'Donnell and Velázquez.

Seville also has a number of street markets selling handicrafts and bric-a-brac – daily handicraft market in the Mercado del Postigo; Wednesday and Thursday,

handicrafts in Rioja and Magdalena, Friday and Saturday in the Plaza del Duque; Thursday, secondhand goods and antiques in Feria; Sunday, antiques and secondhand goods in Alameda de Hércules, and also Parque Alcosa.

What to buy: Antiques around the streets Mateos Gago, Placentines and Rodrigo Caro; **ceramics and tiles** from Santa Ana (factory in Triana) and La Cartuja de Sevilla (factory at Ctra de Merida km 529, tel: 954 392 854); **saddlery and leather items, boots** and **chaps**; **fashion**, Seville's own designers Victorio and Lucchino have a showroom at Sierpes 87; **fans and castanets** and **locally made good**

GIBRALTAR: The Basics

The Place

Gibraltar is one of the last relics of the British Empire. Connoisseurs of anachronisms and quirks of history will find the tiny colony of interest. One-third of the 30,000 population on the Rock, a limestone mass rising to 1,396 ft (426 metres), was formerly composed of British servicemen and their families, but the garrison town atmosphere has declined since Britain had reduced its military presence.

The population is a mixture of Spanish, Moroccan, Jewish, Maltese and Genoese, who speak both English and Spanish although English is the official language. They resolutely oppose Spain's desire to absorb the 2 sq. mile (6 sq. km) peninsula. A democratically-elected House of Assembly led by a Chief Minister rules the colony.

Spain held the Rock until 1704. During the War of the Spanish Succession, an Anglo-Dutch fleet captured it. General Franco tried to force sovereignty to be transferred to Spain by closing the frontier. But his blockade only succeeded in making the Gibraltarians more stubbornly British. Today the colony has become a tourist attraction and is a growing off-shore financial centre.

Planning the Trip

Entry Regulations

EU nationals may present a valid passport or national identity card. Spaniards are required to show a passport. Visas are issued by British Visa issuing posts on Gibraltar's behalf and are usually for a single entry, maximum period of three months. **Immigration Control**, Waterport Police Station, 124 Irish Town, tel: 71543.

Duty free allowance is available for people entering Gibraltar who have not been in Gibraltar during the previous 24 hours.

Tobacco: 200 cigarettes or 50 cigars or 250 grammes of tobacco. **Alcohol:** 1 litre of spirits, liqueur or cordial or 2 litres of fortified or sparkling wine or 2 litres of still wine. **Perfume:** 50 grammes of perfume and 0.25 litres of toilet water.

The above also applies to those returning to Spain, who can import 35,000 pesetas worth of goods on one visit per month, provided they do not reside in Gibraltar or the Campo de Gibraltar.

Gibraltar Customs, Custom House, Waterport, tel: 78879.

Currency

Official currency is the **Gibraltar pound**, which is on a par with the pound Sterling. UK and Gibraltar notes circulate freely, but Gibraltar notes are not exchangeable outside Gibraltar. UK coinage is legal tender. Spanish *pesetas* are widely accepted. There are no restrictions on bringing money in or taking it out.

Banking hours are generally 9am–3.30pm (Monday–Thursday), 9am–3.30pm, 4–6pm (Friday), with variation during summer (July–mid

September). There are branches of Abbey National, Barclays, Lloyds and National Westminster banks, and UK account holders can use their cash cards and current account cheque books in Gibraltar.

Information on cash withdrawls on credit cards is available from banks: Access is represented by Banque Indosuez, 206/210 Main Street (tel: 75090), Visa by Barclays Bank with branches at 84–90 Main Street (tel: 78565), American Express by Bland Travel, Cloister Building, Irish Town (tel: 40748).

Getting There

BY AIR Gibraltar airport offers access to the western end of the Costa del Sol. It is served by British Airways. Coach services are available for passengers travelling to and from the Costa del Sol. **Airport information**, tel: 73026. British Airways, Cloister Building, Irish Town, tel: 79300. There are daily flights to London (Gatwick) plus frequent flights to other destinations such as Manchester, Tangier and Casablanca.
BY SEA A ferry service runs to the Moroccan port of Tangier five times a week in summer, four times in winter. In summer there is also a weekly crossing to Marinasmir. Information from Parodytur, tel: 76070.
BY ROAD The only road access to Gibraltar is via the border with Spain at the crossing with La Linea. The border, (La Verja), is open 24 hours.

Business Hours

Shopping hours are generally 9am or 9.30am–1pm and 3–7pm.

The commercial centre is **Main Street** and **Irish Town**. There are also new shopping complexes at Marina Bay and Sheppard's Marina. On Fridays and Saturdays there is a street market in Cannon Lane, and on Fridays an arts and crafts market at the Boulevard behind the Piazza.

Weights & Measures

Gibraltar officially uses the metric system.

Public Holidays

- **January** New Year's Day (1)
- **March/April** Good Friday, Easter Monday
- **May** May Day (first Monday), Spring Bank Holiday (Last Monday)
- **August** Summer Bank Holiday (Last Monday)
- **December** Christmas Day (25), Boxing Day (26)

Complaints

The Community Advisory Service at City Hall, John Mackintosh Sq., tel: 50788 deals with consumer complaints.

Religious Services

A complete list of places of worship in Gibraltar is available from the Tourist Office. A guided tour of the churches is run once a week starting from the Tourist Office.

Media

Newspapers Gibraltar has several English-language newspapers the most important being *The Gibraltar Chronicle*, founded in 1801. Other publications include *Vox*, *Panorama* and *The New People*.
Television & Radio Gibraltar has its own TV station and two radio stations all broadcasting in English.
GBC Television: Daily broadcasts in English, 7pm–midnight.
Radio Gibraltar: 206m medium wave. Broadcasts 7pm–midnight in English and Spanish.
BFBS Gibraltar: (British Forces Broadcasting Service) – on FM (VHF). There are two stations: bfbs 1 broadcasting music and sport and bfbs 2 broadcasting theatre, current affairs, comedy and music.

Postal Services

The main branch of the Post Office is at 104 Main Street, with two sub-Post Offices at Sand Hill and Glacis Estate. Opening hours are 9am–1pm and 2–5pm Monday–Friday and 10am–1pm Saturday. Post boxes are red with a black base.

Gibraltar stamps are of great interest to collectors and the main Post Office has a philatelic counter for first day covers, gift packs and previous issues, also available by post from Philatelic Bureau, P.O. Box 5662, Gibraltar.

Telecoms

There is International Direct Dialling for all countries. The International Access prefix for all countries is 00 (except Spain), followed by the country code, the province/town prefix and finally the subscribers number, e.g. to phone London 00-44 (UK code)–1 (London code) + subscribers' number. Phone calls to Spain are direct.

Calling Gibraltar from Spain, dial first 9567. To phone Gibraltar from other countries, use the international access prefix + 350 (country code for Gibraltar). Operator-connected telephone booths are available on the ground floor of City Hall at the rear of John Mackintosh Square.

Telegrams, telexes and faxes can be sent from the offices of Gibraltar Telecom International. Main office is at 25 South Barrack Road and branch at 60 Main Street.

Emergencies

Medical Services UK residents are entitled to free medical treatment provided they have a temporary address in Gibraltar. Other EU nationals may receive free treatment on presentation of form E111.

St Bernard's Hospital, tel: 79700. Health Centre, **Casemates Square**, tel: 78337. Open: 9.15am–5.30pm Monday–Friday, 9am–1pm Saturday.

Emergency Numbers
Ambulance/Fire, tel: 199.
Police, tel: 72500.

Getting Around

By Road

Driving is on the right side of the road. A current UK or EU license is valid, other nationals need be in possession of an International Driving Licence obtained in their home country. There are no parking meters in Gibraltar, but fines are imposed for dangerous or illegal parking. Car clamps are also used and cars may be towed away.

Gibraltar is small enough to manage without your own transport, although there are local and international car hire companies.

By Taxi

There are about 112 licensed taxis, with ranks in the town centre and at the airport and frontier, although phone reservations can be made by calling Gibraltar Taxi Association, 12 Cannon Lane, tel: 70027. Fares are not metered but rates are fixed and should be on display at ranks and in the taxi itself. There are surcharges for calls made via the office and from midnight–7am Some taxis offer tours of the Rock; look for a sign on the windscreen saying City Service.

By Bus

Three bus companies operate services around Gibraltar. Information on routes available can be obbtained from the Tourist Office.

Where to Stay

Hotels

Rock Hotel
3 Europa Road.
Tel: 73000.
Gibraltar's grand old colonial-style hotel, opened in 1932, surrounded by gardens on a hillside a short walk from the town centre. Facilities include pool, tennis court and beauty salon. **$$$$**
The Eliott
2 Governor's Parade.
Tel: 70500.
In the centre of the town, the former Holiday Inn is the most modern of Gib's hotels. **$$$$**
Bristol
10 Cathedral Sq.
Tel: 76800.
Basic but adequate old colonial-style hotel in the centre of town. **$$$**

Price Guide

All the prices are for a double room:
$$$$ = Over £80
$$$ = £60–80

Where to Eat

Restaurants

La Bayuca
21 Turnbull's La.
Tel: 75119.
Lunch and dinner. Closed Tuesday. No lunch Sunday. Amex, Diners, Mastercard, Visa.
One of Gibraltar's oldest restaurants, serving international and Mediterranean cuisine. **($$)**
Strings
44 Cornwall's La.
Tel: 78800.
Lunch and dinner. Closed Sunday. Amex, Mastercard, Visa.
Small, cosy and popular, serving bistro like dishes and "specials of the day". **($$)**
El Patio
54 Irish Town.
Tel: 70822.
Lunch and dinner. Closed Sunday, no lunch Saturday. Amex, Mastercard, Visa.
Just off Main Street, specialising in seafood. **($)**

Price Guide

Prices are per person for a three-course meal, not including wine:
Moderate ($$) = £10–£20
Expensive ($$$) = more than £20

Language

Spanish – like French, Italian, Portuguese – is a Romance language, derived from the Latin spoken by the Romans who conquered the Iberian peninsula more than 2000 years ago. The Moors who settled in the peninsula centuries later contributed a great number of new words (see panel). Following the discovery of America, Spaniards took their language with them to the four corners of the globe. Today, Spanish is spoken by 250 million people in north, south and central America and parts of Africa.

In addition to Spanish, which is spoken throughout the country, some regions have a second language. Catalan (spoken in Catalonia), Valenciano (Valencia), Mallorquín (the Balearics) and Gallego (Galicia) are all Romance languages, unlike Euskera, the language of the Basques, which is notoriously complex and difficult—it is unrelated to any other European tongue, and experts are not even sure what its origins are.

Unlike English, Spanish is a phonetic language: words are pronounced exactly as they are spelt, which is why it is somewhat harder for Spaniards to learn English than vice versa (although Spanish distinguishes between the two genders, masculine and feminine, and the subjunctive verb form is an endless source of headaches for students). The English language is one of Britain's biggest exports to Spain. Spaniards spend millions on learning aids, language academies and sending their children to study English in the UK or Ireland, and are eager to practise their linguistic skills with

foreign visitors. Even so, they will be flattered and delighted if you make the effort to communicate in Spanish. You should beware, however, of some misleading "false friends" (see page 354).

The Alphabet

Learning the pronunciation of the Spanish alphabet is a good idea. In particular learn how to spell out your own name. Spanish has a letter that doesn't exist in English, the ñ (pronounced "ny").

a = ah
b = bay
c = thay (strong th as in "thought")
d = day
e = ay
f = effay
g = hay
h = ah-chay
i = ee
j = hotah
k = kah
l = ellay
m = emmay
n = ennay
ñ = enyay
o = oh
p = pay
q = koo
r = error
s = essay
t = tay
u = oo
v = oobay
w = oobay doe-blay
x = ek-kiss
y = ee gree-ay-gah,
z = thay-tah

Basic Rules

English is widely spoken in most tourist areas, but even if you speak no Spanish at all, it is worth trying to master a few simple words and phrases.

As a general rule, the accent falls on the second-to-last syllable, unless it is otherwise marked with an accent (´) or the word ends in D, L, R or Z.

Vowels in Spanish are always pronounced the same way. The double LL is pronounced like the y in "yes", the double RR is rolled, as

in Scots. The H is silent in Spanish, whereas J (and G when it precedes an E or I) is pronounced like a guttural H (as if you were clearing your throat).

When addressing someone you are not familiar with, use the more formal "usted". The informal "tu" is reserved for relatives and friends.

Moorish Connections

The Moors arrived in Spain in 711, and occupied parts of the peninsula for the next eight centuries. They left behind hundreds of Arabic words, many related to farming and crops, as well as place names including those of towns (often identified by the prefix Al-, meaning "the" or Ben-, meaning "son of") and rivers (the prefix Guad- means "river").

Some of these Arabic words passed on to other languages, including French, and from there into English. Among those present in both Spanish and English are sugar (azúcar), coffee (café), apricot (albaricoque), saffron (azafrán), lemon (limón), cotton (algodón), alcohol (alcohol), karat (kilate), cipher (cifra), elixir (elixir), almanac (almanaque), zenith (cenit), and zero (cero).

Words & Phrases

Hello Hola
How are you? ¿Cómo está usted?
How much is it? ¿Cuánto es?
What is your name? ¿Cómo se llama usted?
My name is... Yo me llamo...
Do you speak English? ¿Habla inglés?
I am British/American Yo soy británico/norteamericano
I don't understand No comprendo
Please speak more slowly Hable más despacio, por favor
Can you help me? ¿Me puede ayudar?
I am looking for... Estoy buscando...
Where is...? ¿Dónde está...?
I'm sorry Lo siento
I don't know No lo se
No problem No hay problema
Have a good day Que tenga un

buen día, or Vaya con Diós
That's it Ese es
Here it is Aquí está
There it is Allí está
Let's go Vámonos
See you tomorrow Hasta mañana
See you soon Hasta pronto
Show me the word in the book
Muéstreme la palabra en el libro
At what time? ¿A qué hora?
When? ¿Cuándo?
What time is it? ¿Qué hora es?
yes sí
no no
please por favor
thank you (very much) (muchas) gracias
you're welcome de nada
excuse me perdóneme
hello hola
OK bién
goodbye adiós
good evening/night buenas tardes/noches
here aquí
there allí
today hoy
yesterday ayer
tomorrow mañana **(note: mañana also means "morning")**
now ahora
later después
right away ahora mismo
this morning esta mañana
this afternoon esta tarde
this evening esta tarde
tonight esta noche

On Arrival

I want to get off at... Quiero bajarme en...
Is there a bus to the museum? ¿Hay un autobús al museo?
What street is this? ¿Qué calle es ésta?
Which line do I take for...? ¿Qué línea cojo para...?
How far is...? ¿A qué distancia está...?
airport aeropuerto
customs aduana
train station estación de tren
bus station estación de autobuses
metro station estación de metro
bus autobús
bus stop parada de autobús

Emergencies

Help! ¡Socorro!
Stop! ¡Alto!
Call a doctor Llame a un médico
Call an ambulance Llame a una ambulancia
Call the police Llame a la policia
Call the fire brigade Llame a los bomberos
Where's the nearest telephone? ¿Dónde hay un teléfono?
Where's the nearest hospital? ¿Dónde está el hospital más próximo?
I am sick Estoy enfermo
I have lost my passport/purse He perdido mi pasaporte/bolso

platform apeadero
ticket billete
return ticket billete de ida y vuelta
hitch-hiking auto-stop
toilets servicios
This is the hotel address Ésta es la dirección del hotel
I'd like a (single/double) room Quiero una habitación (sencilla/doble)
... with shower con ducha
... with bath con baño
... with a view con vista
Does that include breakfast? ¿Incluye desayuno?
May I see the room? ¿Puedo ver la habitación?
washbasin lavabo
bed cama
key llave
elevator ascensor
air conditioning aire acondicionado

On the Road

Where is the spare wheel? ¿Dónde está la rueda de repuesto?
Where is the nearest garage? ¿Dónde está el taller más próximo?
Our car has broken down Nuestro coche se ha averiado
I want to have my car repaired Quiero que reparen mi coche

It's not your right of way Usted no tiene prioridad
I think I must have put diesel in my car by mistake Me parece haber echado gasoil por error
the road to... la carretera a...
left izquierda
right derecha
straight on derecho
far lejos
near cerca
opposite frente a
beside al lado de
car park aparcamiento
over there allí
at the end al final
on foot a pie
by car en coche
town map mapa de la ciudad
road map mapa de carreteras
street calle
square plaza
give way ceda el paso
exit salida
dead end calle sin salida
wrong way dirección prohibida
no parking prohibido aparcar
motorway autovía
toll highway autopista
toll peaje
speed limit límite de velocidad
petrol station gasolinera
petrol gasolina
unleaded sin plomo
diesel gasoil
water/oil agua/aceite
air aire
puncture pinchazo
bulb bombilla
wipers limpia-parabrisas

On the Telephone

How do I make an outside call? ¿Cómo hago una llamada exterior?
What is the area code? ¿Cuál es el prefijo?
I want to make an international (local) call Quiero hacer una llamada internacional (local)
I'd like an alarm call for 8 tomorrow morning Quiero que me despierten a las ocho de la mañana
Hello? ¿Dígame?
Who's calling? ¿Quién llama?
Hold on, please Un momento, por favor
I can't hear you No le oigo
Can you hear me? ¿Me oye?

He/she is not here No está aquí
The line is busy La línea está ocupada
**I must have dialled the wrong
number** Debo haber marcado un
número equivocado

Shopping

Where is the nearest bank?
¿Dónde está el banco más
próximo?
I'd like to buy Quiero comprar
How much is it ¿Cuánto es?
Do you accept credit cards?
¿Aceptan tarjeta?
I'm just looking Sólo estoy mirando
Have you got...? ¿Tiene...?
I'll take it Me lo llevo
I'll take this one/that one Me llevo
éste/ese
What size is it? ¿Que talla es?
Anything else? ¿Otra cosa?
size (clothes) talla
small pequeño
large grande
cheap barato
expensive caro
enough suficiente
too much demasiado
a piece una pieza
each cada una/la pieza/la unidad
(eg. melones, 100 ptas la unidad)
bill la factura (shop), la cuenta
(restaurant)
bank banco
bookshop librería
chemist farmacia
hair-dressers peluquería
jewellers joyería
post office correos
shoe shop zapatería
department store grandes almacenes
fresh fresco
frozen congelado
organic biológico
flavour sabor
basket cesta
bag bolsa
bakery panadería
butcher's carnicería
cake shop pastelería
fishmonger's pescadería
grocery verdulería
tobacconist estanco
market mercado
supermarket supermercado
junk shop tienda de segunda mano

Numbers

0	cero
1	uno
2	dos
3	tres
4	cuatro
5	cinco
6	seis
7	siete
8	ocho
9	nueve
10	diez
11	once
12	doce
13	trece
14	catorce
15	quince
16	dieciseis
17	diecisiete
18	dieciocho
19	diecinueve
20	viente
21	veintiuno
30	treinta
40	cuarenta
50	cincuenta
60	sesenta
70	setenta
80	ochenta
90	noventa
100	cien
200	doscientos
500	quinientos
1,000	mil
10,000	diez mil
1,000,000	un millón

Sightseeing

mountain montaña
hill colina
valley valle
river río
lake lago
lookout mirador
city ciudad
small town, village pueblo
old town casco antiguo
monastery monasterio
convent convento
cathedral catedral
church glesia
palace palacio
hospital hospital
town hall ayuntamiento
nave nave
statue estátua

fountain fuente
staircase escalera
tower torre
castle castillo
Iberian ibérico
Phoenician fenicio
Roman romano
Moorish árabe
Romanesque románico
Gothic gótico
museum museo
art gallery galería de arte
exhibition exposición
tourist information office oficina de
turismo
free gratis
open abierto
closed cerrado
every day diario/todos los días
all year todo el año
all day todo el día
swimming pool piscina
to book reservar

Dining Out

In Spanish, el menú is not the main
menu, but a fixed menu offered
each day at a lower price. The main
menu is la carta.
breakfast desayuno
lunch almuerzo/comida
dinner cena
meal comida
first course primer plato
main course plato principal
made to order por encargo
drink included incluida
consumición/bebida
wine list carta de vinos
the bill la cuenta
fork tenedor
knife cuchillo
spoon cuchara
plate plato
glass vaso
wine glass copa
napkin servilleta
ashtray cenicero
waiter, please! camarero, por favor

Menu Decoder

SNACKS

pan **bread**
bollo **bun/roll**
mantequilla **butter**
mermelada **jam**
confitura **jam**

pimienta **pepper**
sal **salt**
azúcar **sugar**
huevos **eggs**
... cocidos   boiled, **cooked**
... con beicon **with bacon**
... con jamón **with ham**
... fritos **fried**
... revueltos **scrambled**
yogúr **yoghurt**
tostada **toast**
sandwich **sandwich in square slices
of bread**
bocadillo **sandwich in a bread roll**

MAIN COURSES

Meat/Carne
buey **beef**
carne picada **ground meat**
cerdo **pork**
chivo **kid**
chorizo **sausage seasoned with
paprika**
chuleta **chop**
cochinillo **suckling pig**
conejo **rabbit**
cordero **lamb**
costilla **rib**
entrecot **beef rib steak**
filete **steak**
abalí **wild boar**
jamón **ham**
jamón cocido **cooked ham**
jamón serrano **cured ham**
jsalchichón **sausage**
lomo **loin**
morcilla **black pudding**
pierna **leg**
riñones **kidneys**
sesos **brains**
solomillo **fillet steak**
ternera **veal or young beef**
lengua **tongue**
a la brasa **charcoal grilled**
al horno **roast**
a la plancha **grilled**
asado **roast**
bién hecho **well done**
en salsa **in sauce**
en su punto **medium**
estofado **stew**
frito **fried**
parrillada **mixed grill**
pinchito **skewer**
Poco hecho **rare**
relleno **stuffed**

Fowl
codorniz **quail**
faisán **pheasant**
pavo **turkey**
pato **duck**
perdiz **partridge**
pintada **guinea fowl**
pollo **chicken**

Fish/Pescado
almeja **clam**
anchoas **anchovies**
anguila **eel**
atún **tuna**
bacalao **cod**
besugo **red bream**
bogavante **lobster**
boquerones **fresh anchovies**
caballa **mackerel**
calamar **squid**
cangrejo **crab**
caracola **sea snail**
cazón **dogfish**
centollo **spider crab**
chopito **baby cuttlefish**
cigala **Dublin Bay prawn/scampi**
dorada **gilt head bream**
fritura **mixed fry**
gamba **shrimp/prawn**
jibia **cuttlefish**
langosta **spiny lobster**
langostino **large prawn**
lenguado **sole**
lubina **sea bass**
mariscada **mixed shellfish**
mariscos **Shellfish**
mejillón **mussel**
merluza **hake**
mero **grouper**

Table Talk

I am a vegetarian Soy
vegetariano
I am on a diet Estoy de
régimen
What do you recommend?
¿Qué recomienda?
**Do you have local
specialities?** ¿Hay
especialidades locales?
I'd like to order Quiero pedir
That is not what I ordered
Ésto no es lo que he pedido
May I have more wine? ¿Me
da más vino?
Enjoy your meal Buen
provecho

ostión **Portuguese oyster**
ostra **oyster**
peregrina **scallop**
pescadilla **small hake**
pez espada **swordfish**
pijota **hake**
pulpo **octopus**
rape **monkfish**
rodaballo **turbot**
salmón **salmon**
salmonete **red mullet**
sardina **sardine**
trucha **trout**

VEGETABLES/CEREALS/
SALADS
vegetables **verduras**
ajo **garlic**
alcachofa **artichoke**
apio **celery**
arroz **rice**
berenjena **eggplant/aubergine**
cebolla **onion**
champiñon **mushroom**
col **cabbage**
coliflor **cauliflower**
crudo **raw**
ensalada **salad**
espárrago **asparagus**
espinaca **spinach**
garbanzo **chick pea**
guisante **pea**
haba **broad bean**
habichuela **bean**
judía **green bean**
lechuga **lettuce**
lenteja **lentil**
maíz **corn/maize**
menestra **cooked mixed
vegetables**
patata **potato**
pepino **cucumber**
pimiento **pepper**
puerro **leek**
rábano **radish**
seta **wild mushroom**
tomate **tomato**
zanahoria **carrot**

FRUIT AND DESSERTS
fruta **fruta**
aguacate **avocado**
albaricoque **apricot**
cereza **cherry**
ciruela **plum**
frambuesa **raspberry**
fresa **strawberry**

granada **pomegranate**
higo **fig**
limón **lemon**
mandarina **tangerine**
manzana **apple**
melocotón **peach**
melón **melon**
naranja **orange**
pasa **raisin**
pera **pear**
piña **pineapple**
plátano **banana**
pomelo **grapefruit**
sandía **watermelon**
uva **grape**
Postre Dessert
tarta **cake**
pastel **pie**
helado **ice cream**
natilla **custard**
flan **caramel custard**
queso **cheese**

Liquid Refreshment

coffee *café*
... black *sólo*
... with milk *con leche*
... decaffeinated *descafeinado*
sugar *azúcar*
tea *té*
milk *leche*
mineral water *agua mineral*
fizzy *con gas*
non-fizzy *sin gas*
juice (fresh) *zumo (natural)*
cold *fresco/frío*
hot *caliente*
beer *cerveza*
... bottled *en botella*
... on tap *de barril*
soft drink *refresco*
diet drink *bebida "light"*
with ice *con hielo*
wine *vino*
red wine *vino tinto*
white *blanco*
rosé *rosado*
dry *seco*
sweet *dulce*
house wine *vino de la casa*
sparkling wine *vino espumoso*
half litre *medio litro*
quarter litre *cuarto de litro*
cheers! *salud*

Days and Months

Days of the week, seasons, and months are not capitalised in Spanish

DAYS OF THE WEEK
Monday *lunes*
Tuesday *martes*
Wednesday *miércoles*
Thursday *jueves*
Friday *viernes*
Saturday *sábado*
Sunday *domingo*

SEASONS
Spring *primavera*
Summer *verano*
Autumn *otoño*
Winter *invierno*

MONTHS
January *enero*
February *febrero*
March *marzo*
April *abril*
May *mayo*
June *junio*
July *julio*
August *agosto*
September *septiembre*
October *octubre*
November *noviembre*
December *diciembre*

False Amigos

"False friends" are words that look like English words but mean something different. Such as:
Constipación **a common cold**
Simpático **friendly**
Tópico **a cliché**
Actualmente **currently**
Sensible **sensitive**
Disgustado **angry**
Embarazada **pregnant**
Suplir **substitute**
Informal **unreliable (to describe a person)**
Rape **monkfish**
Billón **a million million**
Soportar **tolerate**

Further Reading

Although Spain did not figure in the Grand Tour of the early tourists, from the 19th century it attracted a succession of foreign travellers in search of the "exotic". Andalucía in particular awakened their interest. Théophile Gautier, Hans Christian Andersen and Washington Irving were among those to visit the region and their comments make fascinating reading.

Ian Robertson aptly titled his book on the succession of English travellers *Los Curiosos Impertinentes* (The Impertinent Inquisitive Ones, published in Spanish by Serbal, 1988). These impertinent English included Henry Swinburne, Joseph Townsend, and Richard Ford. Ford did most to awaken interest in the region with witty and shrewdly-observed accounts of his travels between 1830 and 1833. This century Gerald Brenan who lived much of his life in Andalucía, stands out as a writer whose great affection for the region did not diminish his critical faculties.

Travel Information

Charming Small Hotel Guide Spain (Duncan Petersen). A survey of small hotels and paradors in Spain, both in cities and in the country.
Special Places to Stay in Spain (Alastair Sawday). Thoroughly-researched guide to small hotels and family-run country inns all over Spain.

General Backgound

As I Walked Out One Midsummer Morning, by Laurie Lee (Penguin). The author's adventures as a young man crossing Spain on foot in the thirties.
The Bible in Spain, by George Borrow. First published 1842. Eccentric, opinionated and entertaining.
Fire In The Blood: The New Spain,

by Ian Gibson (Faber/BBC). A lively
portrait of modern Spain, based on
a popular BBC documentary series.
Handbook for Travellers in Spain,
by Richard Ford. Centaur Press,
1966; and **Gatherings from Spain**.
Dent Everyman, 1970. Accounts of
Spanish travels last century.
Inside Andalucía, by David Baird
(Santana). Entertaining yet profound
– and brilliantly written.
The New Spaniards, by John
Hooper (Penguin). Highly readable
chronicle of modern Spain by a top
British foreign correspondent.
The People of the Sierra, by Julian
A. Pitt-Rivers. Weidenfield &
Nicolson, 1954. Social
anthropologist's dissection of a
remote mountain community.
**The Pueblo: A Mountain Village in
Spain**, by Ronald Fraser. Pantheon.
Villagers of Mijas tell their own
story; and **In Hiding: The Life of
Manuel Cortes**. Penguin, 1982.
How a village mayor stayed hidden
for 30 years for fear of execution.
The Road from Ronda, by Alastair
Boyd. Collins, 1969. Vivid account
of a horse-ride through the Serrania
de Ronda.
South From Granada, by Gerald
Brenan (Cambridge University
Press). An account of the author's
experiences living in an Andalucían
village in the 1920s, a classic on a
lifestyle that is fast disappearing.
Spanish Journeys, by Adam Hopkins
(Penguin). Insightful travelogue by a
top travel writer.
South from Granada, by Gerald
Brenan. Cambridge University
Press, 1988. Classic account of life
in a remote Granada village; and
The Face of Spain (Penguin, 1987).
Brenan's grim view of an
impoverished post-war Spain.
The Story of Spain, by Mark
Williams (Santana). Comprehensive,
and at the same time delightfully
anecdotal and readable look at the
history of Spain.
Tales of the Alhambra, by
Washington Irving (available in
numerous editions). The 19th-
century American author's account
of Moorish legends is still enjoyable.

Culture

Death in the Afternoon, by Ernest
Hemingway (Cape). Hemingway's
explanation of the bullfight,
although much maligned by purists,
is still informative and gripping.
In Search of the Firedance, by
James Woodall (Sinclair-Stevenson).
Flamenco and its origins.
Or I'll Dress You in Mourning, by
Larry Collins and Dominique
Lapierre. Simon & Schuster.
Brilliant insights into Spain's post-
Civil War hardships which moulded
the Andalucían matador El
Cordobés.
White Wall of Spain, by Allen
Josephs (Iowa State University
Press). A thoughtful look at
Andalucían folk culture.

Food and Wine

Cooking in Spain, by Janet Mendel
(Santana). Encyclopedic book of
Spanish cookery with 400 recipes
and colourful insights into local
cuisine.
**Enyclopedia of Spanish and
Portuguese Wine**, by Kathryn
McWhirter and Charles Metcalfe
(Simon & Schuster). An excellent
introduction to the new wines
coming out of Spain.
The Food and Wine of Spain, by
Penelope Casas (Penguin).
Great Spanish recipes from an
American food writer who lived in
Spain for many years.
The La Ina Book of Tapas, by
Elisabeth Luard (Martin). Tasty
survey, with recipes, of those
wonderful Spanish appetisers.
The Wine Atlas of Spain, by
Hubrecht Duijker (Simon and
Schuster). The Spanish wine scene,
written with the traveller in mind.

Other Insight Guides

Europe is comprehensively covered
by the 360 books in Apa
Publications' three series of
guidebooks which embrace the world.
Insight Guides provide the reader
with a full cultural background and
top-quality photography. Titles which
highlight destinations in this part of
Europe include: Spain, Madrid,
Barcelona, Catalonia, Gran Canaria,
Tenerife, Mallorca and Ibiza.

Apa Publications also publish
Insight Pocket Guides, written by
local hosts and containing tailor-
made itineraries to help users get
the most out of a place during a
short stay. Each title also has a
pull-out map. Spanish destinations
in the series include Madrid,
Barcelona, Granada and Seville,
Costa Blanca, Costa del Sol, Ibiza,
Mallorca, Tenerife and Gran
Canaria.

To complete all the needs of
travellers, **Insight Compact Guides**,
in essence mini encylopedias, give
you the facts about a destination in
a very digestible form, supported by
maps and colour photographs.
Titles in the series include
Barcelona, Costa Brava, Gran
Canaria, Mallorca and Tenerife.

ART & PHOTO CREDITS

INSIGHT GUIDE
SOUTHERN SPAIN

Cartographic Editor **Zoë Goodwin**
Production **Stuart A. Everitt**
Design Consultants
Carlotta Junger, Graham Mitchener
Picture Research **Hilary Genin**

Index

Numbers in italics refer to photographs

a

Abd-al-Malik 33
Abd-al-Rahman I 27, 28, 29, 167
Abd-al-Rahman II 30, 167
Abd-al-Rahman III 30, 73, 167, 176, 255
Aben Humeya 227
Abu-al-Abbas 27
Abu-Abd-Allah, Muhammad *see* Boabdil
Abu al-Hasan Ali ibn-Nafi *see* Ziryab
Abu-Ya'qub Yusuf 37, 146
accommodation
  rural tourism 124
agriculture 31, 217
  see also olives
Aguadulce 218
Akhbar Majmua 27
Alalia, Battle of 20
Alcalá de los Gazules *10–11*, 263–4
Alcalá la Real 208
Alcaudete 207
Alessandri, Carlota 115
Alfonso El Batallador 36, 37
Alfonso III 238
Alfonso VI of Léon-Castile 35, 36
Alfonso VIII of Castile 37
Alfonso X (the Wise) 38, 81, 271, 273
  tomb 145
Alfonso XII 257
Alfonso XIII 49
Algeciras 279
Alhama 222
Alhama de Granada 39
Alhambra (Granada) *8–9*, 71, *180–1*, 186–93
  night-time tour 194
  tickets 186, 188–9
  Alcazaba *190*, 190–1
  Gate of Justice (Puerta de la Justica) 189
  Generalife 178, 179, 193
  Museo de la Alhambra 190
  Museum of Fine Art (Museo Bellas Artes) 190
  Palacio de Carlos V 190
  Palacio del Portal 193
  Patio de Comares (Patio de los Mirtos) *134–5*, 192
  Patio de los Leones *182*, 192
  Plaza de los Aljibes 190
  Puerta de las Granadas 189
  Royal Palace (Casa Real or Palacios Nazaries) 188, 191–3
  Sala de Presentación 191
  Torre de Vela 191
almadraba 20
Almanzora valley 222
Almería *216*, *218*, 220–1
  Alcazaba *220*
  Cathedral 221
  Chanca quarter 221
  Paseo de Almería 221
  Rambla del Obispo 220
Almería province 125, *214–15*, 217–23
Almodóvar del Río 143, 176
Almohads 37
Almonaster la Real 289
Almoravids 36, 37
Andalucíans
  character 59–65
  history 19–65
al-Andalus 19, 27
Andarax valley 222
Andújar 211
Angosturo del Guadiaro (Guadiaro Gorge) 236
Antequera 240
  caves *23*, *227*, 240
  museum 240
Aphrodite Kallipygos 22
Arabs 28
Aracena 227, 289
architecture 71, 177
Arcos de la Frontera 264, 277–8
Armada *42–3*, 46–7, 272
artists 162–3
Aroche 289
Augustus 21
auto de fé 39
Avienus 288
Ayamonte 289
azulejos 77, 147, 148, 156

b

Baelo Claudia 23, 279
Baena 177
Baetica 21
Baeza 208
  Casa Juanito (restaurant) 208
  Convento de San Francisco 208

Palacio de Jabalquinto 77, *207*, 208
Plaza de los Leones 208, *210*
Bailén 207
Baños de la Encina 207
Barbarossa 272, 295
beaches 219, 233, 288
Bélmez 212
Belmonte, Juan 82, 83
Benalmádena-Costa 256
Benalmádena-Pueblo 256
Benaoján 263
Benaque 257
Berbers 27, 28, 29
Berja 219
Bienvenida dynasty (bullfighting) 83
billboards (bull) 101
birds 123, 124, 125, 126, 239, 288
  migration 126
biscuits 108
Bismarck, Gunilla von 116, *118*
Bizet 150
Boabdil 40, 183, 222
Bollullos 286
Bolonia *see* Baelo Claudia
Bomberg, David 245
Bonanza 277
Bornos 264
brandy 99, 100, 101
Brenan, Gerald 200, 201, 217, 237
British 115, 118
  in Gibraltar 294
Bubión 199
Bucentaur 272
bullfighting *64*, 65, *78–9*, *80*, 81–5
  museum (Córdoba) 171–2
  Ronda 248
  schools 81, 84

c

Cabo de Gata 125, 219
Cabra 177
Cádiz 271, 273–6
  history 20, 22, 46, 49, 271
  tourist office 276
  Arco de los Blancos 271
  Arco de la Rosa 271
  Caleta (beach) 274
  Columbus monument *268–9*
  Monument to the Cortes (Parliament) 274
  Murallas de San Carlos 274
  Museo Histórico Municipal 275

Museo Provincial 275
New Cathedral (Catedral) 275
Oratorio de San Felipe Neri
276
Oratorio de la Santa Cueva
276
Plaza de España 274
Puerto de Tierra 273
San Felipe Battery 274
Torre Tavira 275
Cádiz, Bay of 272
Caesar, Julius 21
Calar Alto 223
Cambil 212
Camisón, Juan 237
Campo de Dalias 218
Cándido dynasty (bullfighting)
81, 82
Cano, Alonso 163
Cantoria 223
Carmen 150
Carmo see **Carmona**
Carmona (Carmo) 23, 160
church of San Pedro 160
Córdoba gate 160
necropolis 160
Puerta de Sevilla 160
Carratraca 237–8
Carriazo, Mata 19
Cartagena (Carthago Nova) 21
Carthaginians 20
Casares 233–4
Catholic Monarchs 39, 40, 72
cave living 199, *225*, 225–7
caves and grottos *23*, 125,
185, 199, 240
see also **cave living**
Cave of the Bull, El Torcal
240
Caves of Hercules, Cap
Spartel, Morocco 310
Cueva de la Pileta 162, 26–7,
235–6
Cueva de Menga, Antequera
76, *227*, 240
Cueva de Nerja 226, 257
Cueva de Viera 240
Gruta de las Maravillas
(Grotto of the Marvels),
Aracena 227, 289
St Michael's Cave, Gibraltar
299
Cazalla 159
Cazorla *212*
chameleon 128
Charles V 148
Chipiona 277
chiringuitos 106
Christians/Church 23, 28, 29,
30, 32, 33
Reconquest 35–40
churches and chapels
obtaining keys 262
Cabra church 212
Collegiate Church of Sta
María, Osuna 160
Convent of Santa Clara,
Seville 156
El Salvador, Seville 155
El Salvador, Ubeda 209
Espíritu Santo, Ronda 246
Huelma church 212
Jésus del Gran Poder, Seville
156
Nuestra Señora de la Cabeza,
Sierra Morena 211
Oratorio de San Felipe Neri,
Cádiz 276
Oratorio de la Santa Cueva,
Cádiz 276
Royal Chapel (Capilla Real),
Granada 194–5
San Pablo, Córdoba 174
San Pedro, Carmona 160
Sta María, Écija 160
Sta María Alcázar de los
Reales, Ubeda 209
Santa María la Mayor, Ronda
246
Santa Marina, Córdoba 174
climate 314
Cóbdar 223
Columbus, Christopher 45,
146, 151, 284, 285
monument, Cádiz *268–9*
replica of fleet, Muelle de las
Carabelas 285
statue, Palos de la Frontera
284
conflicts, forgotten 62
Constantina 159
conversos 75
Córdoba 23, 36, 167–75
bars 175
crafts 172, 173
flamenco venue 175
market 174
patios 169–70
tourist office 168
Alcázar de los Reyes
Cristianos 169
Ayuntamiento (town hall) 174
Bullfight Museum (Museo
Taurino) *83*, *171*, 171–2
Cathedral 168
church of San Pablo 174
church of Santa Marina 174
Convent of Santa Isabel 174
Fine Arts Museum (Museo
Provincial de Bellas
Artes)
173
Julio Romero de Torres
Museum 173
La Judería (Jewish quarter)
29, 75, *166*, 170–1
La Marina 174
La Mezquita (Great Mosque)
26, 29, *68–9*, 71, *164–5*,
167, 167–8
Museo Arqueológico
(Archaeological Museum)
173
Palacio de Congresos 168
Palacio de Viana 174–5
patios 178, 179
Plaza de la Corredera 174
Plaza del Potro 173
Plaza Tiberiades 171
Puente Romano (Roman
Bridge) 169
Puerta de Almodóvar 170
Restaurant Caballo Rojo
111
Synagogue (Sinagoga) *72*,
170–1
Torre de Calahorra 169
Zoco 172
Córdoba province 175–7
cork 234, 235, 263
corridas 85
Cortes de la Frontera 236, 263
Cortés, Joaquin *89*, 92
Costa de Almería 115
Costa Gaditana 115
Costa del Plástico 218
Costa del Sol 75, 115–18,
253–7
Costa Tropical 115
**Costillares dynasty
(bullfighting)** 82
Coto de Doñana 19, 283–9
courtship 63–4
crafts
Córdoba 172, 173
crusades 37, 40

d

dance see **flamenco**
desert 125
Despeñaperros 128
Díaz, Vázquez 284
Domecq 97, 100, 101, 277
**Dominguín dynasty
(bullfighting)** 81, 85
Don Juan 154

Drake, Sir Francis 46, 100, 272
drink see **sherry, wine**
drugs 118
  Morocco 311
duende 90

e

Écija *160*
  church of Sta María 160
  Palacio de Peñaflor 160
economy 314
El Acebuche 287
El Bosque 249, 278
El Burgo 266
El Cid 35
El Córdobes 176
El Ejido 218
El Greco 157
El Puerto de Santa María 98, 276
  Aguasherry 276
  Ribera del Marisco 276
  wineries 97, 98
El Rocío 64, 287
El Romeral 240
El Torcal *120–1*, 123, *239*, 239–40
Eliot, General 293, 299
  memorial 297
emigration 48
enchufes 61
Enix 218
Estepona 253–4
expatriate community 115, 254
Expo '92 50

f

fairs see **fiestas, fairs and festivals**
Falla, Manuel de 274, 275
  museum 195
Ferdinand I of Léon-Castile 35
Ferdinand III of Castile *38*, 39, 40, 72, 73
  tomb 145
Feria (Seville Fair) 60, *132–3*, 158
festivals see **fiestas, fairs and festivals**
fiestas, fairs and festivals 66–7 317
  Huleva province 287
  Olvera 266
  San Isidro 85
  Seville see **Feria**

Verdiales *65*
fir trees (*Abies pinsapo***)** 126, 236, 249
fish 105, 108–10
fishing 20
flamenco 22, 65, *86–7, 88*, 89–92, 185
fleets 46
flora 125, 128
  see also **national parks, nature parks and nature areas**
  Gibraltar 298
food 30, 105–11
Ford, Richard 22, 48, 59, 143, 187, 245, 249, 265
forests 126
Franco, General Francisco 50
Fraser, Ronald 61
Frigiliana 63
Frontera 271, 278
fruit 110, 222
Fuengirola 255
Fuentevaqueros 195
Fundador brandy 100

g

Gades (now Cádiz) 21, 271
Gadir (now Cádiz) 20, 271
Gallo, Joselito el 82
gardens 178–9
Garganta del Chorro 238
  King's Path (El Camino del Rey) 238, *241*
Garrucha 220
garum 21, 277
Gaucín 234, 262
Gautier, Théophile 231, 245
gazpacho 30, 106
Genalguacil 262
Ghalib, General 32
Gibraltar 27, 48, 293–300, 305
  flora and fauna 298
  history 293
  Alameda Gardens 297
  Apes' Den 298
  Casemates Square 294, 295
  Catalan Bay 300
  Cathedral 295
  Cathedral Square 297
  Frontier, The 296
  Gorham's Cave 296
  Governor's Residence 295
  Main Street *290–1*, 295
  Marina *292*
  Moorish Baths 297
  Moorish Castle *293*
  museum 297

  Notch 300
  St Michael's Cave 299, *300*
  Tower of Homage 300
  Trafalgar Cemetery 295
  Upper Galleries 299
gitano 65
González, Felipe 50, 59
González, Manuel 97
government 314
Goya 157, 287
Granada *34*, 40, 183–95
  flamenco 185
  museums see under **Alhambra**
  tourist office 194
  Abadía de Sacromonte 185–6
  Albaicín 184
  Alhambra see **Alhambra**
  Cathedral (Catedral) *194*
  Corral del Carbón 194
  El Bañuelo (Arab baths) 184
  Generalife 193
  Hospital Real 195
  Hotel Alhambra Palace 183
  Madraza 195
  Manuel de Falla museum 195
  Mirador de San Cristóbal 183
  Monasterio de la Cartuja 195
  Monastery of San Francisco 194
  Queen's House (Callejón de las Monjas) 185
  Royal Chapel (Capilla Real) 194–5
  Sacromonte *86–7*, 90, 185–6
Granada, Kingdom of 39, 183, 200, 231
Granada, War of 74
Grazalema 60, *258–9*, 264–5
grottos see **caves and grottos**
Guadalmedina, Rio 231
Guadalquivir river 141, *143*
Guadix 199, 225, *226*
Guzmán the Good 38, 234
gypsies 65
  cave dwelling 225
  flamenco 22, 89, 185
  Granada 185, 186
Gypsy Kings 91

h

al-Hakam III 32, 72, 167
Hamilcar Barca 20
hams 107, 128, 263
  pata negra 107, 109, 128, 263
  serrano 107, 111, 289
Hannibal 20

Hasdrubal 21
health 316
Hemingway, Ernest 84, 116, 245
Hisham 32
Hisham II 33, 167
Hispalis (now Seville) 23, 141
Hispania 21
history
  early 19–23
  700–1000 27–33
  1000–1491 35–40
  1491 onwards 45–50
Hohenlohe, Prince Alfonso de 115, 116, 117
Hornos 212
Huelva 283
Huelva province 283–9
  deseha 127
  food 108
Huerta de San Vicente 195
Huescar 62
hunting 176, 236
hydros 237

i

Iberians 19
Ibn-Abi Amir see al-Mansur
Ibn-al-Ahmar 39
Ibn-al-Arabi 31
Ibn Al-Khatib 188
Ibn-Ammar 35, 36
ibn-Tashufin, Yusuf 36
ibn-Ziyard, Tariq 27
Ince, Sergeant Major 299
Indalo 226
Indiculus luminosus 29
Indomptable 272
Inquisition 39, 73, 74
Inurria, Mateo 173
Irving, Washington 183, 187
Isabella, Queen 38, 39, 45, 72, 73, 143
Isla Canela 289
Isla Cristina 283, 289
Isla, El Camarón de la 91, 92
Islamic Spain 29, 75
Itálica 20, 22, 76, 159

j

Jábalcuz 212
Jabugo 289
Jaén 136, 210–11
  Arab baths 210
  Cathedral 210, 211
  museum 210
  Santa Catalina 211

Jaén province 207–12
Jerez de la Frontera 54–5, 276
  sherry/brandy 97, 98, 99
  wineries 97
  Real Escuela Andaluza del Arte Ecuestre (Royal Andalucían School of Equestrian Art) 276
Jews 28, 39, 73, 75, 177
  in Córdoba 29, 170
  in Tetouan, Morocco 308
Jimena 212
Jiménez, Juan Ramón 286
Josephs, Allen 64
Juan Carlos I 50
Jubrique 235

l

La Blanca Paloma (The White Dove), Queen of the Marshes 64
La Carolina 211
La Rábida monastery 284
La Rambla 177
language 72, 350
Las Alpujarras 71, 199–201
Las Navas de Tolosa 38
Las Negras 219
latifundia/latifundios 23, 38, 127
Laujar 222
Leal, Valdés 154
Lee, Laurie 271
Lepe 289
Lévi-Provençal 30, 33
liberalism 274
Lijar 62, 223
limpieza de sangre 39, 74, 75
Linares 207
Litri dynasty (bullfighting) 84, 85
Livy 23
Lorca, Federico García 50, 195, 208
  Blood Wedding 219
  museums 195
Los Palacios 159
Lucena 73, 177
Lucía, Paco do 91
lynx 127, 128

m

Macaulay, Rose 223
Machado, Antonio 208
Macharaviaya 256–7
Madinat al-Zahra see Medina Azahara

Maimonides, Moses 73, 171
Mainake 20
Málaga 40, 228–9, 231–3
  beaches 233
  Alcazaba 231
  Cathedral (Catedral) 232, 233
  English Cemetery 232
  Gibralfaro Castle (Castillo de Gibralfaro) 231
  Jardin-Botanico La Concepcíon 179, 232
  Picasso Museum (Museo Picasso) 232
  Plaza de Toros (bullring) 231
Málaga province 233–40
  food 110
  lakes 238
Mañara, Don Miguel de 153, 154
Manolete 174
al-Mansur (Ibn-Abi Amir) 32, 33, 167
Marbella 73, 115, 116, 254–5
  Club 117
Marismas del Odiel 284
Marmolejo 211
Maro 257
Martial 22
Mask of Tharsis, The 19
Matalascañas 287
meal times 105
Medina Azahara 30, 31, 32, 175–6
Medina Sidonia 264
Medina Sidonia, Dukes of 38, 46, 47, 124
Merimée, Prosper 150
Mesas de Villaverde 238
metal mining see mining
Michiner, James 116
Mijas 61, 255–6
Minas de Rio Tinto 289
mining 20, 31, 288, 289
  Rio Tinto 283
Mirador de Puerto Rico 237
Moguer 286
Mojácar 219–20
money 316
Montañés, Juan Martínez 163
Montejaque 263
Montemar 115
Montilla 21, 177
  Las Camachas restaurant 111
Moors 27–33, 73, 76
  artistic influence 70, 71
  flamenco 22
Mora y Aragón, Don Jaime de 116